A HISTORY OF
FOREIGN WORDS
IN ENGLISH

A HISTORY OF
FOREIGN WORDS
IN ENGLISH

BY

MARY S. SERJEANTSON

M.A. (Liverpool), D.Phil. (Oxon).

New York

BARNES & NOBLE, INC.

NEW IMPRESSION 1962

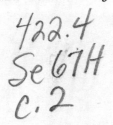

Printed in Great Britain

CONTENTS

PREFACE

The first thing that is wrong in this book is the title. Very many of the words dealt with are certainly not now 'foreign', but have been completely naturalized in English for centuries. But since they are in origin not of the common Germanic stock, the phrase 'foreign words' may stand, and will perhaps be preferred by some to the technical term 'loan-words'.

In a volume which has to cover so long a period as that of the whole history of the English language, the treatment must necessarily be incomplete. Perhaps the time has not yet come for a really comprehensive work—it would need several volumes— on loan-words in English. A great deal of spade-work on individual languages and problems remains to be done. The great Period Dictionaries now being prepared in America, to the publication of which we are looking forward, will be of the utmost value in supplementing the material afforded by the *Oxford English Dictionary* ; and more material may be found in still unpublished records and accounts of early travellers and traders.

The present volume does not limit its attention to foreign words existing in English at the present day. This would give a wrong impression of earlier periods. It does not, however, attempt to trace the history of loan-words in all the local dialects of English at all periods; this requires separate study. Emphasis has been laid throughout on the *first* introductions from individual languages and the *first* appearances of individual words. The greatest amount of space has been devoted to early loans from Latin, French, and Scandinavian, since these languages are the most important sources of our adoptions. Examples of the words in actual use (i.e. quotations from contemporary writers) are given freely, especially in the earlier periods.

In the sections on Old English, all the most important literary texts, glossaries, and other documents have been examined. For Middle English only a comparatively small number of what it is hoped are really representative texts are discussed ; these are of various types and from various areas. This seemed the best method of dealing with the masses of material available. In considering words from Middle English texts it is, of course, safest to take the words as belonging to the time of the *manuscript* used, and not necessarily to that of the *original* document, if the former is a copy. There is obviously always the possibility of changes and additions in copying.

Probably no two people would agree entirely as to what words should be admitted to such a volume as this, especially when the words in question come from the more remote languages such as Chinese, Maori, and so on. Words which are quite familiar to people who live or have travelled in the East, in Australasia, in South America, may be quite unknown and of small interest to those who are familiar only with other parts of the world. My choice of words to be discussed in the sections on the modern period may seem arbitrary, but I have tried to include those which the ordinary English reader is most likely to come across in not too specialized literature.

The appendices on the phonology of Latin, French, and Scandinavian words give, as will be seen, only the main features, and these very briefly ; they are merely intended for reference.

Discussion of controversial matters has been avoided, but references will in some cases be found in footnotes to books or articles dealing with individual points.

The Bibliography gives only the most important of the works which have been consulted. I am most deeply indebted to the Dictionaries mentioned in this list, and in particular to the *Oxford English Dictionary* and the *Shorter Oxford English Dictionary*, without whose help this book could certainly not have been written.

I have to thank my colleague, Dr. E. C. Martin (Reader in Imperial History, University of London), for advice and help in historical matters, and for her patience in answering questions. I should also like to thank my family for much practical assistance, and several generations of students who have helped by asking questions.

M. S. S.

Westfield College
(University of London).
January, 1935.

LIST OF ABBREVIATIONS

A.-N.,	Anglo-Norman	*M.L.G.*,	Middle Low German
Amer.,	American	*Mal.*,	Malay
Arab.,	Arabic	*Med.Lat.*,	Mediaeval Latin
Austr.,	Australian	*Mex.*,	Mexican
Braz.,	Brazilian	*Mod.E.*,	Modern English
C.Fr.,	Central French	*Mod.Gk.*,	Modern Greek
Carib.,	Caribbean	*Mod.Lat.*,	Modern Latin
Ch.,	Chinese	*N.F.*,	Norman-French
Corn.,	Cornish	*O.Du.*,	Old Dutch
Dan.,	Danish	*O.E.*,	Old English
Du.,	Dutch	*O.Fr.*,	Old French
E.E.T.S.,	Early English Text	*O.H.G.*,	Old High German
	Society	*O.Ir.*,	Old Irish
E.Mod.Du.,	Early Modern Dutch	*O.N.*,	Old Norse
E.Span.,	Early Spanish	*O.S.*,	Old Saxon
Eng.,	English	*O. Span.*,	Old Spanish
Flem.,	Flemish	*O.W.*,	Old Welsh
Fr.,	French	*Pers.*,	Persian
Gael.,	Gaelic	*Peruv.*,	Peruvian
Germ.,	German	*Port.*,	Portuguese
Gk.,	Greek	*Pr.O.N.*,	Primitive Old Norse
Gmc.,	Germanic	*Prov.*,	Provençal
Goth.,	Gothic	*Rom.*,	Romance
Hait.,	Haitian	*Russ.*,	Russian
Heb.,	Hebrew	*S.Amer.*,	South American
Hind.,	Hindustani	*Scand.*,	Scandinavian
Hung.,	Hungarian	*Scrt.*,	Sanscrit
Ir.,	Irish	*Singhal.*,	Singhalese
Ital.,	Italian	*Slav.*,	Slavonic
Jap.,	Japanese	*Span.*,	Spanish
Jav.,	Javanese	*Swed.*,	Swedish
L.G.,	Low German	*Turk.*,	Turkish
Lat.,	Latin	*Vulg.Lat.*,	Vulgar Latin
M.Du.,	Middle Dutch	*W.*,	Welsh
M.E.,	Middle English	*W.Afr.*,	West African
M.Flem.,	Middle Flemish	*W.Flem.*,	West Flemish
M.H.G.,	Middle High German		

CHAPTER I

INTRODUCTORY

The English language has throughout its history accepted with comparative equanimity words from other languages with which it has been in contact, and though there have been periods during which speakers and writers of English have made use of foreign words to an exaggerated extent, it is probable that most people will agree that the foreign element in normal English usage has been of value.

Some languages avoid as far as possible the use of alien terms, substituting for them, when an expression for a new object or idea is needed, new words made up of native elements, but England has always welcomed the alien, and many hundreds of words of non-English origin are now part and parcel of our vocabulary, indistinguishable from the native stock except to those with some knowledge of etymology. The language of this country has, it is true, been particularly open to foreign influence, partly through the succession of invaders who came into contact with English speakers during the Middle Ages ; partly through the enterprise of the English themselves, who have carried their language into the far corners of the world, where it has gathered, like a snowball, new matter as it passed on its way. There are few nations and few languages which have had as many opportunities as the English for acquiring new words by the direct influence of other tongues.

The adoption of foreign words in any dialect may come about in different ways, and the extent to which foreign elements become naturalized varies very considerably. Contact between peoples of alien speech may be of several kinds ; they may meet for instance through conquest, through colonization, through trade, or through literature. When one nation subdues another which speaks a different language, the conquerors, if their object has been political power rather than settlement, may constitute an authority, or ruling class, which is in point of view of numbers

1

much in the minority compared with the whole body of the conquered people. In a case like this, it is usually the native language that survives, though the incoming dialect will very probably transfer to the native vocabulary words which express its own methods of government, and other cultural words. This has happened in several instances in Western Europe in the early Middle Ages : the Franks in Latin-speaking Gaul, the Normans in France, the Norman-French in England. In each of these some members of the ruling classes as well as of the subject-classes must have been bilingual, and each in speaking his own language would be liable to introduce into it words, especially of a technical or specialized character, that he has learnt from the other.

This is what takes place when the conquerors who form a governing minority have established themselves in their new country as a separate unity, and have retained little or no connexion with their original home and the speakers of their own language, or have become politically independent. If, however, the conquered country or province does not become an independent state under its new rulers, but is controlled by the original government, so that the ruling class is in constant contact with, and continually reinforced by, people speaking their own language, it has usually happened that the dialect of the rulers has won the day, and has spread throughout the community, absorbing some words from the native speakers, chiefly such as concern local products, natural features, etc., but without necessarily undergoing radical changes in itself. An example of this is afforded by the relative positions of the Romans and Celts in Gaul, where the Latin speech established itself after acquiring a very small proportion of words from the native Gaulish dialect.

A different set of circumstances arises when the invasion is for the purpose of settlement or colonization rather than merely for the sake of political power. If the newcomers arrive in such numbers as to form a majority over the native speakers, and in such military or political strength as to acquire complete control over these, or dispossess them, the dialect of the conquerors or colonists will have the upper hand from the start, wherever they establish themselves. They will, however, adopt from the natives whom they displace words which denote native products, etc., and occasionally native customs, which may have been unfamiliar before. This happened, for instance, when the Anglo-Saxons came to England, eventually in numbers large enough to render the Britons a minority of little importance, or in some areas perhaps to oust them altogether. It has happened again in many areas of European colonization (e.g. the English in Australia), where the language of the newcomers has never shown any likelihood of yielding to the native idiom.

Sometimes warfare aiming at conquest results in a type of immigration, rather than colonization, as in the case of the Scandinavians in this country, where conflict led finally to more or less peaceful settlement, where the invaders established themselves side by side with the natives without overwhelming them or driving them out, and where the race, customs, and even the language, of the two peoples were sufficiently alike to make intercourse between the two, and the subsequent bilingualism, easy and natural. Here the Englishman who acquired Scandinavian (and no doubt also the Scandinavian who learnt English) introduced the new terms into his own language, where they remained even after English had established itself in all the areas of the Nordic settlement, and Englishmen and Danes alike had ceased to be bilingual.

Of course, immigration is not always preceded or accompanied by hostility, and immigrants into a colony with an already constituted authority will usually adopt the general speech of the colony even if their own is an alien one. If the immigrants come in a large enough body to form a small community of their own within the greater one, they are likely to retain their own speech, for a time at least, even though eventually yielding to the pressure of the language spoken all about them. There are many instances of this in the communities of different nationality which have settled in the United States—Jewish, German, Norwegian, etc.—and now are gradually giving up their own dialects, though carrying into their newly acquired English some part of their own vocabulary, some words from which may spread to more distant fields.

For English speakers, trade has always been an important factor in the introduction of new words and of new ideas. Even before English had separated from its Germanic stock it was trade almost as much as conquest which brought into it its first words from other languages, as will be seen in the following chapter, in which the influence of Latin on the Germanic vocabulary will be dealt with. It was trade that in later times brought us acquainted with the words of many another nation in the New World as well as in the old. In this respect trade and scientific exploration go hand in hand, and can hardly be separated ; and the merchant-adventurer holds an important place in the history of the English language.

So far we have considered words borrowed in actual speech. Sometimes, however, loan-words will come into a language from a written source ; in this case they usually pass first into the written language, and thence may or may not pass into the spoken language. Examples of this may be found in plenty in the borrowings from Latin in the later Old English period, when English writers and translators took over, from Latin originals or models, Latin words to serve their purpose, sometimes retaining their original inflexions, sometimes using the appropriate English inflexion. Perhaps the majority of these words remain in the category of what may be called " learned " words, and never reach full currency with the average speaker, if indeed they reach the spoken language at all. We may instance the Old English *aspide* ' asp ', *sanct* ' saint ', *lenticul* ' lentil ', *protomartyr*, *milite* ' soldiery ', *polente, grammatic, circul* ' circle ', *anfiteatra*, *termen* ' fixed point ', as various types of learned words ; and as words which, introduced first from literature, became more or less ' popular ', *cleric* ' clerk, priest ', *offrian* ' to sacrifice ', *apostel*, *nōn* ' noon ', *cucumere* ' cucumber ', *turtur* ' turtle-dove '. In more modern times it is science rather than literature that has been responsible for the introduction of words of a learned type, and English dictionaries, of a general character as well as purely scientific, contain hundreds of words formed directly from Greek or Latin elements, which are never used by the ordinary speaker and may never be seen or heard by him. Here again, some of these words of scientific origin do pass into popular speech, as has obviously happened in such cases as *telephone, telegram, telegraph, gramophone*, and medical terms such as *appendicitis, bronchitis*, which are used by the layman as well as by the specialist.

It happens frequently in the course of the history of our language that a word is borrowed more than once from the same source (or from developments of this source), perhaps once as a popular word and again as a learned or technical one. The Latin word *uncia* was adopted by Germanic (on the continent) as a measure of length, and appears in Old English as *ynce*, Modern English *inch*; a few centuries later, English borrowed the word again, this time in its Romance form, **untsia*, which becomes in Old English *yntse* (now obsolete), used as a measure of weight; the French descendant, *unce, once*, of Romance **untsia*, came into Middle English, again as a measure of weight, and has become Modern English *ounce*; all these were popular loans; but the final version, *uncial*, borrowed in the seventeenth century from Latin *unciālis*, the adjective of *uncia*, is definitely a learned loan.

English has a particularly large number of these 'repeated' loans (in some of which each of the pair or group is of a quite ordinary popular type), owing to the fact of her numerous borrowings from Latin in the Early Middle Ages followed by even more plentiful adoptions from French, which developed from Latin, and further by the continued contact between English and French which has led to many more introductions from French in recent times, by the English habit (renewed in the Renaissance period) of adopting words from Latin, and finally by the fact that even within the Middle English period a word may be borrowed twice over, from different dialects of French. Not very many original Latin words appear in all these five forms in Modern English, since a new loan has often ousted an earlier one, but a large number may be found in two or three of these groups; cf. *catch, chase, capt(ive)* etc.; *mint, money; wine, vine(yard); drake, dragon; master, magistr(ate); trivet, tripod; castle, château; corpse, corps;* and so on.

Some words have entered English, not by direct contact with the language which is their source, but indirectly, through an intervening language. In this way many of the earlier Italian loans came to us through French, the Italian of the Renaissance having reached France first, and thence having passed on to us. In this way, too, the earliest loan-words from the east have come to us through Latin, many of them having already passed through

Greek before reaching Latin. Even in the early centuries of this era, before communication became as simple and rapid as it is to-day, words travelled thousands of miles, westwards from Asia to Europe, across Europe from east to west and from south to north, all round the shores of the Mediterranean, from nation to nation and from generation to generation. Most of these much-travelled words are objects of trade or culture. The word *pepper*, for instance, came first from some eastern language into Greek, thence into Latin and thence into English; *elephant* was first Egyptian, then Greek, Latin, French, and finally English; *camel* was originally Semitic, and this too passed through Greek and Latin before reaching our language. *Albatross* is based ultimately on a Phœnician word which drifted successively into Greek, Arabic, and Portuguese, and then into English. *Apricot* began a long history in Latin, from which it passed in succession to Greek, Arabic, Spanish, French, and English. *Silk* has been Chinese, Greek, Latin, and finally English. *Carat* comes through Greek, Arabic, Italian, and French.

In recent times, English has partially adopted from distant countries many words which are used chiefly or exclusively in connexion with the countries from which they come, by people who themselves know these countries, or in books describing them, either of necessity (for lack of equivalent English terms), or for the sake of local colour. The book about South America will have its *gauchos, lariats, vaqueros, ponchos, cordilleras,* and *llanos*; the Malayan its *amboynas, copra, ihlang-ihlang, mangosteens, krises, parangs,* and *sarongs;* to the Anglo-Indian, his *chota hazris, tiffins, chits, baksheesh, dhobis, punkahs,* are as much a part of his everyday life as his *chutneys* and *curries.*

When used by English speakers, such words practically always adopt English inflexions. It has indeed been usual all through the history of loan-words in our language for them to become rapidly acclimatized enough to be treated grammatically and syntactically as English words. In modern times perhaps this does not mean very much, since so many of the more recent loans are nouns, and English nominal inflexions are so few; but it holds good in the earlier periods, when verbs and adjectives were adopted freely from Latin and French, though occasionally in Late Old English some words of the learned type, borrowed in the written language, may keep their Latin inflexions. A few foreign plurals—chiefly in more recent borrowings from the classical languages—have been retained in English, these having become familiar, to many of those who use them, in the course of a classical education ; such are *agenda, desiderata, data, magi, radii, gladioli, nebulae, criteria, crises, theses ;* some nouns have the foreign plural as well as a native form, sometimes, though not always, with a distinction of meaning, e.g. *appendixes, appendices ; indexes, indices ; formulas, formulae ; funguses, fungi ; geniuses, genii ; hippopotamuses, hippopotami ;* and in words other than Greek or Latin, *cherubs, cherubim ; bandits, banditti ; virtuosos, virtuosi.* But classical words, even the more recent adoptions, which have become entirely popular never have foreign plurals ; we have *irises, crocuses, circuses, villas, spectators, omens, nasturtiums,* not *irides, croci, circi, villae, spectatores, omina, nasturtia.*

Foreign words, when once adopted into English, have always been used freely with native prefixes and suffixes. Adverbs in *-ly*, adjectives in *-ful*, *-less*, abstract nouns in *-ness*, *-ship*, are found with French first elements almost as frequently as with English (e.g. *nicely, pleasantly ; cheerful, beautiful, fruitless ; gentleness, companionship,* etc.) ; and so also the English prefixes *un-, fore-, over-*, etc., may have foreign second elements (e.g. *unaided, unbar, unconscious, forecast, overcharge, overawe,* etc.). Hybrid compounds of noun plus noun, adjective plus noun, etc., are not uncommon ; such are *salt-cellar* (English and French), *heirloom* (French and English), *fainthearted* (French and English), *longlegged* (English and Scandinavian), *blackmail* (English and Scandinavian), as well as the more recent scientific words such as *claustrophobia, Anglophile,* and even *television.* English has, moreover, adopted foreign (especially Latin) prefixes and suffixes, and many of these are living elements which can be used with words from any source (e.g. *pre-, infra-, inter-, -ism, -ize*).

When a foreign word is borrowed, it may or may not retain its original pronunciation in the adopting language. If each of its sounds already exists in the latter, it will probably be adopted in a pretty accurate form ; if, however, some of its sounds are alien to the adopting language, each of these will be replaced by

B

the nearest native sound. Even if some speakers are familiar with, and can pronounce, the dialect from which it comes, their pronunciation will not be generally adopted. Thus there were different pronunciations of some of the French words borrowed in Middle English, the French nasal vowels, for instance, being retained for a time at least by bilingual speakers, while those who spoke only English substituted for them the English non-nasal vowels. Sometimes a foreign word in English will be partly anglicized, even by those who speak the language from which it comes. For instance, the word *garage* is usually pronounced with the first vowel as in English *hat* [æ], and not with the French vowel, but retains the French [ž] for the final consonant, though this sound does not occur as a final consonant in native words. Among some who do not speak Standard English, the word is completely anglicized, the [ž] being replaced by the group [dž] (as in the second syllable of *carriage*), which is common in English in this position. Similarly, the word *voile*, as the name of a material, usually retains its French [wɑ], though somewhat lengthened, but is sometimes heard, in shops, etc., with the anglicized (spelling pronunciation) *oi* [voil] ; while French words with *é, è,* or *ê* have the vowel diphthongized to [ei] (e.g. *fête, fiancé*) since Modern Standard English has normally no long [ē]. Again, the Spanish *ll,* which is an *l* made with the middle of the tongue (in the same position as the consonant *y* [j]) and not with the tip, has the ordinary English *l* substituted for it, in words such as *llama, llano* ; and for the Spanish *ñ* (pronounced like the *gn* in French *montagne*) English people will use the two consonants [nj], sometimes even writing it *ny,* e.g. in *canyon* (Spanish *cañon*).

Once a word has become perfectly assimilated in the spoken language, each of its sounds will follow all the fortunes of that sound in the adopting language ; French *ī* and *ē*, for example, borrowed in the Middle English period, undergo the same developments as the English *ī* and *ē* of that period, the former becoming [ai] as in Present-Day English *line, fine,* the latter [ī] as in *chief, brief.*

Apart from the anglicizing tendency already referred to, the more recently a word has been adopted in English, the more likely it is to retain its original pronunciation, since it will have been affected by fewer purely English changes—changes which have been going on continuously ever since English became an independent language in the fourth or fifth century.

The principal languages which have affected the vocabulary of English have been Scandinavian, French, and Latin, the last most of all. Scandinavian words were borrowed most freely between the ninth century and the twelfth, French words during the twelfth, thirteenth, and fourteenth centuries, but Latin words have been making their way into English, throughout almost the whole period of its history, first into the spoken language, later into written English (through religion, literature, and science), though this latter form of borrowing has given many words also to the spoken language.

During the Modern Period, that is to say after about 1400, the most important period of foreign borrowing was the latter part of the sixteenth century, and the early seventeenth century. Then, as will be seen, many different languages first become represented in the English vocabulary, owing to the remarkable increase in England's direct contacts with foreign countries at this time, which led to direct borrowing from languages which had previously affected the language only indirectly, and also to the appearance of words from languages previously unknown in England or even in Europe.

Before beginning an historical examination of the types of words borrowed from each of the languages which have influenced English, of the circumstances in which such borrowing began, and of the character of the sources in which they are first recorded, it will be well to consider some of the classes of what may be reckoned as loan-words which are not dealt with here.

Phrases from foreign sources are not often fully acclimatized, and are almost always used as aliens—printed in italics, or in inverted commas, and so forth ; such are many French phrases, e.g. *de trop, en règle, tout ensemble, femme de chambre, par excellence, feu de joie, joie de vivre,* and Latin phrases, e.g. *non sequitur, a priori, ad hoc, sine die, sine qua non* (though it is true that to some people such Latin groups have a less foreign atmosphere than the French ones, probably because they are usually pronounced with entirely English sounds).

Secondly, *names of places,* when these are used as the names of products, etc., without, however, the original sense being fully lost. Some place-names have become so thoroughly obscured (through early borrowing and consequently numerous sound-changes, or by dissociation from an original place of manufacture), that they have to be accepted as ordinary loans, e.g. *chest(nut)*, *currant*, *cambric*, *calico*, which should be compared with such forms as *Chablis*, *Moselle*, *Chianti*, and other names of wines, *Angora* (wool), *Morocco* (leather), *Nankin* (china), etc., (some of which may be used either absolutely or attributively, like the last three).

Then there are what are sometimes called ' translation-loans ', especially common in the case of compounds in the older periods of English, when a foreign word expressing a new idea is represented by the nearest equivalent of each of its elements, as when in Old English, for the Latin word *ūni-cornus*, the English form *ān-horn*, = one-horn, is coined ; *all-mihtiġ* for Latin *omnipotens*, *gōd-spell* (Gospel) for Latin *evangelium* (from Greek *eu-angelion* ' good message ').

Another type of word not dealt with in the present volume is to be found in forms borrowed by Standard English from other dialects of English, e.g. words from American English ; or from Scottish or Northern English, such as *bairn*, *raid*, *hale*, which have a typically northern phonological development, or are known to have been widely current in the north before they appear in Standard English. (Words in Scottish, Irish, etc. of non-English origin, are, however, included, since these are really foreign words.)

To conclude this chapter, it must be emphasized that the ' first recorded use ' of a word, especially in the earlier periods, does not necessarily imply ' first use ', (*a*) because a word may be in current use for some time before it appears in any written document, and (*b*) because obviously many words may have been recorded for the first time in documents no longer extant. But in later periods the first occurrence in writing, particularly of words from the more remote languages, or of purely ' learned ' loans, such as some of those mentioned in the concluding chapter, may be in actual fact the first *use* of the word in English speech or writing, or be almost exactly contemporary with this.

And so, leaving more general considerations, we must turn to a more detailed study.

CHAPTER II

LATIN WORDS BEFORE THE CONQUEST

The history of Latin words in English begins in the continental period before the Angles, Saxons, and Jutes crossed the North Sea to settle in this country. From the time of Julius Caesar onwards we have evidence from the Roman historians of contact between the Germanic and the Latin peoples, which led to the adoption of Germanic words into Latin, and of Latin words into Germanic. The Roman armies included northern cohorts, and their familiarity with Latin military terminology and with the names of everyday objects in use in camp and town, served to introduce Latin terms into the native dialects of these soldiers from Nordic tribes. Tacitus mentions Germani who understood Latin, but close acquaintance with it was perhaps not widespread even among members of the legions, a limited, partly technical, vocabulary of Latin words being sufficient for professional needs.

The interchange of words between Germanic and Latin speakers for the first two or three centuries of this era took place in the spoken language ; that is to say, it was not usually Classical Latin which lent and borrowed but the widespread, popular, Vulgar Latin, which was the ancestor of the modern Romance languages, and which, even as early as the third century, was beginning to split up into its different branches in different parts of the Roman Empire. From our point of view the most important of these was the Gallo-Roman, from which came the majority of such early loans into English as show any dialectal variation from Common Romance or Vulgar Latin.

The words adopted from Germanic into Latin for the most part show no particular dialectal characteristics, which indicates that the borrowings date from an early period (perhaps before A.D. 350–400), though some are not recorded until considerably later, appearing for the first time in the individual Romance languages (e.g. in French or Italian). Most of these words are military terms ; there is, for instance, *burgus* (cf. O.E. *burh*

'fortified place, city', Mod.E. *borough* ; Goth. *baurgs*) in the
sense of 'small fort ; watch-tower' (the modern French form
is *bourg*), which appears in second-century inscriptions, and is
used by Vegetius in the fourth century. This writer, however,
implies that the word is not fully naturalized : *castellum
parvulum, quem burgum vocant* 'a little fort, which they call
burgus'. Isidore, more than two hundred years later, has a similar
phrase : *burgos vulgo vocant* 'they call them *burgos* in the vulgar
tongue'. *Drungus* 'a body of soldiers' is used by both Vopiscus
and Vegetius in the fourth century. *Carrago* 'a barricade of
wagons', from *carr* + Gmc. **hagō* 'hedge, barrier', is recorded
by Ammianus Marcellinus about A.D. 400 as a Gothic word.
(The element *carr*, which appears also in Latin as *carrus* 'wagon',
is a Celtic word.) Among terms denoting articles of commerce,
Latin borrowed *spelta*, a kind of grain, 'spelt' (first recorded
A.D. 301, see Walde, *Lat. etymol. Wörterbuch*), *sāpo* 'soap' ; and
among names of animals *alce(s)* 'elk' and *ūrus* 'wild ox'.
Further, Romance used the words *brando* 'sword', *helmo*
'helmet', *gonfalone* 'standard', *mariscalco* 'farrier', *baldo*
'bold', besides several names of colours, which are common to
a number of Romance dialects, and the adoption of which, it
has been suggested, was due to the habit of the Germanic tribes
(mentioned by Tacitus) of painting their wooden shields with
colours. Thus Mod. French has *blanc, brun, gris, bleu*, all of
Germanic origin. It happens not infrequently that a word
borrowed by Romance from Germanic, and established in the
French dialects, was later adopted by English among its loans
from Anglo-Norman or Central French.

It has been indicated above that the first spread of Latin words
into Germanic was due to military influence. After the Roman
soldier came the Roman merchant. From the time of the first
establishment by Julius Caesar of an imperial province in the
neighbourhood of the Rhine, the trade of Italy turned in this
direction, and the inhabitants of the new province quickly learnt
to approve the new stuffs and household vessels, the plants and
their products, the ornaments and the games, which came to
them from the south. Roman coins became generally used, and,
when local mints were eventually set up, classical designs were
followed. Towards the north, beyond the limits of the Roman

province, the spread of objects and ideas, and the words which accompanied them, was slower, and there is a not inconsiderable number of early loan-words from Latin to be found in the southern dialects of Germany, which apparently did not penetrate as far as the shores of the Baltic and the North Sea, and therefore are not found in Old English, or appear there only in a form which makes it certain that they were borrowed after the settlement in this country.

Since the earliest records of English date from the seventh century only, it follows that our evidence for the earliest loan-words from Latin is of an indirect character. Of the Latin words which occur in Old English, a fairly large number occur also in Old High German, in Gothic, in Old Saxon, in Dutch, or other Germanic dialects, and their wide diffusion points to early adoption. Sometimes, instead of or in addition to this, the form which they have assumed in Old English indicates the date of borrowing, since many of the sound-changes characteristic of Old English can be fairly accurately dated, and the absence of certain distinctively English developments in the borrowed words shows the time of their introduction to have been subsequent to such phonological changes. (Cf. the [sk] of *school*, O.E. *scōl*, Lat. *schola*, and of *scuttle*, O.E. *scutel*, Lat. *scutula*, with the [ʃ] of the earlier loan *shrine*, O.E. *scrīn*, Lat. *scrīnium*; when the two first were adopted the tendency for *sk* to become [ʃ] in English was at an end.) Further, the presence or absence in the borrowed words of certain datable developments in Vulgar Latin gives some indication of the date of borrowing; for instance, O.E. *pipor* ' pepper ' must have been adopted before the time of the Vulgar Latin change of intervocalic *p* to *b*, later *v* (cf. Fr. *poivre*), or O.E. would have **pifer* (*f* = *v*); on the other hand, O.E. *cæfester* ' halter ' (Lat. *capistrum*) represents Vulgar Lat. *cabistrum* or *cavistrum*, and so must have been borrowed after the period of this change.

After the English came to this country the chief source of Latin loan-words was the Vulgar Latin used by the Romano-Britons. It is sometimes impossible to distinguish between loans of the later continental period (between 300 and 450) and those of the first centuries of the settlement (450–650), and in some cases, though these are in a minority, words included in the lists representing these two periods respectively (see App. A) might be transferred from one to the other with equal probability of correctness. After about 650, words are introduced which no longer come under the influence of the early Old English sound-changes ; now, too, the source of the loans is Classical Latin as much as, or more than, Vulgar Latin or Romance, owing to the western spread of Latin writings and scholarship. The introduction of Christianity into England during the early seventh century was the starting-point of this new influx, and since much of the early prose of this country is of a religious character, and is partly at least dependent on Latin sources, many of the new Latin words which now appear are of a religious character. Later, 'learned' words relating to scholarship in general appear in English works as the scope of these is widened.

It will be seen that a large majority of the earliest loans are nouns—the names of concrete objects. Adjectives and verbs are rare, and most of the latter are derivatives from nouns (e.g. *pīnian* 'to punish, torment ', from the noun *pīn*, from Lat. *pēna, poena* ' punishment '). More verbs are introduced during the third period (i.e. after 600–650), but even then are less common than nouns ; adjectives are still rare, and such as do occur are often remodelled by the change of a Latin suffix to an English one (e.g. *mechanic-us* ' mechanical' appears as *mechanisċ*, with the substitution of Eng. *-isċ*, Mod. *-ish*, for Lat. *-ic-*). Old English suffixes are used freely to form derivative nouns, adjectives, and adverbs from Latin nouns ; e.g. *pāpdōm* ' papacy', from Lat. *papa* and O.E. *-dōm* (as in *kingdom*) ; *sacerdhād* 'priesthood' ; *regollīċe* 'according to rule'. Hybrid compounds are not un-common, e.g. *sealmsċop* 'psalmist' from Lat. *psalma* and O.E. *sċop* ' poet '.

Not nearly all of the words borrowed before the Conquest have survived to the present day. Many were replaced by introductions from French, which, though coming from the same Latin form as the Old English word, have acquired a distinctive form in French itself. Thus Mod. Eng. *gem* is from Old French *gemme*, from Lat. *gemma* ; the latter had been borrowed by Germanic before the English settlement in England, and appears in Old English as *ǵimm* ; if this had survived it would have been *yim* in Modern English.[1]

The extent to which the individual words are used varies considerably. Some words may be found in almost any Old English text which is examined ; for our knowledge of others we are dependent on a single occurrence, perhaps in a glossary of the tenth or eleventh century, or in a medical prescription. This fact probably does not in all cases reflect the frequency of use in the spoken language, since the distribution of the words in writing naturally depends on the subject dealt with, and the Old English documents, though their scope is fairly wide, do not cover all aspects of ordinary life.

A list of the Old English loans from Latin is given in Appendix A for reference, with their Latin or Romance originals, divided roughly into three periods and classified according to their meaning. It should be noted that a number of words coming into English from Latin were previously adopted into that language from Greek ; this is often the case with words relating to the arts and sciences ; the corresponding Greek forms are given in the lists.

A glance at the list will show the changing character of the loan-words in the different periods. In the earliest stratum there are moderately large groups of military and official and of general trade terms ; a longer list for dress and textiles (twenty-three words), and equally long ones for vessels and receptacles, and for towns, houses, and building. But words for plants and agriculture form the largest group ; many of the plant-names are ultimately of more remote origin than Latin (some are from Egyptian and Asiatic sources) and imply the gradual introduction into Western Europe of plants from the south and east.[2] A number of the animal-names, too, are non-European, and indicate the increasing acquaintance of Europe with the Eastern world.

Of the lists from the second period, the longest are provided by vessels (again) and by plants and agriculture. The number of

---

[1] In the chapters on Old English and in Appendix A the modern English equivalent, if it is derived directly from the O.E. form, is given in small capitals. If a modern derivative exists, though not exactly the same in meaning as the O.E. word, it is added in brackets in small capitals.

[2] On early agriculture and horticulture in England see Hoops, *Waldbäume und Kulturpflanzen*, especially chs. xiii–xv.

vessel-names from this and the earlier period implies a very large variety of these used by Latin-speaking peoples, and only a small number used by the Germanic peoples before they came into contact with the south. Some of these terms survive now as very common words : *cup, bin, chest, pan, pail, pot.* The etymology of many of their Latin or Vulgar Latin forms is doubtful.

In the second period a new class is added : Learning and religion. (For the earliest introductions under the influence of Christianity see the section on Greek.) This includes such words as MONK, NUN, and MINSTER, besides *pinsian* 'to reflect, consider', *glœsan* 'to interpret, gloss', *grœf* 'a style for writing'.

In the third section words relating to religion and learning have very much increased in number. As has already been said, many of these depend directly on written sources, and did not always penetrate into the spoken language. It is not always possible in the Old English texts to distinguish between the foreign words which the writer accepted as English, and those which he still considered foreign, and used, as it were, in italics. There is a fairly large group in this period of words relating to music and poetry—large, that is, when compared with the few words for these in the native vocabulary. (The most important Germanic instrument was the harp (O.E. *hearpe*), and the chief words for 'music' were *glēo* (Mod. Eng. *glee*), *drēam, hleoþor,* and (*ġe*)*sang* (Mod. Eng. *song*). The word *poeta* is not recorded before the Conquest ; the native word was *sċop*.)

For the large number of plant-names which are recorded in Old English we arc indebted in particular to three books of medicine, on which some notes will be given later. It is probable that the plants named were not all grown in England at that time ; some of them are impossible to identify with certainty.

We shall now discuss briefly the Latin element of the chief Old English documents, giving instances of the uses of the foreign words.

Eighth-century Glossaries

We may begin with a group of eighth-century glossaries : the *Corpus, Epinal,* and *Erfurt Glossaries,* lists of Latin words with their Old English equivalents, of which the last two date from about A.D. 700, and are often identical, while the first is a little later and longer than the others, though certainly related to them. Citations are from the *Corpus Glossary* [1] unless a special reference to one of the others is given. The majority of the Latin loan-words which appear in the Old English lists are from the oldest stratum of loans ; some of them are actually the English developments of the Latin words they translate : *buxus*—**box** (tree) (not in *Epinal-Erfurt*) 47 ; *castanea*—**ċiesten** (bēam) ' chestnut ' 47 ; *cerasius*—**ċiser-**(bēam) ' cherry ' 49 ; *coleandrum*—**cellendre** ' coriander ' 53 ; *electrum*—**elotr** ' lupin ' 59 ; *finiculus*—**finugl** ' fennel ' 63 ; *mentha*—**minte** ' mint ' 35 ; *napis*—**naep** ' turnip ' 79. Among the more interesting correspondences are the following :   (A) (= oldest loans) *gladiatores*—**cempan** 67 ; *dulcis sapa*—**caeren** (= ċeren) ' new wine ' 57 ; *caepa*—**ċipe, ynnelaec** ' onion ' 49 (*cīpe* also used to gloss *ascalonia* ' shallot ' : *scolonia*—*cipe* 95 ; *coagolum*—**ċese-**(lyb) ' rennet ' 53 ; *ferculum* ' a dish of food '— **disċ** 63 ; also *paneta* (= *patina*)—**disċ** 85 ; *ebor* ' ivory '—**elpend**(baan) (= elephant tusk) 59 ; *nomisma*—**mynit** ' coin ' [MINT] 81, and *numularius*—**miyniteri** ' moneyer ' 81 ; *lentieula*—**piose** ' PEAS ' 75 ; **popiġ** glosses both *papaver* ' POPPY ' 85 and *cucumis* ' cucumber ' 55 ; *perpendiculum*—**pundur** ' plumbline ' 87 ; *promulgarunt* (pret. pl.)—**sċribun** ' decreed ' 87 ; *bulla*—**siġil** ' seal ' 45 ; *appotheca*—**win**(faet) ' WINE-cask ' 41.

(B) **Byden** glosses the Latin words *doleus* ' a large globular jar ' 35, and *cupa* ' tub, cask ' 53 ; *vestibulum*—**caebrtuun** (= *ċeafortūn* ' hall, court ') 105 ; *fellus*—**catte** ' CAT ' 63 ; *capsis*—**ċest** ' CHEST ' 47 ; *luteum*—**crohha** ' yellow ' 75 ; *concha*—**musclan sċel** ' mussel shell ' 55 ; **seġn** is used for both *labarum* 73 and *vexilla* 105 ; *alea*—**tebl** (= *tæfl* ' die '), *aleator* ' gambler ' 39. Finally **bisċop** appears here, not primarily in the ecclesiastical sense, but in the plant-name *biscopuuyrt* ' BISHOP-wort ' 67, glossing *hibiscum*.

(C) (= third period. Very few of these : *culinia*—**cocas** ' COOKS ' 55 ; *quaternio*—**quatern** (4 on dice) 91 ; *porfyrio*—**feolufer** ' bittern ' 87 ; *immunes* (= *immanes*) **orceas** ' evil

---

[1] Ed. Sweet, *Oldest English Texts*, E.E.T.S., 83, from MS. c.c.c.cbg., cxliv.

spirits ' 69 ; *locusta*—**lopust** ' locust ' 75 ; the last two are not in *Epinal* or *Erfurt*.

An English word is added to the Latin loan in **cyline** ' KILN ', *heorðe* ' hearth ', glossing *fornacula* 65. **Cearricgge**, from Lat. *carrūca*, a four-wheeled travelling-carriage, occurs in all these three glossaries, but is not recorded elsewhere in Old English. The *Epinal Glossary* has *fax*—**fæcilae** ' torch ' 62, which is not in *Corpus*.

The Earlier Verse [1]

Although almost the whole body of pre-Conquest poetry is extant only in copies dating from the early eleventh century, yet the originals of some are undoubtedly to be placed at least as early as the eighth century. *Widsith*, probably the oldest, has, apart from tribal names, only two Latin words : **win-**(*burga*) ' WINE-cities ' (i.e. rejoicing in wine) 20, and **cāsere** ' emperor ' 76. The latter word is used very commonly throughout Old English for the Emperor of the East and the Emperor of the West.[2] (It is also used once with reference to David : *casere creaftig* ' mighty emperor ', Psalm 1, Gr.-W., iii, 2, p. 231.)

In *Beowulf*, the other heroic poems, and the so-called ' elegiac ' poems, the Latin words are still of the popular type adopted into the spoken language in the two earlier periods. They are not very numerous. They are used with no sense of strangeness, but are perfectly at home in the language. The following are the chief ones found in *Beowulf*, with examples of their context : **ancor :** *scip on ancre fæst* 303 ' the ship fast at anchor ' ; **camp :** *in campe gecrong cumbles hyrde* 2505 ' the guardian of the banner fell in the fight ' ; **ċeaster** ' city ' 768 ; **ċeapian :** *maðma hord grimme geceapod* 3012 ' treasure dearly bought ' ; **ċiepan ; dēofol** (see p. 52) : *gegyrwed deofles cræftum and dracan fellum* 2888 ' (a pouch) adorned with devil's skill and with dragon's skins ' : **disċ** and **orc :** *him big stodan bunan and orcas, / discas lagon and dyre sweord* 3047–8 ' goblets and cups stood beside it, dishes lay there and precious swords ' (of the treasure in the dragon's cave) ; **draca,** used for the dragon of the poem by the side of the native

---

[1] References are to lines as given in Grein-Wülcker, *Bibliothek der angelsächsischen Poesie.*

[2] See R. W. Chambers, *Widsith*, pp. 192, 212.

wyrm ; **gīgant** (one of the few late loans in this poem) : *gigantas þa wið gode wunnon* 113 ' giants that fought with God ' ; *giganta weorc* 1562 ' the work of giants ' (of a sword) ; **ġimm :** *heofones gim glad ofer grundas* 2072 ' heaven's jewel glided above the fields ' ; **mīl ; nōn ; sċrīfan :** *ðær abidan sceal . . . miclan domes, / hu him scir metod scrifan wille* 979 ' there he must abide the judgment—how the Creator will pass sentence on him ; **seġn :** *segn eall gylden* 2767 ' a golden banner ' ; **siġle ; strǣt :** *strǣt wæs stanfah* 320 ' the road was paved with stones ' ; in composition with native words, *lagu-strǣt, mere-strǣt* ' sea highway ' (of the ocean) 239, 514 ; **weall :** *wið ðæs recedes weall* 326 ' against the wall of the house ' ; *sænæssas, windige weallas* 572 ' the sea headlands, windy cliffs ' ; **wīc ; wīn :** *druncon win weras* 1233 ' the men drank wine '. **Candel** appears in *Beowulf* in the phrase *roderes candel* 1572 ' heaven's candle, the sun ', and it is in such phrases and with this meaning that this word is always found in Old English verse. Cf. *godes condelle* ' God's candle ' (*Phoenix* 91) ; *seo wlitige wuldres candel* (*Juliana* 454) ' fair candle of glory ' : *heofonlic candel* (*Guthlac* 1264) ' heavenly candle '. It is also used in the same sense in compounds : *dæg-condel* (*Riddle* 88/26) ' day-candle ' ; *frið-candel* (*Genesis* 2539) ' lamp of peace ', etc.

The other heroic and ' elegiac ' poems have nothing to add to these except for **torr,** which occurs in the *Ruin* : *hrofas sind gehrorene hreorge torras* 3 ' the roofs are fallen, the towers in ruin '.

The early Biblical paraphrases—*Genesis, Exodus, Daniel*—have further foreign contributions to make to the vocabulary of English poetry : **ælmesse :** *syle ælmyssan, wes earmra hleo* (*Daniel* 587) ' give alms, be the protector of the poor ' (A.V. ' by shewing mercy to the poor ') ; **clūstor :** *þæt he up heonon ute mihte cuman þurh þas clustro* (*Genesis* 416) ' that he might go up hence through these bars ' (from the speech of Satan in hell) ; **culfre :** *ofer heah wæter haswe culfran* (*Genesis* 1451) ' a grey dove across the towering waves ' (of Noah's dove) ; **earc,** in *Genesis* of Noah's ark, in *Daniel* of the Ark of the Covenant ; **ele**(bēam) ' olive-tree ' (*Genesis* 1473) ; **enġel** ' angel ' ; **esol :** *ongan þa his esolas bætan* (*Gen.* 2866) ' (Abraham) began to bridle his asses ' (the only occurrence of the word in

O.E. verse) : **mæssere** ' priest ', **sācerd** ' priest ' : *bletsian þe pine sacerdos, soðfæst cyning, milde mæsseras* (*Azarias* 148–9) ' Thy priests bless Thee, just King, Thy gentle ministers ' : **segnian :** *he segnade earce innan* (*Gen.* 1365) ' blessed the ark within ' ; **templ :** *sunu Dauides getimbrede tempel* (*Exodus* 391) ' the son of David built a temple '. **Strǣt** is used for the way across the Red Sea : *wegas syndon dryge, haswe herestræta* (*Exodus* 284) ' the ways are dry, the tawny highways '. The tower of Babel is called a *stiðlic stan***torr** in *Genesis* 1700 (' strong tower of stone '). **Seġn** is used for the pillar of fire in *Exodus* (127) ; the word appears elsewhere in the poem in the sense of ' banner '. If the emendation *leon* for *leor* in *Exodus* 319 is correct, as seems certain, this passage gives us the first instance of **lēo** in Old English poetry : *hæfdon him to segne . . . beacen aræred, gyldenne leon* ' they had raised up a banner—a golden lion for a sign '. **Ceaster** is used frequently for ' city '.

The collection of *Riddles* preserved in the Exeter Book may include both eighth and ninth-century poems ; some may be even earlier. They contain few Latin words which do not occur elsewhere in Old English verse, and few which are interesting in other ways. The following are found in the *Riddles* only : **byden :** *bapedan mec in bydene* 28/6 ' bathed me in a butt ' (with reference to the making of mead) ; **cyrten :** *ful cyrtenu ceorles dohter* 26/5 ' a churl's beautiful daughter ' ; **lilie :** *þeah þe lilie sy beorht on blostman* 41/27 ' though the lily be bright of blossom '. All these, however, are to be found in prose. **Līne, pīl,** and **rōse** appear in the *Riddles* for the first time in O.E. verse ; cf. *hildepilas* 16/28 ' javelins ' ; *ic eom stence strengre micle / þonne ricels oþþe rose sy* 41/24 ' I am in scent far stronger than is incense or the rose '. **Gimm** is used in the sense of ' jewel ' : *deora gimmum* 84/36 ' more precious than jewels '. **Earc** is used for a box : *ofte mec bileac . . . ides on earce* 62/2 ' often a woman shut me (i.e. a helmet) up in a box '.

With the poems of Cynewulf and his school, which may be eighth or ninth century, we come to words of a more distinctly theological character, besides other new ones. The signed poems of Cynewulf (*Crist, Elene, Juliana, Fates of the Apostles*) have the following words which do not occur in the texts already discussed : **apòstol :** only in the compound *apostolhād* (*Fates*

14) ' apostleship ', with English suffix : the apostles are referred
to as *æpelingas, pegnas* ' heroes, thanes ', and in other such terms ;
cālend :   *on Maias Kalendas* (*Elene* 1229) ' in the month of
May ' : **carc-** (ern) : *ða wæs mid clustre carcernes duru / behliden*
(*Jul.* 236) ' then the prison-door was closed with a bar ' ; (*be*)-
clȳsan (< *clūs* ' barrier ') :   *geatu stondað beclysed* (*Crist* 323)
' the gates stand barred ') ; **culpe :** *ne ic culpan in þe . . . æfre
onfunde* (*Crist* 177) ' I have never found any fault in thee ' ;
mūr : *burston muras and stanas* (*Crist* 177) ' walls and stones
burst asunder ' ; **pundrian :** *eow sceal . . . apundrad weorðan*
(*Elene* 580) ' shall be apportioned (i.e. weighed out) to you ' ;
scrift, in the sense of ' confessor ' : *ne mæg þurh þæt flæsc se
scrift geseon on þære sawle* (*Crist* 1306) ' the confessor cannot see
through the flesh into the soul ' ; **senoð :** *þæt ge seonoð-domas
rihte reccen* (*El.* 552) ' that you may report the decrees of the
synod correctly ' ; **sȳfre :**   *unsyfre folc* (*Crist* 1232) ' an
intemperate people '.   **Draca** is used in *Elene* for the devil :
dreogaþ deaþ-cwale in dracan fæðme (*El.* 766) ' endure the
torments of hell in the devil's embrace '. **Rex** is used twice in
Elene (e.g. *ece rex, meotud milde* 1042 ' the eternal king, the kind
creator ') ;   the word seems never to have been adopted into
English, and is probably used here deliberately as a foreign word,
though such usages are not found elsewhere in Cynewulf. (Ge)-
segnian means ' mark with the sign of the Cross ' in *Crist* 1342.

The story of St. Andrew in the poem of *Andreas* has the words
martyr : *martyra mægen unlytel* 878 ' a great company of
martyrs ' (also in the verse life of St. Guthlac) ;   **marman-**
(stān) :   *geher ðu, marmanstan, meotudes rædum* 1500 ' hear
thou, marble, the commands of the Creator ' (St. Andrew orders
the marble pillars to pour forth a flood) ; and **tīgle :** *tigelfagan
trafu* 844 ' buildings gay with tiles '.

The *Phoenix*, though partly dependent on a Latin original,
has not many Latin words, and hardly any which have not
appeared before. The bird itself is called **fenix :** *fugel feþrum
strong, se is Fenix haten* 86 ' a bird strong in feathers, which is
called Phoenix '. This word does occur elsewhere in Old English,
for instance in Ælfric's Grammar (*c.* 1000). Another bird-name
is **pēa :** (of the phoenix) *se fugel is on hiwe . . . onlicost pean* 312
' the bird is in colour . . . most like to a peacock '. **Tapur,** like

candel (see p. 19), is used with reference to the sun : *hwonne swegles tapur ofer holm-þræce hædre blice* 114 ' when the sun's taper shines forth serenely over the tossing waves '. **Solor** is used of the phoenix's nest : *se fugel ofer heanne beam hus getimbreþ, and gewicaþ ðær sylf in ðam solere* 204 ' the bird builds a nest in a lofty tree, and dwells there in that upper room '.

The verse life of St. Guthlac has the words **mynster, regol,** and **mūtian :** *under haligra hyrda gewealdum in mynsterum* 387 ' under the authority of holy pastors, in monasteries ' ; *þæt ic forbær rume regulas geongra monna* 460 ' I preferred the lax rules of young men ' : *þas woruld-gestreon bemutad weorþað* 42 ' the treasures of the world shall be changed '.

The rest of the Old English verse will be dealt with later.

The Early Ninth-century Prose

In the legal documents of the late eighth and early ninth centuries [1] we find a fair number of words of the commonest and earliest type. Some, such as *butter, cheese, wine, taper, pound,* and also **sester,** occur in bequests : **wīn :** *mittan fulne huniges oðða tuegen uuines* 37 (805–31) ' a measure full of honey or two of wine ' ; **tapur :** *ðritig teapera, gif hit wintres deg sie* 41 (835) ; **sester, butere :** *sester fulne huniges, sester fulne butran, sester fulne saltes* 41 (835) ' a jar full of honey, one of butter, and one of salt ' ; **čēse :** *x hennfuglas and x pund caeses* 37 (805–31) ' 10 hens and 10 pounds of cheese ' ; *selle mon uuege cæsa and fisces and butran and aegera* 37 (805–31) ' there shall be given a wey of cheeses and fish and butter and eggs '. Ecclesiastical terms occur : **ælmesse :** *ageofan hio þa ilcan elmessan* 45 (871–89) ' let them give the same alms ' ; **mæsse :** *ðaet eghwilc messepriost gesinge fore osuulfes sawle twa messan* 37 (805–31) ' that each mass-priest should sing for Oswulf's soul two masses '. **Diacon** and **passiōn** are both learned words : *and aeghwilc diacon arede twa passione fore his sawle* 37 (805–31) ' let each deacon read two Passions for his soul '. **Port** occurs in the compound *portwara* ' citizens ' 24 (839).

The *Kentish Glosses* [2] of MS. Cotton Vespasian D VI, from the first half of the ninth century, have little of interest for us, but

---

[1] Quoted from Sweet, *Oldest English Texts*, ref. number of charter and date.
[2] Wright-Wülcker, *Vocabularies*, i. Ref. to column.

they supply five words which do not occur in the earlier *Corpus Glossary* : **æced** ' vinegar ' (glossing *acetum*) 66 ; **pytt** : *puteus angustus—neare pyt* 79 ' narrow pit ' ; **sæc** = *sacculum* 62 ; **tæpped** : *tapetibus pictis—gemetum tepedum* 62 ' embroidered carpets ' ; **trifot** ' tribute ' : *tributis—trifetum, gafol* 68 (*gafol* is the native English word).

The *Vespasian Psalter*,[1] an interlinear English version of the psalms and canticles, from the first half of the ninth century, has some examples of the earliest recorded occurrence of Latin words in English, besides showing some interesting usages of words we have already noted elsewhere. The writer shows little inclination to use the words of Latin origin which correspond to the Latin words he is translating, though it happens occasionally in the case of the more exotic words such as *timpane, ysope*. **Assa** appears in *wilde assan* = *onagri* 335 ; **ċeafor-**(tūn) in *in midle ceafurtunes ðines* = *in medio atrio tuo* 290 ' in the midst of thy court ' ; **calic** : *dryhten dael erfewordnisse minre and celces mines* 202 ' the Lord is the portion of my inheritance and of my cup ' ; **ceder** : *gebriceð dryhten ceder-beamas ðes muntes* (= *cedros Libani*) 222 ' the Lord breaks the cedar-trees of the mountain ' ; **cerubin**, probably to be regarded as still a ' foreign ' word : *ðu sites ofer cerubin* 302 ' Thou sittest above the cherubim ' : **cocer** : *gearwadon strelas heara in cocere* (= *in faretra*) ' they have prepared their arrows within the quiver ' ; **culfre** : *fiðru swe swe culfran* 261 ' wings like a dove " ; **gīgant** : *gefaeh swe swe gigant to earnenne on weg* 209 ' rejoiced as a giant to run his course ' ; **ġimm** is used in *ofer gold and gim* ' above gold and precious stone ', where the Latin has *super aurum et topazion* 368 ; **lēo** : *swe swe lea in bedcleofan his* 197 ' like a lion in his den ' ; **mūl** : *swe swe hors and mul* 227 ' like horse and mule ' ; **munt** : *and geherde mec of munte ðæm halgan his* 189 ' and heard me out of his holy hill ' ; **mirra** : *mirra and dropa and smiring from hreglum from stepum elpanbaennum* 249 ' myrrh and " drops " and cassia from thy garments out of the ivory steps' ; **palm** : *se rihtwisa swe swe palma bloweð* 321 ' the righteous shall flourish like a palm-tree ' ; **plant** : *bearn ðin swe swe neowe plant ele-trea* 377 ' thy children like new olive-tree plants ' ; **portic** : *oððæt ic ingæ in godes halig portic* 289 (= *in sanctuarium*

c   [1] Sweet, *Oldest English Texts*. Ref. page.

dei) ' until I go into the sanctuary of God ' ;   **salm :**   *noman ðinum salm ic cweoðu* 209 ' I will sing a new song to thy name ' ; **tiġle :**   *adrugade swe swe tigule megen min* 213 ' my strength is dried up like a tile ' ;   **torr :**   *tor strengu from onsiene feondas* 269 ' a tower of strength in the presence of my enemies ' ;   **turtur :** *speara gemoeted him hus and turtur nest* 307 ' the sparrow has found him a house and the turtle-dove a nest ' ;   **ymen :**   *niowne ymen gode urum* 241 ' a new song unto our God ' ;   **ysope :**   *ðu onstrigdes mec mid ysopan* 257 ' thou hast washed me with hyssop '.   (It will have been observed that a considerable proportion of these words occur in similes.)   Further, there is a little group of musical instruments :   **timpana :**   *in midle iungra plægiendra timpanan* 279 ' in the midst of the young ones playing on the timbrels ' ;   **organa :**   *in salum in midle hire we hengan organan ure* 385 ' on the willows in the midst of her we hung up our instruments ' ;   **cymbala :**   *hergað hine in cymbalan wel hleoðriendum* 401 ' praise him upon the well-sounding cymbals ' ; **citere :**   *aris wuldor min, aris hearpe and citere* 265 ' arise, my glory, arise, harp and cither ' (= *psalterium et cythara*).   All of these words except *culfre, gīgant, gimm, lēo, ceafortūn,* seem to be recorded first in English prose in the *Vespasian Psalter.* There are naturally fewer of the ' every-day ' words in this text than in some others, and more ' learned ' words.

THE PROSE OF KING ALFRED'S TIME

We must first consider King Alfred's own writings.   Since a considerable part of these consists of translations from Latin, one might expect them to reflect the Latin vocabulary of the originals.   This does not, in fact, often happen ; it is least rare in the *Orosius,* where the subject-matter introduces such foreign ideas as *consul, triumph, dictator.*   These are of the type of ' learned ' words which were never naturalized in English.

King Alfred's translation of Gregory's *Liber Pastoralis* [1] is usually considered to be his first extant work.   Here are some of the learned words which he uses in it ; it will be seen that an explanation often accompanies them.   **Aðamans :**   *se hearda*

[1] Ed. Sweet, *Gregory's Pastoral Care,* E.E.T.S., 45, 50, from MS. Cott. Tiberius B. XI.   Ref. to page.   The Latin, where quoted, is from the edition of the *Liber Pastoralis* in Migne's *Patrologia.*

stan, se þe adamans hatte 270 ' the hard stone which is called adamant ' (the Latin has *durus adamas*) ;   **carbunculus** and **iacinctus :**   *on gimma gecynde carbunculus bið diorra ðonne iacinctus* 411 ' among gems the carbuncle is more precious than the jacinth ' ;   **chōr :**   *se psalmscop cwæþ . . . Lofiað God mid tympanan and on choro . . . on ðæm chore bioð monege men gegadrode anes hwæt to singanne anum wordum and anre stemne* 346 ' the psalmist said, Praise God with the timbrel and in the chorus . . . in the chorus many men are gathered to sing something in the same words and with one voice ' (but the Latin has the same comment :   *in choro autem voces societate concordant*) ;   **cymen :**   *ge tiogoðiað eowre mintan and eowerne kymen* 439 ' you tithe your mint and your cummin ' (Lat. *cyminum*) ;   **epistola :** *on his epistolan to Galatum* 116 ' in his epistle to the Galatians ' ;   **magister :**   *he cyðde ðæt he wæs magister and ealdormonn* 116 ' he showed that he was master and chief ' ;   **manna :**   *se sweta mete þe hie heton monna* 124 ' the sweet food which they called manna ' (the *Vespasian Psalter* has *heofonlic hlaf* ' heavenly bread ' for manna 297) ;   **purpura :**   *purpura, ðæt is kynelic hrægl* 84 ' purple, that is a royal robe ' ;   **sācerd :**   *sacerdas, ðæt is on Englisc clænseras* 138 ' *sacerdas* (= priests), that is in English purifiers ' ;   **sōn :**   *ðæt hie noht ungelice ðæm sone ne singað þe he wilnað* 174 ' that they sing sounds not unlike those which he desires.'

We may add to these some examples of words of a more ordinary character, either recorded in this text for the first time or illustrating interesting uses :   **alter :**   *Godes alter* 216, etc., ' God's altar ' ;   the native word is *weofod, weobud*, which is also used in the text ;   **apostol,** common throughout King Alfred's writings ; **carcern :**   *bendas and karcernu* 204 ' bonds and prisons ' (= *vincula et carceres*) ;   **ċēac :**   *beforan ðæm temple stod æren ceac* 104 ' before the temple stood a brazen laver ' ;   **ċēas :**   *ða wrohtgeornan þe cease wyrceað* 176 ' the quarrelsome who stir up strife ' ;   **ċeaster** is the regular equivalent of *civitas* ' city ' : *ða ceastre Hierusalem* 160 ' the city of Jerusalem ' ;   it is also used to translate *castra* :   *he arærð ceastre wið Hierusalem* 162 ' he sets up a camp against Jerusalem ' (= *castra erigit*), and also *templum* :   *on þære Godes ceastre* 252 (= *in templum Dei*) ; **cōc :**   *koka aldermon towearp ða burg æt Hierusalem* 310 ' the prince of cooks cast down the city at Jerusalem ' (= *princeps cocorum* ; the Vulgate has *regis quoque* . . .) ; **fefer** : *an lytel fefres* 228 ' a little fever ' ; **fic** : *swæ se fiicbeam oferscedoð ðæt land* 336 ' as the fig-tree overshadows the land ' ; **impian** : *hiene selfne fæstlice geimpað on eorðlicum weorcum* 132 ' grafts himself firmly into earthly works ' (= *inserit*) ; **martyr** : *he underfeng martyrdom* 52 ' he underwent martyrdom ' ; **mentel** : *forcearf his mentles ænne læppan* 196 ' cut off the border of his cloak ' (= *oram chlamydis*) ; **offrung** : *ryhtwisra monna offrung* 368 ' the offering of righteous men ' ; **olfend** : *ðæt hi forswulgun ðone olpend* 439 ' that they should swallow the camel ' ; **pāpa** : *dryhtnes cempa, Rome papa* 8 ' the Lord's champion, the Pope of Rome ' ; **pile** : *ðeah ðu portige ðone dysegan on pilan swæ mon corn deð mid pilstafe* 266 ' though you pound the foolish in a mortar as one does corn with a pestle ' ; **pinsian** : *pinsige ælc mon hiene selfne georne* 62 ' let every man consider himself carefully ' ; **plantian** : *to plantianne . . . swa se ceorl deð his ortgeard* 292 ' to plant as the churl does his garden ' ; **pyngan** : *hine pynge mid sumum wordum* 296 ' may prick him with words ' ; **pyle** : *wa ðæm ðe willað under ælcne elnbogan lecgean pyle* 142 ' woe to them that wish to lay a pillow under each elbow ' ; **sicor** : *ne bio we no ðæs sicore* 425 ' let us not be sure of it ' ; **solor** : *on ðæm solore ðæs modes* 22 ' in the upper chamber of the mind ' (cf. the use in the *Phoenix*, above) ; **strǣt** : *æt ælcre stræte ende* 132 ' at the end of every street ' (= *in capite omnium platearum*) ; **tapor** : *hie hiene onælð mid ðæm tapore ðæs godcundan liegges* 258 ' they kindle him with the taper of the divine fire ' ; **templ** : in the sense of tabernacle : *Moyses oft eode in and ut on ðæt templ* 100 ' Moses often went in and out of the temple ' (= *tabernaculum*).

This is a long list, but the *Pastoral Care*, since it is the first considerable piece of connected prose in English (the *Vespasian Psalter* being only an interlinear gloss), deserves special attention.

The translation of the fifth-century *Historia adversus Paganos* of Paulus Orosius [1] gives us a number of words connected with Roman history and customs ; like the ' foreign ' words referred to in the *Pastoral Care*, these sometimes have a note of explanation : **anfiteatra** : *heora godas bædon þæt him man*

---

[1] Ed. Sweet, E.E.T.S., 79.

worhte anfiteatra 102 (this has the Latin plural ending) 'asked their gods that amphitheatres should be made for them'; **bibliothece :** *and hiora bibliotheco wearð onbærned from ligette* 270 'and their library was burned up by lightning'; **cohorte :** *he hæfde eahta and eahtatig coortana þæt we nu truman hataþ* 240 'he had 88 cohorts, which we now call *truman*'; **consul :** *him ða Romane . . . ladteowas gesetton, þe hie consules heton* 68 'the Romans appointed leaders whom they called consuls' (cf. the later *Cleopatra Gloss*, which for *consul* has *gearcyning* or *heretoga* 375) ; **istoria :** *ic sceal eac þy lator Romana istoria asecgan* 160 'I shall relate the history of the Romans later' (cf. *stǽr*, also from Lat. *historia*, but adopted into English through Irish ; see p. 59) ; **legie :** *hi hæfdon eahta legian* 160 'they had eight legions'; **palendse :** *æt þæs caseres palendsan* 272 'at the Emperor's palace'; **philosoph :** *hie sealdon Demostanase philosophe* 124 'they gave to Demosthenes the philosopher'; **talente :** *on ælcre anre talentan wæs lxxx punda* 170 'in each talent was 80 pounds'; **tictator :** *heora tictator, Camillis hatte* 92 'their dictator, called Camillus'; **triumphe :** *ðæt hie triumphan heton, þæt wæs . . .* 70 'which they called a triumph, that was . . .'

The following uses are worth noting : **cāsern** for the feminine of *cāsere* (with the Germanic feminine suffix) : *hie heton his wif casern* 266 'they called his wife Empress'; **ćest :** *twa cista, þa wæron attres fulle* 258 'two boxes which were full of poison' (= *arca*) ; **cyperen :** *ealle þa onlicnessa . . . ge ærene, ge cyprene* 216 'all the images, both of iron and of copper'; **elpend :** *he* [Pyrrhus] *hæfde xx elpenda* 154 'he had 20 elephants'; **lēo :** *þæm Minotauro . . . þæt wæs healf mon, healf leo* 42 'the Minotaur, which was half man, half lion'; **mattuc :** *and siþþan mid mattucum heawan* 186 'and afterwards to cut it up with mattocks'; **mydd :** *þrio mydd gyldenra hringa* 190 'three bushels of gold rings' (= *tres modios*) ; **nunne** is used for a vestal virgin : *Caperronie wæs haten heora goda nunne* 162 'one of the "nuns" of their gods was called Caperronia'; **offrian :** *hie him þagit ofreden and bloten* 162 'they still made offerings and sacrifices to them' (*blōtan* is the native verb) ; **port,** in the sense of 'haven' rather than 'town' : *an port . . . þone man hæt Sciringes heal* 19 'a port called S.'; **scōl :** *þære*

scole þe he on leornede 284 ' the school he learned in ' ; (ā)**spendan** :
þonne his gestreon beoð þus eall aspended 21 ' when his wealth
is all spent in this way ' ; **spynge** : *for þon þe elpendes hyd wile
drincan wætan, gelice ond spynge deð* 23Q ' because an elephant's
hide will absorb moisture as a sponge does ' ; **tigle** : *he is geworht
of tigelan and of eorðtyrewan* 74 ' it [the wall of Babylon] is all
made of bricks and bitumen ' ; **tunece** : *hie him sendon ane
tunecan* 234 ' they sent him a toga ' ; **yndse** : *ælc wifmon hæfde
ane yndsan goldes* 196 ' each woman had an ounce of gold '
(= *auri uncias*).

The Old English version of Bede's *Historia Ecclesiastica* [1]
contains, as its subject would suggest, a large number of
ecclesiastical terms. Such words as *ælmesse, abbud, abbudisse,
engel, mæsse, munuc, mynster, nunne, sācerd, salm,* are common.
There are a good many learned words, usually following Bede's
Latin : **antemn, letania** : *þeosne letaniam and ontemn gehleoðre
stefne sungon*   60 ' they sang this litany and antiphon with
harmonious voices ' (= *laetaniam consona uoce modularentur*) ;
archidiacon : *þæs gelæredestan Bonefatius archidiacones* 454 ' of
Boniface the learned archdeacon ' ; **balsam** : *hordærn balsami*
(with Latin ending) 174 ' a store of balsam ' (= *opobalsami
cellaria*) ; **canon** : *þæt halige gewrit se canan* 486 ' the holy
scripture, the canon ' (= *scriptura sancta*) ; **capitol** : *swa we
ær in þæm uferan kapitule cwædon* 84 ' as we said in the last
chapter ' ; **comēta** : *neowe steorra, se is cweden cometa* 298 ' a new
star, which is called *comet* ' ; **crisma** : *under crisman* 404 ' attired
in the chrisom ' (= *in albis*) ; **discipul** : *heo gesomnodon micelne
þreat discipula* 258 ' they gathered a throng of disciples ' ;
King Alfred does not seem to use *leornung-cniht*, the usual term
in the Gospels for ' disciple ' ; he has, however, *leornung-mon*
(applied to a woman) in the phrase *discipula and leornung-mon
regollices lifes* Bede 236 (= *discipula uitae regularis*) ; **domne** :
her resteð domne Agustinus 106 ' here lies the lord Augustine '
(= *hic requiescit domnus Augustinus*) ; *min domne, hwæt is þis
fyr?*   214 ' my lord, what is this fire ? ' (= *domine*) ; **eretic** :
wið Ðeodorum and Theodoreti and Iiba þæm ereticum 312
' against Th. and T. and I., heretics ' ; **grammatic** : *grammatic-
cræft tydon and lærdon* 258 ' taught grammar ' ; **martyr** : *ða*

---

[1] Ed. Miller, E.E.T.S., 95–6, 110–11. Ref. to page.

prowunge para haligra martyra 40 ' the passion of the holy martyrs ' ; *prowunge* is the native word equivalent to *martyrdom* ; for *martyr* the word *prowere* is often used ; **meter-fers :** *we . . . awriton, ge meter-fersum ge geradre spræce* 366 ' we have written, both in verse and in prose ' (= *et uersibus heroicis et simplici oratione*) ; *meterfersum asang and geradre spræce gesette* 448 (= *et uersibus exametris, et prosa composuit*) ; *meter-cræft = metricæ ars* 258 ; **nōn :** *þy feorðan wic-dæge . . . fæston to nones* 162 ' the fourth week-day they fasted till noon ' ; **subdiacon :** *to subdiacone gehalgad* 254 ' ordained subdeacon ' ; **tabul :** *gehalgadne tabul on wigbedes gewrixle* 416 ' a consecrated table in place of an altar ' (= *tabulam altaris uice*) ; **tra**(*isc*) : *on gelicnesse þæs traiscan wæles wundade* 154 ' wounded in the manner of the tragic slaughter ' (= *tragica caede*) ; but this should perhaps be *trōisc* = Trojan, which is the word used in another, similar, passage (306).

The following may also be noted : **ampelle :** *genom his ompellan and sumne dæl þæs eles sende in þone sæ* 200 ' took his flask and poured some of the oil into the sea ' ; **ancor :** *þa ongunnon þa scipmen þa oncras upp teon* 200 ' then the sailors began to draw up the anchors ' ; **crisp :** *and hæfde crispe loccas fægre* 390 ' and had pretty curly hair ' ; **crūċ :** *þa aðenede se biscop hine in cruce* 372 ' the bishop prostrated himself in the form of a cross ' ; **fers :** *þa fers and þa word þe he næfre gehyrde* 344 ' the verses and the words which he had never heard ' ; **meregrota :** *on ðam beoþ oft gemettan ða betstan meregrotan* 26 ' in these are often found the best pearls ' ; **portic :** *in þære cirican norðportice* 106 ' in the north porch of the church ' ; **prafost :** *prafost and ealdormon* 232, *profost and regolweard* 360 (= *propositus* of a monastery) ; **regol :** *þeodscipe regollices liifes* 226 ' the discipline of regular life ' ; **seġn,** used by the side of *tācn* to translate *uexilla,* cf. 144, 146, 184 ; **strǣt :** *ceastre and torras and stræte and brycge on heora rice geworhte wæron* 44 ' towns and towers and roads and bridges were made in their country ' (= *stratae*).

King Alfred's translation of Boethius's *Consolation of Philosophy* [1] (and we include here the verse as well as the prose version of the *Metra*) has very few words of Latin origin which

---

[1] Ed. Sedgefield, Oxford, 1899.

do not occur in his other writings. **Consul** (as in *Orosius*) has an explanatory note : *þa wæs sum consul, þæt we heretoha hata∂* 7 ' there was a certain consul, which we call *heretoga* ' ; **culpian** is found in this text and apparently nowhere else in Old English : *þæt mon scyle culpian to þæm þe him gifan scyle* 71 ' that a man must cringe to one who may give to him ' ; **læden** has here the sense of ' Latin ', but *bōclæden* is used also for ' Latin ' (i.e. ' book Latin '), and occasionally in Old English *læden* is used for ' language ' in general ; cf. the references to Ælfric's *Heptateuch* below ; **must** occurs here in the phrase *þeah þe wel lyste wearmes mustes* 12 ' though you much desire new wine '. The remaining words of interest in *Boethius* are a small group of bird and animal names : **cypera :** *þonne eow fon lyste∂ leax o∂∂e cyperan* 176 ' when you wish to catch " lax " or " kipper " ' (i.e. salmon at two different stages) ; **tigris :** *swiftran þonne tigris . . . strengran þonne leo* 72 ' swifter than the tiger, stronger than the lion ' ; **ultor :** *se ultor sceolde forlætan ∂æt he ne slat ∂a lifre Sticces* 102 ' the vulture is said to have stopped tearing the liver of S.' (when it heard the music of Orpheus).

Finally, from the version of St. Augustine's *Soliloquies* only two words need be mentioned : **inseġl :** *gyf ∂ines hlafordes ærendgewrit and hys insegel to ∂e cym∂* 24 (the first occurrence) ' if thy lord's letter and his seal come to thee ' ; **line :** *be anre linan . . . wæs awriten* 21 ' in one line was written ' (see also *Riddles*), where *līne* is used in the same sense).

Leaving King Alfred's own work, we may turn to the O.E. *Martyrology*,[1] which perhaps dates from his reign, though the manuscripts in which it is extant are all at least a century later. This text has the words **rōse** and **lilie :** *swa swote swa rosan blostman ond lilian* 198 ' as sweet as the blossoms of rose and lily ' ; also **marm(ar),** which has not so far been referred to in the sections on prose : *þeah hit wære marmarstanes* 74 ' though it were of marble ' ; **candel** is used in its concrete sense : *swa hwelc mon swa condella onbærne* 116 ' as though one were burning a candle ' ; **cæppa :** *þa dyde Albanus on hine þæs preostes cæppan* 100 ' then A. put on him the priest's cope ' ; **crēda :** *gif he song his credan* 144 ' if he sang his creed ' ; **relic :** *eall godes folc mid eadmodlice relicgonge* 62 ' all the people of God in a humble

[1] Ed. Herzfeld, E.E.T.S., 116. Ref. to page.

visiting of relics ' ; **sealticge :** *sellan anre sealticgan hire plegan
to mede* 156 ' to give to a dancer as a reward for her dancing ' ;
piċ and **draca** have already been noted in the section on the earlier
verse : *of þære com gan micel draca ond abat þone þriddan dæl
þæs hæðnan folces* 90 ' out of it came a huge dragon and eat up
a third part of the heathen people ' ; *þa het se casere meltan
on hwere lead ond scipteoran ond pic* 96 ' then the Emperor
ordered lead and tar and pitch to be melted in a cauldron '.
The English equivalents given for the Latin names of the arts
show that abstract native words could be constructed and used
instead of adopting Latin ones : *arythmetica,* þæt is þonne
rymcræft ; *astrologia,* þæt is þonne tungolcræft ; *astronomia,*
þæt is tungla gang ; *geometrica,* þæt ys eorð-gemet 212 ;
mechanica, þæt is weoruld-weorces cræft ; *medicina,* þæt is
læce-domes cræft 214 ; *musica,* þæt ys dreamcræft 212.

The translation of Gregory's *Dialogues* by Wærferth, Bishop of
Worcester, is another important prose work of Alfred's time.
Perhaps the most interesting point about the Latin element in
its vocabulary is the variation in the three manuscripts. The
Oxford MS. (Bodl. Hatton 76) sometimes has a native word
where the Cambridge MS. (C.C.C. S 10) has one of Latin origin
and (more rarely) vice versa. The British Museum MS. (Cott.
Otho C. I) usually has the same word as the Cambridge MS.
(these two MSS. are very close in other respects), but occasionally
agrees with Hatton against Cbg. It has been suggested that
Hatton represents a revision of the version in the other two MSS.

The following are the chief instances :—

(A) Latin word in Cbg. :—

Cbg.	B.M.	Hatton
bydene	bydene	ele-treddan 50
bydenu	bydenu	kyfa 57
calicas	calicas	scencea 127
candele	candele	leoht(es) 143, 144
carcern	carcern	cweartern 107
epistolan	epistolan	ærend-gewrite 38
militisces (mannes)	militisces (mannes)	þegenes 77, 78
spertan (= spyrtan)	spertan	wylian 110

Cbg.	B.M.	Hatton
tapor	tapor	weocon 44
torre	torre	stypele(s) 170, 3

(B) English word in Cbg. :—

beode	mysan	mysan 143
beode	beode	mysan 143
gebletsodon	gesenodon	gesenodon 124
god-webbenum	god-webbenum	pællenum 131
lof-sang	lof-sang	(beod)-fers 62
(ge)cide	(ge)cide	ceaste 64

Sometimes Cbg. uses both a loan-word and the corresponding native word in the same passage : **calic** (here in the sense of 'lamp', not 'cup' as in the list above) : *þone tobrocenan calic þære ærran gesynto eft ageaf* 50 'gave back the broken lamp as whole as before' ; elsewhere in this chapter *glæsen leoht-fæt* ; here the variation depends on the Latin original, which has *calicem* in the sentence quoted, but *lampas vitrea* later in the passage. **Mēse :** *þa [grenan wyrta] to ure mysan bringeð* 181 'shall bring green vegetables to our table' ; but *beode* is used on the same page.

The word **templ** is used in this text with reference to the temple of God and to that of Apollo. **Solor**, which usually has the meaning of 'upper room, solar' (cf. *gestod in þam solore þæs Mynstres* 119 'stood in the upper room of the monastery') once translates *palatium* : *þeowode in þam solore þære Con-stantinopoliscan byrig* 248 'should serve in the palace of the city of Constantinople'.

The following loan-words appear here for the first time in English prose, though some have been noted earlier in glossaries : **cancer :** *gestanden on þa breost mid cancre þære wunde* 278 'afflicted in the breast with cancer' ; **leahtric :** *þa geseah heo æne leahtric* 30 'then she saw a lettuce' ; **cycene :** *þa awurpon hie þæt . . . in þa cycenan* 123 'they threw it into the kitchen' ; **cymbala :** *þa stod þær semninga sum man mid anum apan . . . and sloh cymbalan* 62 'all at once there stood there a man with an ape and struck cymbals' ; **cemes :** *butan his kemese* 68 'without his shirt' ; **dalmatica :** *man alegde ofer þa bære . . .*

his dalmatican 329 ' they laid his dalmatic over the bier ' ;
dihtian : *him to gehet his writere and him dihtode* 193 ' he
summoned his scribe and dictated to him ' ; **fenester :** *oð þæt
hit becom upp to þam fenestrum* 220 ' until it came up to the
windows ' ; **matta :** *þæt hine man alegde in his cytan on þa
meattan* 125 ' that he should be laid on the mat in his cell ' ;
mæslere : *ga to Abundium þam mæslere* 228 ' go to A. the
sacristan ' (= *vade ad Acontium mansionarium*) ; **scrin :** *forlet
þa scrine his feoh-gestreones* 52 ' left his treasure-chest ' ;
milit(isc) : *þa wæron militisce men farende* 194 ' there were
soldiers travelling ' (= *milites*) ; **spyrte :** *twa spyrtan fulle metes*
203 ' two baskets full of food ' ; **traht :** *in þam godspelles trahtum
þe ic self awrat* 283 ' in the commentary on the Gospel, which
I wrote myself ' ; **trahtian,** here ' to discuss ' : *ongunnon trahtian,
hwæðer hi mihton . . . þæt unmæte stanclif onweg aleoðian* 213
' they began to discuss whether they could remove the huge rock '.

The Anglo-Saxon Chronicle,[1] the first part of which was
compiled during King Alfred's reign, does not give us many words
of special interest until the eleventh century. The following
words from the ninth and tenth centuries, not very common in
Old English generally, may be mentioned :—

Ninth Century : **cometa** (evidently a foreign word here) :
*se steorra þe mon on boclæden hæt cometa, same man cwepaþ on
Englisc þæt hit feaxede steorra sie* 892 ' the star which is called
' cometa ' in Latin, while in English men say that it is the star
with hair ' ; **crisma :** *his crism-lising wæs æt Weþmor* 878 ' the
putting off of his baptismal robe was at Wedmore ' ; **cumpæder**
(recorded here only) : *Æþered his cumpæder* 894 ' Æþered his
godfather ' ; **domne :** *þa was domne Leo pape on Rome* 853
' then was lord Leo pope at Rome ' ; **legat :** *þæt seo abbot beo
gehealden for legat of Rome* 675 ' that the abbot should be
recognized as papal legate ' ; **scōl :** *þy ilcan geare forborn
Ongolcynnes scolu* 816 ' in the same year the English school
(at Rome) was burnt down ' ; **senoþ :** *her wæs geflitfullic senoþ
æt Cealchyþe* 785 ' in this year there was a disputatious synod at
Chelsea '. Tenth Century : **mynetere :** *and an myneter in Stan-
ford* 963 ' and one maker of coins at Stamford ' ; **Pentecosten :**

---

[1] Ed. Plummer, *Two Anglo-Saxon Chronicles Parallel.* Ref. to year of
Chronicle.

Pentecostenes dæg 973 'the day of Pentecost' ; **portic :** *binnan Gleawcestre on þam east portice sancte Petres cyrcean* 918 'at Gloucester in the east porch of St. Peter's church' ; **sanct** (usually used attributively) : *he is nu æfter deaðe heofonlic sanct* 979 'he is now after death a heavenly saint' ; **clēric :** *draf ut þa clerca of þe biscoprice* 963 'drove out the clergy from the bishopric'.

THE OLD ENGLISH GOSPEL VERSIONS

Of the Old English translations of the four Gospels [1] the oldest is the interlinear Northumbrian version in the Latin Lindisfarne Gospels, added to the Latin in the middle of the tenth century. A little later in date is the interlinear gloss in the Rushworth Manuscript, in which the Gospel of St. Matthew is in a Midland dialect, while those of St. Mark, St. Luke, and St. John are in a southern Northumbrian dialect, and are largely dependent on the Lindisfarne gloss. The late West Saxon version is from about 1050, but may be considered here with the others. Taking *St. Matthew* first, we find that each of the versions has its own peculiarities. In Lindisfarne alone of the translations are the following words (though some are found elsewhere in Old English) : **ćealcian** 'to whitewash' : *byrgennum oferhiudum vel uta gecælcad sepulchres* xxiii, 27 (= painted or whitewashed on the outside), Rush. and LWS. Gospels *(be)hwitum* ; **ceulas** 'baskets' xv, 37 where Rush. has *sperta*, LWSG. *wilian* ; **cilic :** *in cilic and in asca* xi, 21 'in sackcloth and ashes', where Rush. has *in wite* (= in torment), and LWSG. *on hæran* (= in haircloth) ; **cuopel,** apparently from Med. Lat. *caupulus* : *in lytlum scipe* vel *cuople* viii, 23 (= *in nauicula*), where the others use *scip* ; **cursumbor,** where the others have *recels*, the usual native word for incense, ii, 11 ; **mīl** (here equivalent to Lat. *mille* 'thousand', rather than 'mile') : *suachua ðec genedes mile strædena* v, 41 'whosoever shall compel thee to go a thousand paces', where Rush. has *þusend steppan*, and LWSG. *þusend stapa* ; **nōn :** *to huil nones* xxvii, 45 'at noontide', Rush. and LWSG. *nigoþan tid* 'ninth hour' ; **pīnian :** *ðu cuome hider ær*

---

[1] Ed. Skeat, *The Gospel according to St. Matthew*, etc. Ref. to chapter and verse.

tid to pinienne usih viii, 29 'art thou come hither to torment us before the time', where Rush. has *tinterga* and LWSG. *preagenne*, all in the sense of 'torment'; **plæce**: *in huommum ðara plæcena* vel *worðum* vi, 5 'in the corners of the streets' (the word *worð* is used for a street in a town or for the hall or *atrium* of a house), where Rush. has *worðana*, LWSG. *stræta*; **port** 'gate': *inngeonges ðerh nearuo port* vel *dure* vel *gæt* vii, 13 'enter ye in at the strait gate', the others having only *geat*; **seternes-**(*dæg*): *to sunnadæg* vel *to seternes-dæg* xii, 8 (= *sabbati*), where the others have *reste-, ræste- dæg*; **camell**: *hrægl of camella herum* ii, 4 'a garment of the hair of camels', Rush. and LWSG. using *olfend* (see below); **trahtian**: *ðæt is getrahtet, mið us god* i, 23 'which is, being interpreted, God with us', for the *gereht* of the others. In Mt. viii, 5 Lindisfarne has **centur** for 'centurion', but explains it, *þæt is hundraðes monna hlaferd* 'lord of a hundred men', and has also the phrase *ðæm aldormenn* v, 8, where Rush. has *centurio*; in both passages LWSG. has *hundredes ealdor*.

Lind. and Rush. agree against LWSG. in having **cælic** (LWSG. *drinc*) in Mt. x, 42. Rush. has the following forms where different words occur in Lind. and LWSG.: **diner**: *þa geþingádun wið þæm wyrhtum be dinere* Mt. xx, 2 'they agreed with the workmen for a penny', Lind. *of pening*, LWSG. *ænne penig*; **discipul**: *discipuli* vel *his pægnas* Mt. v, 1 Lind. *ðeignas*, LWSG. *leornung-cnihtas*; **pipere**: *piperas* Mt. ix, 23, Lind. *beameras*, LWSG. *hwistleras*; **sperta**: Mt. xv, 37 and xvi, 10, for which Lind. has *ceulas* and *monda*, and LWSG. *wilian*; **sȳfer**: *unsyfernisse* Mt. xxiii, 27, Lind. *unclænæ*, LWSG. *fylþe*; **torcul**: *gedælf in ðæm torcul* Mt. xxi, 33 'digged a wine-press in it', Lind. *win-trog*, LWSG. *win-wringan*; **synagoge**: *lærende in heora synagogum* vel *somnungum* Mt. iv, 23 'teaching in their synagogues or congregations', the others (*ge*)*somnungum*; **tæppel-**(bred): *ne þurh eorðæ forðon þi hio is fot-scamel* (the word used by Lind. and LWSG.) vel *tæppel-bred his fota* v, 35 'nor by the earth for it is his footstool'.

The considerably later *Late West-Saxon Gospels* have the following individual forms: **altāre** Mt. v, 24, the others *wigbed, weofud*; **coccel** 'tares' Mt. xiii, 25, Lind. *wynnung* vel *sifþe*, Rush. *weod*; **fann**: *ðæs fann ys on his hand* Mt. iii, 12,

Lind. omits, Rush. *windiu scofel* (but *fann* in Lind. Lu. iii, 17) ;
milite : *þa milite geworhton þyrnenne coronan* Mt. xxvii, 27
'the soldiers made a crown of thorns' (cf. *Vercelli Homilies,*
below) ; **munt :** *he astah on þone munt* Mt. v, 1 'he went up into
the mountain', Lind. *mōr*, Rush. *dūn* ; **pytt :** *hig feallaþ begen
on ænne pytt* Mt. xv, 14 'both shall fall into the ditch', others
sēaþ, but Rush. has *pytt* as an alternative to *seaþ* in xii, 11.

For the remaining three gospels we must content ourselves
with giving lists of words (with one reference to each) which
occur in Lindisfarne and not in LWSG., and vice versa. (Rush.
may be assumed to have the same word as Lind. except where
otherwise stated.)

1.   Lindisfarne :—

      assald ' ass ' Lu. xiii, 15.
      camell ' camel ' Mk. i, 6.
      casering, a coin, Lu. xv, 8.
      cawl ' basket ' Mk. vi, 43.
      celmert-(monn) ' hired man ' Mk. i, 20, etc.
      corona ' crown ' J. xix, 2.
      cunele ' thyme ', Lu. xi, 42.
      cyrtel ' coat ' Mk. vi, 9.
      discipul ' disciple ' Lu. vi, 40.
      lopestre ' locust ' Mk. i, 6.
      magistre ' master ' Lu. vi, 40.
      pic ' pinnacle ' Lu. iv, 9.
      pis(lic) ' heavy ' Mk. xiv, 40.
      plætse ' street ' Mk. vi, 56.
      plett ' sheepfold ' J. x, 1.
      purble ' purple ' J. xix, 5.
      regol-(weard) ' ruler, nobleman ' J. iv, 46.
      segne ' net ' J. xxi, 8 (Rush. *nett*).
      stole ' robe ' Mk. xii, 38.
      torr ' tower ' Mk. xii, 1.
      trahtian ' interpret ' J. i, 41.
      turtur ' turtle-dove ' Lu. ii, 4.

2.   Late West-Saxon Gospels :—

      altare ' altar ' Lu. xi, 51.
      alewe ' aloe ' J. xix, 39.

box ' box ' J. xix, 39.
byden ' pot, measure ' J. ii, 6.
candel-(stæf) ' candlestick ' Mk. iv, 21.
calc ' sandal ' Mk. vi, 9.
cocc ' cock ' J. xiii, 38.
cypa ' basket ' Lu. ix, 17.
castel ' village ' Mk. vi, 6.
dihtan ' to order ' J. xviii, 14.
flasce ' bottle ' Mk. xiv, 13.
mangung ' merchandise ' J. ii, 16.
mese ' table ' Mk. vii, 28, etc.
minte ' mint ' Lu. xi, 42.
munt ' mountain ' Mk. iii, 13.
nard ' spikenard ' Mk. xiv, 3.
offrung ' sacrifice ' Mk. ix, 49.
olfend ' camel ' Mk. i, 6.
paradis ' paradise ' Lu. xxiii, 43.
purpur ' purple ' J. xix, 2.
sætern-(dæg) ' Saturday, Sabbath ' Lu. xxiii, 54.
scrin ' coffer ' J. xii, 6.
seam ' wallet ' Lu. xxii, 35.
sicol ' sickle ' Mk. iv, 29.
spynge ' sponge ' Mk. xv, 36.
titul ' title ' Mk. xv, 26 (not in Rush.)
toll-(scamol) ' treasury ' Mk. xii, 41.
turtle ' turtle-dove ' Lu. ii, 4.

These lists are the same in length, but differ in that the first
has a fair proportion of words which occur nowhere in Old English
except in the Lindisfarne and Rushworth Gospels. *Cāsering*,
translating *drachma*, is found in the Rushworth version of
St. Matthew as well as in the three gospels referred to in the
lists ; the word is recorded also in the fragment of Old High
German epic poetry known as the *Hildebrandslied*, in the form
cheisuring. For *drachma* LWSG. has the native word *sċilling*.
Celmert-monn [1] ' hired servant ', represented in LWSG. by
hyra, hyremonn, yrðling, is apparently from a Vulgar Latin
form *collimbertus* of Lat. *collibertus* ' fellow-freedman '. *Plætse*,

---

[1] See Jordan, *Eigentümlichkeiten des anglischen Wortschatzes*, p. 82.

plæce, from a Romance form of Lat. *platea*, occurs in Lind.,
Rush., and also in another northern document, the *Durham
Ritual*. *Plett* ' sheepfold ' (LWSG. *sceapa-falde*) seems to be from
Lat. *plecta* ' hurdle '. *Purple*, with dissimilation of *r* to *l*, takes the
place of the usual O.E. *purpur* ; cf. the alternative forms *turtur*
and *turtle* ; the latter is, however, fairly common.

A few of the correspondencies between Latin loan-words and
native words are worth noting. For *altare* of LWSG., the other
Gospels have *wigbed*, *weofud*, and this word is retained in the
twelfth-century Hatton MS. of the Gospels, though this usually
follows the LWSG. The word *bæzere*, *bæpzere* ' baptist ' corresponds to the native *fullwihtere*, which appears in LWSG.,
though this also has *bezera*. For *box*, in *sealf-box* (Mk. xiv, 3)
' box of ointment ', LWSG. has *stænne-fæt*. For *candel-stæf*
' candelabrum ' Lind. has *leht-isern* (= light-iron). For *lilie* in
sceawiaþ þa lilian hu hi wexaþ Mk. xii, 27, Lind. has simply
wyrta ' flowers '. LWSG. uses *gærstapan*, usually ' grasshoppers '
for the Latin *locustas*, Lind. *lopestro* Mk. i, 6. *Munt* occurs in
all the versions, but though it is the usual word in LWSG.,
Lind. more often has *mōr*. For the ' learned ' word *osanna*
Mk. xi, 10 Lind. uses the native exclamation *lā hæl*. The word
pīslīc (with Gmc. suffix, from Lat. *pēns-us*) ' heavy ' occurs in
Mk. xiv, 40, *ego hiora pislico* ' their eyes were heavy ' ; this
is in Lind. ; LWSG. has *gehefegode* (P.P.). Where LWSG.
has *sicol* ' sickle ', Lind. has *rīp-īsern* ' reaping-tool '. For *torr*
in Lind. Mk. xii, 1, LWSG. has *stypel* (cf. *Gregory's Dialogues*,
above). *Leorning-cniht* is the usual word in LWSG. for
' disciple '. For the learned *paradis* in LWSG., Lind. has *nercsna-
wong*, a Germanic word whose etymology remains a puzzle.
For the Latin *supra pinnam templi* Lu. iv, 9, Lind. has *ofer
horn-pic temples*, LWSG. *ofer þæs temples hricg*. For *sēam*
(V.Lat. *sauma*) in Lind. (Lu. xxii, 35) *buta seame and met-bælig*
' without purse and scrip ', LWSG. has *seod* ' pocket, purse '.
Apostol is used in all the versions, but LWSG. has *ærenddraca*
' messenger ' at least once (J. xiii, 16). The native word for
corona (Lind. J. xix, 2, *corona of þornum* ' crown of thorns ')
is *cyne-helm* (LWSG.) or, as Lind. gives as an alternative, *siǵ-beǵ*
' circlet of victory '. *Cocc* replaces the Gmc. *hona* in J. xiii, 38.
The foreign *mangung* for *negotiatio* is found in LWSG. ; Lind.

has the earlier and commoner loan-word *ceping*. Finally we note
that Lind. and Rush. use the form *cælc* for ' cup ' (Lat. *calic-em*),
and LWSG. *calix*, the latter indicating a re-borrowing from Latin
at a later date.

LATE TENTH CENTURY

The tenth-century glosses in MS. Harley 3376 give a few new
words, chiefly of a learned type : **cassan** (pl.) glosses *casses,
retia* 200 ; **casul** appears as the equivalent of *byrrum* 196 ; **ćetel**
of *caldaria* 197 ; **ciper-**(*sealf*) ' henna ointment ' for *ciprum*
205 ; **circul** for *circulus* 204 ; **platung(um)** for *brateolis, laminis*
196 ; **tunne** for *cantarus* 198. **Cōcere** ' cook ' (with Gmc. suffix
-*ere* ; cf. *cōc*, already referred to) appears in the compound
cocor-panne, for *frixorium* 243. **Scriptor,** in the compound *tid-
scriptor* for *chronographius* 204, is perhaps purely Latin. English
equivalents given for the loan-word **sicul** (glossing *falx*) are
wingeard-seax, rifter (' vineyard-knife, reaper ').

The *Blickling Homilies* [1] of the late tenth century have no new
introductions, except perhaps **lāur** (*mid lawere gebeagod* 187
' crowned with laurel ') and **spica,** unless the latter is to be
considered a foreign word : *ele and nardus and spica, seo is brunes
heowes and godes stences* 73 ' oil and nard and spikenard, which is
of a dark colour and has a good perfume '. The following uses
should be noted : **binn :** *arweorþian we Crist on binne asetene* 11
' let us honour Christ laid in a manger ' ; **cantic :** *on hire cantice
gefeonde . . . sang and þus cwæþ* 5 ' rejoicing in her song, sang
and said thus '. **Gigant** is used for Goliath : *he þone gigant
ofwearp* 31 ' he overthrew the giant '. **Discipul** is the regular
word for ' disciple '.

The form **orgel,** as distinct from *organe*, appears in a tenth-
century gloss in the Blickling MS., in which the Homilies are
also found : *organo—orgeldreame* 150 ' the sound of a musical
instrument '.

The *Vercelli Homilies,* [2] probably of the late tenth century, give
us the word **evangeliste :** *sægð oðer euuangeliste, þæt . . .* 12
' another evangelist says that . . .', perhaps not to be regarded as

---

[1] Ed. Morris, E.E.T.S., 58.
[2] Ed. Förster, *Bibliothek der ags. Prosa*, xii (first half). Ref. to page.

D

an English word. **Sȳfer**(*licnesse*) (with a double Gmc. suffix) is used in the sense of ' sincerity ' (59). **Milite** appears several times for ' soldiers ' : *wæron þa milite þæs ge-refan men* 34 ' the soldiers were men of the reeve's ' ; an adjectival form of this word (*militisc*) has already appeared in Wærferth's translation of Gregory's *Dialogues*, and *milite* occurs again in the eleventh century *St. Matthew* (see above).

THE WORKS OF ÆLFRIC

Ælfric, abbot of Eynsham, is the most notable writer of the late tenth and early eleventh century. Trained in the school of Æþelwold at Winchester, he represents a fine product of the monastic revival of the late tenth century. His works are varied, including science and grammar as well as sermons and other religious writings.

The homilies,[1] being of a popular character, contain few unusual Latin words, and some words of a learned type are explained : *he is cweden protomartyr, þæt is se forma cyðere* (Catholic Homilies, 50) ' he is called protomartyr, that is the first witness ' ; *betwux dracum and aspidum and eallum wyrmcynne* 486 ' among dragons and asps and all kinds of serpents ' ; and even *discipuli, þæt sind leorning-cnihtas* 26 ' disciples, that is learners '. **Crēda** must have been a familiar word, and this is used without comment, or without explicit comment : *þone geleafan þe on ðam credan stent* 274 ' the faith which is to be found in the Creed '. Ælfric uses the form **pistol** rather than the more learned *epistol* : *Hieronimus se halga sacerd awrat ænne pistol* 436 ' Jeremy the holy priest wrote a letter '. **Arc** is, however, a learned form, of more recent introduction than *earc* : *God beleac hi bynnan þam arce* 22 ' God shut them into the ark '. The word **regol** is used in the compound *regol-sticca* in its original sense of ' carpenter's rule ' 362. **Cranic** ' chronicle ' appears three times in Ælfric (e.g. *swa swa Hieronimus sæde syððan on his cranice* Hom. on St. John xvi ' as Jeremy afterwards said in his chronicle '), but is found otherwise only in a late gloss (Napier, *Anecdota Oxoniensia* vii, 24 : *cranic-writere—chronographorum*).

---

[1] Ed. Thorpe, *Homilies of the Anglo-Saxon Church.* Ref. to page.

Ælfric's *Saints' Lives* [1] have much the same type of vocabulary as the *Homilies*, but with more words for household and other ordinary objects. **Altāre** is used by the side of *weofed*. **Caric** occurs in this text only : *genam ænne lytelne tænel mid caricum gefylledne* 44 (pt. 3) ' he took a little basket filled with figs '. **Carte** is found several times for ' a paper, a deed ' : *awrat on anre cartan* 82 ' wrote on a piece of paper '. **Cristalle** occurs in *an wurðlic weorc . . . of glitniendum cristallan* 132 ' a fine piece of work of shining crystal '. **Fant :** *to geleafan bringan and on fante fullian* 85 ' bring to the faith and baptize in the font '. **Mechanisc** (with Gmc. suffix) is found here alone : *an wurðlic weorc on mechanisc geweorc* 132 ' constructed by mechanical craft '. **Mynecen** is common throughout : *modor ofer manega mynecena* 94 ' mother over many nuns '. **Sanct** is used fairly often (= *se hālga*) : *þa mynstermenn noldon . . . þone sanct underfon* 136 (pt. 3) ' the monks would not receive the holy man ' ; so also is **āspendan :** *aspende . . . ma þonne twa hund punda* 132 ' spent more than two hundred pounds '. **Tālent :** *þone onfangenan talent fram his hlaforde* (pt. 3) ' the talent received from his master '.   Note also the following : **buteruc** ' leather bottle ' : *nan win buton on anum gewealdenan butruce* 164 ' no wine except in a little bottle ' ; **cuppe,** a late borrowing compared with *cupp* and *copp* : *ne mage ge samod drincon ures drihtnes calic and ðæs deofles cuppan* 378 ' you cannot drink the Lord's chalice and the devil's cup ' ; **cyċene :** *eode him to kicenan . . . and began to etanne* 264 ' went to the kitchen and began to eat ' ; **foca** ' a cake baked on the hearth ' : *geseah þær licgan ænne snaw-hwitne focan* 394 ' saw lying there a snow-white loaf ' ; **lenticul :** *feawa lenticula, mid wætere ofgotene* 44 (pt. 3) ' a few lentils soaked in water ' (cf. *lenticula, þæt syndon pysan* 48 ' lentils, that is, peas ') ; **mōr :** *þa hæðenan . . . mid morberium gebyldon þa ylpas, forðan þe mor-berian him is metta leofost* 104 (pt. 3) ' the heathen encourage the elephants with mulberries, because mulberries are their favourite food ' (Ælfric always uses *ylp* rather than *ylpend*, cf. *ylp is ormæte deor, mare þonne sum hus* 104 (pt. 3) ' the elephant is a huge beast, bigger than some houses ') ; **mynet-(īsen) :** *man awende mynet-isena on his dagum* 516 ' the coinage was changed in his day ' ; **ōrel :** *geglængde me mid orle of golde*

[1] Ed. Skeat, E.E.T.S., 76, 82, 94, 114.

awefen 172 ' adorned me with a veil woven of gold ' ; **post :**
þæt hus wearþ forburnon buton þam anum poste 140 (pt. 3) ' the
house was burned except for the one post ' ; **tabula :** *on anum
leadenum tabulan ealle mid stafon agrofon* 508 ' on a leaden tablet
engraved with letters '.

Ælfric's translation of the *Heptateuch*,[1] his *Preface to Genesis*,
and his short treatise *On the Old and New Testament*, contain
a number of Biblical words, among which it is sometimes hard
to distinguish real loans from merely *ad hoc* usages of foreign
words. Among the latter we may class names of foreign plants,
etc., such as *cucumeres, stacten*, though some seem to be used as
English.words : **coriandre :** *swilce coriandran sæd* 310 ' like
coriander seed ' ; **lactūca :** *ðeorfe hlafas mid ðære lactucan þe
on felda wyxt* 243 ' unleavened bread with the lettuce that grows
in the field ' ; **polente :** *polentan ðæes ylcan geares* 384 ' parched
corn of the same year ' ; **por-**(*lēac*) and **enne-**(*lēac*) ' leek ' and
' onion ' 309. **Læfel** translates Latin *scyphum* : *and nim minne
sylfrena læfel* 193 ' and take my silver cup ' ; **orc** is used for
crater 272 ; **(e)arc** is Noah's ark, but the *arca foederis* is usually
scrīn. **Organe** occurs in reference to Jubal, *þe wæs fæder hearpera
and þære þe organon macodon* 94 ' who was the father of harpers
and those who made music ' ; another manuscript has *fæder
hearpera and organystra*. For ' Sabbath ' Ælfric uses *Sæternesdæg*.
Leden means both ' speech ' and ' Latin ' (see also p. 30) :
swilce edischenna, ðæt is on Leden coturnix 253 ' also quails, that
is in Latin coturnix'. **Fals** (a noun) means ' fraud ' : *hwi tyhð
ure hlaford us swa miceles falses ?* 193 ' why does our Lord accuse
us of so great a fraud ? ' Further we have in the essay on the
Testaments : **titelian :** *twa bec . . . man getitelode him* 557 ' two
books were ascribed to him ' ; and the foreign plural **seraphin :**
þa twa seraphin soðlice getacnodon . . . 1161 ' the two seraphs
betokened . . .' And finally we observe that **fers** is used in the
Preface to Genesis in the sense of a ' verse ' in the Bible : *on
þære bec on þam forman ferse* 56 ' in the first verse of the book '.

Ælfric's *Hexameron*,[2] besides telling the story of the Creation,
has some comments on natural history. Thus we have **pard** and
tigris, though hardly as English words : *ða swiftan tigres and*

---

[1] Ed. Crawford, E.E.T.S., 160.
[2] Ed. Crawford, *Bibliothek der ags. Prosa*, x.

ða syllican pardes 275 ' swift tigers and strange leopards ', as well
as *ylp* (e.g. *ða ylpas beoð swa mycele swylce oðre muntas* 289
' the elephants are as big as mountains '). **Paradis** varies between
English and Latin inflexions : *to ðam upplican Paradise* 512 ' to
Paradise above ', but *God hi ða gebrohte binnan Paradisum, ðæt
we hatað on Englisc Neorxnawang* 427 ' God brought them into
Paradise, which we call in English *Neorxnawang* '

Eastern Themes

Still more names of plants and other things of Eastern origin
are to be found in two prose pieces in MS. Cotton Vitellius
A XV, the *Wonders of the East* and the (spurious) *Letter of
Alexander to Aristotle*,[1] probably of the late tenth century. The
first has **lāur** (also in the *Blickling Homilies*) : *on þisse stowe beoð
treowcynn þa beoð lawern-beame* 61 ' in this place there are kinds
of trees which are laurel-trees ' ; **ostre :** *se nænine operne mete
ne þige buton sæ-ostrum* 63 ' who eat no other food but sea-
oysters ' ; **pipor :** *on þam landum bið ,pipores genihtsumnis* 53
' in those countries is plenty of pepper '.

Alexander's letter has the following Latin words, which seem
to be used as English, besides some obviously regarded as foreign :
canna : *fen and cannon and hread-wæteru* 30 ' fen and reeds
and reedy marshes ' ; **columne :** *þar wæron gyldene columnan
swiðe micle* 6 ' there were very large golden columns ' ; besides
sēam : *þridde healf þusend mula ðe þa seamas wægon* 13 ' 2,500
mules which carried the baggage ' ; **epistol :** *ða sealde he me
gewrit and ænne epistolan* 28 ' then he gave me a writing and
a letter ' ; also the animals *lēo, olfend, elpend, mūl.* The following
retain Latin inflexions : balzamum, cristallum, smaragdus,
cypressus, eclypsis, tigris, pardus, scorpiones, unio, carbunculis.

Later Verse

The Old English verse *Psalter* contains a good many Latin
words which occur nowhere else in the verse, and some of them
nowhere in the prose. Among the less frequent may be mentioned
aspide, basilisca (*þu miht* . . . *basiliscan tredan* 90/13 ' you may

---

[1] Ed. Rypins, E.E.T.S., 161.

tread upon the adder '), **ceder, cōc** (*swylce hi on cocer-pannan cocas gehyrstan* 101/3 'as though cooks roasted them in a pan '), **sallettan** (*singað him and salletað* 104/2 'sing and play upon the harp ').

The word **pandher** occurs in a fragment of a bestiary ; **tæfl** and **teosol** in the Gnomic Verses of the Exeter Book, the former apparently used here attributively : *tæfles monnes, þonne he teoselum weorpeð* 185 'the gamester when he throws dice '. But for the most part the new words of the later verse are simply those of prose, and add nothing to the poetic vocabulary as such. This is particularly true of the technical *Menologium*, perhaps of the late tenth century, which uses such words as **bises** 'leap-year' (Lat. *bissextus*), **kālend, circul** 'zodiac ' ; it has also all the Latin names of the months, but these (as in the *Martyrologium* of an earlier date) are still in their Latin forms and cannot claim to be naturalized.

ELEVENTH CENTURY PROSE

The collection of homilies edited under the title of *Wulfstans Homilien* [1] are certainly not all by this writer, who was a slightly later contemporary of Ælfric, and Archbishop of York. Possibly the first five sermons in the collection are his. It will be seen that only two of the few interesting Latin words in these homilies come in this group : **Crisma :** *ðonne se sacerd smyreð mid þam halgan crisman breost and sculdru* v, 35, 'when the priest anoints breast and shoulders with the holy oil ' ; **crismale :** *mid þam crismale . . . man tacnað þæne cristenan cynehelm* v, 36, 'by the chrisom the Christian crown is signified ' ; **fals :** *þæt an mynet gange ofer ealle þas þeode buton ælcon false* L 272 'that one coinage should be used throughout this people without any fraud ' ; **idol :** *ne ænig man idola weorðje æfre* x, 71 'that no man should ever worship idols ' ; **letanie :** *ga man mid reliquium ut and mid letanian* xxxv, 170 'let there be a procession with relics and litanies ' ; **orgel :** *hwær ys heora prass and orgol ?* xxx, 148 'where is their splendour and pride ? ' ; **pinsian :** *hu swiðe man pinsað þa sawle on domes dæg* xlvi, 239 'how severely the soul will be judged on the day of doom ' ; **pipe :** *hearpe and pipe*

---

[1] Ed. Napier, *Wulfstans Homilien*. Ref. to homily and page.

and mistlic gliwgamen vi, 46 ' harp and pipe and joyous music
of many kinds ' ; **rabbian :** *ac læt þone deofol Antecrist rabbian
and wedan* xiii, 84 ' but let the devil Antechrist rage and rave '.

The prose dialogue of *Salomon and Saturnus* [1] has little of
interest, but the word **ynċe** occurs in it—an early loan from Lat.
uncia—in the sense of ' inch ' : [Adam] *wæs vi and cx ynca lang*
180 ' Adam was 116 inches long '. It is to be found earlier in the
Laws of Ethelbert and of Alfred. Examples of *yntse* ' ounce ',
a later loan from *uncia*, have already been given.

The prose *Life of St. Guthlac* [2] has the word **ċeren** ' new wine ',
otherwise recorded only in glossaries, and in the *Leechbooks*
(dealt with later) : *Mid þam cerenum þære godspellican swetnysse*
72 ' with the new wine of the sweetness of the Gospel '. We
may note also the use of **fers :** *sona swa he þæt fyrmeste fers sang
þæs sealmes* 44 ' as soon as he has sung the first verse of the
psalm ' ; **ymen :** *ða hæfde he his sealmes geleornod and canticas
and ymnas* 18 ' then he had learnt his psalms and canticles and
hymns '.

An English version of Defensor's *Liber Scintillarum*,[3] a com-
pilation consisting of extracts from the Bible and the writings
of the Fathers of the Church, has a few interesting forms :
mæġester (as well as the later **magister**) : *hefe mægster-domes* 120
' the weight of responsibility ' ; *nys leorning-cniht ofer magister
fullfremed* 204 ' the disciple is not raised above his master ' ; **plūm**
' down ' : *plum-feþera hnescnysse* 144 ' the softness of down ' ;
sacc : *doð eow saccas þa na ealdian* 156 ' make for yourselves
purses which do not grow old ' ; **sēam :** *seam assan* 190 ' the
burden of an ass ' ; **seolc :** *on seolce and on cild claþum* 87 ' in
silk and in swaddling-clothes '.

The interlinear version of the Benedictine Rule in MS. Cott.
Tiberius A III [4] has not very many Latin words ; most of them
are in the more technical parts, especially those dealing with
the divine offices. The following should be noted : **antemn** 38 ;
capitol (= *lectio*) 44 ; **cufl :** *genoh bið munece twa tunican and
twa cuflan habban* 92 ' it is enough for a monk to have two habits
and two cowls ' ; **grēf :** *sex, græf, nædl* 93 ' knife, style, needle '

---

[1] Ed. Kemble, for the Ælfric Society, from MS. Cotton Vitellius A xv.
[2] Ed. Goodwin (1848), from MS. Cott. Vesp. D xxi.
[3] Ed. Rhodes, E.E.T.S. 93, from MS. Royal 7 C iv.
[4] Ed. Logeman, E.E.T.S. 90.

(in a list of a monk's requirements) ; **reps :** *mid heora repsum* 39 ' with their responses ' (=*responsoriis*) ; **scamol :** *ofor rædinc-scamol* 38 ' on the reading-stool ' ; **scyrtan :** *sum ðinc of rædingum is to scyrtanne* 42 ' some part of the lesson is to be curtailed ' ; **socc :** *soccas and hosan* 92 ' shoes and hose ' (= *pedules et caligas* ').

Byrhtferþ's Manual [1] claims attention as a technical treatise on astronomy, mathematics, prosody, and other matters. In many instances he uses actual Latin forms without any English equivalent ; he says himself : *me ys neod þæt ic menge þæt Lyden amang þissum Englisce* ' I am compelled to mix Latin with the English '. Very frequent loan-words are **circul** ' zodiac ', **cleric** ' clerk ', **cyrten** ' perfect, exact ', **scrutnian** ' examine ', **trahtnian** ' explain '. The following words are rare in Old English : **cyrriol :** *þa æðelan munecas þære tide lof mid kyrriole . . . gewurðiað* 126 ' the good monks honour the praise of that hour with the Kyrie Eleison ' ; **declinan :** *þa naman and þa binaman and heora declinunga* 94 ' the nouns and pronouns and their declensions ' ; **epact :** *þisra epacta gerynu apinsiun* 36 ' ponder the mysteries of these epacts ' ; **termen :** *þanne byð mycel gedwyld on þam Easterlicne termene* 72 ' then there will be much error in the date of Easter '.

Then, finally, there are three books on medicine, the *Leech Book,* the *Herbarium Apuleii,* and the *Medicina de Quadrupedibus.* [2] All depend on Latin originals, and their chief value lies in the large number of plant-names which they record. Some of these occur fairly often in Old English, others are to be found in glossaries, others in these medical works alone. Among the rarer names we find (*a*) in the *Leech Book* : **cuneglæsse** ' hound's tongue ' 110 ; **safine** ' savin ' 100 ; **nefte** ' catmint ' 62 ; **alewe** ' aloe ' 60 ; **aprotane** ' southernwood ' 60 ; **slarege** ' salvia sclarea ' 58 ; **saluie** ' sage ' 50 ; **celeþenie** ' celandine ' 26 ; **bete** ' beetroot ' 18 ; **rude** ' rue ' 18 ; (*b*) from the *Herbarium* : **amigdal** ' almond ' 104 ; **berbena** ' verbena ' 170 ; **dracentse** ' dragon-wort ' 106 ; **elehtre** ' lupin ' 148 ; **organe** ' marjoram ' 216 ; **petersilie** ' parsley ' 240. From the *Medicina de Quadrupedibus* we get **croh** ' saffron ' 348.

---

[1] Ed. Crawford, E.E.T.S., 177.
[2] Ed. Cockayne, *Leechdoms, Wortcunning and Starcraft.* Rolls Series.

Besides these there are many words, some of which are of Latin origin, referring to the preparing of prescriptions, such as names of vessels and instruments ; **ampulle, ċetel, ċēac, cuculere,** etc., besides **trifulian** ' to pound up ', **trimessa** ' drachm ', **plaster,** etc.

The eleventh century glosses,[1] which contain a vast amount of matter, give no opportunity of seeing words in actual use, but they include a number of words which are rare or not recorded elsewhere. A gloss to the Latin text of Ælfric's *Colloquy* (a Latin dialogue designed for teaching purposes) supplies the following : **capitol :** *primam missam—capitolmæssan* 101 ; **claustor :** *in claustrum—to claustre* 103 ; **culter :** *cultro—cultre* 90 ; **lamprēde :** *murenas—lampredan* 94 ; **mangere :** *mercator—mangere* 96 ; **ostre :** *ostreas—ostran* 94 ; **pīne-***(wincle)* ; *torniculi—pine-winclan* 94 ; **cocc** ' cockle ' : *neptigalli sæcoccas* 94.

The *Cleopatra Gloss* (in MS. Cott. Cleop. A III) is probably of the early eleventh century. It contains some hundreds of words, with a good proportion of foreign loan-words. The following will give some idea of the variety : **āmel** ' vessel for holy water ' : *amulas—amelas* 348 ; **ampulle :** *legithum* [= *lecythum*]—*ampellan, elefæt* ; **calu** ' bald ' : *caluus—calo* 276 ; **campian** ' to fight ' : *agonizans—campiende* 341 ; **catt :** *muriceps—cat* 445 ; **cempa :** *anthletarum—cempena* 345 ; **centaur :** *centauri—þæs centaures* 374 ; **cemes** ' shirt ' : *camisa—cemes* 362 ; **ċietel :** *caldaria—citel* 363 ; **ċeren :** *carene—cerenes, hunigteares* 370 ; **codd-** *(æppel)* ' quince ' : *malum cidonium, siue malum cotonium, id est codæppel* 411 ; **cuclere :** *coclear—cuclere* 281 ; **draca :** *Leuiathan—se draca* 489 ; **fīfele :** *fibule—fifele* 403 ; **glædene :** *gladiolum—glædene* 416 ; **læfel :** *aquemanile—læuel* 350 ; **lēo :** *leunculi—leonhwelpes* 434 ; **mōre :** *pastinaca—weal[h]more* 271 ; **munt :** *alpes—munt iofes* (= Jovis) 355 ; **nōt** ' note ' : *notariorum—not-writera* 451 ; **orc** ' devil ' : *orcus—orc, þyrs, heldeofol* 459 ; **pālent :** *ad palatinas—to ðæm palentlicum* 342 ; **paper :** *papirus—paper* 523 ; **plūm :** *plumnus—plum-treow* 269 ; **seġn** ' standard ' : *aquile—segn* 275 ; **tapor :** *papirus—taper* 267 ; **tæfl :** *alea—tæfl* 267.

From the *Royal Gloss* (in MS. 1829, Royal Library, Brussels) : **calcatrippe :** *heraclea—calcatrippe* 298 ; **cerfille :** *brassica—*

---

[1] Wright-Wülcker, *Anglo-Saxon and Old English Vocabularies*, vol. i.

wudu-cerfille 296 (also glosses *pastinaca* 299) ; **delfin :** *pina—delfin, mere-swin* 293 ; **glædene :** *scilla et gladiola—gladene* 301 ; **lufestice :** *lubestica—lufestice* 301 ; **punt :** *trabaria, caudex—punt* 287 ; **rædic :** *raphanus—ancre, þæt is rædic* 300.

Finally there is the so-called Vocabulary of Ælfric, probably having no connexion with him, or perhaps based on a glossary of his but with very many additions. This is a classified glossary, divided into animals, plants, parts of the body, weapons, and so forth. The highest proportion of Latin words comes in the *Nomina Vasorum*, where out of fifty-nine entries twenty-six are Latin, or Latin-English hybrids ; in addition, several are of unknown origin. Here are some selections from the glossary : **balsminte :** *sisimbrium—balsminte* 136 ; **box :** *pixis—bixen box* ' a box of box-wood ' 124 ; **canne** ' cup ' : *crater, uel canna—canne* 122 ; **cāsere :** *imperatrix, uel Augusta—caseres wif* 155 ; **ċipp** ' plough-share ' : *dentale—cipp* 106 ; **corn** ' cornel ' : *cornus—corn-treow* 138 ; **cost** ' costmary ' : *costus—cost* 133 ; **cyrten :** *uenusto—ic cyrtenlæce* ' I beautify ' 178 ; **magdala :** *amigdala—magdala-treow* 139 ; **malwe** ' mallow ' : *màlua—malwe* 139 ; **mōraþ :** *carenum—moraþ* 128 ; **munt :** *oreades—munt-ælfen* 189 ' mountain elves ' ; **næpte :** *nepita—næpte* 133 ; **persoc :** *persicarius—persoc-treow* 138 ; **pervince :** *uinca—peruincæ* 136 ; **pilstre :** *pila—pilstre* 141 ; **pisle** ' warm room ' : *scriptorium—pisle, fer-hus* 186 ; **port :** *castellum—wic uel lytel port* 140 ; **post :** *basis—post* 164 ; **pumic :** *pumex—pumic-stan* 148 ; **reps :** *responsorium—reps* 129 ; **side, seolc :** *bombyx—sid-wyrm uel seolc-wyrm* 121 ; **solsece :** *solsequium uel heliotropium—solsece uel sigel-hwerfe* 133 ; **suftlēre :** *subtalares—swyftleares* 125 ; **sūtere :** *sutrina domus—sutera hus* 186 ; **suðeriġe :** *satirion—suðerige* 137 ; **tolnere :** *telonearius—tolnere uel tollere* 171.

The Anglo-Saxon Chronicle in the Eleventh Century

This account of Latin loan-words in Old English may fittingly be concluded with some notes on the vocabulary of the Chronicle [1] in the eleventh century, since this text more than any other in Old English seems to look forward into the Middle English

---

[1] For the earlier part of the Chronicle see above, p. 33.

period. It is with this text, too, that the account of the French
loan-words will begin, since the history of French words in English
is not limited to post-Conquest days. And here, also, as will be
seen later, are to be found the majority of Scandinavian loan-
words recorded before the Conquest. Many of the ecclesiastical
terms common in other prose of the period occur in the Chronicle,
e.g. *ancor-(setl)*, *ælmes(ful)*, *calic*, *candel-mæsse*, *clerec*, *crisma*
(*se forlet his crisman and his hrode . . . and feng to his spere* 1056,
' he left the chrisom and the rood and took the spear '), *offrian*,
prouost (*þa cusan þa munecas to abbot Brand prouost* 1066 ' the
monks chose Brand the provost to be abbot '), *regul*, etc.   In
addition to these the following appear :   **Advent :**   *Osmund
biscop of Searbyrig innon Aduent forðferde* E 1099 ' Osmund,
Bishop of Salisbury, died during Advent ' ;   **cantel-cāp** (= *cantere*
+ *cāp*, and elsewhere *cantercæppe*) ' priest's cope ' :   *cantelcapas
and reafas* E 1070 ' copes and vestments ' ;   **capellān :**   *þær
Rannulf his capellane þæt biscoprice on Dunholme geaf* E 1099
' gave Ranulf his chaplain the bishopric of Durham ' ;   **capitula**
in the sense of ' ecclesiastical chapter ' :   *þe abbot eode into
capitulan* E 1083 ' the abbot went into the chapter ' ;   **chōr,**
in the sense of ' choir ' (part of church) :   *þa Francisce men
bræcen þone chor* E 1083 ' the French destroyed the choir ' ;
decānus :   *se þe wæs decanus æt Cristes cyrcan* D 1020 ' who was
Dean of Christ Church ' ;   **grād :**   *swa þæt ðet blod com of ðam
weofode uppon þam gradan* E 1083 ' so that the blood came from
the altar on to the steps '.   **Corōna** is used by the side of the native
cynehelm :   *þa corona him on heafode settan* D 1066 ' to place the
crown on his head '.   **Mæġester** is used in quite a general sense :
þonne wæs he mægster on þisum lande E 1086 ' then was he master
in this country ' ;   the more usual, but not exclusive, earlier
sense was ' teacher '.   **Pālant** is used of a foreign palace :   *se
casere gaderode unarimedlice fyrde ongean Baldewine of Brycge,
þurh þæt þæt he bræc þæne palant æt Neomagan* C 1049 ' the
Emperor gathered a huge army against Baldwin from Bruges,
because he destroyed the palace at Nijmegen.   **Port** is a
common term for a town or city :   *Rannulf eorl gaderade mycele
fyrde to Hereford port* C 1055 ' Earl Ranulf gathered a large
army at the city of Hereford ' ;   *of porte and of uppelande* E 1087
' from town and country ', etc.   **Pyleċe** has the sense of ' fur robe '

in *on merðene pyleceon and gra-schynnene* D 1075 ' in robes of
marten-skins and of grey fur ' (*gra-schynnene* is from Old Norse,
see p. 69). **Sester** is still used as a measure for wheat : *se
sester hwætes eode to lx penega* E 1043 ' a sester of wheat went
up to 60 pence '.

This brings to an end the survey of the pre-Conquest Latin
words in English. The influence of Latin is felt next in a less
direct way, since it comes through French dialects developed
from Romance, and not immediately from Classical Latin,
Vulgar Latin, or Common Romance. This stratum of Latin words
begins before the Conquest, but since there can be no real
dividing-line between pre- and post-Conquest French loans,
such words will all be dealt with in a later chapter.

It is perhaps surprising that so few of the early Latin loan-
words have survived into Modern or even into Middle English.
The majority of them were replaced by the corresponding
French forms. Others were only technical, learned words and
were not really established even in the written language. In
other cases the objects the words denoted themselves passed out
of use (e.g. some of the weights and measures, vessels, garments).
The list of Latin words in Appendix A, in which the modern
descendants, where they exist, are indicated, shows that many
of the words which still survive are frequently-used, popular
words. Altogether rather more than a hundred are in use to-day
in Standard English (others, e.g. some plant-names, survive in
provincial dialects), of which the following are among the most
common : belt, box, butter, candle, cat, chalk, cheap, cheese,
cock, cook, cup, fan, fever, inch, kitchen, mile, mill, pan, pea,
pear, pepper, pail, pipe, pit, poppy, post, sack, school, silk, sock,
spend, stop, wall.

Although some words were adopted direct from Latin in the
Middle English period, the next time any very large number was
introduced was in the Renaissance period, when, as in Later
Old English, the terms borrowed were of a literary and
learned type.

Chapter III

OTHER FOREIGN ELEMENTS BEFORE THE CONQUEST

A

The Greek Element

It has already been pointed out that a not inconsiderable number of words borrowed by English from Latin had previously been adopted into Latin from Greek. But there is a small number of words borrowed by Germanic direct from Greek. They are early loans, and it seems possible that some at least were adopted first by the Goths, and that from Gothic they spread to other Germanic dialects. The words in question are all from ecclesiastical Greek, and are the product of Christianity, but they must have been learnt by most of the Germanic peoples before these became Christians themselves.

The Greek forms are *aggelos* ' messenger, angel ', *diabolos* ' adversary, Satan ', *kuriakon* ' the Lord's house ', *presbyter* ' elder, priest '. Of all but the first the phonological development is hardly clear, so that the exact story of their introduction into Old English cannot be told. The Old English forms are respectively *enġel, dēofol, ċiriċe (ċyriċe), prēost*. Modern English Devil, Church, Priest, are the direct descendants of the O.E. words, but *angel* is from French (from Lat. *angelus*, itself a loan-word from the Greek).

Engel appears first in prose in the *Vespasian Psalter, hwoene læssan from englum* 194 ' a little lower than the angels ', but is probably earlier in the Cædmonian poems, for instance in *Genesis* : *þæt his engyl ongan ofermod wesan* 262 ' that his angel began to be overweening '. It is used almost exclusively in the Biblical sense throughout Old English, and it is not necessary to give many examples : *englas stigon up and ofdune on ða hlæddre* (Alfred's translation of the *Cura Pastoralis* 100) ' angels went up and down on the ladder ' ; *he þær fram Godes ængle þæt bebod underfeng* (Wærferth : *Gregory's Dialogues*, 13) ' he received the

command from God's angel ' ;   *he gesceop tyn engla werod, þæt
sind englas and heah-englas, throni, dominationes, principatus,
potestates, uirtutes, cherubim, seraphim* (Ælfric :   *Cath. Homilies,
10)* ' He created ten orders of angels, these are angels and
archangels, thrones, etc.' ;   *Gabrihel his heahengel* (Ælfric :
Homily on the B.V.M., 32) ;   *buton lichoman swa swa synd ænglas
on heofonum* (Ælfric :   *Saints' Lives*, 14) ' without bodies, as are
the angels in heaven '.   The original Greek sense of ' messenger '
appears in *engel min befora onsione ðin* (Lindisfarne, Mark i, 2)
' (I will send) my messenger before thy face '.   The nearest
equivalent native word is *ār*, used both for ' angel ' and for
' messenger, herald ' ;   this is from the same source as *ærend*
' message ' (Mod. Eng. *errand*).

Dēofol ' devil, evil spirit, Satan ' is common in early and later
verse, as well as in prose.   It appears in the early *Corpus Glossary*
(*c.* 750) :   *orcus—ðyrs, hel-diobul* 83, *ðyrs* being a native word for
an evil spirit or ogre.   (Cf. the *Cleopatra Gloss.*, p. 47 above,
where the Latin loan-word *orc* is equated with *ðyrs* and *hel-
dēofol*.)   In translations from Latin it corresponds to *diabolus*
or to *daemonium* :   *from hryre and diofle middeglicum* (= a ruina
et daemonio meridiano) *Vesp. Psalter* 319 ' from destruction and
the evil one at noon-day ' ;   *þa sona eode se deofol in þone mæsse-
preost* (Dial. 73) ' then suddenly the devil entered into this
priest ' (= hunc simul repente diabolus invasit) ;   *cum, deoful,
hider and unsco me* (Dial. 221) ' come hither, devil, and unshoe
me ' (= veni, diabole, discalcea me) ;   of demoniacal possession :
alle yfle hæbbende and diowbla hæbbende (Lind. Mark i, 32) ' all
those who were sick and possessed of devils '.

Ċiriċe is used both of the building and of the spiritual body :
to godes ciricum in supregum and in cent (Charter 45 in O.E.T.,
871–889) ' to God's churches in Surrey and in Kent ' ;   *þær he
ær het getimbrian cyrican of treowe* (Chron. E. 626) ' where before
he had had a wooden church built ' ;   *ane gastlice modor, seo is
ecclesia genamod, þæt is godes cyrice* (Wulfstan x, 67) ' one
spiritual mother, who is called *ecclesia*, that is the Church of
God ' ;   *cyrice is þære sawle scip* (Wulfstan xlvi, 232) ' the church
is the ship of the soul '.

In the *Lindisfarne Gospels* (Luke vii, 5) *cirice*, as an alternative
to *somnung* (= assembly), translates *synagogam* :   *somnung* vel

cirica he getimbrode us ' he has built us a synagogue '. In Ælfric's
Vocabulary appears *ecclesia—circe*, and also *basilica—cinges hof*
[= king's court] uel *circe* 184, with two late Latin meanings of
basilica. Once at least the word is used of a heathen place of
worship, for which *templ* is the usual word : *gebletsode Romulus
. . . mid para sweora blode þa cyrican* (*Orosius* 66) ' Romulus
consecrated the temples with the blood of their fathers-in-law '.

Prēost is the ordinary word for a priest of the Christian religion.
The compound *mæsse-preost* is used for one who was competent
to celebrate Mass, having attained the necessary orders. *Mæsse-
preost* often translates *presbyter*, the uncompounded word
clericus : *sum wæs . . . bescoren preost* (Bede 428) ' one was
a tonsured priest ' (= adtonsus ut clericus) ; *mid ane oððe mid
twam his preosta* (Bede 162) ' with one or two of his priests '
(= cum uno clerico aut duobus) ; *ic Beda Cristes peow and
mæssepreost* (Bede 2) = Baeda famulus Christi et presbyter ;
Gaudentius se mæsse-preost (Dial. 56) = Gaudentius presbyter ;
but this is not an invariable rule, cf. *þas hatheortan preostes
unstilnysse* (Dial. 65) ' the raging of the furious priest '
(= presbyteri furentis insaniam). Either may translate *sacerdos*
(for which also the Latin loan-word *sācerd* is found) ; *yfle preostas
bioð folces hryre* (*Cura Past.* 30) ' evil priests are the people's
destruction ' (= sacerdotes mali) ; *wære sum mæsse-preost,
se mid his preostum . . .* (Dial. 224) ' there was a certain mass-
priest, who with his priests . . . (= quidam venerabilis sacerdos
erat, qui cum clericis suis). Note also : *þær wæs Wilfrid preost
þe siððon wæs biscop* (Chron. E. 656) ' then was Wilfrid a priest,
who was afterwards a bishop) ; *Columba messapreost com to
Pyhtum* (Chron. E. 565) ' Columba the priest came to the Picts '.
In Ælfric's *Vocabulary* the following group appears : *presbiter—
mæssepreost* : *sacellanus—handpreost* ; *clericus—preost, uel
pingere* (i.e. a priest in his office of advocate or intercessor) ; for
hand-preost cf. Chron. F. 1051 : *Stigand þe was þes cinges ræd-
gifa and hand-preost* ' Stigand, who was the king's advisor and
chaplain '.

Mæsse-preost is used occasionally of a priest of the Jews :
æd-eau ðec ðæm measse-preost (Lindisfarne Mt. viii, 4) ' show
thyself to the priest '. For priests of pagan religions the Latin
loan *sācerd* is used.

The Greek words which came into Old English by way of Latin are given with the corresponding Latin words in Appendix A. But the introduction of these from Greek into Latin and thence into English is not the whole of the story. Greek itself borrowed a considerable number of words from Eastern languages, especially names for plants and animals which were imported into Greece, or became known there through travellers and writers, and these were transmitted into English through Latin. Sanscrit supplied Gk. *panthēra* (O.E. *panther*), *margaron*, *-ītēs* (O.E. *meregrota* ' pearl '), and *peperi* (O.E. *pipor* ' pepper ')— a highly contrasted group. From Iranian came *pardos* (O.E. *pard* ' leopard ') and *tīgris* (O.E. *tigris* ' tiger '), but also *paradeisos* (O.E. *paradis* ' paradise ') the original sense being ' enclosure, park, garden '. Probably from Asia Minor, Greek borrowed the plant-names *puxos* (O.E. *box*), *kastanon* (O.E. *ċiesten* ' chestnut '), *kerasion* (O.E. *ċiris* ' cherry '), *kudōniā* (O.E. *codd-æppel* ' quince '), *pisos* (O.E. *pise* ' pea '), *proumnon* (O.E. *plūm* ' plum '). *Rhodon* (O.E. *rōse*), and also, curiously enough, *boutūron* (O.E. *butere* ' butter ') are from some Western Asiatic language, besides *pelekān* (O.E. *pellicān*), which is certainly connected with another foreign word in Greek, *pelekus* ' axe ' (cf. Assyrian *pilaqqi* ' axe '). A Place-Name is the source of Gk. *sabanon* (O.E. *saban* ' sheet ') ;   cf. Arab. *sabanijjat*, stuff made at Saban, near Baghdad.

The contact of European languages with Semitic also began very early, and is continued in the early centuries of this era through the medium of the Hebrew Bible, whence several Semitic words found their way into Greek and thence farther afield. The plant-names *kumīnon* (O.E. *cymen* ' cummin '), *hussōpos* (O.E. *ysope* ' hyssop '), *sturax* a kind of resin (O.E. *stōr* ' incense '), and *balsamon* (O.E. *balsam*), are all Semitic ; hence also comes the stone *iaspis* (O.E. *ġeaspis* ' jasper ') and the *kamēlos* (O.E. *camell*). A later loan from the same group of languages is Gk. *abbas* (O.E. *abbod* ' abbot ') from Syriac *abbā*, originally ' father ', but acquiring the sense of ' head of a group of monks ' with the rise of monasticism, which had its origin in Syria.

There are at least three early loans from Egyptian into Greek, which penetrated into Western European languages :   Gk.

khartēs (O.E. *carte* ' paper '), *sināpu* (O.E. *senep* ' mustard ').
and *el-ephas*—the origin of the *el* is doubtful—(O.E. *elpend*
' elephant') ; for the last, cf. Egyptian *āb*, Coptic *eb(o)u* ' elephant,
ivory '.

Some North African dialect apparently produced *orīganon*
(O.E. *organe* ' marjoram '), since the plant is believed to have
come from that area.

Thus early loans from the East, if not direct, are fairly
numerous. The next non-European words that will have to be
considered are those from Arabic, which make a surprisingly
large group in the Middle English vocabulary.

B

THE CELTIC ELEMENT

Three different strata of Celtic loan-words may be recognized
in Old English. In the first place there are a few early continental
loans, borrowed from Old Celtic, and common to all or most of
the Germanic languages ; secondly, there are words adopted from
the Britons by the English after the middle of the fifth century ;
thirdly, there is a group of ecclesiastical and religious terms introduced by Irish missionaries. Almost all the Celtic loan-words
became established as popular words ; there is very little
' learned ' element, such as there is in the case of Latin, since
nearly all the words, with the exception of a few in the third
period, passed from mouth to mouth, and not through the
influence of literature.

Of the first group the earliest is the Gmc. **rīki-* ' kingdom '
(cognate with Lat. *rēx*), which appears in Old English as *rīce*
(surviving now only as the second element of *bishop*RIC), in
Old High German as *rīhhi* (Mod. German *Reich*). Old English
has also an adjective *rīce* (O.H.G. *rīhhi*, Goth. *reiks*) ' powerful ',
from the same source. Both these words are very common in
O.E. Mod. Eng. *rich* is from French, borrowed from Germanic,
and thus of the same origin.

O.E. **ambeht** ' servant ;   service, office ' is from a Gmc.

E

ambaht, which is probably direct from Celtic, but may have come through Lat. *ambactus*. (From this Latin form, through Romance and Spanish, Mod. Eng. *ambassador* is derived.) Gothic has the word in the form *andbahts* ; O.H.G. has *ampaht*, O.S. *ambahteo*. It is common in Old English, both as an independent word and in compounds : *ambeht-secg, -mann, -þegn, -scealc*, etc., implying ' servant, attendant '. In the *Lindisfarne Gospels* the word corresponds to Latin *minister* and *discipulus* : *allra hlætmest and allra embehtmonn* Mk. ix, 35 ' last of all and servant of all ' : *in onsione ðara ambihta* vel *ðara ðegna his* J. xx, 30 ' in the presence of his disciples '. *Ambeht* is found both in heroic and in purely religious verse : *ic eom Hroðgares ar and ombiht* Beowulf 336 ' I am Hrothgar's messenger and servant ' : *eom ic . . . his ombeht-hera, þeow geðyldig* Guthlac 571 ' I am his servant, his patient minister '. For the sense of ' ministry ', cf. *læste þu georne his ambyhto* Genesis 518 ' perform his ministry diligently '.

The O.E. **dūn** ' mountain, hill ' (Mod. Eng. DOWN, n., and also the adverb, which is from O.E. *of dūne* ' from the hill ') is often considered to be of Celtic origin. Corresponding forms are found in a number of West Germanic languages, so the loan, if it is one, must be of the continental period. Moreover, the O.E. vowel tells against borrowing from British, since in this dialect Celtic *ū* had become *ǖ*, perhaps had even become unrounded to *ī*, some time before the English settlement. O.Irish *dūn*, from which the Germanic word might have been borrowed, has the meaning of ' fortified place, enclosed town ', and this is the sense of the corresponding word in other Celtic languages. This does not fit in well with the significance of Gmc. *dūn*, and though there is some slight evidence for a Celtic use of the word in the sense of ' fortified *hill* ', this is not found until the fifth century, and is even then doubtful. On the whole it is better to regard the Celtic origin of O.E. *dūn* as non-proven.[1]

Words borrowed from the Britons after the settlement are chiefly the names of natural objects, animals, and things of everyday use. **Bratt** ' a cloak ' is found in the *Lindisfarne Gospels*, in company with *hrægl* and *hæcla*, as a translation of *pallium* (Mt. v, 40) ; the word survives in provincial dialect. **Binn**

---

[1] See Förster, *Keltisches Wortgut in Altenglischen*, p. 166 ff.

' BIN, manger ' may be either a continental loan from Gallo-Roman, or a loan from O.Brit. *bennā ; it has been noted in the previous chapter. **Bannoc** occurs only once in Old English, in a gloss to one of the works of Aldhelm, where it seems to mean ' a bit, piece ' (of a cake or loaf) ; it is probably from O.Brit. *bannōc ' a bit, drop '. **Gafeluc** ' a small spear ' may be from Old British (it occurs in Ælfric's *Vocabulary* 143, glossing *hastilia*) ; so also may **dunn** ' dark-coloured, grey, DUN ', which is found in Charters referring to *tunecan*, and also to *stān* ' stone '.

Of names of animals, **brocc** ' badger, BROCK ' is almost certainly from Old British (Ælfric's *Vocabulary* 119 : *taxus—broc* ; also in *Med. de Quadrupedibus* : *taxonem, þæt ys broc on Englisc*) ; **assa** ' ASS ', already dealt with under Latin loan-words, and ultimately from Lat. *asinus*, may possibly have come into English through Old Welsh *assen*.

Altogether the Celtic words of these two types are surprisingly few and doubtful. There are more certain loans to be noted under the heading of natural objects, but most of these occur only in Place-Names. Two at least, however, are to be found in the *Lindisfarne Gospels*, **carr** ' rock ', and **luh** ' lake ' : *cephas þæt is getrahtad carr* J. i, 42 ' Cephas, which is by interpretation a stone ' (so Rushworth ; LWSG. has *petrus*) ; *geheawen of carre vel stane* Mk. xv, 46 ' hewn out of stone ' (the others have *of stane*). **Luh**, also found in Northumbrian only, is the usual word in the *Lindisfarne Gospels* (rare in Rushworth) for ' lake, inland sea ', also ' strait ' : *before-fara hine ofer luh vel lytel sæ* Mt. xiv, 22 ' to go before him across the lake ' (Rush. *ofer sæ*, LWSG. *ofer muþan* ' arm of the sea ') ; it is from Old Welsh *luch* ; cf. Gaelic *loch*. **Torr** [1] ' a rock, rocky peak, hill ' from O.Brit. *torr, is found as a gloss to *scopulum* in Ælfric's *Vocabulary* 147 and other glosses, and also in the metrical version of the Metres of Boethius : *atrendlod of ðæm torr* Met. 5–17 ' rolled down from the tor ' (of a stone) ; it is fairly common in delimitations of boundaries in Old English charters. This word is found in modern Place-Names, especially in the south-west, but also in the north. More widespread in modern Place-Names is *combe, coomb(e)*, O.E. **cumb,** from O.Brit. *kumbā (cf. Welsh *cwm*). This also is most common in the south-west, but is to be

[1] See Förster, *Englische Studien*, liv, 103.

found occasionally all over England, except perhaps in the East Midlands. O.E. **funta,** which seems to have come to us from Celtic, but is ultimately from Lat. *fontana,* is found in a few names, such as Mottisfont, Havant, Chalfont.[1]

Besides these words, which were probably adopted into the ordinary English vocabulary before being used to form Place-Names, there are a number of names of districts, places, hills, rivers and forests which were taken over directly by the English from the Britons. *Kent, Leeds* (formerly the name of a district), *Lindsey* and *Kesteven* (two divisions of Lincolnshire), are all from earlier Celtic forms, as are also the names of the two Northumbrian kingdoms, *Deira* and *Bernicia.* DEVON and CORNWALL are formed from Celtic tribal names. Celtic names of rivers are to be found in all parts of England [2]; several have simply the sense of 'water' and occur repeatedly; such are Avon, Stour, and the varying developments of O.Brit. *Isca :* Esk, Usk, Exe, etc. Some are descriptive, such as Cam 'crooked', Dee 'holy', Dove 'black', and so on. Not infrequently a river has given its name to a town or village, as in the case of Dover (from Brit. *Dobrā* = water). Hill-names, too, fairly often survived the English invasion, and these sometimes became also Place-Names (e.g. Kinver, Clun, Penn).

Of Place-Names other than those of the types referred to in the last paragraph, the chief survivors are the names of the most important Romano-British towns, though many of them have an English suffix added : London, Reculver, Lympne, Win(chester),[3] Salis(bury), Ciren(cester), Catterick, Carlisle, Lich(field) Ilk(ley), and so on. Besides these, Celtic town and village names occur in varying numbers in many parts of England. They are most common in the west, from Cumberland and Westmorland down to Devon, where the proportion of Celtic to English names is, however, surprisingly small, as has recently been shown in the English Place-Name Society's volumes on this county.

Finally we come to the very few Old English loan-words from Old Irish, introduced by Irish missionaries during the seventh century. The one which occurs most commonly in Old English

---

[1] On this and other Celtic Place-Names see especially Ekwall, *The Celtic Element,* in *Introduction to the Survey of English Place-Names,* pp. 14 ff.
[2] Ekwall, *English River-Names.*
[3] For *chester,* O.E. ċeaster, see p. 25.

is **drȳ** ' a magician, sorcerer ', from O.Ir. *drui* (pl. *druid*). It
translates *magus* and *maleficus* ; the native equivalent is
scinlǣca. Here are some examples of the use of the word : *hie
Simon þone dry swiþe heredon* Blickling Homs. 173 ' they praised
Simon the magician ' (= *Simon magus*) ; *fela þinga dydan þa
geogeleras on Egyptalanda þurh dry-cræft* Wulfstan xvi, 98 ' the
jugglers did many things in the land of Egypt by their magic ' ;
bisuicen wæs from drygum vel tungul-cræftum Lind. Mt. ii, 16
' was deceived by the magi or astronomers ' (= *a magis*) ; *sio*
[Circe] *hi sceolde bion swiðe dry-cræftigu* Boeth. 116 ' she is said
to have been much skilled in magic arts ' ; *hi þær þa dryas
ongunnon ferian geond þæt wæter* Dial. 73 ' the magicians began
to carry them across the water ' (= *malefici*) ; *þæt heo wære
dryegge ond scinlæce* Mart. 28 ' that she was a sorceress and a
witch ' (*-icge, -ecge* is a personal suffix) ; *her bioð þa mæstan
dryicgan and scinlacan* Verc. Homs. 77 ' here are the greatest
magicians and sorcerers '.

The word **clucge** ' a bell ' is recorded only once in Old English :
sweg and hleoðor heora clucgan Bede 340 ' the music and melody
of their bell ' (= *campanae sonum*). It is known that bells were
in use in Irish monasteries from a very early period, and many of
the great bell-towers survive in all parts of Ireland. St. Patrick's
own small bell, enclosed in a shrine, is preserved in the National
Museum of Ireland. O.E. has also a native word, *belle* ' BELL ',
which is found in some manuscripts in the passage from the O.E.
Bede just quoted, and also in Ælfric's *Vocabulary* as a gloss for
tintinnabulum, and in the *Lambeth Psalter* for *cymbalum* : *heriaþ
hine on bellum* 150 ' praise him with bells '.

Ancor ' a hermit, anchorite ', probably entered England from
Ireland (O.Ir. *anchara*, from Latin from Gk. *anachorēta*), where
devotion to the life of a hermit was common. It occurs more
often in compounds than independently, e.g. *in medmyclum
ealonde . . . ancor-lif lædde* Bede 360 ' he led the life of a hermit
in a small island '.

The remaining words are also ultimately of Latin origin, though
they came into English through Irish. The first is **stǣr** ' history '
(Vulgar Lat. *stōria*, fr. Lat. *historia*). The Irish form is *stoir*, and
the process of development of this to O.E. *stǣr* is doubtful,
though the ascription of the Old English word to this source

seems certain. The word occurs frequently in the O.E. version of Bede's *Ecclesiastical History* : *þara abbuda stær and spel þisses mynstres* Bede 484 ' the story and narrative of the abbots of this monastery ' ; *in þis user ciriclice stær* Bede 282 ' historiae nostrae ecclesiasticae ' ; also in other writings : *on Ongelcynnes stere, þæt is on historia Anglorum* Mart. 86 ' in the history of the English ' ; in the Harley Gloss : *commentarius—stærtractere* 207 ' expounder of history '. ' Historian ' is *stær-writere* : *ic, swa soð-sagol stær-writere* Bede 206 ' I, as a truth-telling historian '.

Æstel ' a bookmark ', recorded once only, in King Alfred's preface to his translation of Gregory's *Cura Pastoralis* (*on ælcre* [*bec*] *bið an æstel* 6 ' in each book is a bookmark '), is from Lat. *hastula* ' a slip of wood ', but probably by way of Irish. Another word relating to books is **cine**, glossing *quaternio*, and apparently meaning a sheet of parchment folded in four ; it is from O.Ir. *cīn*, itself from Lat. *quīna* ' five each '.

Finally there is the disputed word **cros** ' CROSS of stone ', from Lat. *crux, cruc-em*, which may have come into English through Irish (O.Ir. *cross*) or through Scandinavian. The popularity of the stone cross in Ireland, and the influence of Celtic art on the carved crosses of England, added to the non-religious character of the words introduced by Danes and Norse-men and of their usual activities in this country, make the former the more probable. The word is rare in Old English ; it is found in the name *Normannes cros* (a hundred-name, now Norman Cross, near Peterborough) three times in the tenth century, e.g. in the *Anglo-Saxon Chronicle* E 963. Another instance from the *Chronicle* occurs only in a charter (*and swa to Grætecros* ' and so to Great Cross ' Chron. E 656) which may be an addition by the twelfth century scribe of this part. Other *Cross*-names are recorded from the end of the eleventh century onwards, but its first appearances in literature are in the first manuscript of Laȝamon's *Brut*, of about 1200 : *he* [King Oswald] *lette sone arere : a muchel cros and mare* 31386 (MS. *crost*), and in a slightly different sense in the twelfth century *St. Katherine* (see below, p. 77). The O.E. word which it finally almost entirely displaced was *rōd*, Mod. Eng. ROOD.

The next Celtic loan-words do not appear in English until the end of the Middle English period, and these will be discussed later.

Chapter IV

THE SCANDINAVIAN ELEMENT

The Scandinavian element in English is due in the first place to the Viking invasions of England in the eighth, ninth, and eleventh centuries, and their forcible settlement in parts of the country, but also, and in much greater degree, to the peaceful association of Englishman and Scandinavian during the eleventh and twelfth centuries. These dates are, of course, only approximate, but they serve to indicate roughly the two strata of Norwegian and Danish loan-words in Old English.

The first written record of a Viking attack on England is in the *Anglo-Saxon Chronicle*, where under the year 787 we read ' In this year King Breohtric married Eadburg, the daughter of Offa. And in his days there first came three ships of the North-men from Hereðaland. . . . These were the first Danish ships that came to England ' (Laud MS.). Further raids (in which the monasteries of Lindisfarne and Wearmouth were plundered) are recorded in 793 and 794, though in the latter year many of the attacking ships were wrecked by a storm. In the year 832, when we have the next reference to the Northmen, the assault was directed against a part farther south : ' in this year the heathen men plundered Sheppey '. After this the attacks became more frequent and more widely dispersed, and brought the invaders in larger numbers. In the year 851 the Danes for the first time wintered in England, instead of confining themselves to their former brief incursions, and not long after this the first permanent Danish settlements on English territory were made.

There were two main lines of attack and settlement—that of the Norwegians, who, sailing round the north of Scotland, established themselves in the Western Isles, in Ireland, and in North-West England and part of Wales, and that of the Danes, who struck into the East Midlands and Yorkshire. The English had insufficient political unity to resist effectively, but towards the end of the ninth century the vigour of Alfred of Wessex prevented the invaders from obtaining a hold over the whole of the country. Through his military skill and courage and his political ability the continuous fighting was brought to an end for a time, and the Northmen settled down more or less peacefully to trade and agriculture and the building of towns, in the area known as the Danelaw, which included the East Midlands, north as far as the Tees, west as far as the Pennines, Nottingham, and Bedford, south as far as the Thames.

After the death of Alfred in 900 his descendants acquired some increased authority over the Danelaw, where Englishmen and Scandinavians were now living side by side, apparently on friendly terms. But at the end of the tenth century a further invasion from the continent brought a new danger. In the tragic reign of Ethelred the Unready, England, and especially Wessex, suffered continuous attacks from Scandinavians who were seeking now for political power as much as for material plunder. If they were repulsed at all it was by payments of money, not by force of arms, and the effects of the enormous bribes which were repeatedly paid were of very short duration. The end of the fighting came at last in 1016 when, after a last struggle between the Danish Cnut and the English Edmund (son of Ethelred), the kingdom was divided between these two. The death of Edmund in the same year left Cnut as undisputed king of the whole of England as well as of Denmark and Norway, and from this time onwards we hear of no more Danish invasions.

During the rest of the eleventh century the Scandinavians gradually became absorbed into England and English life, and eventually, though perhaps not until the next century, their language was given up for English and disappeared, but not without leaving a distinct impression upon English, just as the Scandinavian legal and political customs left their mark upon English social life. For some time the Danes must have been bilingual, and no doubt many of their English neighbours and fellow-villagers and townsmen learnt to speak Danish. Inter-marriage between the two races was common, and this encouraged the tendency to bilingualism. Scandinavian terms learnt by Englishmen were introduced by them into their own tongue, and became established there. This was especially easy since the Scandinavian dialects at this period had considerable resemblance to the English dialects, particularly in vocabulary ; the speakers of both were to some extent mutually intelligible ; thus words introduced from one to the other language would carry with them little of the feeling of foreign words. In some cases the corresponding words in the two languages were practically identical, and it is sometimes impossible to know whether a particular word in Middle English is a loan-word or not. It happens not infrequently that a Scandinavian word has a slightly different sense from that of its English cognate, which sometimes led to the borrowing of *meanings* of words instead of words themselves.

The Scandinavian invaders and settlers did not speak a uniform dialect, though the varieties were not very strikingly differentiated. The Norwegians and Danes spoke respectively a West Scandinavian and an East Scandinavian dialect. The former is now represented by Modern Norwegian and Icelandic, the latter by Danish and Swedish. It is not always possible to assign a loan-word with certainty to one or other of these two dialects, but occasionally a definite phonological distinction enables us to do so.

The first period of Scandinavian loan-words, up to about the second decade of the eleventh century, seems to have introduced very few words into English, to judge by those which are recorded in writing at that period. Of these about fifty were still in use in Middle English, and about twenty-five have survived to the present day. The extant documents may be misleading as to the number of words borrowed before 1016, since practically all the written material of the early eleventh century which we now have comes from the south of the country and not from the Danelaw. But it is improbable that there was very much genuine word-borrowing until the more settled conditions after 1016 had come into being. The earliest loans, as will be seen, are of a more or less technical character, having to do chiefly with the sea and with legal customs ; those adopted before about 1150 are partly of a similar character, though some more miscellaneous words occur ; the later (M.E.) adoptions have no such limitations, and embrace even the most commonplace words, no introduction of new objects or ideas being implied. Hundreds of Scandinavian words are recorded for the first time in the thirteenth century, but many of these were doubtless in

use in some parts of the country earlier than this. As has already
been said of the tenth and early eleventh centuries, only a little
East Midland material is extant from the eleventh and twelfth
centuries, and in any case the type of word being borrowed at
this period was not such as would readily find its way into
literature.

THE EARLIEST LOANS FROM SCANDINAVIAN

Of the earliest loans and those of the second period the greater
number are to be found in the *Anglo-Saxon Chronicle* and the
Laws ; some appear only in vocabularies ; a few are confined
to Northumbrian texts such as the Lindisfarne and Rushworth
Gospels and the Durham Ritual.

About thirty words may be ascribed to the period before
1016. This includes the names of four types of ships : **barða,
barda** ' a beaked ship ' (O.N. *barð* ' armed prow ', *barði* ' a ram ;
a kind of ship '), found only in glosses and translating *rostrata
nauis* (*Harley* and *Royal Glosses*) and *dromo* (Ælf. Voc. 181 ;
here equated with *æsc*, a common native name for the Danish
ships) ; **cnearr** (O.N. *knǫrr*, a small ship, trading vessel), in the
poem known as the *Battle of Brunanburh* (under the year 937
in the Chronicle) : *cread cnear on flot* ' the ship hastened out to
sea ' ; *gewitan him þa Norðmen nægled cnearrum* ' the Northmen departed in their nailed ships ' (both passages refer to the
ships of the Danes) ; **floege** ' a little ship ' (cf. Icelandic *fley*
' ship ' [1]), only in Lind. J. vi, 22 : *floege* uel *lyttel scip*, translating
nauicula ; this word is found at least once in Middle English,
fleyne (pl.) in the romance of *Octavian* (southern version, *c.* 1350) ;
scegð, a light ship, both in glossaries and in the Chronicle :
scapha, uel trieris—litel scip uel sceigð (Ælf. Voc. 165) ; *trieris—
scægþ* (*Royal Gloss.* 289) ; *of x hidon ænne scegð* (Chron. E 1008)
' one ship for every ten hides ' ; the corresponding passage in
the Latin version (in F) has *unam magnam nauem quæ Anglice
nominatur scegþ* ; cf. also *wicing* [= Viking] uel *scegðman*,
glossing *pirata uel piraticus* (Ælf. Voc. 111).

Ten words denoting persons were now borrowed : **bōnda,
hūsbōnda, -bunda** ' householder, HUSBAND ' (M.E. *bōnde*

---

[1] The O.N. form was probably *fløy*.

' husbandman ') : *swa ymbe friþes bote swa þam bondan sy selost and þam þeofon sy latost* (*Laws of Æthelred* vi, 32) ' so concerning (the maintenance of) public safety in such a way as may be best for the householder and worst for the thief ' ; *an his manna wolde wician æt anes bundan huse his unþances . . . and se husbunda ofsloh þone oðerne* (Chron. E 1048) ' one of his men wished to stop at a man's house against his will . . . and the master of the house slew the other '. A feminine form appears to be used in Ælfric's *Heptateuch* : *ða Israeliscan wif biddaþ æt ðam Egiptiscean wifon æt hira nehgeburon and æt hira husbondum* (= Lat. *hospita*) *sylfrene fatu* (Exod. iii, 22) ' the Israelitish women shall ask the Egyptian women, their neighbours, and the mistresses of houses, for silver cups '. *Husbond* with the sense of ' householder ' is still found in Chaucer. **Dreng** ' warrior ' (O.N. *drengr*) only in the poem of the *Battle of Maldon* : *forlet þa drenga sum daroð of handa/fleogan of folman* 149 ' one of the warriors let a javelin from his hand fly from his palm ' ; this survives in earlier Middle English, e.g. in Laȝamon's *Brut* (*dring*) and *Havelok* (*dreng*). **Feolaga** ' FELLOW ', colleague, mate ' (O.N.) *fēlagi*) : and *wurdon feolagan and wed-broþra* (Chron. D 1016. ' and became fellows and sworn brothers ' (of Edmund and Cnut) ; also the compound *feolag-sċip* : *ic wille þat min and Ulfketels felageschipe stonde* (from a Charter in Thorpe's *Diplomatarium Aevi Saxonici*, p. 573). **Hold,** a title, ' vassal ' (O.N. *hǫldr*) : *Ysopa hold and Oscytel hold* (Chron. A 905) ; *him cierde to Ðurferþ eorl and þa holdas* (Chron. A 921) ' Earl Thurferth and the " holds " turned to him ' ; the high rank of the hold is indicated by the fact that his wergeld was four thousand *þrymsas* (= 1,000 shillings) ; the word occurs also in Lind. Mk. vi, 21 : *symbel worhte ðæm aldormannum and holdum and forwostum Galileæs* (= cenam fecit principibus et tribunis et primis Galileae). **Liesing** ' a freedman ' (O.N. *leysingr*, with approximation to O.E. *līesan* ' to set free ') seems to be recorded once only : *buton ðam ceorle ðe on gafollande sit and heora liesengum* (Laws of Alfred and Guthrum, 880–890, but MS. *c.* 1125) ' except the commoner who is settled on tributary land, and their freedmen [i.e. of the Danes] '. **Niðing** ' villain ' (O.N. *nīðingr*) : *wælreaf is nīðinges dæd* (Laws of Æthelstan iv, 7, *c.* 1000) ' robbing the slain is the act of a villain ' ; *se cing þa*

and eall here cwædon Swegen for niðing (Chron. C 1049) 'the king
and all the army declared Sweyn a villain' ; also *unnīðing* 'an
honest man' : *bead þæt ælc man þe wære unniðing sceolde cuman
to him* (Chron. E 1087) 'ordered that every honest man should
come to him' ; *nīðing* is fairly common in Middle English.
Đir 'maid-servant' (O.N. *þīr-r*), in the Lindisfarne and
Rushworth Gospels, as an alternative to the native *þignen*,
translating *ancilla* (John xviii, 17). **Đræl** 'servant, slave,
'THRALL' (O.N. *þræll*), in Lind. and Rush. Mt. x, 24 : *allra ðræl
vel esne* (= omnium servus) ; also Rush. J. viii, 34 : *se ðe doeð
synne ðræl is synnes* 'he who sins is the servant of sin' ; *þeah
þræla hwylc hlaforde æthleape and of cristendome to wicinge
weorðe* (Wulfstan 162) 'if any slave escapes from his master
and from Christianity becomes a pirate' ; it is common in Middle
English. **Ūtlaga** 'outlaw' (O.N. *ūt-lagi*, cf. *lagu*, below), a
common term : *þa cwæð man Swegen eorl utlah* (Chron. E 1048)
'Earl Sweyn was pronounced an outlaw' ; hence the verb
ūtlagian : *on þis ylcan geare man geutlagode Osgod Clapan* (Chron.
C 1046) 'in the same year Osgod Clapa was outlawed'.

Other social and legal terms are : *(brȳd)*-**hlōp** 'bridal, wedding'
(O.N. *brūð-hlaup*, with the cognate English word substituted for
the first element), in the Gospels, translating *nuptiae* (Rush.
L. xvii, 27, etc.), and in the Chronicle : *þe wæron æt þam brydlope
æt Norðwic* (D 1076) 'who were at the wedding at Norwich'.
Bȳ 'a dwelling' (O.N. *bȳ-r*) : *se ðe hus oððe lytel by hæfde in
byrgennum* (Lind. Mk. v, 3) 'who had a house or little dwelling
among the tombs' (= domicilium) ;   M.E. has the word
occasionally, e.g. in the *Cursor Mundi* : *siþen he come vntill a bij*
13290 ; it survives now only in the compound *by-law* = town-
law, except in Place-Names, of which it is a common element
in the north and east. **Cann** (O.N. *kanna*) is a legal term signifying
'cognizance, averment' :   *gif he þanne þæt ne mæge gecyþan
mid rihtre canne* (Laws of Hlothhere and Eadric, but a twelfth
century MS.) 'if he cannot prove this by a lawful declaration' ;
mynstres aldor hine cænne in preostes canne (Laws of Wihtred 17)
'the head of a monastery shall clear himself by the same formula
of averment as a priest' (twelfth century MS. from a late sixth
century original). **Griþ** (O.N. *grið*) 'truce ; peace, protection'
is used for a temporary cessation of warfare, as compared with

the native *friþ*, which means a condition of peace in general :
he þa þæs cynges worde and his witena grið wið hi gesætte (Chron.
E. 1002) ' with the consent of the king and his council he made
a truce with them ' ; *we willaþ wið þam golde grið fæstnian*
(Maldon 35) ' we will make a truce for this gold ' ; *griþ* also
signifies ' security, safety ' (in a more localized or personal sense
than *friþ*, which is rather ' public safety ') guaranteed within
certain local or temporal limits, or by the protection of a king
or other person : *wæs þær ealne þone winter on þæs cynges griðe*
(Chron. E 1048) ' he was there all the winter under the king's
protection ' ; it occurs fairly commonly in M.E., often in the
formula *griþ and friþ*. **Husting** ' a court, assembly, tribunal '
(O.N. *hūs-ðing*, apparently as held in a building, compared with
a ' thing ' in the open) is found in the Laws and the Chronicle :
genamon þu þone biscop leaddon hinc to heora hustinga (Chron.
E 1012) ' took the bishop and led him to their assembly '
(i.e. of the Danish army) (MS. F *in concilium suum*) ; it is
also used in Latin documents for the council of the City of
London ; it is not used in the wider sense of the national
assembly. Middle English has it in Laȝamon's *Brut* : *eoden to
sumne/hulden muchel husting* 2324 (the later version has the
French *conseil*).

Lagu ' LAW ' (O.N. *lǫg*, pl.) is one of the commonest
Scandinavian loans in O.E., and one of the most important.
It is used for a decree, enactment, for a code of laws or legal
system, and for an area under a specific legal system : *he niwade
þær Cnutes lage* (Chron. E 1064) ' he renewed the laws of Cnut ' ;
nu is seo ealde lagu geendod æfter Cristes tocyme (Ælfric's Pastoral
Epistles, 380) ' now is the old law ended after Christ's advent ' ;
þær hæfþ ane lage earm and se welega (Be Domes Dæge, 163)
' there poor and rich have one law ' ; *he sætte mycel deor-frið
and he lægde laga þær-wið* (Chron. E 1086) ' he established
protection for game and made laws concerning it ' ; *gylde lah-
slitte inne on Deone lage and wite mid Englum* (Laws of Edward
and Guthrum) ' pay the fine in the Danelaw and the corresponding
fine among the English '.

Ōran, pl. (O.N. *aurar*, O.Swed. *öre*), and **marc** (O.N. *mark*)
are used first in the Laws of Alfred and Guthrum, and fairly
often later for weights or values of silver or gold ; the *mark*

had eight times the value of the *ōra* ;   Chadwick (*Studies in Anglo-Saxon Institutions*, p. 24) gives the value of the *ōra* as 16 pence or 20 pence, according to two different reckonings which seem to have been in use : *he . . . astealde þa swiðe strang gyld . . . þæt wæs viii marc æt ha* (Chron. C 1040) ' he levied a heavy tax, which was eight marks per man ' ;   *twelf orena mid Denum and xxx scillinga mid Englum* (Laws of Alfred and Guthrum, vii) ' twelve oras among the Danes and thirty shillings among the English ' ;   *þæt wæs an gylden calic on fif marcon* (Chron. D 1058) ' it was a golden cup worth five marks '.   **Targe,** a small shield, is found translating *parma, scuto*, in the Brussels Gloss, and *clipeus* in the ninth century ;   cf. also *ic ge-ann Ælmere minen disc-ðene mines taregan* (Charter in Kemble's *Codex Diplomaticus*, III, 363) ' I bequeath my small shield to Ælmer my dish-bearer ' ;   the word was supplanted in Middle English by the French *targe* with [dž], itself borrowed from Germanic.   The word **wǣpen-tǣc** ' WAPENTAKE ' is from O.N. *vāpna-tak* ' a taking or touching of weapons ', but with the native form substituted for the Scandinavian in the first element ; it denotes a sub-division of a shire, and under Danish influence it took the place of the ' hundred ' in the northern counties, in some of which it still survives : *þæt man hæbbe gemot on ælcum wæpentace* (Laws of Æthelred, iii, 3) ' that a meeting should be held in each wapentake '.   **Wrang** ' WRONG ' (O.Norwegian *vrang*) : *unrihtdeman, ðe wendaþ wrang to rihte and riht to wrange* (Wulfstan 203) ' unjust judges, who turn wrong to right and right to wrong ' ;   also ' rough, uneven ' : *to ðam feorðan þorne on wrangan hylle* (*Codex Diplomaticus*, V, 297).

A small group of miscellaneous words completes this section, four from the *Lindisfarne Gospels*, one from the *Durham Ritual*, and one from the *Battle of Maldon*.   The last-named gives us **ceallian** ' to CALL ' (O.N. *kalla*) : *ongan ceallian þa ofer cald wæter* 91 ' began to call then across the cold river ' ;   the Durham Ritual has **efne** ' material ' (O.N. *efni*), and **farnian** ' to prosper ' (O.N. *farna-sk*) : *hal me do uel farniga me* ' make me prosperous ' : Lind. has **sparrian** ' to bar ' (O.N. *sparra*), M.E. *sparren, sperren* : *gesparrado dure ðin* (Lind. Mt. vi, 6) ' thy door being shut ' ; **ðweng** ' band ' (O.N. *þveng* ' thong '), Mt. xxiii, 5 (*ðuencgo*, = *philacteria*) ;   **sang** ' bed ' (O.N. *sǣng*) :   *song uel bedd* Lk.

xxii, 12 (= *stratum*) ; **eggian** ' EGG on ', Mk. xv, 11, where
ge-eggedon glosses *concitaverunt.*

What appears to be a very early loan is **eorcnan-***stān* ' precious
stone ' (O.N. *jarkna-steinn*), which is to be found in the earlier
verse, such as *Elene, Phoenix, Ruin,* and even (*eorclan-*) in
Beowulf ; it is believed to have come to Scandinavia from the
East, presumably by the medium of trade ; the Chaldean word
for ' topaz ' is *jarkān.*

SCANDINAVIAN WORDS OF THE SECOND PERIOD

The second period of Scandinavian loans may be reckoned
as extending from 1016 until about 1150—approximately the
beginning of the M.E. period. About thirty-three words belong
here, of which rather less than a third did not survive this period,
while twelve are in common use to-day ; *crooked, die, knife,
haven, hit, root, sale, score, skin, snare, take, they.* The following
are nouns denoting for the most part commonplace objects :
cnīf ' KNIFE ' (O.N. *knīf-r*) appears first in the eleventh century,
e.g. glossing *artavus* (= *cultellus*), Wright-Wülcker, I, 329, and
in a charm in MS. Cott. Vitellius E xviii : *writ pisne circul mid
pines cnifes orde* (Cockayne, *Leechdoms* I, 395). The native word
was *seax.* **Scinn** ' SKIN ' (O.N. *skinn*) and the compound **grā-
scinnen** ' of grey fur ' (O.N. *grā-skinn*) are in the Chronicle :
*geafon him myccla geofa . . . on scynnan mid pælle betogen, on
mærðerne pyleceon and gra-schynnene and hearma scynnene*
(Chron. D 1075) ' gave him rich gifts—skins covered with purple,
and robes of marten-skins and of grey fur and of ermine ' ;
it does not become common in M.E. before the fourteenth century.
Skin replaced O.E. *fell* and *hȳd,* ' FELL ', ' HIDE ', which were used
for the skins both of men and of animals, but in Modern English
have become restricted to the latter. **Rōt** ' ROOT ' (O.N. *rōt*)
occurs only in the compound *rōt-fæst* ' root-fast ', and this not
till the twelfth century ; *pa bepohte he him pæt gif he mihte ben
rot-fest on Engleland pæt he mihte habben eal his wille* (Chron.
E 1127) ' he bethought himself that if he could become
established in England he might have all his desire ' ; but
Middle English has it fairly frequently from Orm (c. 1200)
onwards. O.E. had *wyrt* for ' root ', the same word as that for

a plant. **Snearu** ' SNARE ' (O.N. *snara*) appears as a gloss for *laquem* (' for birds and hares ') in the Brussels Gloss to Aldhelm (p. 429). **Lit** ' colour, dye ' (O.N. *litr*), now obsolete except in provincial dialects, is quoted by Napier [1] from an early twelfth century manuscript, Cott. Vespasian D XIV, in the British Museum : *swa swa se litigere þe lufeð ælces heowes lit* ' like the dyer who loves colours of every hue ' ; the word is next recorded in the thirteenth century (*in kides blod he wenten it*—i.e. turned it about—*ðo was ðor-on an rewli lit* Genesis and Exodus 1068) ; it is not at all common in Middle English. **Loft** (O.N. *lopt*) is recorded once in Old English, where it has the sense of ' air ' (cf. O.E. *lyft*) : *heo ne liþ on namum þinge ac on lofte heo stynt* (Ælfric's *Hexameron*) ' [the earth] rests on nothing, but stands in the air ' ; in M.E. it has the meaning of ' upper room, LOFT ' (as in O.Norse, as well as ' air '), and is fairly common ; it is also used in the phrases *bi loft, on loft* ' on high, ' ALOFT '. **Læst** ' a fault, sin ' (O.N. *lǫstr*) has been noted by Napier in an eleventh century MS. (Bodl. Hatton 114) : *þæt he ure neoda gecnawe and ure læsta gebete* ' that He may know our needs and amend our faults ' ; it appears again in the late twelfth century, and later in Middle English.

The three verbs **diegan** ' DIE ', **hittan** ' to come upon, meet with, [HIT] ', and **tacan** ' touch, TAKE ', have all survived to modern times. O.N. *deyja* had an O.E. cognate which might have been the ancestor of the M.E. form *deien, deȝen*, but seems to have disappeared early, and the word *dēȝen*, etc., from the eleventh century onwards is almost certainly from the Scandinavian. The first occurrence of it is in Eadwine's *Canterbury Psalter* [2] 105/13 : *hredlice dydon* ' soon they died ' (= cito defecerunt) : it is a very common word in Middle English, and eventually took the place of *sweltan* and *steorfan* (the latter now has a restricted meaning, STARVE). **Hittan** (O.N. *hitta*) is not recorded in its usual modern sense until the fourteenth century ; in its single occurrence in Old English it means ' to come upon ' or ' fall upon ' : *Da com Harold ure cyng on unwær on þa Normenn, and hytte hi begeondan Eoferwic* (Chron. D 1066) ' then Harold our king came unexpectedly on the Northmen

---

[1] *Contributions to Old English Lexicography*, 1906.
[2] Ed. Harsley, E.E.T.S., 92.

beyond York ' (Chron. E has *gemette*). **Tacan** (O.N. *taka*), which
after the M.E. period entirely replaced O.E. *niman*, is found first
in the Chronicle (D) in the year 1072 : *se kyng nam heora scypa
and wæpna and manega sceattas and þa menn ealle he toc* 'the
king seized their ships and weapons and much money, and he
took all the men ' ; three special phrases, adapted from Old
Norse, are also found in O.E. : *toc to uuerrien him* (Chron. 1135)
'took to making war upon him' (O.N. *taka at*) ; *þet land-folc
him wið toc* (Chron. 1127) ' the people accepted him ' (O.N. *taka
við*) ; cf. also *tacan on* (O.N. *taka á*) ' to touch ' : *sona swa
þæt ele toc on þæt wæter* (MS. C.C.C. Cambridge 303, early twelfth
century, p. 179 [1]) ' as soon as the oil touched the water ' ; the
first of these at least survives in Middle English : *token to ʒeien*
(St. Katherine, 2060) ' began to cry '.

Three adjectives, *(ʒe)***crōcod** ' CROOKED ', **ragg**(*iʒ*) ' rough,
shaggy ', and **witter** ' wise ' were retained in M.E. The first
must be derived from *crōk* (O.N. *krōkr* ' crook ') which is
frequently found in M.E., and it is probably owing to chance that
the noun has not been recorded in O.E. The adjective is indeed
found once only, in MS. C.C.C. Cambridge 303,[2] referring to
a cripple ; it appears next in the late twelfth century *Lambeth
Homilies*. **Raggiʒ** (with an English suffix) is also from a noun :
O.N. *rǫgg* ' tuft ' (M.E. *ragge* ' RAG ') ; it occurs in the *Brussels
Gloss* to Aldhelm, for *setosa*. **Witter** (O.N. *vitr*) is equally rare in
O.E., occurring only in the Chronicle : *wislice hine bepohte swa he
full witter wæs* (D 1067) ' prudently bethought himself, being very
wise'. This is used also in Middle English, especially in earlier texts.

As in the first period, we have also in the second a number of
words denoting things connected with the sea. None of these
survived the O.E. period except **hæfen** ' HAVEN ' (O.N. *hǫfn*) :
*he geaf into Cristes cyrican on Cantware-byri þa hæfenan on
Sandwic* (Chron. A 1031) ' he gave to Christ Church, Canterbury,
the port of Sandwich '. Others are : **hā** ' thole ' (O.N. *hā-r*)
and **hamele** ' oar-loop ' (O.N. *hamla*), occurring once each in the
Chronicle, in the same passage of different manuscripts : *man
geald xvi scipan æt ælcere hamulan viii marc* (Chron. E 1039) ' they
paid for 16 ships at 8 marks per man ' ; *þæt wæs viii marc æt ha*

---

[1] See Napier, *Contributions to O.E. Lexicography.*
[2] See Björkman, *Scandinavian Loan-words*, p. 35, n. 2.

(Chron. C 1040) 'that was 8 marks per man'; the Chronicle also has **hā-sǣta** 'rower' (O.N. *hā-seti*), but with English second element : *and sceolde man setton oðre eorlas and oðre hasæton to þam scipum* (Chron. E 1052). **Liþ** 'a fleet' (O.N. *lið*) and **lips-mann** 'sailor' both occur in the Chronicle, the latter being the earlier : *Leofric eorl and mæst ealle þa þegenas benorðan Temese and þa liðsmenn on Lunden gecuron Harald to healdes ealles Englalandes* (E 1036) 'Earl Leofric and almost all the thanes north of the Thames and the seamen of London chose Harold to be ruler of all England'; *þæt lið wende ongean to Sandwic* (Chron. D 1052) 'the fleet went again to Sandwich'; the word is not·uncommon in the Chronicle (all MSS.). **Wranga** 'hold of a ship' (O.N. *vrǫng*) occurs in *Ælf. Voc.* 182 (printed as *pranga* in Wright-Wülcker).

Among words relating to law and social life we find five denoting persons : *carl, būtse-carl, hūs-carl, hofding, swegen.* **Carl** corresponds to O.E. *ċeorl*; it is used sometimes alone, sometimes as the first element of a compound, to denote 'man, male' (e.g. *carl-cat, carl-fugol*); note also *carles wǣn* 'churl's waggon, Charles's wain', of the star, in Cockayne's *Leechdoms* III 270. **Būtse-carl** (O.N. *būza* 'boat') is apparently a regular sailor of the king's own fleet (not a member of the national levy) and corresponds to the **hūs-carl** of the king's standing army (see Bosworth-Toller, Supplement); both are used in the Chronicle : *ealle þa butsecarlas of Hæstingan* (C 1052) 'all the seamen from Hastings'; *þa hwile com Tostig eorl into Humbran mid lx scipum . . . and þa butse-carlas hine for-socan* (D, E 1066); *man gerædde þa þæt Ælfgifu Hardacnutes modor sæte on Winceastre mid þæs cynges hus-carlum hyra suna* (Chron. E 1036) 'it was decided that Ælfgifu, Harðacnut's mother, should remain in Winchester with the house-carls of the king her son'. **Hofding** 'leader, ringleader' (O.N. *hǫf-ðingi*) is used in the second sense in Chron. D 1076 : *Rawulf eorl and Rogcer eorl wæron hofdingas æt þisan unræde* 'the earls Ralph and Roger were ringleaders in this conspiracy'. **Swegen** (O.N. *sveinn* 'man') is found several times as a personal name before the Conquest, but otherwise is recorded only in the compound *bātswegen* 'boatman, BOATSWAIN' in a charter printed by Earle [1] : *on Wycinges batswegenes*

---

[1] Handbook to the Land-Charters and other Saxonic Documents, p. 254.

gewittnisse ' on the testimony of Wicing the boatman '. The O.E. cognate is *swān*.

Fylcian ' to marshal, arrange ' (O.N. *fylkja*) is found in the Chronicle only : *þær his liþ fylcade* (C 1066) ' marshalled his fleet there '. **Gærsume** ' treasure ' (O.N. *gersumi*), which survived for a time in Middle English, occurs a number of times in the Chronicle, e.g. *ealle þa betstan gærsaman þe Cnut cyng ahte* (D 1035) ' all the best treasures that King Cnut possessed ' ; *sceawode þæt madme-hus and þa gersuman þa his fæder ær gegaderode . . . on golde and on seolfre and on faton and pællan and on gimman* (E 1086) ' inspected the treasure-house and the treasures which his father had collected—gold and silver and vessels and silks and gems '. **Māl** ' suit, cause ; terms, pay ' (O.N. *māl*) is to be found in the Cleopatra Gloss, and also in the Chronicle : *on þyson ylcan geare Eadwerd cing scylode ix scypa of male* (Chron. 1086) ' in this same year King Edward paid off nine ships ' (cf. the O.N. phrase *skilja af máli*, in the same sense) ; *scip-lið gewende to Legeceastre and ðær abiden heora males* (C 1055) ' the fleet went to Chester and there waited for their pay ' ; it is found occasionally in Middle English (*māl, mōl*), and, in a northern form, it appears in Mod. Eng. *black*MAIL. **Manslot** (O.N. *manns-hlutr*) has been noted by Napier [1] in MS. C.C.C. Oxford 197 (twelfth century) ; it seems to signify ' portion of land allotted to the head of a family ' ; the same MS. gives us **sceppe,** a measure for wheat or malt (O.N. *skeppa*, otherwise not recorded until the fifteenth century, when it has the sense of ' basket ', and now familiar as ' SKEP ') ; and **scoru** ' SCORE ' (O.N. *skor*) : *v scora scæp* ' five score sheep '.

Another trading term is **sala** ' SALE ' (O.N. *sala*), found in O.E. only in *Ælf. Voc.* 180, where it is equivalent to *uenditio*.

Two war-terms remain : **orrest** ' battle ' (O.N. *orrosta*) : *hine on orreste ofer-com* (Chron. E 1096) ' overcame him in battle ' ; **tapor-æx** ' a small axe ' (O.N. *tapar-øx*) : *swa feorr swa mæg an taperæx beon geworpen* (Thorpe, *Diplomatarium* 317) ; *and þar beo an mann stande on þan scipe and habbe ane taper-æx on his hande* (Chron. A 1031) ' let there be a man standing on the ship with an axe in his hand '. This word is particularly interesting as it is the first certain example of a Slavonic word in English ;

---

[1] *Contributions to O.E. Lexicography*, p. 43, q.v.

Russian *topór*, or rather its ancestor, found its way into Scandinavian, and thence into English. The word, however, did not survive in Middle English.

Finally we come to a form in Old English which *may* be of Scandinavian origin, and if so is the first appearance of a very important loan-word. This is the form *þæge* 'they, these', possibly identical with the M.E. *þei* from Scand. *þeir* (see p. 81). *Đæge* appears in two texts : the *Late West Saxon Gospels* : *sume ðæge wæron hæðene* John xii, 20 'some of them were heathen', and in the prose *Salomon and Saturnus* [1] : *ic ðe secge, fram iiii steorrum. Sage me, hwæt hatton page?* (p. 178) 'I tell you, from four stars. Tell me, what are they called ? '

These, then, complete the earlier loans from Scandinavian, so far as they are actually recorded, though, as has already been said, it is possible that some of those not occurring in writing before the M.E. period were already in use in the spoken language.

SCANDINAVIAN WORDS IN MIDDLE ENGLISH

During the Middle English period the proportion of Scandinavian loan-words used in a specific text varies according to the part of the country from which it comes, the literature and documents of the North, North-West, North-East, and East Midlands having many more Norse and Danish words than those of the South and South Midlands. A certain number of Scandinavian words are found even in the south in early Middle English, for the most part those which have already appeared in Old English ; words which drift down to the south as the M.E. period goes on are chiefly, though not exclusively, such as still remain in Modern English.

It has already been indicated that sometimes the meaning of a Scandinavian word becomes attached to the cognate English word, though the Norse word itself is not borrowed ; this has happened, for instance, in the case of O.E. *eorl* (M.E. *erl*) 'man, warrior', which after the Danish influence began was used for 'chief, ruler of a shire' (O.N. *jarl*) ; cf. also O.E. *drēam* 'music, joyful sound, revelry', which acquired its modern meaning of 'vision' through the influence of the related O.N. *draumr* ; the old sense of *drēam* still remains throughout the M.E. period,

[1] See p. 45.

but the word is used in the modern sense in *Havelok the Dane*
in the late thirteenth century : *a selkuth drem me dremede nou*
1284 ' a strange dream I dreamed '. The O.E. words with this
significance were *swefn*, still in use in Chaucer's writings, and
mǣtan vb., *mǣting* n. (M.E. *mēte*, *mēting*, *-ung*).

Scandinavian accidence had very little effect on English
grammar. Rarely, Norse inflexions are retained in English, but
as an integral part of the word ; e.g. the O.N. nominative (masc.)
-r in *hāgher* ' skilful ' (O.N. *hāg-r*), the neuter *-t* in *want* (O.N.
van-t ' lacking '), or the genitive *-ar* in the (remodelled) *nihter-tale*
(' night-time ', *Havelok*, Chaucer, etc.), O.N. *náttar þeli.*

Beginning at about 1150 we shall now consider the
Scandinavian element in some representative texts from different
parts of the country, down to the time of Chaucer.

The *Peterborough Chronicle* (MS. E of the *Anglo-Saxon
Chronicle*) was continued longer than any of the other versions
of the Chronicle, the last part, from 1132 onwards, having been
written about 1154. This final section, in spite of its place of
origin, has very few Scandinavian words which have not appeared
before in English. The pronoun **bāðe** ' BOTH ' is usually considered to be from O.N. *bāðir*, though in some areas at least it
may come from O.E. *bā þā* (' both ' + demonstrative) : *bathe
be nihtes & be daies* 1137 ' both by night and by day ' ; *hæfde
ða baðe togedere þone kinerice on Scotlande & þone eorldom on
Englelande* 1124 ' he had both together the kingdom in Scotland
and the earldom in England '. O.N. *brenna* probably gave rise
to M.E. **brennen** ' burn ' (cf. O.E. *bærnan, biernan*) : *þa ræueden
hi & brendon alle the tunes* 1137 ' they plundered and burnt all
the towns '. **Hærnes** ' brains ' (O.W. Scand. *hiarni*) occurs in :
and uurythen to ðæt it gæde to þe hærnes 1137 ' and twisted (a
cord) until it went to the brain '. The conjunction and preposition
till ' to, TILL ', identical with a form which had existed as a
native word in early Old English, was introduced from
Scandinavian in the twelfth century (O.N. *til*) : *dide ælle in
prisun til hi iafen up here castles* 1137 ' put them all in prison until
they gave up their castles '. The word is common in Middle
English in northern texts, and survives in Modern Standard
English as a conjunction.

One other word which we still use, and whose initial [sk]

gives it a Scandinavian flavour, may be mentioned here as illustrating one special tendency in the M.E. period. This is SCATTER, which first appears in the Chronicle : *he todæld it & scatered sotlice* 1137 ' he spent and scattered it foolishly ' ; it is actually from an O.E. **sċaterian*, now SHATTER, and there happens to be no Scandinavian form from which it could be derived. But fairly often there were cognate forms in English and Scandinavian which were distinguished only or mainly by the *sċ-* (*sh*) of the former compared with the *sk-* of the latter, and the initial consonants were sometimes interchanged, the Norse consonant-group being used in English. Thus O.E. *sċiftan* ' SHIFT ' corresponded to O.N. *skifta*, and M.E. has both *shift* and *skift*. Other such doublets are M.E. *schei, skei* ' SHY, timid ' (O.E. *sċēoh*, Dan. *skȳ*) ; *shēr, skēr* ' clear ' (O.E. *sċǣr*, O.N. *skǣr*). Through the existence of such pairs it became natural among bilingual speakers to reconstruct similar pairs by supplying the missing one of the pair, such as *skateren* by the side of *shateren*, or (in the other direction) *schimeren* ' SHIMMER ' by the side of *skimeren* (O.Swed. *skimra*), or *schele* beside *skele, skile* (O.N. *skil* ' reason, SKILL '). Similarly a Scandinavian initial *g* might be substituted for the corresponding English ȝ (= *y-* [j]), since the one is often equivalent to the other in cognates. This, it seems, was what happened in *give* (cf. O.E. *ġefan*, O.N. *gefa*), which eventually took the place of M.E. ȝ*eve*, ȝ*ive*, *yive*.

Two other early Middle English texts which contain very few Scandinavian loan-words are the collection of homilies in MS. Bodley 343,[1] and the *History of the Holy Rood-Tree*.[2] The first has only **witer** (O.N. *vitr* ' wise, knowing ; evident ' ; see above, p. 71), in an adverbial form with English suffix : *witer-lice metezung is alræ mæzene moder* 90 ' surely moderation is the mother of all virtues ' ; the latter has the verb **dēȝen** and the noun **rōt,** both already found in O.E. (see above) : *for þan ðe ic nu deȝen sceal* 14 ' because I must now die ' ; *þa roten fordruȝode wæron* 4 ' the roots had dried up '. The vocabulary of both these texts gives a decidedly archaic impression.

The brief *Hymns of St. Godric*,[3] dating from about 1170, give

---

[1] Ed. Belfour, E.E.T.S., 137.   [2] Ed. Napier, E.E.T.S., 103.
    Ed. Hall, *Selections from Early Middle English*.

the form **burth** ' birth ' (O.N. *burðr*) ; the O.E. form is (*ǧe*)*byrd*. (M.E. and Mod.E. *birth* is from O.Swed. *byrþ*.)

A group of three alliterative legends in MS. Royal 17 A xxvii and MS. Bodley 34 have a larger number of Norse words, many of them dating from the Old English period. These are the legends of *St. Katherine, St. Margaret,* and *St. Juliana.*[1] To judge from their dialect they are from a west midland area. They probably date from before 1200, though the MSS. are early thirteenth century ; they might be considered here, or at the beginning of the next section. Of words already dealt with, they have (to give their modern forms) *both, die, law, knife* (*mid kenre pikes pen eni cnif* Kath. 1929 (of St. Katherine's wheel) ' with sharper spikes than any knife '), *egg* vb. (*he forgulte him anan þurh eggunge of eue* Jul. 60 ' he sinned through the instigation of Eve '), *fellow* (*weoren as feolahes þurh muche freontschipe* Jul. 4 ' were as fellows through great friendship ' ; *englene feolahe and archanglene freonð* Bodl. Jul. 49, where Royal has *ifere*, O.E. *ǧeféra*, ' fellow of angels and friend of archangels '), *haven* (*lead me . . . to þe hauene of heale* Jul. 42 ' lead me to the haven of salvation '), *root, take, thrall, call* (*heo bigon to cleopien ant callen þus to criste* Marg. 3) ; besides *grið* (*schulen gledien igodes grið* Marg. 21 ' shall be glad in the keeping of God '), and *witterlic*, which have not survived. Besides these we find the following words : **bond** ' BOND ' (O.N. *band*) Marg. 13 ; **bōn** ' prayer, BOON ' (O.N. *bōn*, cf. O.E. *bēn*) : *þæt mi bone mote þurh þurlen þe weolcne* Marg. 7 ' that my prayer might pierce the sky ' ; **bule** ' BULL ' (O. East Scand. *bule* ; this occurs already as a Place-Name element in O.E.) : *helle bule haueð ouercomen* Jul. 54 ' has overcome the bull of hell ' ; **crōk** ' CROOK ; evil device ' (O.N. *krōkr*) : *wite me from his lað ant wið his crefti crokes* Jul. 34 ' protect me from his hate and from his cunning devices ' ; **gapen** ' gaze, GAPE at ' (cf. Swed. *gapa*) : *þes keiser bicapede hem* Kath. 1255 ' this emperor gazed at them ' ; **casten** ' CAST ' (O.N. *kasta*) : *het hire þrefter kasten in cwalmhus* Kath. 1547 ' ordered her afterwards to be cast into the torture-house ' ; also *akesten* ' to overcome, cast down ' : *ouercomen ant akasten hare þreo cunne fan* Marg. 1 ' to overcome and cast down

---

[1] *St. Katherine*, ed. Einenkel, E.E.T.S., 80 ; the other two ed. Cockayne, E.E.T.S. 13 and 51. Quotations are from MS. Royal unless otherwise stated.

their three kinds of foes ' ; **lān** ' LOAN, reward ' (O.N. *lán*) :
to leosan ower swinkes lan Kath. 805 ' to lose the reward of your
labour ' ; **mēoc** ' MEEK ' (O.N. *mjúkr*) : *marherete mildest and
meidene meokest* Marg. 4 ' Margaret mildest and meekest of
maidens ' ; **wanten** ' WANT ' (O.N. *vanta*) : *neauer of þi wil ne
schal þe nawt wontin* Jul. 22 ' never shall anything you desire
be wanting '. These eight words and the eleven first mentioned
have all survived to the present day ; the following eleven do
not now occur in Standard English : **grā** ' grey ; unfriendly,
hostile ', as noun ' evil spirit ' (O.N. *grá-r*) : *of þat grisliche gra
weren agrisen swiðe* Jul. 53 ' were much affrighted by that
grisly devil ' ; **greiþen** ' to prepare ' (O.N. *greiða*) : *he greiðið
þe o grome nu alles cunnes pinen* Jul. Bodl. 35 ' he is preparing
for you now in anger all kinds of torture ' ; **hap** ' luck, success '
(O.N. *happ*) : *bisohte him help & hap* Kath. 184 ' asked for help
and success ' ; but the related HAPPY and HAPPEN are now in use;
keiser ' emperor ' ; **liðen** ' listen ' : *lusteð me leoue men ant
lideð ane hwile* Jul. 72 ' listen to me, dear men, and hearken
for a while ' ; **lire** ' face, skin ' (O.N. *hlýr*) : *to-limede hire ant
teleac lið ba ant lire* Jul. 58 ' tore her to pieces and rent limbs
and skin ' ; **mensk** ' grace, honour, dignity ' (cf. O.Swed.
mænska ' goodness ') : *te murðe þat lið to meiðhades menske*
Jul. 18 ' the joy that waits on maiden's grace ' ; *nowcin* ' hardship, pain ' (O.N. *nauðsyn*) : *ne niht nis ter neauer ne neauer
na nowcin* Kath. 1683 ' there is never night or pain ' ; **skēr**
' pure, clear ' (O.N. *skǽr*) : *þat ne schulen ha beon sker of ure
weorre* Jul. 50 ' that they shall not be quit of our war ' ; **stōr**
' strong, great ' (O.N. *stórr*) : *is nu se storliche unstrenget ower
strengðe* Kath. 1269 ' is your strength now so greatly enfeebled ' ;
þwert ' across ' (O.N. *þvert*, neut. acc. of *þverr*) ; **wandraþ**
' suffering ' (O.N. *vandrǽpi* ' difficulty ') : *to wurchen ow al þat
wandrepe* Jul. 22 ' to cause you all that suffering '. Finally there
is the O.N. noun-suffix *-lēc, -leik* (O.N. *-leikr*) ' -ness ' : *þe beoð
wiðuten godleic & empti wiðinnen* Kath. 838 ' which are without
goodness and empty within ' ; *ich am gomeful and gled lauerd of
þi godlec* Marg. 10 ' I am joyous and glad, Lord, for Thy goodness ' ; *feirlec and strencðe beoð his schrudes* Marg. 19 ' fairness
and strength are His garments '.

This group, especially the legend of St. Margaret, has frequent

examples of pairs, usually with little difference in meaning, and
often simply for the sake of the alliteration ;   here we may find
Scandinavian and native words side by side :   *wið gersum ant
wið golde* ;   *ouercomen ant akasten* ;   *to cleopien ant callen* ;   *his
þral ant his þeowe,* and so forth.

The alliterative gnomic verses known as the *Proverbs of
Alfred,*[1] a southern text, the manuscript of which dates from
before 1200, has very few Scandinavian words :   **again**
' AGAINst ' (not necessarily Scandinavian, but probably affected
by Scand. influence ; the usual native form is *aʒein*), **fro** ' from,
FRO ' (in *to and fro* ;   O.N. *frá*), **ille** adv. ' ILL ' (O.N. *illr,
illa*), **þoh** ' THOUGH ' (O.N. **þóh*) ;   also **grip,** and **late** ' to let '
(cf. the cognate O.E. *lǽtan,* M.E. *lēte*) : *wose lat is wif his maister
wurþen* 358 ' whoso lets his wife become his master ' (this form
of the third person singular, however, may be English).

Another text which is also southern but from a definitely
south-eastern area, is a prose dialogue (between Reason and
Man's Soul) in MS. Stowe 340, published under the title of
Vices and Virtues.[2]   In addition to BOTH, NAY, THRALL, and
grip, this document has two words not referred to. before :
kanunk ' canon ' (O.N. *kanunkr,* from Lat. *canonicus*) : *munekes
kanunekes, ancres & eremites* 35 ;   and **skent-ing** ' amusement '
(O.N. *skemta* vb.) : *gleues & skentinges . . . & alle ðo þing ðe
ʒeu hier gladien mai* 69 ' joys and pleasures and all those things
that may please you here '.

Nor is there a larger proportion of Norse words in either of
the two late twelfth-century collections of sermons known as
the *Lambeth Homilies* [3] and the *Trinity Homilies.*[4]   The former,
besides CROOKED, BOTH, LAW, LOW, and **grip,** gives us the two
important words **skill** and **wing.** The first is from O.N. *skil,*
and in Middle English has the senses of ' skill, discrimination,
reason ' : *þet wes al mid muchele skile* 59 ' that was all with much
reason ' ; also *unskile* : *forʒef us ure unskile* 65 ' forgive us our
folly ' ; *wing* is from O.N. *vengr* : *a vuhel com flon from houene
into orðe. her uette feþer-home and wenge* 81 ' a bird came flying
from heaven to earth ; here he brought plumage and wings ' ;
O.E. generally uses *feþera.*

[1] Ed. Borgström, Lund, 1908.   [2] Ed. Holthausen, E.E.T.S., 89.
[3] Ed. Morris, E.E.T.S., 53.   [4] Ed. Morris, E.E.T.S., 29.

The *Trinity Homilies* have even fewer Scandinavian words, the most interesting being several examples of the verb **egg,** e.g. *þat man eggeð his negebure to done or to speken him harm* 13 ' that a man eggs on his neighbour to do or speak harm to him '.

The long epic poem known as the *Brut*,[1] by the Worcester-shire poet Laȝamon, written in the late twelfth century, and a fine example of Middle English heroic verse, contains over 16,000 long lines, but has altogether less than forty Norse words. Most of them are words which are common generally in Middle English : BOTH (also the native *ba, boa, beie*, etc.) ; **bōnde,** and **hūsbōnde** ' HUSBAND ', ' householder ' (*of æuer elche huse : þat husbonde wunede* iii, 285 ' from every house in which a husbandman lived ') ; BOON (*þe king uor his fader bone : ȝette hire hir bone* II, 200 ' the king at his father's request granted her boon ') ; **brunie** ' coat of mail ' ; **griþ** (often in the formula *griþ and friþ* ; cf. also *æuere he hæhte ælcne mon chireche-griþ halden* II, 514 ' always he bade every man respect the protection of the Church ') ; KNIFE ; DIE ; **hail** adj. (' whole, safe ' : O.E. *hāl* ' WHOLE ' is also used by Laȝamon ; note also *Leofue freond wæs hail / þe oðer sæið drinc hail* II, 175 ' Dear friend, be in health ! The other says Drink hail ! ' and cf. *wassail*) ; **dring** ' warrior ' (O.N. *drengr*) ; **gersum** ; **greiðen** ; HIT (*þe eotend smat after biliue : & noht hine ne hutte* III, 35 ' the giant aimed a blow at him quickly, and did not hit him '), **hustinge** (cf. above, p. 67) ; **kaiser** ; LOW (*þe hehȝe & þa laȝe* II, 541 ' the high and the low ') ; LAW ; OUTLAW ; **mensk** ' honour ' ; **niðing** ; ROOT ; **stōr** ' strong, great ' ; SWAIN ; TAKE ; **witer** ' wise ' (*heo was witer heo was wis* I, 409 ' she was wise and clever ').

Besides these there are seven others, less frequently found in M.E., which also occur in the *Brut* : **attlen** ' to go, turn ; to think, purpose ' (O.N. *ǽtla* ; (to the reader) *lete we nu þene eotend bilafuen : and atlien to þan kinge* III, 32 ' let us now leave the giant, and turn to the king ') ; **farcost** ' a kind of boat ; condition, circumstances ' (O.N. *farkostr*) : *haures he sende : to hirede þes kinges / to witen of his farcost* I, 63 ' he sent spies to the king's court to learn his position ' ; **skēr** ' quit, free ' (*habbeð iqueðen us scere* II, 108 ' has pronounced us free ') ; **skenting** (*þer wunede þe king al þene winter a skenting* III, 230 ' the king

---

[1] Ed. Madden, London, 3 vols, 1847.

stayed there all the winter amusing himself ') ; **wandreþ** (*mid wandreðe & mid sare* II, 97 ' with misery and pain ').

It is interesting to note that another version of Laȝamon's *Brut*, made about fifty years later (edited with the earlier MS.), retains most, though not quite all, of these words, and has besides : CAST, LEG (O.N. *leggr* ; *his legges he helede mid hosen of stele* II, 463 ; the earlier version has *sconken* ' SHANKS '), **may** ' maiden ', THEY (occasionally), THURSday (*þorisdei*, O.N. *Ðors-* ; the early version has the native *Ðunres-dæi*).

In contrast to all the southern and midland documents so far discussed, we now turn to a work from the north-east midlands : the *Ormulum*,[1] written about the year 1200 by Orm, a canon-regular of the order of St. Augustine. It consists of paraphrases of and commentaries on the Gospels used at Mass, and contains some 10,000 long lines, in an unrhymed metre imitating the Latin *septenarius*. This is the first Middle English text to contain any considerable number of Scandinavian words, and it is for this reason, as well as others, of some importance linguistically, if not otherwise. It has about 120 words which may with some certainty be considered Scandinavian, besides others which are doubtful ; some (A) survive in Modern Standard English ; (B) some may be found all over the country in Middle English ; (C) some are limited to the northern and north midland areas in M.E. ; (D) some occur in this text only in M.E. (though some of these have survived in modern dialects). The use of the plural pronouns *they, their, them*, should be especially noted, since these forms eventually spread into all dialects, ousting the native forms. Lists of the most interesting of the Norse words in the *Ormulum* are given here, with illustrations of the use of some of them ; except in list A the spelling is that of Orm (note that a double consonant indicates that the preceding vowel is short).

(A) Most of these have been mentioned earlier as occurring in Old or Early Middle English ; the O.N. forms will therefore not be given in all cases : ANGER vb. (O.N. *angra*) ; AYE (Orm *aȝȝ*, O.N. *ei*) ; AWE (Orm *aȝhe*, O.N. *agi*, cf. O.E. *eȝe*) ; BAND ; BOTH ;

[1] Ed. Holt, 1878, 2 vols. See also Brate, *Nordische Lehnwörter im Orrmulum*. Halle Beiträge, x, pp. 1–80.

BAIT vb. (Orm *beȝȝten,* O.N. *beita* 'to cause to bite'; cf.
O.E. *bātian*); BLOOM 'flower' (O.N. *blōm*); BOON; BOOTH
(O. Swed. *bóþ* 'booth, stall'; BOUND (in the phrases *bound for,
outward bound*; Orm *būn* 'ready', O.N. *búinn*); BULL; CROOK;
DIE; EGG (on); FLIT (O.N. *flytja*); FRO; GUEST (the consonant
at least is Scandinavian; O.N. *gestr*; cf. O.E. *ġest*); GAIN
(O.N. *gegna*); HAIL 'salute'; ILL; KINDLE; KNIFE; LAW;
LOFT; LOW; MEEK; 'RAISE (O.N. *reisa*); ROOT; SCATHE(less)
(O.N. *skaði* 'harm'); SCARE (Orm *skerren* vb., cf. O.N.
skjarr 'timid'); SKILL; SKIN; SLEUTH(hound) (Orm *slōþ*
'track'; O.N. *slóð*); TAKE; THEY (O.N. *þeȝȝ, þeȝȝr, þeȝȝm*);
TILL; THOUGH; THRIVE; WAND; WANT; WING; WRONG.

Examples: *þatt mihhte ohht anngrenn oþre* I, 12 'that might
in any way anger another'; *dreding and aȝhe* I, 249 'dread and
awe'; *þeȝȝ dursten beȝȝtenn menn / Forr æþelike giltte* I, 354
'they durst punish men for public guilt'; *Forr Nazaræþ
bitacneþþ uss Onn Ennglissh brodd & blome* II, 19 'for Nazareth
betokens in English shoot and blossom'; *Forr þatt teȝȝ turrndenn
Godess hus Inntill huccsteres boþe* II, 196 'because they turned
the House of God into a huckster's booth'; *& Abraham wass
forrþrihht bun To don Drihhtiness wille* II, 156 'A. was straightway ready to do the Lord's will'; *& ȝiff he seoþ þe mann
forrdredd, He wile himm skerrenn mare* I, 132 'and if he sees the
man frightened, he will scare him more'; *aȝȝ follȝhenn soþ
meocnesses sloþ* I, 111 'ever to follow the path of true meekness';
all swa summ win wass wannt tatt follc II, 146 'when wine was
wanting to the people' (the word *want* has the neuter *t* of the O.N.
adj. *van-r, van-t* 'lacking'; this is kept in the M.E. verb *wanten,*
which also occurs in Orm).

(B) Words which occur in M.E. in any part of the country:
brennen 'burn'; **greȝȝþen** 'prepare'; **griþþ; haȝherr** 'skilful,
dexterous' (O.N. *hag-r*; note the retention in English of the
Scand. *-r* of the nom. masc. sing.); **keȝȝsere; kidde; lasst**
'fault'; **kanunnkess** 'canon' (O.N. *kanunkr,* from Lat.
canonicus); **-leȝȝc; make** 'wife, mate' (possibly English, but
perhaps from O.N. *maki*); **māl** 'speech, payment'; **may**
'maiden'; **orrest** 'contest' (recorded in O.E., but not again
in M.E.); **sēr** 'separate'; **skemmting; summ** 'as' (cf. the
dialectal *how-some-ever*); **tīþende; wanndraþ; witerr.**

Examples : *& forrþi þatt Sannt Anndrew wass Rihht god and hazherr hunnte* II, 114 'because St. Andrew was a good and skilful hunter' ; *o þatt kezʒseress time* I, 121 'in that emperor's time' (Orm also uses the O.E. form *cāsere* ; see above, p. 18 and below, p. 107, note) ; *inn orresst ʒæn þe deofell* II, 81 'in strife against the devil'.

(C) Words which are found in northern texts : **Addlen** 'earn' (O.N. *ǫðla-sk*) ; **beʒʒsk** 'harsh' (O.N. *beisk-r*) ; **biggen** 'dwell' (O.N. *byggja*) ; **brāþ** 'angry' (O.N. *bráþ-r*) ; **brodd** 'sprout, spike' (O.N. *broddr*) ; **bulaxe** 'axe' (O.Dan. *buløx*) ; **fere** 'power' (O.N. *føri*) ; **forrgarrt** 'destroyed, condemned' (P.P. of *forgaren*, from O.Swed. *gøra* 'to do') ; **gǣte**(*lǣs*) 'without care' (O.N. *gǽta* 'heed') ; **gloppnenn** 'to be terrified' (O.N. *glúpna* 'to be surprised') ; **gres** 'grass' (Swed. *gräs* ; cf. O.E. *grǣs*, M.E. *gras*) ; **hæþelig** 'scornfully', *hǽþing* 'scorn' (O.N. *háþ*, *hǽþa* 'scorn') ; **heþen** 'hence' (O.N. *heðan*) ; **hōf** 'measure, reason' (O.N. *hóf*) ; **immess** 'variously' (O.N. *ýmiss*) ; **lesske** 'loin' (O.Swed. *liuske*) ; **leʒhe** 'hire, pay' (O.N. *leiga*) ; **leʒʒk** 'play, sport', **leʒʒkenn** 'to play' (O.N. *leikr*, *leika*) ; **leʒʒtenn** 'to look for' (O.N. *leita* : cf. O.E. *wlātian*) ; **loʒhe** 'fire' (O.N. *logi*) ; **merrke** 'mark' (O.N. *merki* ; cf. O.E. *mearc*) ; **mineþþ** 'has in mind' (O.N. *minna*) ; **nowwt** 'oxen' (O.N. *naut* ; cf. O.E. *nēat*, *nīeten*) ; **occ** 'and' (O.N. *ok*) ; **radd** 'afraid' (O.N. *hrǽddr*) ; **rāþ** 'counsel' (O.N. *ráþ*) ; **rō** 'quiet, peace' (O.N. *ró*) ; **rōs** 'praise' (O.N. *hrós*) ; **sammtale** 'agreed' (O.N. *saman* 'together') ; **sīt** 'pain, illness' (O.N. *sýta* 'to afflict') ; **skēt** 'quickly' (O.N. *skiótr*) ; **skiledd** 'divided' (O.N. *skil* 'discernment, discrimination') ; **skir** 'clean' (O.N. *skír* ; cf. O.E. *scīr*) ; **sterrne** 'star' (O.N. *stjarna* ; cf. O.E. *steorre*) ; **þrinne** 'three' (O.N. *þrinnr*) ; **ummbe** 'about' (O.N. *umb*) ; **upp-brixle** 'object of reproach' (O.N. *brigsli*) ; **heþen** 'whence' (O.N. *hvapan*).

Examples : *Itt ise full bitterr & full beʒʒsc* I, 232 ; *lokepþ hwære I bigge* II, 99 'look where I live' ; *wiþþ skarn, wiþþ hæpinng, ne wiþþ idell* I, 152 'in scorn, contempt or idleness' ; *heore leʒhe birrþ hemm beon Rædiʒ þann itt iss addledd* I, 215 'their pay should be ready for them when it is earned' ; *Onn idell, & wiþþutenn ned, Alls iff he wollde leʒʒkenn* II, 64 'idly and needlessly, as if he wished to jest' ; *all swa summ þe nowwt i ploh*

II, 199 'like the oxen in the plough'; *to brukenn resste & ro wiþþ himm* III, 319 'to enjoy peace and rest with him'; *to rosenn off þin haʒherrleʒʒc* I, 169 'to boast of thy skill'; *newe steorrne ʒaff he þeʒʒm* II, 30 'He gave them a new star'; *mid þrinne lakess lakedd* II, 30 'presented with three gifts'.

(D) Words which occur only in Orm in M.E. : **Afell** 'strength' (O.N. *afl*); **ammbohht** 'maidservant' (O.N. *ambótt*; originally Celtic; see O.E. *ambeht*): **bennkedd** 'provided with benches' (O.Swed. *bænker* 'bench'); **broþ-fall** 'epilepsy' (O.N. *brot-fall*); **dowwnenn** 'to smell' (O.N. *daunn* n.); **ēpenn** 'to cry' (O.N. *øpa*); **glūternesse** 'gluttony' (O.N. *glutr* 'extravagance'); **nāþe** 'grace' (O.N. *náp*); **rowwst** 'voice' (O.N. *raust*); **sannen** 'to prove' (O.N. *sanna*); **skirrpeþþ** 'rejects' (O.N. *skirpa*); **sowwþ** 'sheep' (O.N. *souþr*); **trigg** 'truth' (O.N. *tryggr*; cf. O.E. *trēowe* TRUE); **ūsell** 'wretched' (O.N. *úsǽll*).

Examples : *Loc her icc amm ammbohht all bun To follʒhenn Godess wille* I, 79 'look, here I am, a handmaid ready to follow the will of God'; *wiþþ þrinne bennkess bennkedd* II, 175 'supplied with three benches'; *recless smec Is god & swet to dowwnenn* 'the smoke of incense is good and sweet to smell'; *þe rowwst iss herrd off ænne mann Ðatt epeþþ þuss i wesste* I, 320 'the voice is heard of a man that cries thus in the desert'; *draf hemm alle samenn ut, & nowwt & sowwþess alle* II, 188 'drove them out all together, and all the cattle and sheep'; *trigg & trowe griþþ and friþþ* Preface 69 'faithful and true peace and security'.

1200–1250

The most important prose work of Early Middle English is the *Ancrene Riwle* or *Rule of Recluses*. It is almost certainly a product of the twelfth century, but although it is extant in a number of manuscripts none of these is earlier than the first quarter of the thirteenth century. The only one which has yet been printed [1] is of about 1220–1230, and since it is at present uncertain how far the vocabulary of this agrees with the original, it is dealt with here as a thirteenth-century text. It is a work of considerable length, amounting to 215 pages in print. Altogether it contains

---

[1] Nero A XIV in the British Museum. Ed. Morton, Camden Society, 1853.

something over thirty different Scandinavian words, by no means a high proportion. The work is probably from the West Midlands.

The following words are still current : anger, boon, both, cast, crooked, die, droop, egg (on), fellow, gain, knife, meek, root, skill, thrall, Thursday, (a)thwart, wing, want ; besides these we have **algate, fīken** ' to hurry about ', **garsum, greiþ(en), griþ, hāwer** ' skilful ' (O.N. *hágr*), **lāt, -lēc, liten** ' to dye ' (cf. *lit* ' colour ', earlier in this chapter), **mensk, skēr,** (for)**swīðen** ' to burn up ', **tiðing, witnen** ' to witness ', **wondreþ,** none of which are peculiar to the Rule, but for the most part common enough in Middle English.

Here are some examples of their use : **algate :** *his abbod bed allegate þet he scholde siggen* 314 ' his abbot told him that he should by all means confess ' ; **angres-ful :** *forto beon so angresful þerefter nis nout God icweme* 370 ' to be so anxious concerning it is not pleasing to God ' ; **crōked :** *of crokede & of kene uondunges* 102 ' of malicious and sharp temptations ' ; **drūp(i) :** *makeð drupie chere* 88 ' assumes a drooping air ' ; **eggen :** *to eggen us to gode* 146 ' to incite us to good ' ; **fīken :** *fikeð mid te heaued & stingeð mid te teile* 206 ' moves the head about quickly and stings with the tail ' ; **garsum :** *ne he ne bereð no garsum bute gnedeliche his spense* 350 ' he carries no money but his bare expenses ' ; **hāwur :** *ofte a ful hawur smið smeoðið a ful woc knif* 52 ' often a skilful smith forges a weak knife ' ; **lāt :** *of tollinde lokunges ne lates* 51 ' of enticing looks or behaviour ' ; **liten :** *þus he liteð cruelte mid heowe of rihtwisnesse* 268 ' he colours cruelty with the tint of goodness ' ; **mēoken** ' to make meek ' : *makieð edmod & meokeð our heorte* 278 ' make your heart humble and meek ' ; **skēr :** *beoð al sker of his atter* 136 ' be all free from his venom ' ; **skil** ' reason ' : *hwon þe olde unwine isihð ure skile slepen* 272 ' when the old enemy sees our reason asleep ' ; **tiðing :** *no tale ne tiðinge of þe world* 70 ; **þwert :** *attri speche is eresie & þwert-ouer leasunge* 82 ' poisonous speech is heresy and direct lying ' ; **wing :** *þe hwingen þet bereð ham upward* 130 ' the wings that bear them upward ' ; **witnen :** *ase holi writ witneð* 286 ' as holy writ testifies ' ; **wandreþ :** *wondreðe & weane ine licome & ine soule* 156 ' misery and woe in body and soul ' ; **wanten :** *þenc euer hwat þe wonteþ of holinesse* 276 ' think always how much holiness is wanting in you '.

Among other religious writings of the period may be mentioned two much briefer documents, also from the west : a small collection of homilies in MS. Cotton Vespasian A XXII, and an attractive homiletic allegory known as *Sawles Warde*,[1] 'the guardianship of the soul', which treats of the house of Man, wherein the Soul is the treasure, Wit is the husband, Will the wayward wife, and the Five Senses are the five servants. This contains the following Scandinavian words : **drūpnen :** *iseh ow iffruhte ant somdel drupnin* 259 ' I saw you in fear and somewhat depressed ' ; **hūsbōnde** ' householder ' ; **keiser :** ȝarowe forte demen . . . *kinges ant keiseres* 261 ' ready to judge kings and emperors ' ; **-lēc :** *þe feierlec of hare wlite* 261 ' the fairness of her face ' ; **lahe** ' low ' ; **mēoc ; nowcin** ' hardship ' ; **weng :** *to witen us on euch side under godes wengen* 253 ' to guard us on each side under the wings of God ' ; **wandraþ ; wanten ; witterlich.**

In the *Vespasian Homilies* we find very few Norse words : **gate** (not common except in the north) : *me sceolden anon eter gat ȝemete* 23 ' they should meet him presently at the gate ' ; **griþ :** *wið wam we ne muȝe grið ne sibbe macie* 243 ' with whom we should make neither truce nor peace ' ; **lage** ' law ' ; **wrang-**(seht) ' enmity ' (O.N. *rang-sáttr*) : *twan hlaforde þe wransehte bien samod* 241 ' two lords who are at enmity with each other ' ; **witer-**(lich) : *witodlice he cumð an ende þisser world* 231 ' certainly he shall come at the end of this world '.

A decidedly different type of literature is to be found in the Middle English Romances, one of the earliest of which is *King Horn*,[2] written apparently in the South-East Midlands in the first half of the thirteenth century. It cannot be said, however, that the Scandinavian element of the vocabulary of this romance, at least, differs much from that of the religious works already discussed. Here are to be found such words as : both, cast, die, fellow, haven, husband (*husebonde*, not in the sense of ' householder '), ill· (adv.), knife, law, low, meek(ness), take, thrall, till, wrong. Slightly less usual are **brunie** (*his brunie he gan lace* 717 ' he began to lace his mail-shirt ') ; **flitten** ' FLIT ' (*wel sone bute þu flitte* 711 ' unless you withdrew at once ') ; **gate** ' GATE ' (*suppe com in atte gate* 1078 ' then came in at the gate ', but the

---

[1] Both ed. Morris, E.E.T.S., 34.   [2] Ed. Hall, Oxford, 1901.

native ʒate is also used) ; **hitten** ' HIT ' (wiþ swerde ihc þe anhitte 712 ' I hit at you with a sword ') ; **nevenen** ' to name ' (wel bruc þu þin euening 206 ' may you live up to your name ') ; **nīþing** (þanne spak þe gode kyng, Iwis he nas no niþing 196 ' then spoke the good king, certainly he was no villain ') ; **bitaken** (bitok him þi lond werie 785 ' took upon himself to defend your land ') ; **tīþing** (site stille, sire king, & herkne þis typyng 806 ' sit still, sir king, and hearken to these tidings ') ; **þriven :** (of all þat were aliue Ne miʒte þer non þriue 620).

In the dialogue between The Owl and the Nightingale,[1] a poem of nearly 1,400 lines in rhymed couplets, the Scandinavian element is very small ; in fact, the poem has remarkably few foreign words of any kind (see p. 128, on the French element). The forms which do appear are the following : **bōnde** (swa deþ moni bonde-man 1577 ' as many a husbandman does ') ; **bōþe** ' BOOTH ' ; **cogge** ' COG ' (O.Dan. kogge) ; **crōked** (cliures scharpe & wel icroked 1676 ' claws sharp and very crooked ') ; **ille** (al þat heo spekeþ hit is him ille 1536 ' all that she speaks is amiss to him ') ; **laten** ' let ' ; **nai** (nay, nay, sede þe niʒtingale 543) ; **skenten** ' to please ' (þe more ich singe þe more I mai, An skente hi mid mine songe 449 ' the more I sing the more I may, and please them with my song '), **skenting** ' amusement ' ; **skēren** ' to purify, rid ' (þar-of þu, wrecche, moste þe skere 1302 ' there-of, wretch, you must rid yourself ') ; **skil** ' reason, SKILL ' ; **stōr** (wundere me þungþ wel starc & stor 1473 ' it seems to me a great and mighty marvel ') ; **þoʒ** ' though '.

Two pieces of about 1250, both from the East Midlands, have a higher proportion of Scandinavian words. These are a paraphrase of Genesis and Exodus [2] in rhymed couplets (4,162 lines) and a Bestiary,[3] partly rhymed, partly alliterative (802 lines). The dialects of these two are very similar. Genesis and Exodus has over sixty distinct Scandinavian words : **age** ' AWE ' (but also the native eige, O.E. eġe) ; **ai** ' AYE ' ; **anger** ' grief, ANGER ' : and dede hire sorge and anger mune 972 ' and did remember her sorrow and grief ' (the sense ' anger ' is not recorded till the late fourteenth century) ; **biggen** ' dwell ' : And ðor he biggede in

---

[1] Ed. Wells, Boston, 1907.
[2] MS. C.C.C. Cambridge. Ed. Morris, E.E.T.S., 7.
[3] MS. Arundel 292. Ed. Hall, Selections from Early Middle English.

G

a caue 1137 ' and there he dwelt in a cave ' ; also **bigging** ' stay,
sojourn, residence ;   dwelling-place, house ' :   *long bigging is
here nogt god* 718 ' it is not good to stay here long ' ;   *ðo was
non biging of al egipte lich-les* 3163 ' then was no house in all
Egypt without a corpse ' ; **birþe** ' BIRTH ' : *ðe fader luuede esau
wel / for firme birðe* 1484 ' the father loved Esau well, as eldest
born ' ; **blōmen** ' to BLOOM ' : *orest it blomede, and siðen bar / ðe
beries ripe* 2061 ' first it bloomed, and then it bore the berries
ripe ' ; **bond** ' BOND ' : *And bondes ben leid on Symeon* 2230 ;
BOON ; BOTH ; **brennen** : *an swiðe ferli sigt ðor-bi, / fier brennen
on ðe grene leaf* 2777 ' a marvellous sight there, fire burning in
the green foliage ' ; **callen** ' to CALL, summon, name ' :   *quor-at
calles ðu me?* 3237 ' wherefore do you call me ? ' ; *Jacob calde
ðat stede betel* 1631 ' Jacob called that place Bethel ' ;   also
bi-callen ' accuse ' : *ðis sonde hem ouertakeð raðe / And bi-calleð
of harme and scaðe* 2314 ' this messenger overtakes them quickly,
and accuses them of wrong-doing and injury ' ; DIE ; FELLOW :
min mog, min neue. and felage 1761 ' my kinsman, my nephew
and companion ' ; **fēr** ' sound, whole ' (O.N. *førr*) : *Al hol and
fer he wiste it sen* 2812 ' afterwards he knew it all whole and
sound ' ; **flitten** ' FLIT ; remove ' : *Niðede ðat folk [ðat] him fel
wel, / And deden him flitten hise ostel* 1522 ' the people were envious
because he prospered, and made him remove his dwelling ' ;
FRO : *for God led hem fro helle nigt / to paradises leue ligt* 89 ' for
God led them from the night of hell to the dear light of Paradise ';
garen, geren ' to prepare, do, perform, cause ' (O.Swed. *gøra*) :
sone o-morwen he gan him garen 1417 ' straightway in the morning
he prepared himself ' ; **gestning** :   *at heg tide and at gestning*
1507 ' at festival and entertainment ' ;   probably **glenten** ' to
move quickly, slip aside ;   to glance, look, shine, GLINT ' (cf.
Swed. dial. *glänta*) : *ghe glente and ðhogte, migte it nogt ben* 1029
' she looked (in astonishment) and thought it might not be ' ;
greiþen ; gres : *trees it for-brac and gres and corn* 3049 ' trees
it destroyed and grass and corn ' ; **griÐ :** *wopen of wigte and tol
of griÐ* 469 ' weapons of war and tools of peace ' ; **heil** adj. :
*Good is, quað Joseph, to dremen of win, / Heilnesse an blisse is
ðer-in* 2068 ' It is good, said Joseph, to dream of wine ;   health
and happiness are therein ' ; **heðen, hweðen, ðeðen** ' hence,
whence, thence ' ; **hilen** ' hide, cover ' (O.N. *hylja*) : *It mai*

ben hoten heuene-Rof, / It hiled al ðis werldes drof 102 ' it may be
called the roof of heaven ; it covers all the compass of this
world ' ; **ille** adj. and adv. : *And quo-so wile cursing maken, /
Ille cursing sal taken* 4038 ' and who-so utters a curse, an evil
curse shall fall upon him ' ; perhaps **kide** ' KID ' (Dan. *kid*) :
two kides he fette and brogt es hire 1535 ' two kids he fetched
and brought them to her ' ; **kippen** ' to seize ' (O.N. *kippa*) :
so manige dead ðor kipte 3164 ' so many Death seized there ' ;
LAW ; **laten** ' let ' ; **lit** ' colour ' ; **lote** ' face, cheer ' ; **merke**
' mark, sign ' ; **mōl** ' speech ' (O.N. *mál*) : *ðes frenkis men o
france moal / it nennen un iur natural* 81 ' these Frenchmen in
the speech of France call it *un jour naturel* ' ; **gate** ' way ' :
sore he gunen for-dredde ben,/for ne cuðen ne gate flen 3224 ' they
began to be much afraid, for they could in no way escape ' ;
nīðing ' villain ', but here ' villainy, meanness ' ; **oc** ' also ' ;
ōr ' before ' ; **sperren** ' to close, bar ' ; **ransaken** ' to search,
RANSACK ' (O.N. *rann-saka* ' to search a house ') : *he gan hem
ransaken on and on* 2323 ' he began to search them one by one ' ;
rapen ' hasten ' ; **scaðe** : *He ben cumen to mirie dale, / An ðere
he werken sckaðe and bale*, 850 ' they are come to a pleasant
valley, and there they do harm and injury ' ; **skil** ' reason, skill ' :
a spirit ful of wit and sckil 203 ' of wisdom and reason ' ; **seck**
' sack ' ; SISTER ; **skie** ' cloud ' (SKY) : *Bi-foren hem fleg an
skige brigt* 3255 ' before them flew a bright cloud ' ; **tīnen** ' to
lose ' (O.N. *týna*) : *ðu tines vn-ended blisce* 3518 ' you will lose
unending bliss ' (cf. dial. *tyne*) ; TAKE ; **lōwe** ' flame ' : *and al-so
hege ðe lowe sal gon, / So ðe flod flet de dunes on* 643 ' and the
flame shall rise as high as the flood stood on the mountains ' ;
twinne ' two ' (TWIN) (O.N. *tvinnr*) : *Heft haueð he mad her vii
alter / And on ilc brend eft twin der* 402 ' again he has made here
seven altars, and burnt on each two beasts ' ; THOUGH ; THRALL ;
ðwert ' perverse ' : *his herte ðo wurð ðwert and hard* 3099 ' his
heart became perverse and hard ' ; **uggen** ' to fear ', **ugli**
' horrible, fearful ' (UGLY) (O.N. *uggr* ' fear ', *ugga* ' be afraid ') :
ðo cam on him ugging and frigt 950 ' then fear and dread came
upon him ' ; *And wurð sone an uglike snake* 2805 ' and became
at once a horrible snake ' ; the word *ugge* ' fear ' is recorded
first in English in the prose piece entitled *A Lovesong to our Lord*,
of the early part of the twelfth century (Morris, E.E.T.S., 34,

p. 209) ; the modern sense 'repulsive in appearance' is not found until the fourteenth century, but it is not always easy then to distinguish this sense from that of 'frightful, terrible, etc.' ; **wanten** ' to be wanting ' ; **will** ' astray ' (O.N. *villr*) : *wimman wið childe, one and sori, / In ðe diserd, wil and weri* 975 (of Hagar and Ishmael) ' woman and child, alone and sad, in the desert wandering and weary ' ; WINDOW (O.N. *vindauga*, lit. ' wind-eye ') [1] : *Fowerti dais after ðis / Arches windoge undon it is* 602 ' forty days after this the window of the ark is undone ' ; **witterlich ; wand** ' WAND '.

The *Bestiary*, a translation of a Latin *Physiologus*, is an account of the habits and character of a number of animals, birds, etc., with allegorical interpretations. The following are the Scandinavian words to be found in it : AYE ; **ande** ' breath ' (O.N. *andi*) ; BOON ; BOTH ; **brennen ; brō** ' eyebrow ' (O.N. *brá*, cf. O.E. *brēow*) : *he is blac so bro of qual* 194 (of the panther) ' it is black as brow of whale ' ; CALL ; **derf** ' bold ' (O.N. *djarfr*) : *derflike wiðuten dred* 313 ' bravely, without fear ' ; **fēȝen** ' to cleanse ' (O.N. *fǽggja*) : *feg ðe ðus of ði brest filde* 160 ' cleanse yourself thus of the poison of your heart ' ; **fiken** ' to fidget, fuss and hurry about' (O.N. *fikia-sk*) ; FRO ; GAPE ; **gres ; heil** ' sound ' ; ILL ; **ket** ' flesh ' (O.N. *kiǫt*) : *he tireð on his ket* 336 ' he tears at its flesh ' ; LAW ; **leið** (O.N. *leiðr*, cf. O.E. *lāþ*) : *seftes . . . leiðe & lodlike* 356 ' creatures hideous and loathly ' ; **oc** ' also ' ; **or** ' before ' ; **rapelike** ' hastily ' ; **reisen** ' rouse, RAISE ' ; **rennen** ' run ' ; **scaðe :** *sipes ge sinkeð & scaðe ðus werkeð* 447 ' ships she sinks, and thus does harm ' ; **skenting** ' amusement ' ; (un)**skil ; skīe** ' SKY ' : *ðurh skies sixe and seuene* 50 ' through six and seven skies ' (cf. the earlier meaning, ' cloud ', in *Genesis and Exodus*, above ; this sense is found as late as Skelton) ; **swiðen** ' to burn ; to light up ' (O.N. *svípa*) ; TAKE ; TILL ; **twinne** ' two ' ; **ðeðen ;** THOUGH ; **wille** ' astray ' ; **wrong** ' twisted' (WRONG).

1250–1300

To the second half of the thirteenth century may probably be ascribed the Romance of *Havelok the Dane*.[2] This has associations

---

[1] The Ancrene Riwle, referred to above, uses *þurle, eie-þurle*, for window, but the Titus MS. of this text, which has many northern features, has *windohe*.
[2] Ed. Skeat and Sisam, Oxford, 1923.

with Lincoln and Grimsby, and the large number of Norse and
Danish words to be found in it certainly indicates an area in
which Scandinavian influence was strong. The poem, which was
written for popular reading or recitation, has 3,000 lines in
rhyming couplets.

The vocabulary not infrequently has the cognate English as
well as a Norse form, but sometimes the English forms are due
to the scribe and not to the author ; this is obviously the case
in some of the rhymes, for instance in lines 360–1, where the MS.
rhymes *boþe–rede* (O.E. *rǣdan* ' advise '), impossible unless it
is assumed that the original had the form *rōþe* (O.N. *ráða*) ;
again, in lines 1397–8 [1] occurs the rhyme *name—Rauen* (a personal
name, Hugh Raven), and in 2528–9 *cauen—name*, which apparently
disguise a form *naven* (O.N. *nafn* 'name '), not elsewhere recorded
in M.E., but corresponding to the verb *nevenen* ' to name '.

It is unnecessary to quote all the Scandinavian words (of
which there are over 120) in this text. Many of them are such
as occur generally in Middle English. The following list gives
some of the less common and more interesting : **asken** ' ashes '
(O.N. *ask-* ; cf. the native *æsc* ' ASH ') 2841 ; AWE ; **beiten :**
þanne men doth þe bere beyte 1840 ' when men bait the bear ' ;
perhaps BIG : *Bernard stirt* [= started] *up, þat was ful big* 1774 ;
bleike ' pale ' (O.N. *bleik-r* ; the text has also the native *blāke*) :
þat weren for hunger grene and bleike 470 ; **bloute** 1910 ' soft,
pulpy ' (O.N. *blautr*) : *he maden here backes al-so bloute* 1910
(by beating them) ' they made their backs as soft ' ; **bōne**
' equipped ' (O.N. *bóenn*, p.p. of *bóa* ' to prepare ') ; **bulder-**
(stone) ' BOULDER ' ; CLUB (O.N. *klubba*) : *he dredden him so þef
doth clubbe* 2289 ' they dreaded him as a thief does a club ' ;
coupe ' buy, pay for ' (O.N. *kaupa* ; like O.E. *ćēapian*, this is
ultimately Latin) ; **crūs** ' fierce ' (O.N. *krús*) : *And drive hem
ut, þei he weren crus, / So dogges ut of milne-hus* 1966 ' drove
them out, though they were fierce, like dogs out of a mill-house ' ;
frest ' delay ' (O.N. *frest*) ; **frie** ' to blame ' (O.N. *frýja*) ;
dreng ' a free tenant ' (already in O.E., = ' warrior ') ; **garen**
' to prepare ; to cause ' : *þer-on he garte þe erl suere* ; **gate**
' way ' [2] : *Thou canst* [= knowest] *ful wel þe rihte gate / To*

---

[1] See note in edition cited above.
[2] *Gate* is, of course, common in northern towns in the sense of " street ".

Lincolne 846 ; **genge** ' retinue, household ' (O.N. *gengi*) ; **geten** ' to GET ' (O.N. *geta* ; cf. the English *-ġetan* (only in compounds in O.E.), M.E. ӡ*eten,* which would have given Mod. E. *yet) ; **gēten** ' to watch, guard ' (O.N. *gǽta*) : *þat he sholde on ilke wise / Denemark yeme and gete so* 2960 ' that he should in the same way guard and look after Denmark ' ; **goulen** ' to scream ' (O.N. *gaula*) : *hwi grete ye and goulen nou ?* 454 ' why do you cry and scream ? ' ; **kaske** ' vigorous ' (O.N. *kask-r*) : *þe laddes were kaske and teyte* 1841 ' the young men were vigorous and active ' ; **keuel** ' a gag ' (O.N. *kefli*) ; KINDLE ; **kippen** ' to seize ' ; **kirke** ' church ' (O.N. *kirkja*; in northern areas this cannot always be distinguished from the northern form of O.E. *ċiriċe* ; the latter, however, would be *chirche* in *Havelok*) ; **kiste** ' chest ' ; **lenge** ' prolong ' (O.N. *lengja*) ; **leyk, leyken** ' play ' ; **liften** ' to LIFT ' (O.N. *lypta*) : *þat mouhte it liften to his kne* 1028 ; **loupe** ' to run, rush ' : *and bigan til him to loupe* 1801 (O.N. *laupa* ; cf. O.E. *hlēapan*, M.E. *lēpe,* which also occurs in *Havelok*) ; **lurken** ' to LURK ' : *he made hem lurken and crepen in wros* 68 ' he made them lurk in hiding, and creep into holes ' ; **mirk** ' MIRK ' : *Jesu Crist, that makede mone / On þe mirke niht to shine* 404 ; **rig** ' back ' (O.N. *hrygg-r* ; cf. the native *ridge*) : *And caste brinie up-on his rig* 1775 ' cast his shirt of mail upon his back ' ; **rippe** ' basket ' (O.N. *hrip*) ; **rowte** ' to roar ' (O.N. *rauta*) ; SCABBED (Dan. *skab*) ; SEEM ; **serk** ' shirt ' (O.N. *serk-r*) ; **span-**(new) (O.N. *span-nýr*) : *and bouhte him clopes, al span-newe* 968 ; STACK (O.N. *stakk-r*) ; **sternes** ' stars ' ; **stith** ' anvil ' (O.N. *steði* ; cf. Mod. E. *stithy*) : *And beten on him so doth þe smith / With þe hamer on þe stith* 1877 ; **teyte** ' active ' (O.N. *teitr*) ; **tinte** ' lost ' : *þat he ne tinte no catel* 2023 ; **þarne** ' to lose ' (O.N. *þarfna*) ; **þei** ' THEY ' (beside the native *he* ' they ') ; **þerne** ' serving-maid ' (O.N. *þerna*) ; **þrinne** ' three ' (cf. *twinne* ' two ' in *Gen. and Exod.*) ; **to-rīuen** ' to rend ' (O.N. *rífa*) ; **wayke** ' weak ' (O.N. *veik-r* ; O.E. *wāc* becomes M.E. *wōk*) ; **wesseylen** ' to drink healths ' ; **wiht** ' courageous and active ' (O.N. *vig-t,* with neuter ending) ; **wrō** ' corner ' (O.N. *wrá), etc., etc.

As an example of a different and less ' popular ' type of romance we may take *Floris and Blauncheflur,*[1] translated in the south

---

[1] Ed. Lumby, E.E.T.S., 14.

or central East Midlands from a French version of the story.
Close adherence to the French original perhaps accounts for the
small Scandinavian element and the large proportion of French
words. Of the former we have :   **brenne, caste, felawe, gate**
(also *ʒate*), **gersume, gestning** (*he hopede come to þat gesninge* 82
' he hoped to come to that entertainment '), **hail** ' health-
drinking ' (*He let fulle a cupe of win,* / ' *Dame,*' *he sede,* ' *þis
hail is þin* ' 56 ' he had a cup filled with wine, " Lady," he said,
" I drink to your health " '), **hauene, may** ' maiden ' (*Đus herinne
þis oþer day* / *Sat blauncheflur, þat faire may* 46), **marc, stōre**
' strong ' (*Fram flore into flore* / *þe strimes urneþ store* 228 (of
the system of hot-water pipes in the palace at Babylon) ' from
floor to floor the streams flow strongly '), **tīþing.** In at least one
case (here shown by the rhyme) the scribe has replaced a
Scandinavian word by an English one :   *þo floriz iherde his
lemman nempne* / *So blisful him þuʒte þilke steucne* 53 ' when
Floris heard his love named, that voice seemed blissful to him ',
where we should read *neuene* for *nempne.*

From quite a different part of the country—Gloucestershire—
comes a rhymed history of England, which goes by the name of
Robert of Gloucester's Chronicle.[1] This was for the most part
composed towards the end of the thirteenth century, and the
oldest manuscript now extant is of the early fourteenth century.
The Scandinavian element is inconsiderable. The following words
occur : HIT ; BOON ; BOTH ; **brenne ;** CAST ; DIE ; FELLOW ; **fyki**
(' to move quickly, fidget ') ; **greiþen ;** HAVEN ; HAIL (*dronk hir
heil* 2521 ;   also *washayl* 2514) ;   HUSBAND (in the sense of
' husbandman '); LOW; MARK (amount of money); MEEK; ROOT;
SKULL (its earliest appearance ;   cf. Swed. dial. *skulle*) ;   SKULK
(cf. Norw. dial. *skulka*) ; **skēre** ' to exculpate ' ; SLY ; SWAIN ;
TAKE; THRALL; WING; **wōn** ' provision, store ' (O.N.*ván*). It will
be observed that very few are now obsolete. Later manuscripts
of this Chronicle introduce a few more Norse words :   **atwynne**
' in two ' 3333 (where A—the earliest MS.—has *atuo*) ;   **blōme**
' to BLOOM ' (A : *blowe*) ;   **bole** ' BULL ' 2497 ;   *burþe* ' birth ' ;
cally ' to CALL ' (A : *clupie,* O.E. *cleopian*) ;   on **loft** ' ALOFT '
(A : *on luft*) ;   **ōr** ' before ' (A : *er*) ;   **sistre**(n) ' SISTER ' (A :
sostren) ;   **þrōf** ' THROVE ' (A : *þeu*).

<hr>

[1] Rolls Series.

Similarly, in the *Southern Legend Collection* [1] in MS. Laud 108, written also in the South-West Midlands, the first thousand lines show only eleven Scandinavian words ; these are of the same character as those in *Robert of Gloucester* : BOON, BOTH, **brenne,** CAST, DIE, FELLOW, **greiþen,** LAW, MARK, SKIN, TAKE.

The South Midland poetical version of the story of *Iacob and Iosep,*[2] in addition to CAST, DIE, LAW, **skēre** (*ȝif ȝe of Egipte lond wolleþ faren skere* 438 ' if you want to go out of the land of Egypt unhindered '), TAKE (*he toc his beuerene hat* 517 ' he took his beaver hat '), WRONG (*in þe prison liþ mid ful muche wronge* 274), has the pronoun **þei** ' THEY ' five times (but the usual southern *hī* fifty-six times, according to the editor), and the noun **brunie** ' shirt of mail ' 407.

FOURTEENTH AND EARLY FIFTEENTH CENTURIES

To illustrate the Scandinavian element in the vocabulary of this period, we shall make a somewhat arbitrary choice among a very large number of writings in great variety. The following come from different parts of the country, and represent various types of literature : the *Cursor Mundi*, Richard Rolle (Epistles and Lyrics), two of the poems of the Ireland Manuscript (*The Anturs of Arther*, and *Sir Amadace*), Robert of Brunne's *Handlyng Synne*, the Prose Psalter of MS. Brit. Mus. Additional 17376, the *Aȝenbite of Inwit*, the *Festial* of John Mirk, the poems of William Herebert, and finally some London documents.

The first-named, a chronicle of the world, beginning with the Creation, was written in the North of England, probably in the first quarter of the fourteenth century. The oldest and fullest version (that in MS. Cotton Vespasian A III) [3] consists of nearly 30,000 lines. The following Norse words occur in the first thousand lines : AYE, **and** ' breath ' (*þis aand þat men draus oft / Betakens wynd þat blaws o loft* 531 ' this breath that men constantly draw betokens the wind that blows aloft ') ; **at** ' that ' relat. pron. and conj. (*to þis palais at was sua rike* 415 ' to this palace which was so splendid ') ; AWE ; perhaps **barn** ' bairn ' (*þar sal ȝe find sumkin dedis / þat iesus did in hys barn-hedis* 166

---

[1] Ed. Horstmann, E.E.T.S., 87.   [2] Ed. Napier, Oxford.
[3] Ed. Miller, E.E.T.S. 7 vols.

' there shall you find certain deeds that Jesus did in His child-
hood ') ; **bath** ' both ' ; BIRTH ; **brāþ**(li) ' violently ' (O.N.
bráþ-r) ; CALL ; CAST ; CROOK (*For of alle als scheus þe bok /
Mast he cuth o crafte and crok* 700 ' for as the book shows he knew
most of all of craft and cunning ') ; **dil** ' to hide ' (O.N. *dylja* ;
How Iuus wit þer gret vnschill / Wend his vprisyng to dill
202 ' how the Jews in their folly thought to conceal His
resurrection ') ; **fēr** ' sound ' (*How he heled on al vnfere* 187
' how He healed all the sick ') ; **fil** ' villain ' ; FRO ; (a)GAIN ;
garen ; **gate** (*nan-gat* ' in no way ' 421) ; GET (*o me seruis sal he non
gette* 460 ' of me he shall get no service ') ; **graiþ**(li) ' with skilful
design ' ; **gress** ; **griþ** (*þas oþer gastes þat fell him wiht / þe quilk
for-sok godds grith* 492 ' those other spirits that fell with him,
that forsook the peace of God ') ; **hap** ' success ' ; ILL ; **laire**
' clay ' (O.N. *leir* ; *O watur his blod, his fless o leir. / His hete
of fir, hijs and of air* 519 (of the making of man) ' of water his
blood, his flesh of clay, his warmth of fire, his breath of air ') ;
LAW ; LOW ; MEEK ; **mensk** vb. ' to honour ' ; **merc** ; **myn** ' to
think ' (*In hir wirschip wald i bigyn / A lastand warc apon to
myn* 112 ' in her honour I would begin to think upon an enduring
work ') ; **neuen** ' to name ' ; RAISE ; **renn** ' to run ' ; ROOT ;
samer-tale ' harmonious ' (*þe bestes self war samer-tale* 683) ;
sēr ' many, various ' (*sanges sere of selcuth rime, / Inglis, frankys
and latine* 23 ' many songs of rare rhyme, English, French, and
Latin ') ; SKILL ; SLY ; **stad** ' established ' ; **stern** ' star ' (*þe
firmament, þat is to say, / þe li[f]t wit sterns, gret and smal*) ; TAKE ;
TILL ' to ' ; THEY–THEIR–THEM ; **tint** ' lost ' ; **thrin** ' three '
(*þe elementz first in dais thrin* 353, of the Creation) ; **twin** ' two '
(*he fordestend twin creature / to serue him in þat hali ture* 417 ;
twins in the modern sense are *twinlinges* 3445) ; **þowf** ' though ' ;
thethen ; **tīt** ' quickly ' ; **þrā** ' bold, severe, cruel ' (O.N. *þrá-r*
' obstinate ') ; **wān** ' provision quantity ' ; WANT ; **will** ' astray ' ;
witer (*Ne þe nedder was noght bittur þan / þowf he was euer wittur*
698, of the serpent in Paradise) ; WRONG.

This long list by no means exhausts the Norse words used in
the *Cursor Mundi*. The following list gives some of the more
interesting to be found in the remaining 29,000 lines of the poem :
bī ' town ', **aghtel** ' to intend ' (dial. *ettle*), **bait** ' food ', **brixel**
' strife ', **busk** ' prepare ' (O.N. *búa-sk*), **carp** ' boast, talk ', **derf,**

dring ' man ', **gleg** ' quick, sharp ', **hething** ' scorn ', **kist** ' chest ', **loft** ' garret, LOFT ', **māl** ' payment ', **nightertale, nocin** ' hardship ' (cf. *St. Margaret*, above), **ransak, rō** ' rest ', **rōs** ' praise ', **serk** ' shirt ' ; SISTER, **sīt** ' sorrow ', SKY, SLAUGHTER, **snaip** ' to blame, disgrace ', **steþi** ' stithy ', **thorsday, thuert, waike** ' weak ', WAND. It will be noticed that many of these are now obsolete, or survive only in local dialects.

The romance of *The Anturs of Arther at the Tarne Wathelyne* [1] has, on account of local references, been assigned to the neighbourhood of Carlisle. The poem contains 715 lines, and there is a fairly large number of Scandinavian words. Many of these are common in Middle English generally (though not always in precisely these forms) : **kest** ' cast ', **grythe, loe** ' low ', **lauyst** ' lowest ', **bigg** ' dwell, build ', **callus** ' calls ', **droup, brenne, gersum, lates** ' looks, behaviour ', **mekenes, tithing, dee** ' die ', **wrang, gete, witturly, wontut** ' wanted '. Less widespread are the pronoun **thay,** the adverbs **hethun** and **quethun** ' whence ', besides **agaynes** ' AGAINST ', **bonk** ' bank ', **barn** ' child ', **bounn** ' ready ', **busk** ' prepare, equip ', **carp** ' talk ', **coup** ' buy, pay for ', **derfly** ' boldly ', **gayne** ' ready, direct ', **gate** ' way ', **ger** ' make, cause ', **gēte** ' guard ', **graiþ** ' ready ', **hillyng** ' covering ', **lain** ' deny ', **laykes** ' games ', **laythe** ' loathsome ' (cf. native *lāð, lōð*), **myn** ' remember ', **merke** ' mark, sign ', **myrke** ' dark ', **radd** ' afraid ', **raiken** ' go, move quickly ', **scōgh** ' wood ' (O.N. *skógr*), **sīte** ' sorrow ', **skrīken** ' shriek ' (the Modern English word is from O.E. *scrīcan*), **snaype(ly)** ' keenly, painfully ', **thro(li)** ' earnestly ', **tynte** ' lost ', **waythe** ' hunting ' (O.N. *veið-r*), **wōthe** ' danger ' (O.N. *váði*).

Examples of use : **barn :** *of qwom that blisfulle barne in Bedelem was born* xviii ; **busk :** *his basnet was busket ful bene* xxx ' his bacinet was properly arrayed ' ; **bigg :** *By a lauryel ho lay, vndur a lefe sale, / Of box and of barbere, byggyt ful bene* vi ' by a laurel she lay, under a pleasant arbour, carefully constructed of box and barberry ' ; **carp :** *to carpe with ʒour qwene* xi ; **droup :** *Thay questun, thay quellun, / By frythun, by fellun, / The dere in the dellun / Thay droupen and daren* iv ' they hunt and kill, by woods and hills, the deer in the dells they cower and

---

[1] Ed. Robson, *Three Early English Metrical Romances.* Camden Society, 1842. Ref. stanza. The MS. is of the fifteenth century.

lurk ' ; **gate :** *And thus Dame Gaynour the gode, gayli ho glidus /
The gatys with Syr Gawan* iii ; **ger :** *Fro cite I schalle sayntes ger
seke sone for thi sake* xvii ' from the city I shall have saints
visited (i.e. pilgrimages made) soon for thy sake ' ; **gēte :** *gete
the wele, Syr Gawan, the boldest of Bretan* xxiii ' guard thee well,
Sir Gawain, the boldest of Britain ' ; **graiþ :** *Syr Gawan,
graythist on grene* i ; **myn :** *myn the with massus* xviii ; **myrke :**
The day wex as dyrke [= dark] / *As the mydnyȝte myrke* vi ;
raiken : *And rayket to hit in a res, for he was neuyr radde* ix ' and
went to it [i.e. the ghost] in a rush, for he was never afraid ' ;
scōgh : *Alle dyrkyns the dere, in the dym scoghes* v ' all the deer
hide in the dim woods ' ; **sīt :** ' *say me,' quod Gaynour,* ' *quat
myȝte saue the from site*' xvii ' "tell me ", said Guinevere, " what
might save thee from sorrow " ' ; **skrīken :** *The bryddus in the
boes . . . Thay skryken in the scoes* x ' the birds in the boughs,
they shriek in the forests ' ; **snaype :** *For the snyterand snaue
that snaypely hom snellus* vii ' for the driving snow, that painfully whirls them on ' ; **waythe :** *ȝe, we ar in wudlond . . . and
walkes on owre wayth* xxxiv ' yes, we are in the woodland, and
go on our hunting ' ; **wōth :** *schalle be woundut, iwis, wothelik*
xxiv ' shall certainly be sorely wounded '.

The story of *Sir Amadace*, which is extant in the same
manuscript, is probably from the North-West Midlands. This
poem is a little longer than the last, and the number of
Scandinavian words is rather less. The more usual are : **agayn,
awe, bothe, bowne, dee** ' die ', **felau,** (thus)**gate** ' in this way ',
gere ' cause ', **gete** ' get ', **happe** ' success ', **ille, kesten, meke**
' meek ', **skille** (and *vnskille*), **take, thay,** etc., **tille, tithing,
wān, wōne** ' supposition, thought '. Besides these we find :
bain ' obedient, ready ' (O.N. *beinn*) : *And haue seruandis fulle
bayne* xlvii ; **gere** ' GEAR, equipment, array ' (O.N. *gøri*) : *He
come in als gay gere, / Ryȝte as he an angelle were* lvi ; **hething**
' contempt ' : *Bothe in hething and in scorne* ii ; **kist** ' chest '
(O.N. *kista* ; cf. O.E. *ćest*, from which the modern form is
derived) : *kistes and cofurs bothe ther stode* xliv ; **lain** ' to deny ' :
Sertan is noȝte to layne xlvii ' certainly it is not to be denied ' ;
līth ' listen, hear ' : *Now listun and ȝe may lithe* xxiii ; **naut**
' oxen ' : *Hors and naute, shepe and sqwyne* [= swine] xv ; **stad**
' standing, established ' : *In stid quere þou art stadde* xlii ; **sum**

' as ' :   *with tunge sum I the telle* lxix ;   (*als*)**tite** ' quickly ' :
hasteli and alstite lvi ;   **will** ' wild, bewildered, astray ' :   *Quen
folus may walke full wille of wone* xxxiv ' when fools may walk
all wild of wit '.

One of the most important writers of the North Midlands in the
fourteenth century was Richard Rolle, hermit and mystic, most
of whose works survive in many manuscripts, some of which
have not retained the dialectal features of the originals.   To
illustrate this writer's vocabulary, a number of lyrics and three
epistles (*Form of Living, Ego Dormio,* and *Commandment of
Love*) in MS. Cambridge Dd v, 64 have been chosen.[1]   In these
documents the Scandinavian element is fairly large ; the following
words occur :   **agaynes, ay, band, barn** ' child ', **bath** ' both ',
bygge, cal, egg vb., **fā** ' few ' (O.N. *fār*), **felaw, fra** ' from ', **gar**
' make ', **gate,** (for)**gete, gildre** ' snare ' (O.N. *gildra*), **hethyng,
hethen** ' hence ', **ill, kindle, law, layne** ' deny, conceal ', **lift,
meke, myrke, neven** ' name ', **radde** ' afraid ', **raise, renne, rōsen**
' to glorify ', **rote, sēme** ' seem ', **sēr, skylle, sterne** ' star ', **take,
till** ' to ', **thai—thayr—thaim, tīn** ' lose ', **tyte** ' quickly , **ugly**
' horrible, hideous ', **waik** ' weak ', **wandreth** ' misery ', **wyterly**
' certainly '.

Examples :   *like til barnes, þat lufes mare an appel þan a castel*
41 ' like children, who prefer an apple to a castle ' ;   *when he
egges vs till ouremykel ees & rest of body* 13 ' when he incites us to
over-much ease and rest of body ' ;   *for þai sal be brether & felaws
with awngels & haly men* 20 ' they shall be brothers and fellows
of angels and holy men ' ;   *þe whylk myght gar all men wonder
on þam* ' which might make all men wonder at them ' ;   *þis
gylder layes oure enmy to take vs with* 6 ;   *þat þe fyre of hys lufe
kyndell oure hert* 9 ' that the fire of His love may kindle our
heart ' ;   *ne þai may lyft þair will to ȝerne þe lofe of godd* 4 ' nor
may they lift their will to desire the love of God ' ;   *meke men
and wymen, Criste dowues* 51 ' meek men and women, Christ's
doves ' ;   *to ńeven his name with-outen reverence* 22 ;   *vggly ymages
for to make vs radde* 15 ;   *thorow þe ioy of a raysed thoght* 46
' through the joy of an exalted thought ' ;   *all þat roses þar
awne state before all other* 62 ' all who exalt their own state before
all others ' ;   *many er war* [= worse] *þan þai seme, & many er*

---

[1] Ed. Horstmann, *Richard Rolle of Hampole*, London, 1895. Ref. page.

better þan þai seme 18 ;   *sere men in erth has sere gyftes* 29 ;   *if þai had knawne skyll and halden discrecion* 6 ;   *in fyrst degre er men lickend to þe sternes* 34 ;   *we haue a lange way till heuen* 6 ' we have a long road to heaven ' ;   *For he þat hase noght Ihesu Criste, he tynes all þat he has* 4 ;   *þai þat er wys, & wil not tyte trow till all spirites* 12 ' those that are wise, and will not quickly believe in all spirits ' ;   *þe vgly felyschip of þe deuels* 37 ;   *þat þai er sa wayke with-in þair hert* 3.

The next author is from the West Midlands :   John Mirk, a canon-regular of Lilleshall, in North-East Shropshire.   His writings date from about, or very shortly after, 1400.   The *Festial*, his most important work, is a collection of sermons for the Church's year, of a popular character, and containing many illustrative tales as well as legends of the Saints.   He employs rather fewer Scandinavian words than Rolle, and most of those which occur are still in use. Here is the list :   **agaynys** ' AGAINST ' (but usually the native **aȝeynys,** etc.) ;   (al)**gate** ' always ' (also *allway*) ;   **anger** ' ANGER ' (not ' grief ') : *he snorted at þe nose, and frope at þe mowth for angur* 53 (also *anangren* ' to anger ') ; **ask** ' ash ' :   *brent hom all to cold colys and askes* 146 (also *Aske Wanysday*) ; **atwyn** ' in two ' ;   AWE ;   AYE ;   **bone** ' BOON ' ;   BOND ; **bōnd** ' servant ' ;   **bonke** ' bank ' (the modern form is from the eastern type) ;   BOTH ;   **bōþe** ' BOOTH ' (in the compound *toll-boþe* ' tax-collector's office ') ;   **brenne ;**   BULL ;   **burthe** ' birth ' ; BIG :   *mony a byge and a strong I haue ouercom* 201 ;   CALL ;   CAST ; **crōke, crōket** ' CROOKED ' ;   DIE ;   **drowpe** ' DROOP, be cheerless ' : *he þat wyll take þys to hert, he schall haue bettyr lust . . . to drowpe þen to daunce* 65 ;   EGG :   *eggys and chese byn molton flesche* 84 ; **felaw** ' FELLOW ' ;   **frope** ' FROTH ' (O.N. *froða*), also vb. ;   *hys mowþe fropys* 84 ;   GET ;   **grayþe** adj. :   *suche prestys as con not make a grayþe vnswar* 124 ' such priests as cannot make a ready answer ' ;   **gresse** (also the English *gras* ' GRASS ') ;   HAPPEN ; HAIL ! ;   **heþen** ' hence ' ;   **hylling :**   *to haue deth in mynde and þe hyllyng of hure graue* 291 ' to have death in mind and the covering of their grave ' ;   **hytten** ' HIT ' ;   **kake** ' CAKE ' :   *our old fadres wolden ete þes dayes kakes bakyn yn þe ymbres* 254 ' our forefathers would eat on those days cakes baked in the embers ' ; KNIFE ;   LAW ;   LEG ;   **lousen** ' to loose ' :   *he lowsyd monkynd out of hys bondys* ;   MEEK ;   **mynnyng** ' remembrance ' ;   NAY ;

raggyd : *thow hast þy cloþe raggyd* 113 ' you have your clothing ragged ' ; **rapen** ' hasten ' ; **rauting** ' making a noise ' : *in rawtyng, in reuelyng* 63 ' in riot, in revelling ' ; RAISE ; **ren** ' run ' ; RANSACK ; ROOT ; **scolle** ' skull ' ; **sekkes** (also the native SACK) ; **scrapen** ' SCRAPE ' (O.N. *skrapa* ; cf. the native M.E. *schrapen*) ; SEEM ; **skath** ' injury ' ; **skerre** ' rock, rocky island ' : *bryngyth þe schip to ʒondyr skerre fast by* 206 ; SKILL ; SKIN ; **sparren** ' to shut, bar ' ; SISTER ; TAKE ; TILL prep. ; **þay, þei,** etc. (but Gen. and Dat. *hore, hure, hom*) ; THRALL ; THURSday ; WANT ; WING.

The South Lincolnshire writer, Robert of Brunne, of the first half of the fourteenth century, makes surprisingly little use of Scandinavian forms. The first thousand lines of his chief work, the *Handlyng Synne*,[1] or *Treatise on Sin*, has only eighteen different Norse words. A number of these occur in rhyme, rather as though it was for this purpose he employed them. This is the list : (a)**beyted** ' enticed ' ; BOTH ; **brenne ;** CAST ; **frastys** (O.N. *freista* ' try, tempt ') ; **felaushepe ; gest** ' GUEST ' ; **hansel** ' gift ; first appearance or occurrence ' (O.N. *hand-sal*) ; LAW ; **late** ' let ' ; **layþ ; lowe** ' fire ' ; RAISE ; SKILL ; TAKE ; (as)**tyte** ' quickly ' ; THEY (but gen. and dat. *hem, here*) ; **weyue** ' WAIVE, turn aside '.

Another West Midland writer, but from an area farther south than that of Mirk, is William Herebert, a Franciscan friar of Hereford, who died in 1333, and was thus a contemporary of Robert of Brunne. Some examples of his verse translations of Latin hymns are extant.[2] The Scandinavian words in these are but few, the list containing only eleven ; of these only two are now obsolete : BOON, BOTH, CALL, CROOK (' evil device '), DIE, **grith,** LAW, MEEK, ROOT, TAKE, **skēr** (*of sunne make ous sker* 24 ' make us free from sin ').

Turning eastwards again we come to the mid-fourteenth century *Prose Psalter*,[3] probably from the southern part of the Central Midlands. Here again the Scandinavian element is not large, and all but a few of the words still survive in Standard English, the exceptions being **biggen** ' to build ', **brenne, gress,**

---

[1] Ed. Furnivall, E.E.T.S., 119, 123.
[2] Ed. Carleton Brown, *Religious Lyrics of the Fourteenth Century*, pp. 15–29.
[3] Ed. Bülbring, E.E.T.S., 97. Ref. psalm and verse.

hillen ' conceal ', **lowe** ' fire '. Besides these, this text has : bull, cast, crooked, die, fellow, haven, kid, law, leg, lift, low, meek, root, rotten, skin, slaughter, take, thrall, wing.

Examples : *Bot ʒif ʒour Lord haue bigged þe hous, in vain hij trauaileden þat it sett* 126/1 ' unless the Lord has built the house, in vain have they worked that set it up ' ; *as a poudre, þat þe wynde casteþ fram þe face of þerþe* 1/5 ' like dust that the wind casts from the face of the earth ' ; *And hij ioiden, for þe flodes were still : and God lad hem to þe hauen of her wille* 106/29 ; *þou for-ʒef þe wikednes of þy folk, and hilled alle her synʒes* 84/2 ' Thou didst forgive the wickedness of Thy people and conceal all their sins ' ; *y ne shal nouʒt taken chalues of þyn hous, ne kiddes of þyn flokkes* 49/10 ' I shall not take calves from thy house, nor kids from thy flocks ' ; *ne wele-likeing ne shal nouʒt be to hym in manner legges* 146/11 ; *y lifted my soule to þe* 142/10 ; *As þe fur þat brenneþ þe wode, and as lowe brennand þe mounteins* 82/13 ' like fire that burns the wood, and flame burning the mountains ' ; *rotennes entred in my bones* (p. 185) ; *spredand out þe heuen as a skyn* ' spreading out the heaven like a skin ' ; *as shepe of slaʒtter* 43/24 ' as a sheep for slaughter ' ; *Joseph was solde to þral þurth hem* 104/16 ' J. was sold as a slave by them ' ; *As þe egle clepand hir briddes to fleʒe . . . He sprad out his wenges* (p. 186) ' like the eagle calling her young birds to fly, He spread out His wings '.

The chief representative of the Kentish dialect of the fourteenth century, the *Aʒenbite of Inwit,*[1] or *Remorse of Conscience,* written at Canterbury by Dan Michel of Northgate, contains very few Norse forms. The only certain ones are (in 267 printed pages) : HUSBAND : *wymmen þet heþ housebounde* 48 ; **greiþen :** *agrayþeþ his herte* 119 ' makes ready his heart ' ; HAVEN : *to þe hauene of helpe þet is to Iesus crist* 183 ; **laʒe** ' LAW ' ; MEEK : *god þet loueþ Mueknesse and zoþnesse* 64 ' God that loves meekness and truth ' ; **kesten** ' cast ' ; ROOT ; SKILL ; SKIN : *ine ane ssepes scinne* 44 ' in a sheep's skin ' ; **scot** ' tax ' : *þis is þet scot þet me ofte payþ* 51 ' this is the tax that one often pays ' ; **þrel** ' thrall ' ; **uelage** ' fellow ' ; WING ; **wrang** ' WRONG '.

Finally, we must examine a few documents from the City of London, and consider briefly the Scandinavian element in the

---

[1] Ed. Morris, E.E.T.S., 23.

writings of Chaucer as a representative London poet. There
are few or no documents until the latter part of the fourteenth
century that can be definitely ascribed to the dialect of London.
A collection of seventy-five documents, from 1384 to 1425,
including letters, accounts, wills, and other official papers, has
recently been edited.[1] In these occur the following words, which
still survive :   again(st) (but usually *ayeins*, etc.), bond(man),
both, call, cast, fellow, get, law, low, ragg(ed) ' spiky ', root,
scot ' tax ', seem, skill, slaughter, sister (but usually *soster*,
O.E. *sweoster*), take, they—their—them, Thurs(day) ; besides
brenne, renne, tithinges, and **husteng** (now only in *hustings*, in
a rather different sense) : *be þeir dede enrolled in þe hustenge of
London* (Letters, xv, 5) ; cf. this word in Old English (p. 67).

Chaucer, in the *Prologue to the Canterbury Tales*, uses twenty-
seven definitely Scandinavian words :   **agayn** prep., **algate,**
AWE, BIG, CAKE, CALL, **carp,** DROOP, FELLOW, GEAR, GET, HAVEN,
KNIFE, LAW, LEG, LOW, MEEK, MIRE, **nightertale, renne,** ROOT,
SCATHE, SEEM, **snybben** (Dan. *snibba* ; cf. SNUB, which seems to
be related), TAKE, THEY (but not *their* and *them*), THRIFT.
The *Parliament of Fowls* adds to this list **brenne,** DIE, **hap,**
GATE, on-**lofte,** SKILL, WILL, WRONG.   Elsewhere in Chaucer we
find the following :   **anger**(ly) ' grievously ', **atwynne, baiten**
' feed ', BOON, **carl, egge**(ment) ' incitement ' (with French
suffix), **geste** ' GUEST ', **greiþen, gres, laten** ' let ', **laus** ' loose ',
may ' maiden ', **marc** (money), (ouer)**thwart, rape** ' hasten ',
RAISE, **rowte** ' snore ', **scalle** ' scab ', **skye** (in the sense of
' cloud ' : *And het a certeyn wynd to go, / And blew so hidously,
and hye, / That hit ne lefte not a skye / In al the welken longe and
brood* H. of Fame III 408-11), SLY, SPAN-newe, **styth** ' anvil ',
store ' stubborn ', THRIVE, TWIN ' two ', **wayke** ' weak ', WAIVE,
wone ' plenty '.

OTHER SCANDINAVIAN LOANS

The texts which have been discussed have provided examples
of most of the Scandinavian words which were borrowed in the
Old and Middle English periods.   To make the list more complete,

---

[1] *London Documents*, 1384-1425, ed. R. W. Chambers and M. Daunt,
Oxford, 1931.

the following may be added, all dating from M.E. times, and all pretty certainly from Scandinavian : **kilt** vb. (O.Dan. *kilte* ; the noun, derived from the verb, does not appear till the eighteenth century) ; **ling** ' heather ' (O.N. *lyng*) ; **rein**(deer) (O.N. *hreinn*, cognate with O.E. *hrān*) ; probably **rub** vb. ; **scab ; scant** (O.N. *skann-t*, with neuter ending -*t*, as in *want*) ; **scrap** (O.N. *skrap*) ; **skirt** (O.N. *skyrta* ; the native cognate is *shirt*) ; **stab ; swirl ; tang** (O.N. *tangi*) ; probably **tangle** vb. (the noun is from the verb, and is seventeenth century) ; **wicker ;** perhaps **snarl** ' tangle '.

Since the Middle English period a number of Scandinavian words have entered English. In the fifteenth century : **link, silt.** Sixteenth century : **batten** ' feed ', **scud,** perhaps **wad, scrag, smelt** (of ore), perhaps **yaw** (nautical), **rowan, rug, slag, kink, skit, snag, scuffle, snug, scrub, simper.** Seventeenth century : **troll, oaf, squall, keg, skittles, gauntlet** (in the phrase *to run the gauntlet,* first in 1661, but in its earlier form **gantlope** (from Swed. *gatlopp*) in 1646 ; note that the other *gauntlet,* which has influenced this, is from French), **smut, bum**(boat), perhaps **nudge, skewer** n. (1679), **rune** (1690) ; the cognate word existed in O.E., *rūn* ; this would have become [raun] in Modern English, cf. the archaic *round* ' to whisper ', from O.E. *rūnian*). Eighteenth century : **cosy, muggy, tungsten** (Swedish, from *tung* ' heavy ' + *sten* ' stone ') and **trap** (rock). Nineteenth century : **vole** (1805, first as *vole-mouse*), **floe, nag** vb., **palstave** (1851, in archæological use), **ski** (1885).

This does not include words which are now dialectal or archaic, such as **daggle, scaur,** and Milton's **scrannel ;** or words denoting things especially connected with Scandinavia, Iceland, etc., such as **marram**(grass), **fiord, auk, maelstrom, voe, loom** ' guillemot ' (all seventeenth-century) ; **saga** (1709), **kraken, skald, desman** (musk-rat, from Swed. *desman-råtta*), **jokul** (all eighteenth-century) ; and finally **rorqual** (whale) 1827, and **storthing** 1834.

Chapter V

THE FRENCH ELEMENT

It is curious that the introduction of French words into English was due in the first place to men of the same race as those who brought Scandinavian words to England. While Norwegians and Danes were fighting their way into this country, similar settlements were being made by the Vikings in the northern part of the kingdom of the Franks, and under the name of Normandy a strong feudal dukedom was established there, founded upon French culture and Northern strength.

The Normans adopted the French language, which they spoke with certain distinguishing characteristics, and it was this dialect which was carried into England in the eleventh century, and which developed there into a specific variety known as Anglo-Norman. From Anglo-Norman numerous words passed into English. Later, this influence was reinforced by new introductions from France, both from Norman-French and from the more southerly Central French, and also (though these are not common) from the speech of southern France, the *langue d'oc* or *Provençal*.

After the Norman Conquest Anglo-Norman was, for 300 years, the official language of the court, of justice, and of politics, and its influence on written English can be traced to an ever-increasing extent during all this period. By the time English had replaced Anglo-Norman in official use in the late fourteenth century, many hundreds of words had become surely established in the English vocabulary, and we find that Chaucer and Langland, for example, use something like 10 per cent of French words.

But it is perhaps the earliest appearance of these foreigners, and the gradual creeping in of one word after another, which are the most interesting parts of the history of the French influence on English, and to begin at the beginning we have to turn back to a period a hundred years earlier than the Norman Conquest.

By the end of the tenth century, communication between the
countries on either side of the English Channel was fairly close
in matters of trade as well as in matters of religion, the latter
helped particularly at this time by the new impetus given to
English monasticism by the French Cluniac Order. During the
earlier part of the eleventh century, Edward, the son of
Ethelred the Unready and of the daughter of a Norman duke,
was being brought up in Normandy, the Scandinavians having
gained the ascendancy in England, and when he at last came to
the throne in 1042 the influence of his upbringing naturally
remained, and his friends and supporters, both spiritual and
temporal, were French. This certainly prepared the way for
the Norman Conquest, and among other products of France
the speech of William the Conqueror and his followers was by
no means unfamiliar to many Englishmen at the time of the
Battle of Hastings.

One or two of the early loans from French are a little doubtful ;
so **prūd, prūt** ' PROUD ' (and the noun *prȳd* ' PRIDE '), which is
probably from a French form of Vulgar Latin *prōd-is*, and is
common in O.E. in the eleventh century ;   and **sot** ' foolish ',
which is either directly from Vulgar Lat. *sottus*, or from French
sōt of the same origin ;   probably two forms existed in Old
English, one with a short vowel, from Latin, the other, with a
long vowel, from French. The word **sott** occurs, for instance, in
the so-called *Vocabulary of Ælfric*, as well as elsewhere in the
eleventh century. Apparently French is the word **tūr** (cf. the
early loan *torr*, from Lat. *turr-is*), which appears already in
the *Durham Ritual* of the late tenth century.

The eleventh-century *Vocabulary of Ælfric* just mentioned has
the French **capun** ' CAPON ', glossing *capo* and *gallinaccus* (132),
and **tumb-**(ere) ' dancer ' (with English personal suffix, from
O.Fr. *tomb-er*), for *saltator* 150. This word occurs also in the
Late West Saxon Gospels :   *þære herodiadiscan dohtor inneode
and tumbode* (=saltasset) Mk. vi, 22 ' the daughter of Herodias
went in and danced ' (the Lindisfarne Gospels have *plægede*) ;
so also in the corresponding passage in Mt. xiv, 6. One very early
French word is to be found in the Lindisfarne and Rushworth
Gospels :   **fræpgian** (O.Fr. *frapp-er*), once translating *accusāre*
(Mt. xii, 10), and once apparently in the sense of ' to reverence,

honour ' :   *hia gefræppegedon sunu minne* Mk. xii, 6 ' they have
reverenced my son ' (= reuerebuntur).[1]   The verb **servian**
(O.Fr. *serv-er*) has been noted in an eleventh-century version of
the pseudo-Matthew Gospel :   *oðerne dæl þæm þe gode ane
serueden* 11. 48–9 [2] ' another part to those who served God only ' ;
an earlier copy has *þeowedon*, a common English word in this
sense.   Two names for articles of food are also to be found in
eleventh-century documents : **gingifer** ' ginger ', in a prescription
in the *Leechbook*, and **bacun** ' BACON ', quoted by Napier
(*Contrib. to O.E. Lexicography*, p. 56) as glossing the English
word *flicce* ' flitch ' in one of a series of entries relating to Bury
St. Edmunds at the end of a manuscript of the Benedictine
Rule in Corpus Christi College, Oxford.

The various versions of the Chronicle provide a few French
words during the eleventh century : **prut,** already mentioned, in
the phrase *prutne here* F 1005 (the E version has *rancne here*) ;
the weapon-name **arblast** occurs in D 1079 :   *wearð þærrihte
mid anan arblaste ofscoten* ' was at once shot by an arbalest ' ;
serfise ' SERVICE ' in A 1070 :   *þam biscopan ðe þar cumene
wæran be ðas arcebiscop Landfrances hæse þa serfise to donde*
' the bishops who had come there at the bidding of Archbishop
Lanfranc to render service ' ;   two names of buildings are **prisun**
' PRISON ' and **castel** ' CASTLE ' :   *& gefeng Rogcer eorl his mæg
& sette on prisun* D 1076 ' took Earl Roger his kinsman and put
him in prison ' ;   *worhton castelas wide geond þas þeode* D 1066
' built castles throughout the country ' ;   *hi comon þa to þam
castele to Tonebricge* E 1087 ' they came to the castle of
Tonbridge ' ;   Old English had a word *castel* (from Lat. *castellum*),
but this has the sense of ' village ' (see above, p. 37) ;   *castel*
in the new sense is evidently a Norman introduction.   The E
manuscript or Peterborough version of the Chronicle is written
in the same hand from the beginning up to 1121, so eleventh-
century and earlier entries should perhaps be regarded as dating
only from the twelfth century.   Besides **castel** (*þa hæfdon þa
welisce menn gewroht ænne castel on Herefordscire* 1048 ' the
Welshman had built a castle in Herefordshire '), we note **market,**
dated 963 but only in a charter which is probably a late eleventh

---

[1] Or has the glossator mistaken the Latin word for a form of *reverberāre*,
and is the meaning here simply ' to strike, beat ' ?
[2] See Swaen, *Englische Studien*, xlix, 353.

century or twelfth-century addition : *ic gife þone tun þe man cleopað Vndela . . . market & toll* ' I give to the town which is called Oundle a market and the right of taking tolls ' ; **tūr,** with reference to the Tower of London : *þone weall þe hi worhton onbutan pone tur* 1097 ' the rampart which they built about the tower ' ; the title **cancelere** ' chancellor ' [1] : *& Rodbeard his cancelere þæt biscoprice on Lincolne* 1093 ' and to R. his chancellor the bishopric of Lincoln ' ; lastly, the two names **Bataille** (of Battle Abbey, near the site of the Battle of Hastings) : *he let halgian þæt mynster æt þære Bataille* 1094 ' he ordered the monastery to be consecrated at Battle ', and **Malueisin,** which is the name of a castle, but which is translated in the Chronicle itself : *þa het makian ænne castel toforan Bebbaburh, & hine on his spæce Malueisin het pæt is on Englisc Yfel nehhebur* 1095 ' he ordered a castle to be built near Bamburough, and called it in his language Malvoisin, which is in English Evil Neighbour '.

Later in the twelfth century, until the Peterborough Chronicle comes to an end in 1154, French words become more numerous. They may be classified as follows :—

(A) Words denoting person or rank : **abbat** ' ABBOT ' (cf. O.E. *abbod,* directly from Latin) 1123 ; **canonie** ' canon ' : *he was canonie of an mynstre Cicc* 1123 ' he was canon of a monastery called Cicc ' ; **capelein** ' chaplain ' (see note on *cancelere* above) : *Turstein . . . se wæs æror þæs cynges capelein* 1114 ' Thurstan, who had previously been the king's chaplain ' ; **cardinal :** *sende se papa of Rome to ðise lande an cardinal* 1125 ; **clerc** (cf. the Latin loan *clēric, -oc* in O.E.) : *þa cusen* [= chose] *hi an clerc Willelm of Curboil wæs gehaten* 1125 ; **cuntesse** ' COUNTESS ' and **emperice :** *þe hefde ben Emperice in Alamánie & nu wæs cuntesse in Angou* 1140 ' who had been Empress of Germany and now was Countess of Anjou ' [2] ; **duc** ' DUKE ': *se duc of Sicilie* 1129 ; **legat** ' LEGATE ': *com an legat of Rome Henri wæs gehaten* 1123 ' a legate called Henry came from Rome ' ; **prior :** *prior on Cantwarbyrig* 1107 ' prior of Canterbury '. The following three terms denote assemblies or groups : **curt** ' COURT ' : *& to king*

---

[1] The modern form is from the Central French dialect, with *ch-* for the northern *c-*. See Appendix D.

[2] The O.E. *cāsere* (from Latin), used normally of the Emperor of Rome, is still used (once) in this part of the Chronicle : *his dohter þæt he æror hafde giuen þone kasere Heanri of Loherenge to wife* 1126. M.E. often has *keiser,* a Scand. loan, ultimately from Latin, but also of course *Emperor.*

bletcæd in Lundene . . . & held þær micel curt 1154 ' was consecrated king in London, and held a great court there ' ; **cap(i)tel**
' chapter (of monks) : *swa swa hi hæfden cosen ærcebiscop æror
in here capitele* 1123 ' as they had chosen an archbishop earlier
in their chapter ' ; *bærnde eall þæt mynstre of Burh & eallæ þa
husas butan se captelhus & se slæpperne* 1116 ' the whole of the
monastery of Peterborough was burnt and all the buildings
except the chapter-house and the dormitory '.

   (B) Finance :   **rent :**   *wrohte on þe circe & sette þarto landes
& rentes* 1137 ' worked on the church and endowed it with lands
and rents ' ;   **tenserie** ' payment for protection ' :   *hi læiden
gæildes' on the tunes . . . & clepeden it tenserie* (Low Lat.
tenseria) 1137 ' they imposed taxes on the towns, and called it
" tenserie " ' ;   **tresor :**   *he hadde get his tresor* 1137 ' he had
obtained his treasure ' (cf. the Scand. loan-word *gærsum, gersum*,
which was finally supplanted by *tresor*).

   (C) Buildings :   **crucet-**(hūs) ' torture-house ' (fr. French
from Lat. *cruciātus*) 1137 ;   **celle** ' CELL ' : *ealle þa priores muneces
& canonias þa wæron on ealle þa cellas on Englaland* 1129.

   (D) Law and social relations :   **acorden** ' to come to terms,
agree ; reconcile ' (cf. the O.E. term *sæhtnian*) :   *se ærcebiscop
. . . wearð þurh þone papan wið þone cyng acordad* 1120 ' the
archbishop was reconciled with the king through the pope's
intervention ' ;   *manega him to gebugen & wið hine acordedan*
1119 ' many went over to his side and came to terms with him ' ;
iustise ' JUSTICE ' :   *he dide god iustise & makede pais* 1140
' he administered justice well and made peaceful conditions ' ;
pais ' peace ' (cf. Scand. *grip*, and O.E. *friþ*) :   *alle diden him
manred & suoren þe pais to halden* 1140 ' all did him homage and
swore to keep the peace ' ;   **priuilegie :**   *he for to Rome . . . &
begæt thare priulegies* 1137 ' he went to Rome and there obtained
privileges '.

   (E) Religion :   **cariteð** [1] ' charity ; provision, sustenance, given

---

[1] O.Fr. *carite*(*t*), Lat. *caritāt-em*. Final *-t, -d* after a vowel were lost in French
about the beginning of the twelfth century, having first become open consonants, *-þ, -ð* ; this stage lasted longer in Anglo-Norman, and M.E. has
a number of examples showing this final þ, ð : *natiuiteð*, also in the Chronicle ;
cariteþ, by the side of *karite*, in *Vices and Virtues* ; *cariteþ* in Orm ; and *feið*
and *plenteð* in *Genesis and Exodus* (see all these below). *Feið* ' FAITH ' is the only
one in which this *-th* has survived ; the others were reborrowed with O.Fr.
final *-é*, Mod. Eng. *-y*.

for charity ' : *heold mycel carited in the hus* 1137 ' provided much
cheer in the monastery ' ; **miracle :** *maket þur ure Drihtin
wunderlice & manifældlice miracles* 1137 ' through our Lord
performed wonderful and many miracles ' (O.E. uses the word
wundor ' WONDER ' in this sense) ; **nativiteð :** *On þisum geare
to Natiuiteð* 1102, 1105 ' in this year at the Nativity ' ;
processiun : *he wæs mid procession underfangan to abbat* 1103
' he was received as abbot with a procession ' (this text also
uses the Latin form *processionem*).

(F) Military : **Standard** (the stem of this word had been
borrowed by French from Germanic ; it is the same word as
stand) : *flemdon þe king æt te Standard* 1138 ' routed the king at
the (battle of the) Standard '. The O.E. words in this sense are
segn (a Latin loan), *cumbol*, chiefly poetical, *tācen* ' TOKEN ', and
þûf, the latter meaning originally ' a tuft ' ; Mod. Eng *flag*
(not recorded in this sense till the fifteenth century) is Germanic,
but most words denoting flags of various types came from French
into English, e.g. *ensign, banner, pennon*, though some of them,
like *standard*, were adopted first by French or Vulgar Latin
from Germanic, e.g. *banner, gonfalon.*

The three legends of *St. Margaret, St. Katherine,* and
St. Juliana, already referred to in the previous chapter, have
a rather higher proportion of French words than of Scandinavian.
In a rough classification they are as follows : (A) Persons :
baptist : *sein iuhan þe baptiste* Jul. 41 (the native word was
fulwihtere, fulluhtere, which is not used in M.E., though the noun
fulluht, and the verb *fulhen, fulwen* are common, and are both
used in these legends ; *cristnien* occurs also in O. and M.E. ;
baptist and *baptise* do not become common till the modern
period) ; **clerc** ' learned man, CLERK ' : *fifti scolmeistres, / of alle
þe creftes / þæt clerc ah to cunnen* Kath. 523 ' fifty schoolmasters,
of all the sciences which a clerk ought to know ' ; **dame** (as a
form of address) : *hu nu, dame, dotestu* Kath. 2080 ' how now,
lady, are you mad ? ' (king to queen) ; **grandame :** *in hire
grandame hus* Marg. 22 (the O.E. term for ' grandmother ' was
eald-mōdor) ; **meister :** *hwa sende þe to me ant is meister ouer þe*
Jul. 40 ' who sent thee to me and is master over thee ? ' (this
is really not distinguishable from the M.E. development of O.E.
mægester, which was borrowed direct from Latin) ; **pilegrim**

(O.F. *pelegrin, from Lat. *peregrīnum* 'stranger') : *as pilegrimes, þe wel witen, seggeð* Kath. 2470 ' as pilgrims say, who know well ' ; **prince** : *þe prude prince* Kath. 579 ; *of þæt heðene folc patriarke ant prince* Marg. 2 ; **prophete** : *Abacuc þe prophete* Kath. 1826 ; **seint** : *sein iuan* Jul. 40 ' St. John ' ; **sire** : *þi sire sathan þat tu leuest uppon* Jul. 54 ' Satan your lord, in whom you believe ' ; **curt** ' COURT ' : *tu schalt, þu motild, / to curt cumen* Kath. 397 ' thou shalt, babbler, come to court '.

(B) Finance : **rente** : *heh mon of cunne ant eke riche of rente* Jul. 4 ' a man of noble blood and rich in rents ' ; **riche, poure** : *þæt poure ba and riche* ' both poor and rich ' Kath. 50 ; *þat refde þen riche iob his ahte* Jul. 40 ' that deprived rich Job of his possessions '.

(C) Buildings : **castel** : *castel of strencðe aȝein þe stronge* Marg. 11 ; **chapel** : *hwa so omi nome makeð chapele oðer chirche* Marg. 20 ' whoever in my name makes a chapel or a church ' ; **postel** ' post ' : *in te twa stanene postles* Jul. 56 ' on the two stone posts ' ; **prisun** : *into darc hus & prisunes pine* Jul. 30 ; **tūr.**

(D) Law and social relations : **crūnen** vb., **crūne** n. : *to eche wunnen icrunet* Marg. 1 ' crowned in eternal bliss ' ; *& te an toc ane guldene crune, & sette on hire heauet* Kath. 1570 ' and the one took a golden crown and set it on her head ' ; **place** : *ȝef he come in place* Kath. 1309 ' in public ' ; **selen** ' to SEAL ' : *isealede writes* Kath. 407 ' sealed letters ' (*St. Margaret* has the verb *seilien* and the noun *inseil*, from O.E. *siglian, insegl*, direct from Latin) ; **serven** : *softe me bið euch derf hwen ich him serue* Jul. 18 ; also (with Eng. prefix) *of-serven* ' deserve ' : *þu hauest inoh min freontschipe of-seruet* Jul. 34 ' you have enough deserved my friendship ' ; **servise** ; **sputen, desputen** : *nan swa deope ilearet þæt durste sputin wið us* Kath. 1308 ' none so deeply learned that he dare dispute with us ' ; *þæt ha beo ear ouercumen wið desputinge* Kath. 561 ' that she may first be overcome by argument ' ; **warant** : *widewene warant ant meidenes mede* Marg. 8 ' safeguard of widows and maiden's reward '.

(E) Religion : **grace** : *hefde þe grace of þen hali gost* Marg. 2 ; **lei** ' law, religion ' (O.Fr. *lei*, from Lat. *legem*) : *leaffule in godes lei* Kath. 164 ' faithful in the law of God ' ; **merci** : *ant merce wummon haue of mi wrechedom* Jul. 48 ' and have mercy, woman, on my misery ' ; **merciable** ' pitiful ' : *ne beoð cristene . . .*

merciable ant milzful Jul. 52 ' are not Christians merciful and
pitiful ? ' ;   **miracle** (also the native term *wunder*) ;   **parais :**
paraises ʒeten aren ʒarewe iopeɲet Marg. 12 ' the gates of Paradise
are ready opened ' ;   **passiun :** *prowede, oðer polede pine oðer
passiun* Kath. 1157 ' suffered, or endured pain or passion ' (the
native *prowien* vb., *prowung* n., remained in use till the later
thirteenth century) ;   **salve** ' salvation ', **salven** ' to save ' :
rihtwise weole & sunfule salue Jul. 64 ' the riches of the righteous
and the salvation of the sinful ' ;   *us for to saluin & makien us
stronge* Kath. 1025 ' to save us and make us strong ' ;   **maumet**
' heathen idol ' (from the personal name *Mahomet*) : *to makien
swucche maumez of treo oðer of stan* Kath. 265 ' to make such
idols of wood or stone ' ;   **ymage :** *ichulle leten makien þe of gold
an ymage* Kath. 1465 ' I shall have an image of gold made '.

(F) Military .   **werre** ' WAR ', **werrien** ' to make war against '
(ultimately of Germanic origin).

(G) Nature :   **bēst :** *þu bittre baleful beast* Kath. 2038 ' thou
bitter baleful beast ' (O.E. *dēor* later acquired the specialized
sense of ' deer ', but all through M.E. the meaning ' beast ' is
common) ;   **leun** ' LION ' : *daniel bimong þe wode leuns* Jul. 32
' Daniel among the raging lions ' (this form replaced the O.E.
lēo, from Latin) ;   **aromat** ' aromatic herb ' : *wið smirles of
aromaz swote smellinde* Kath. 2194 ' with sweet-smelling ointment
of aromatic herbs ' ;   **oil** (O.Fr. *oile* ; cf. O.E. *ele*, from Latin
oleum) : *þe floweð ut wið þe eoile* Kath. 2483 ' which flows out
with the oil ' ;   **rose :** *as lilie ileid to rose* Kath. 1423 ' like lily
laid with rose ' ;   **marbre** ' marble ' : *of marbre-ston a temple* ;
flum ' river ' : *iflum iurdan* Jul. 62 ' in the river Jordan '.

(H) Clothes, textiles, etc. :   **ciclatun, sendal :** *wið ciclatouns
& cendals & deorewurðe claðes* [— precious garments] Jul. 9
(*cendal* in MS. Bodley ; not in Royal) ;   **mantel :** *hudden hare
heauet . . . under hare mantles* Marg. 7 ' hid their heads under
their mantles ' ;   **purpre** ' purple silk ' : *wið purpre wið pal &
wið ciclatun* Jul. 8.

(J) Household and other objects :   **basin :** *his twa ehnen . . .
brad as bascins* Marg. 9 ' his two eyes, broad as basins ' ;
furneis : *þat ferliche fur i þe furneise* Jul. 32 ' the dreadful fire
in the furnace ' (O.E. has *ofen* ' OVEN ' in this sense) ;   **lamp :**
makeð chapele oðer chirche oðer ifindeð in ham liht oðer lampe

Marg. 20 'makes a chapel or church or provides in them light or lamp'.

(K) Physical action, appearance, faculty, etc. :   **cachen** ' CATCH ' (cf. O.E. *læċċan*, now *latch*) :   *ʒef ha keccheð me nu ne findi neauer leche* Jul. 72 ' if they catch me now I shall never find a doctor' (i.e. shall never recover) ; **changen** : *þa he þis iherde changede his chere* Marg. 3 ' when he heard this his face changed ' ; **chere** ' face, appearance ' ; **savour** : *swotest to smeallen . . . his swote sauur* Marg. 4 ' sweetest to smell . . . his sweet savour ' ; also **sauure** ' savoury ' Kath. 1527 ; **semblant** : *þæt hit ne sem, nowðer ne suteli omi samblant þæt ich derf drehe* Marg. 5 ' that it may not seem, or appear in my face, that I am suffering pain '.

(M) Moral and intellectual :   **clergesse** ' female scholar ' : *anlepi dohter icuret clergesse* Kath. 75 ' an only daughter, an eminent scholar ' ; **clergie** ' science ' :   *clerkes . . . swiðe crefti of alle clergies* Kath. 585 ;   **cravant** ' defeated, coward(ly) ' (later *craven* ; the etymology is doubtful ; it seems to have some connexion with O.Fr. *creant*) :   *al ha icneowen ham crauant & ouercumen* Kath. 132 ' all acknowledged themselves defeated and overcome ' ; *ich am kempe ant he is crauant* Marg. 11 ' I am a warrior and he is a craven ' ; **dout** ' doubt, fear ' : *cum nu, & beo þu na þing o dute* Kath. 2430 ' come now, and be not in doubt ' ; **gin** ' device ; snare ' : *þis pinfulle gin, o swuch wise iginet* Kath. 1955 (of St. Katherine's wheel) ' this painful device, contrived in such a way ' ; **hardi** : *se swiðe wilcweme & se hardi* Kath. 1729 ' well-pleasing and brave ' ; **meistrie** ' mastery ' : *cweðen hire þe meistrie* Kath. 133 ' ascribed to her the mastery ' ; **orgel** ' pride ' : *his egede orhel ferliche afallet* Marg. 11 ' his foolish pride suddenly cast down ' ; **pēs** [1] : *custe ham a cos of pes* Jul. 74 ' kissed them with a kiss of peace ' ; **reisun** ' reason, answer ' : *to ʒelden reisun for ham* Kath. 2216 ' to give an answer to them '.

(X) Miscellaneous :   **Feverer** ' February ' : *of feouereles moneð* Jul. 78 (MS. Bodley has *feouerreres*) ; **Latin** : *lewede men þat understonden ne mahen latines ledene* (on the meaning of O.E. *læden, leden* see p. 30 ; it seems to have always the sense of ' speech ' in M.E.).

It is apparent from the number of groups already necessary to classify the French words in these early texts, that English

─────────

[1] For this form compared with *pais*, see Appendix D.

borrowings from French are by no means limited in character.
Nor do the majority of them necessarily imply the introduction
of new objects and ideas from the Continent, since the new word
quite often replaces an old one. The most distinctive group in
Early Middle English (and this is due to the character of much
of the earliest M.E. literature) is that under the heading of
Religion. We may notice already, however, numerous words
for different classes of persons, for titles, etc., and the beginning
of the plentiful supply of words for clothes, etc., which become
very much increased in number in later Middle English.

The short verse text known as the *Proverbs of Alfred* (see
p. 79) has very few French words : (A) CLERK ; COMPANY.
(B) POOR ; RICH ; MULTIPLY (*multeplien heure god* 634 ' to multiply
their goods '). (K) (*bi*)**cacchen.** (M) AMEND ; **dote** ' fool ' (*ich
telle him for a dote* 457 ' I reckon him a fool ' , GENTLE (*gentile
man*) ; **gentelerie** ' gentle-ness, gentility ' (*þuru þis lore ant
genteleri / he amendit huge companie* 668) ; **gīle** ' GUILE'; **scarnen**
' scorn ' ; **orgul** ' pride '.

The south-eastern *Vices and Virtues* (see p. 79) has many of
the French words which have already been noted, as well as
a few new ones. Taking the same classification as before : (A)
clerc ; ermite (*ancres & eremites* 35) ; **pilegrime** (*pilegrimes
ðe lateþ her awen eard* 35 ' who leave their own country ') ;
profiete ; seint ; spuse ; virgine. (B) Finance : **besant** (*ða
fif gildenene besantes* 17 ' the five golden bezants ' ; from
O.Fr., from Lat. *bezantius* (*nummus*) ' coin of Byzantium ') ;
rente (*tunes, oðe oðre þinges þe rentes ʒiueð* 77 ' towns or other
things that yield rents ') ; **richesse** ' RICHES ' (not originally
a plural) (*ʒie riche menn ðe habbeð swa michele blisse of ʒeuer
michele richeise* 69 ' you rich men who have so much happiness
in your riches ').

(C) Buildings, etc. : **castel ; hermitorie** (*munec mai ut-faren
mid ileaue in to hermitorie* 73 ' a monk may, with permission, go
out into a hermitage ' ; **tūr** : (*hlauerd, bie ure tur of strengþe* 107
' Lord, be our tower of strength ').

(D) Law and social relations : **crūne** (*ðe mann ðe is aʒeanes
ðe kinge & wile his curune him benemen* 15 ' the man who is
against the king and wishes to take his crown ' ; **menstre** ' office '
(later *mester*) (*ʒif he bie of heiʒe menstre* 7 ' if he be of high office ' ;

obedience ' obedience ;   command, authority ' (*ʒif he hafð sum
hei obedience* 7 ' if he has some high command ') ;   **pleiten** ' to
plead ' (*wa ʒeu ðe beplaitið ʒeuer emcristen* 81 ' woe to you who
plead against your fellow Christian) ;   **servise.**

(E) Religion :   **casten** ' chasten, chastise ' (*he besohte at gode
þat naht ne scolde reinin for ðe folke to kastien* 143 ' he besought
God that it should not rain, to punish the people ') ;   **discipline**
(*nemeð discipline of alle ðe misdades ðe ʒe deð* 125 ' make a
discipline of all the misdeeds which you do ') ;   **religiun** (*nimeð*
[= take] *ðe cloðes of religiun* 5) ;   **religius** (*ðane religiuse man ðe
alle woreld-þing for godes luue hafð forlaten* 3 ' the religious man,
who has left all worldly things for the love of God ').

(G) Nature :   **lion** (*alswa ðe lyon ðe gað abuten þe dier hem to
forswoleʒen* 139 ' like the lion that goes about the beasts to devour
them ') ;   **roche** ' rock ' (*ðo stan-roches of ðe harde hierte* 45 ' the
stony rocks of the hard heart ') ;   **senevei** ' mustard ' (*ðe seneueies
corne* 29 ' the mustard-seed ').

(J) Household :   **lamp.**

(K) Physical :   (*ā*)**côfrian** ' recover '.

(M) Moral and intellectual :   **cariteþ,** also **carite** (see note,
p. 108) :   (*Cristes kariteþ, ðat is godes luue & mannes* 19 ' Christ's
charity, that is the love of God and man ' ;   *se ðe wuneð on karite,
he wuneð on gode* 37 ' he who dwells in charity, dwells in God ') ;
and also the Central French form **charite** ;   **grace** ;   **maistre**
' mastery ' ;   **sermun** (*ðurh haliʒe writes oðer ðurh hali sermuns*
35 ' by holy writings or holy sermons ').

The *Lambeth* and *Trinity Homilies,* of the late twelfth century,
have a vocabulary of rather similar type, with a slightly higher
proportion of French words. In the Lambeth group the following
are to be found (there are no entries under (F) Military, or (H)
Clothes) :

(A) **erite** ' heretic ' (or this may be directly from Lat.
haereticus) ;   DISCIPLE (cf. O.E. *discipul,* from Lat.) ;   CLERK ;
MINISTER (*godes minist[re] he scal mundian efre* 115 ' God's
minister He shall ever protect ') ;   CATCH-POLL, literally ' chase-
chicken ' (*Matheus þet wes cachepol þene he iwende to god-spellere*
97 ' Matthew who was a catch-poll when he became an
evangelist ') ;   JUGGLER (*þa liʒeres and þa wohdemeres and þa
iuguleres and þa oðer sottes* 29 ' the liars and false judges and

jugglers and other fools ') ; **meister** (*þa welle bi-wisten xii meister
deoflen* 41 ' twelve master-devils guarded the well ') ; PATRIARCH ;
PROPHET ; ROBBER (*rubberes and þa reueres and þa þeoues* 29
' robbers and plunderers and thieves ') ; SAINT ; SPOUSE.

(B) POVERTY (*þer scal beon worldwunne wiðuten pouerte* 143
' there shall be joy without poverty ' ; RICH.

(C) CASTLE (*heauekes and hundes, castles and tunes* 49 ' hawks
and hounds, castles and towns ' ; but also at least once (p. 3)
in the sense ' village ', where it represents O.E. **castel,** a Latin
loan) ; **gerner** ' granary ' (O.Fr. *gerner, grenier,* from Med. Lat.
grānārium) (*þet corn me deð in to gerner* 85 ' men put corn into
the granary ') ; PRISON.

(D) **crūne ; livreisun** ' award ' (*in þe deie of liureisun hwense
god almihtin wule windwin þet er wes iþorschen* 85 ' in the day of
judgement, when almighty God will winnow what has been
threshed ') ; SERVICE.

(E) **archangel** (but usually this text has the O.E. *engel*) ;
circumcisiun ;   grace ;   merci ;   ureisun ' ORISON ' (*þe halie
ureisuns þe me singeð in halie chirche* 51) ; **parais** (*þet wes eorðliche
parais* 129 ' that was the earthly paradise '), but also the O.E.
(Latin) form *paradis* ;   **passiun** (*Vre drihtnes halie passiun,
þet is his halie prowunge* 119) ; **processiun ; sacren** vb., **sacrament**
(*þe halie sacramens þe me sacreð in alesnesse of alle sunneres* 51
' the holy sacraments which are consecrated for the redemption
of all sinners ') ;   **sauter** ' psalter ' (the development of Fr. *-lt-*
to *-ut-* goes back at least as far as the eighth century).

(G) **flum** ' river ' ;   **mont** (*uppon ane dune þat is þe mont of
synai* 87 ' on a hill which is Mt. Sinai ') ; **blanchet** ' white flour '
(*þas wimmen heo smurieð heom mid blanchet þet is þes deofles
sape* 53 ' these women smear themselves with powder, which is
the devil's soap ') ;   **frut** ' FRUIT ' (*alse me saweð sed on ane time
and gedereð þet frut on oðer time* 135 ' as one sows seed at one time,
and gathers the fruit at another time ') ;   **oli** ' oil ' ;   **arabisz**
(O.Fr. *Arabis*), **mule** ' MULE ' (cf. O.E. *mūl*, from Latin), **palefrei**
(O.Fr. *palefrei*(*d*), from L.Lat. *paraveredus* ' PALFREY ' ;   *he mihte
ridan ʒif he walde on riche stede and palefrai and mule and arabisz*
5 ' he might if he wished ride on a fine horse or palfrey or mule
or Arab steed ').

(J) **bar** (*tobrec þa irene barren of helle* 131 ' broke the iron bars of hell ') ; **table** (*drihten him bi-tahte twa stanene tables* 11 ' the Lord gave him two tables of stone ' ; *ec he writ heo in his tables* 21 ' also he wrote it in his tablets ').

(K) FEEBLE (*þa bi-come his licome swiðe feble* 47 ' then his body became very feeble ').

(M) CHARITY (Lamb. has both *charite* and *cherite*) ; the A.-N. form *carite* is no longer used) ; **large** ' generous ' (*þe Men ful of milce* [= pity] *and þe large Men* 143) ; **lechur** ; **pēs** ; **prūd** ; **sermonen** ' to preach, talk ' ; **sot** ' fool ', **asottien** ' become foolish ' ; **uers** ' VERSE ' (cf. O.E. *fers*, direct from Latin).

This text not infrequently has O.E. forms which were even as early as this often replaced by French words, e.g. *lēo* ' lion ', *inseil* ' seal ', *engel* ' angel ', etc.

The *Trinity Homilies* contain many of these words, besides some others. The following are the most noteworthy instances : (A) **maisterling** (with English suffix ; *ge maisterlinges of pesternesse openeð giwer gaten* 113 ' you princes of darkness open your gates ') ; **eremite** ' hermit ' ; **barun** ' BARON ' (*ne was þe engel isend ne to kinge ne to eorle ne to barun* 35). `

(C) **sepulcre** ' SEPULCHRE '.

(D) CUSTOM (*it is custume þat ech chirch-socne goð þis dai a processiun* 89 ' it is the custom that each parish goes on a procession this day ') ; HONOUR (*noht for godes luue ac . . . for onur to hauen* 83 ' not for the love of God, but in order to get honour ') ; **waiten** ' to watch, WAIT, for, heed ' (*bitrumede þat child and waiteden hit on eche wise* 87 ' supported the child and tended it in every way ').

(E) **absolucion** ; **calice** ' chalice ' (the Central French form *chalice* is not recorded till the fourteenth century) ; **chastien** ' CHASTEN ' (cf. *casten* in *Vices and Virtues*) ; PENITENCE ; also **aduent,** with explanation : *todai is cumen ðe holie tid þat me clepeð aduent . . . þat is seggen on englis ure louerd ihesu cristes to-cume* 3.

(G) **langust** ' locust ' ; **leun** ' lion ' (cf. *leo* in Lamb. Hom.) ; OLIVE, PALM (*sum palm-twig, and sum boh* [= bough] *of oliue* 89).

(K) **aisie** ' at ease ' (O.Fr. *aisié*) ; **meseise** ' unease ' ; **struien** ' destroy ' (*þat he sholde fare to þe burh of ierusalem and strugen it* 51 ' that he should go to the city of Jerusalem and destroy it ').

(L) Food : **feste** ' FEAST '.

(M) **mesure** ' moderation ; MEASURE ' ; **orgel, orguil** ' pride '
(*worldes richeise weched orgel on mannes heorte* 43 ' worldly riches
kindle pride in man's heart ' ;   **proue** ' try, test, PROVE ' (*proue
ech man himseluen* 93 ' let each man try himself ') :   ROBBERY
(*oder purh piefes oder purh roberie* 61 ' through thieves or
robbery ') ;   VERSE (*elch of hem wrot his uers and sainte peter he
wrot pat formeste* 17 ' each of them wrote his verse, and St. Peter
wrote the first ').

Laȝamon's poem, *The Brut* (see p. 80), is very different
from the Middle English texts already dealt with in this chapter,
but the French element does not differ as widely as the matter and
its treatment, except that the number of words under (E)
Religion is fewer. The second version, about fifty years later
than the early one, has considerably more French words, and
a comparison of the two is well worth while.[1] Many of the
English words in the first text which are replaced by French words
in the second are words which do not occur at all in later M.E.,
and had presumably become archaic or obsolete when the second
version was made.

First, then, the French forms in MS. Caligula, *c.* 1200 :   (A)
Persons :   **admirail** ' Saracen king, emir ' (ADMIRAL) ;   **barun**
' BARON ' ; CARDINAL ; CLERK ; duc ' DUKE ' ; **dusze-pers,** the ' twelve
peers ' of Charlemagne (but this is rather a quotation from French
than a real loan : *twelfe iferan* [= companions], *pa Freinsce
heo cleopeden* [= called them] *dusze pers* I, 69) ; **ermite** ' HERMIT ';
LEGATE ;   **machun** ' mason ' (*hornes per bleouwen, machunnes
heowen* I, 223) (of building a castle) ' horns were blowing, masons
hewing ') ;   PILGRIM ;   PRELATE ;   PRIMATE ;   SAINT ;   **senatur**
' SENATOR ' (of Rome), also **senaht** ' SENATE ' ;   SIRE.

(B) Finance :   POOR ;   RICH. This text also has the word
riche in the sense of ' powerful ', and as a noun meaning ' realm ' ;
these are from the O.E. *rīce* (see p. 55).

(C) Buildings, etc. :   CASTLE ; **postel** (MS. Otho, the later version,
has POST) ;   **tūr, tour** (also *turre*, probably direct from Latin).

(D) Social :   **crūn** ' CROWN ' (but here in the sense of ' head ') ;
seruise (in MS. Caligula the word is used only of worship in a
(heathen) temple, e.g. *pe king bi-gon seruise* I, 344).

---

[1] See especially on the vocabulary of the two MSS., H. C. Wyld, *Studies in
the Diction of Laȝamon's Brut*, Language, vi, March, 1930.

(E) Religion :   ANGEL ;   **maumet, mahimet, mahun** ' idol ' ;
PROCESSION.

(F) Military :   **legiun** ' Roman legion ' (*For ilke legiuns, heo
clupeden Kair-Usk Kaerliun* I, 257 ' for the same legions they
called Caer-Usk Caerleon ') ; **weorre** ' WAR ', **weorrien** vb. (once
where Otho has *werre*, Calig. has the native *comp*).

(G) Nature :   **flum, flom** ' river ' ;   **gingiuere** ' ginger ' ;   **liun**
(Calig. also uses O.E. *leo* ;   Otho has *lion* and *leo*) ;   **licoriz**
' liquorice ' ;   **montaine ;   olifant** ' elephant ' (*anne scelde gode
he was al clane of olifantes bane* II, 576 ' a good shield, it was all
throughout of ivory ').

(H) Clothes, etc. :   **cheisil** (O.Fr. *chainsil*, a linen material)
II, 575 ; MANTLE ; **purpre** ' purple silk ' (*pælles and purpras &
guldene ponewæs* I, 100 " pall and purple and golden pennies ').

(J) Household, etc. :   **caðel** (Otho *catel*) ' goods, property,
chattels ' ;   **coriun,** a musical instrument (*of fiðele & of coriun*
I, 298) ;   **timpe** ' tambour ' ;   GYVES (*giues swiðe grete heo duden
an his foten* II, 218 ' great gyves they put on his feet ') ; CABLE
(*he hihte hondlien kablen, teon seiles to toppa* I, 57 ' he ordered the
cables to be handled, the sails to be hoisted to the tops ') ; **māl**
' coffer ' (surviving in *mail, mail-bag*, etc.).

(K) Physical :   ARRIVE ;   CATCH ;   **freche** ' FRESH '; **grauen**
' enGRAVE ' ; **soffri** ' suffer ' ; **striuing** ' STRIVING ' (in one passage,
Calig. has *flit*, for which Otho has *strīf*) ;   WAIT, ' be in
expectation '.

(M) Moral and intellectual :   ASTRONOMY (*to lokien in þan
steorren . . . þe craft is ihate Astronomie* II, 598) ; **ginne** ' trap,
device ' (here in a non-material sense) ; **latinier** ' interpreter '
(*he wes þe bezste latimer þat ær com her*) ; **scarn** ' scorn ' (*mucchel
hoker & scarn* II, 301 ' much contempt and scorn ' ;   O.Fr.
escarnir ;   Otho has the later **scorn**, from O.Fr. *escorner*) ;
sot ' fool '.

The later manuscript of Laȝamon has the following words of
French origin which do not occur in the earlier one :—

(A) CHIEFTAIN (*ouer eche ferde / anne cheueteine* I, 251 ;
MS. Caligula has the native *hertoȝe*, O.E. *here-toga*) ; **conseil**
' COUNCIL ' I, 98 (MS. Calig. has *husting*, a Norse loan, see p. 67) ;
rout ' assembly, company ' (*and sone a-ȝein come cnihtes to
route* III, 7 ' knights came again soon into a company ', MS.

Calig. *hīreden* ; also *route of wolves*, Calig. *weored*, a common
O.E. word for ' band, host ').

(B) Finance : **tresor**, if this is the correct reading in III, 154
þe king of [tr]esur ne rohte (MS. damaged) ' the king cared not
for treasure ' ; Calig. *æhte*, a native word ; **truage** ' tribute '
(O.Fr. *treuage*, fr. *treu*, Lat. *tribūt-um*, + -*age* ; *truage of þis
londe* II, 630 ; Calig. *gauel*, O.E. *gafol*).

(C) Buildings : ABBEY (*Bangor was on abbey* III, 191 ; Calig.
munucclif, O.E. *munuc-līf*) ; CHAPEL (Calig. *chireche*) ; **prisun**
' PRISON ' (I, 43, where Calig. has *quarcerne*, which Otho also uses
elsewhere ; this is perhaps a blend of O.E. *cweartern* and the
Lat. loan *carcern*, or it may be merely a graphical mistake
for the former); **nonnerie** ' NUNNERY ' (Calig. *munstre*, O.E.
mynster).

(D) Social : GRANT (*ʒef þou þis wolt granti me* II, 167 ' if you
will grant me this ' ; here and elsewhere Calig. has *ʒette*, etc.,
O.E. *ǵēatan*, which Otho also uses sometimes) ; HONOUR ;
HOSTAGE (*four and twenti hostages / Childrich þar bi-tahte* II, 454
' 24 hostages Childric gave ' ; Calig. *gisles*, O.E. *ǵīsel*, which is
also to be found in Otho) ; SERVE (*he bad him þat he moste
sarui him a wile* I, 169 ' he asked him that he might serve him for
a while ', Calig. *hēren*, which is its usual word, though it has
þæinen, O.E. *þeǵnian*, in II, 612, where Calig. has *saruy*).

(E) Religion : GRACE (Calig. *milce*) ; IMAGE (*makede tweie
ymages þane drake iliche* II, 339 ' made two images like the
dragon ', Calig. *imaken*, O.E. *ǵemaca*).

(F) Military : **gisarme** ' battle-axe ' (Calig. *axe*, *wi-æx*) ;
arsoun ' saddle-bow ' (*he ladde by his harsun* I, 96 ' he led [him]
by his saddle-bow ' ; Calig. *on his exle* ' at his shoulder ') ;
pensile ' small flag ' (O.Fr. *penoncel* ; *þe king he sette up on an
hulle mid mony pensiles* III, 84 ' he set the king up on a hill with
many flags ' ; Calig. *here-marken*) ; **spiare** ' spy ' (*his spiares
come and tolde to þan kinge* III, 39), Calig. *hauwæres*, O.E. *hāwere*
' one who sees, spectator, spy '.

(G) Nature : **contre** ' COUNTRY ' I, 54 (Calig. has *montaine*
here) ; **mont, mount** ' MOUNT ', several times where Calig. has
munt, which is probably the O.E. loan-word from Latin ; but
usually Otho has *hull* for Caligula's *munt* ; PARK (*ʒe honteþ
in þis kinges parc* I, 61 ' you are hunting in the king's park ' ;

I

Calig. *friðe*) ;   **marbre** ' marble ' (*postes longe of marbre stones stronge* I, 56 ;   Calig. *marmon stane*, see *mearm-* in Chapter II).

(H) Clothes :   **atyr** ' ATTIRE ' ;   GUISE (Calig. *wisen*).

(J) Household :   **coupe** ' cup ' (Calig. *bolle*).

(K) Physical :   **ascapede** ' ESCAPED ' (Calig. *at-breac* I, 68) ; **aspien** ' see, ESPY ' (Calig. *hoʒien*) ;   CHANGE ;   CRY (*for þene deolfulle cri* II, 75 ;   here Calig. has *sorhʒen* ' sorrow ', elsewhere *grure*, O.E. *gryre*) ;   DELAY (*þat hii come to Ambres-buri wiþ houte delaie* II, 308) ;   PASS (*paisi ouer bieres* I, 57 ' to pass over the waves ', Calig. *līðen*) ;   ROLL   ' rub, burnish ' (*hie rollede wepne* 512) ;   **siwen** ' follow ' [enSUE] : *ich þe wolle siwi* I, 59 ' I will follow you ', Calig. *mid fare* ;   in II, 264 Otho has *siwede* for Caligula's *after wende*.

(M) Moral and intellectual :   **deol** ' sorrow ' (*hit was a deolful þing* I, 294 Calig. *ladlich* ' loathly ') ;   **fausien** ' fail ' (*and his here-burne gon to fausie* II, 584 ' his coat of mail began to fail ' ; Calig. has *falsie*, which is from or influenced by O.E. *fals* ' falseness, fraud ', direct from Lat. *falsus*) ;   **folie** ' FOLLY ' I, 128 (Calig. *soth-scipe, sot* being an older loan from Fr. or V.Lat.) ;   **gyle** ' GUILE ' (Calig. *vuele* ' evil ') :   **lettre** ' LETTER ' (*one derne lettre ʒeo sende him to reade* I, 192 ' a secret letter she sent him to read ' ; Calig. *stille boc-runen* = ' book-runes ') ;   **paie** ' to please, satisfy, PAY ' ; **pais** ' peace ', for *griþ* or *friþ* in Caligula ;   also the verb **paisi** for *sæhtnien* in Caligula.

In contrast to the high proportion of Norse loan-words to be found in Orm's *Ormulum*, this writer uses only eleven words of French origin.   Comparing this with the comparatively large number in the early manuscript of Laʒamon's *Brut*, of about the same date, and with the far larger number in the western *Ancrene Riwle*, next to be discussed, little, if any, later in date, we are led to the conclusion that the French influence travelled more quickly across country to the West Midlands than up-country to the North-East Midlands.

The following are Orm's French words : PROPHET ; BEZANT ; RICH ;   CASTLE (*to timmbrenn himm . . . An casstell ʒæn þe defell* II, 277 ' to build for him a castle against the devil ') ; CROWN ; **kariteþ** ' charity ' ;   **orgel** ' pride ' ;   **scarn, scarnedd ; flumm** ' river ' ;   **gyn** ' device ' ;   **bulten** ' to sift, boult ' (O.Fr. *bulter* ; *bulltedd bræd* I, 32 ' bread made of boulted flour ').

1200–1250

We shall begin this half-century with another Western text, the Nero manuscript of the *Ancrene Riwle* (see p. 84), which has far more French words than any so far dealt with. It is, indeed, a long work, but even so the proportion is high. Since this is one of the most important works in Middle English it will be treated at some length. The number of technical religious terms is very noticeable, as is also the number of abstract terms included under (M) Moral and Intellectual, which is now sub-divided.

(A) Persons : **ame** ' friend ' (O.Fr. *ami* ; *ame dogge, go herut* 290 ' friend dog, go out ') ; also **belami** ' fair friend ' (*nai, belami, nai!* 338) ; perhaps **baban** ' baby ' (*weope efter him, ase doð þet lutel baban efter his moder* 234 ' weep for him, as the little baby does for his mother ') ; **baptist ; burgeis** (*hit is hurgeises riht for to beren purses* 168 ' it is a burgess's right to carry purses ') ; **champiun** (*þuruh þe tentaciuns, ipreoued to treowe champiuns* 236 ' proved by temptations to be true champions ') ; **chaumberling ;** DAME ; **deciple ;** EMPEROR (*þuruh Julianes heste þe Amperur* 244) ; **eremite** (*mon bi him one, eremite oðer ancre* 12) ; EVANGELIST (another MS. has the Eng. word *godspellere*) ; **fisicien** ' PHYSICIAN ' ; HARLOT (*beggen as on harlot . . . his liueneð* 356 ' to beg his living like a vagabond ') ; **iuglurs** ' jugglers ' ; **kunseiler** (*Luue is his chaumberling & kunsiler* 410 ' Love is his chamberlain and councillor ') ; MANCIPLE (*þe ȝiure glutun is þes feondes manciple* 214 ' the greedy glutton is the devil's purveyor ') ; MERCER ; **meistre ; mesire ; messager** ' MESSENGER ' ; **nurice** ' NURSE ' (*rockeð hit ȝeornliche ase nurice* 82 ' rocks it diligently like a nurse ') ; **paroschian** ' PARISHIONER ' ; PERSON ; PILGRIM (*þe gode pilegrim halt euer his rihte wei uorðward* 348 ' the good pilgrim ever keeps his direct way forward ') ; **prechur ; prelat ; prisun** ' prisoner ' ; PROPHET ; RECLUSE ; ROBBER ; SAINT ; SERVANT ; SPOUSE ; **wardein** (*þe heorte wardeins beoð þe vif wittes* 48 ' the guardians of the heart are the five wits '). **Curt** ' COURT ' ; **mester** (*holde euerich his owene mester* 72 ' let every one keep to his own business ') ; **press** (*me is loð presse* 168 ' a crowd is hateful to me ').

(B) Finance : ADVERSITY, PROSPERITY, (*in aduersite, & in prosperite* 194) ; **cwite** ' quit ', **acwiten, cwitaunce** (*ponewes*

to uorte acwiten . . . *him mid* 124 ' pennies to set him free ') ;
dette, dettur (*þe dette þet tu owest me* 126) ; PAY (*er he hefde al
his ransun fulliche ipaied* 124 ' before he had paid all his ransom
in full ') ; RANSOM ; RELIEF ' alms ' ; RENT ; **spense** (*he ne
bereð no garsum bute gnedeliche his spense* 350 ' he carries no money
but his bare expenses ').

(C) Buildings, etc. : CASTLE ; CELLAR (*iðe celere oðer iðe
kuchene* 214 ' in the cellar or in the kitchen ') ; CELL ' store-
house ' (*þe celles of his aromaz* 152 ' his store-houses of aromatic
herbs ') ; **cite** ' CITY ' ; **kuuent** ' convent ' ; **gernere** ' granary ' ;
giste ' lodging ' (*halt forð his rute & hieð toward his giste* 350
' holds ·on his way, and hastens towards his lodging ') ; **kernel**
' battlement ' (O.Fr. *crenel* ; *halt hire heaued baldeliche uorð vt
iþen open kernel* 62 ' holds her head boldly forth in the open
battlement ') ; **loggen** ' camp, LODGE ' (*we beoð ilogged her bi
þe, þet ert ston of help* 264 ' we are encamped here beside thee,
that art a stone of help ') ; PARLOUR (*al beon heo lutle, þe parluris
lest & nerewest* 50 ' let them (the windows) be little, the parlour's
smallest and narrowest ') ; **pilare** ' PILLAR ' ; SEPULCHRE ; **tur**
' TOWER ' (*euer so herre tur, so haueð more wind* 226 ' the higher
the tower, the greater the wind ').

(D) Law and social relations : **baundun** (*þe terme is ine Godes
honden and nout i þine baundune* 338 ' the appointed time is in
the hands of God and not in your power ') ; **crune ; culvert**
' villainous ' (O.Fr., from Lat. *collibertus* ;   cf. O.E. *ćelmert*,
see p. 37) ; DEGREE ; GIBBET (*hongen on a gibet* 116) ; GRANT ;
juggen ' JUDGE ', **jugement** ' JUDGEMENT ' (*nis þer no riht dom,
ne no riht gugement* 118 ' there is no just sentence and no right
judgement ') ; **noces** ' marriage ' ; SERVE, SERVICE ; TERM
' appointed time ' ; **trone** (*sette þe ine trone & quene crune on
heaued* 40 ' placed thee on a throne and a queen's crown on thy
head ').

(E) Religion : ANNIVERSARY (*ine anniuersaries, þet is in
mune-dawes* (= days of remembrance) 22) ; **caliz** ' chalice ' ;
canoniel ' canonical ' ; **creoiz** (O.Fr. *crois, cruiz* ; *makieð on
ower muþe mit te þume a creoiz* 18 ' make the sign of the cross on
your mouth with the thumb ' ; also Eng. *rode-tokne*), **creoisen**
' to make the sign of the cross on ' ; CRUCIFIX ; **chastien ;
eresi** (*Eresie* . . . *ne rixleð nout in Engelond* 82 ' heresy has not

got the upper hand in England ') ;   **feste** ' festival ' ;   **grace**
(*þurh his grace* ;   cf. *ower graces stondinde biuore mete & efter* 44
' your graces, standing, before food and after ') ;   **misericorde**
(*þe six werkes of misericorde* 30 ' the six works of mercy ') ;
ORDER ; **parais** (*Ne kumeð non into Parais bute þuruh þisse leitinde
sweord* 356 ' none comes into Paradise but past this flaming
sword ') ;   PURGATORY ;   RELIGION, RELIGIOUS n. ;   RULE (*þeos
riwle is euere wiðinnen & rihteð þe heorte* 2) ;   **sacren** ' to
consecrate ',   **sacrament.**   ABSOLUTION ; REMISSION ; SALVATION.
ADVENT ; ASSUMPTION ; NATIVITY.   AVE ;   COLLECT ;   **cump(e)lie**
' compline ' ;   HOUR (*an oðer wise siggen hire ures* 6 ' to say her
hours in another way ') ;   **imne** ' hymn ' ;   **letanie** ' litany ' ;
nocturne ;   oreisun ;   paternostre ;   sauter ' psalter ' ;   **uers**
' VERSE ',   **uerset, uersalien** ' to say versicles '.

(F) Military : ASSAIL, ASSAULT (*þes deofles assauz beoð
ofte strengest* 196 ' the assaults of the devil are often strongest ') ;
baret ' strife ' ;   **calenge** ' to challenge ' ;   **gunfaneur** ' standard-
bearer ' (*schrift, lo nu, is gunfaneur, & bereð her þe banere biuoren
alle Godes ferde* 300 ' Lo, now, confession is a standard-bearer,
and carries the banner before all God's army ') ;   **quarreau**
' quarry, stone ' (*þeo hwile þæt me mit quarreaus wiðuten asaileð
þene castel* 62) ;   **skirmen** ' fight ' (cf. *skirmish* ;   *þe wreðfule . . .
skirmeð mid kniues* 212 ' the wrathful fight with knives ') ;
turnement ' TOURNAMENT '.

(G) Nature : AIR ;   DESERT ;   ROCK ;   BEAST ;   SCORPION
(*þisse deouel scorpiun, attri iteiled* 206 ' this scorpion, the
devil, poison-tailed ') ;   LION ;   UNICORN (*mon wroð is wulf oðer
leun oðer unicorne* 120 ' an angry man is a wolf or a lion or a
unicorn ' ;   in Old English a translated form, *ān-horn*, was
used) ;   **corbin** ' raven ' ;   **flur** ' FLOUR ',   **fluren** ' to FLOWER,
flourish ' ;   FRUIT (*swete frut, þet me clepeð figes* 150) ;   **aromat ;**
FIG, **figer** ' fig-tree ' ;   **clou de gilofre** ' clove ' ;   **gingiuere**
' ginger ' ;   **bame** ' balm ' ;   **eisil** ' vinegar ' (this is recorded earlier,
in the twelfth century Hatton MS. of the Gospels : **aisil**) ;   **licur**
' liquor ' ;   **eoli** ' oil ' ;   **piment** ' spiced drink ' (*piment of swete
huni luue, eisil of sur nið* [= hatred] 404) ;   SPICE (*hope is a
swete spice wiðinne þe heorte*).

(H) Clothes, etc. :   **abit** ' HABIT ' 12 ;   **atiffen** ' adorn ' (*lat
oðre atiffen hore bodi* 360) ;   ORNAMENT (*þe ueire urnemenz þet*

bitocneð blisse 302 'the fair ornaments that typify bliss ') ;
VESTMENT (*ne nout ne underuo ʒe þe chirche uestimenz* 418 ' do
not take charge of the church vestments ') ; **broche** (*ring ne
broche nabbe ʒe* 41 ' have neither ring nor brooch ') ; **stamin**
' shirt of linen and woollen ' (O.Fr. *estamine*) ; VAMP (A.-N.
*vampé, from O.Fr. *avan-pié*) ' front part of shoe or stocking '
(*hosen wiðuten uaumpez* 420). **achate** ' agate '.

(J) Household and other objects : **ampuile** ' phial ' ; **beaubelet**
' jewel ' ; **buste** ' box ' (O.Fr. *boiste*) ; **cage** ' CAGE ' (*brid ine
cage* 102) ; **chetel** ' chattels ' (*to dealen his feder chetel* 224 ' to
distribute his father's goods ') ; **crecche** (O.Fr. *crache, creche*)
' crib ' ; **kuvertur** ' covering ' (O.Fr. *coverture*) ; **druerie** ' token
of love ' (*þis was his driwerie* 250) ; **giuegoue** ' joujou, gewgaw '
(*worldes weole & wunne & wurschipe & oðer swuche giuegouen*
196) ; **scorge** ' SCOURGE ' ; SPONGE (O.Fr. *esponge* ; cf. O.E.
spynge, from Latin) ; **trufle** ' trifle '.

(K) Physical action, appearance, faculty, etc. : **aboutien**
' to stick out, lean out ' ; **aspien** ' spy on ' ; **avancen** ' to
advance ' ; **awaitien** ' to lie in ambush ' (AWAIT) ; **babelinde**
' chattering ' ; **buffeten** ' to BUFFET ' ; CATCH (*heo hunteð efter
pris & keccheð lastunge* 66 ' she pursues praise and catches
blame ' ; *kauhte mid his cleafres* 102 ' caught with his claws ') ;
CHANGE ; DEPART ; **despoilen** ' rob, DESPOIL ' ; **disturben, sturben**
' DISTURB ' (*ne muhte letten him of his beoden ne disturben him*
162 ' might not hinder him in his prayers, nor disturb him ' ;
entermeten (O.Fr. *entremetre*) ' to meddle with, take part in '
(*ʒif heo entermeteð hire of þinges wiðuten* 172) ; **frot**(ung) ' rubbing,
friction ' (O.Fr. *froter*) ; **jurneie** ' JOURNEY ' ; **lacen** ' to LACE ' ;
parten ' PART, depart ' ; **recoilen** ' to drive back ; RECOIL ' ;
regiben (O.Fr. *regiber*) ' to kick ' (*hit regibbeð anon, ase uet kelf*
138 ' then it kicks, like a fat calf ') ; ROB ; **rute** ' way, road ' ;
SIGN (*makien signes touward hire* 70) ; **soilen** ' to SOIL ' ;
STRIVE ; **trussen** ' to pack up ', **trusseau** ' pack, bundle ' (*itrussed
mid trusseaus* 168). **Anguisus** ' painful ' (*þe anguisus deaðe
þæt he schulde þolien* 112) ; **baraine** ' BARREN ' ; **chere ; cwoint**
' brisk, active, skilful ; elegant ; clever ; famous ; well-known '
(O.Fr. *coint*, from Lat. *cognitus*), Mod. Eng. *quaint* ; **eise** ' at
ease ' ; **meseise** ' uneasy ' ; FEEBLE ; **feblesce** (*þet we iknowen
ure owune feblesce & ure owune muchele unstrencðe & ure owune*

wocnesse 232 ' that we may know our own feebleness and great lack of strength and weakness ') ; LARGE (*a large creoiz* 18) ; NOISE ; **semblaunt** ' appearance ' ; SILENCE ; **tendre** ' TENDER ' ; UNSTABLE ; CHARGE ' burden ' ; **charoin** ' carcase, carrion ' (the latter form from A.-N. *caroigne* ; cf. Central Fr. *charoigne*) ; HAUNCH ; **sauur** ' SAVOUR '.

(L) Food : DIET ; PITTANCE (*was euer iȝiuen . . . so poure pitaunce* 114) ; **potage** (*hwoso is euer feble eteð potage* 412).

(M) Moral and intellectual : (i) States of mind, qualities, etc. : ABSTINENCE ; AFFECTION ; **anui** ' trouble, worry ' (*in þe anui of pisse worlde* 374) ; **asprete** ' bitterness ' ; **chastete** ' CHASTITY ' ; **cherite** ; COMFORT (*froure & cumfort* 176, the first being O.E. *frōfor* ' comfort ') ; **kunscence** ' consciousness ' ; **contumace** ' CONTUMACY ' ; **creaunt** ' craven ' ; **cruel, cruelte** ; **cuueiten** ' COVET ' ; **daunger** ' arrogance ', **dangerus** (*ful itowen, dangerus, & erueð for te paien* 108 ' perverse, domineering, and difficult to please '), Mod. Eng. *dangerous* ; **debonerte** ; **debonere** ' gentle, meek, well-mannered ' (*þet debonere child hwon hit is ibeaten . . . cusseð þe ȝerd* [= kisses the rod] 186) ; **deinte** ' value, dignity ' (*me let lesse deinte to þinge þet me haueð ofte* 412 ' one ascribes less value to a thing one has often ') ; **delice** ' pleasure ' ; **delit** ' DELIGHT ' (*a swetnesse & a delit of heorte* 102) ; **desperance** ' despair ' (*ȝe muhten sone uallen . . . in desperaunce, þet is in unhope* 8) ; **deuocion** ' DEVOTION ' ; **deuout** ' DEVOUT ' ; **dute** ' fear, DOUBT ' ; **folie** ; **folherdi** ' FOOLHARDY ' ; **gelus** ' JEALOUS ' ; **gentile** (*noble men & gentile ne bereð nout packes* 166) ; **genterise** ' nobility ' ; **gile** ' GUILE ' ; **glorie** ; **glutun** ' GLUTTON ' ; IGNORANCE (*ignorance : þet is unwisdom & unwitenesse* 278) ; IMPATIENCE ; **inobedience** (*inobedience : þet is þet child ne buhð* [= obeys] *nout his eldre* 198) ; **ipocrite, ipocrisie** ; JOY ; **largesse** ' generosity ' ; **kurteisie** ' COURTESY ' ; **merci, merciable** ' merciful ' ; **mesure** ' moderation ' 336 (*þe middel weie of mesure is euer guldene* 336) ; NOBLE, **noblesce** ' nobility ' ; OBEDIENCE ; **orhel** ' pride ' ; **pacience** (*pacience, þet is polemodnesse* 181) ; PENITENCE ; PERFECTION ; **peis** ' peace ' ; PRESUMPTION ; PURITY (*purete of heorte : þet is cleane, schir inwit* 4 ' purity of heart, that is a clean, clear conscience ') ; SCORN (*þe sixte Bacbitunge, þe seoueðe Upbrud oðer Schornunge* 200 ' the sixth backbiting, the seventh reproach or scorn ') ; **trecherie, treitre** (*heo biswikeð ou & is ower treitre* 194 ' she betrays you and is your traitor ') ; **vilte** ' meanness ' ; **vngracius** ' ungrateful person '.

(M) (ii) Mental action, or action directed to the mind : **affaiten** ' dispose ' ; **akointed** ' acquainted ' ; **ameistren** ' to master ' ; **asaumple** ' example ' ; **attente** ' endeavour, attempt ' ; **bisamplen** ' to moralize ' ; BLAME ; BLASPHEMY ; COGITATION (*cogitaciuns, þet beoð fleoinde þouhtes* [= flying thoughts] 288) ; **kunsent** ' CONSENT '; CONTEMPLATION ; **counsail** ' advice ' ; COUPLE vb. (*hwi Isaie ueieð hope & silence & kupleð boðe togederes* 78 ' why Isaiah connects hope and silence and couples them together ') ; **defaut** ' fault ' ; DISCIPLINE ; **deskumfit** ' discomforted ' ; FAME ' reputation ' ; **fantesme** ' phantom ' ; **grucchen** ' to grumble ' (O.Fr. *grouchier*) ; MEDITATION ; OBSERVANCE ; **paien** ' please ; PAY ' ; **pleinte** ' complaint ' ; **preche** ' PREACH ' ; **preisen** ' to PRAISE ' ; **pris** ' praise ' ; PROFESSION (*makien professiun* 6) ; PROPHECY ; **preoue** ' proof ' ; **scandle** ' scandal ' ; SIMONY ; TEMPT, TEMPTATION ; TRIBU-LATION ; **trublen** ' TROUBLE ' ; WITNESS.

(M) (iii) Other abstractions : **astat** ' state, estate ' ; **capital** adj. (*al wiðuten eddren capitalen* 258 ' without the chief veins ') ; **cas** ' happening ', **auenture** ' happening, event ' (*swuch cas and swuch auenture* 340) ; CAUSE (*cause is, hwi þu hit dudest* 320 ' " cause " is why you did a thing ') ; CIRCUMSTANCE ; **efficace** ' effect ' ; **encheisun** ' reason ' ; **manere** ' MANNER ' ; **materie** ' matter ' ; MERIT ; POINT (*þu ert in Eue point : þu lokest o þen eppel* 52 ' you are in the same case as Eve, you are looking at the apple ') ; **priuite** ' secrecy ', **priueement** ' privately ' ; PRIVILEGE ; **propre** ' suitable ' ; **reisun** ' reason ' (*þis is nu þe reisun of þe veiunge* [= joining] 78) ; **spece** ' kind ' (*þe spece of prude þet ich cleopede presumciun* 208 ' the species of pride which I called presumption ') ; **special** (*bute he habbe leaue special of ower meistre* 56 ' unless he have special leave from your master ').

(M) (iv) Writing, learning, painting, and other arts : ARTICLE ; **augrim** ' algorism, arithmetic ' ; **autorite** ' (written) authority ' ; **chapitre** ' CHAPTER ' ; CLAUSE ; **clergesse** ' learned woman ' ; **descriuen** ' describe ' ; **distinctiun** ' DISTINCTION, section ' ; **enbreuen** ' to write ' (*þet þe deouel naueð enbreued on his rolle* 344) ; FIGURE (*figures of augrim* 214) ; **lescun** ' LESSON ' ; **lettre** (*ge ne schulen senden lettres ne underuon lettres ne writen buten* *leaue* 422) ; **pagine** ' page ' ; **peintung** (*Ine schelde beoð preo þinges, þet treo* [= wood], *and þet leðer, & þe peintunge* 392) ; **peinture** ' *wo and wunne* [= joy] *ipisse worlde al nis bute ase a scheadewe ; al nis bute ase a peinture* 242) ; **depeinten** ' to depict ' ; **cwaer** ' book ' (O.Fr. *quaier*, Lat. *quaternus*) (*þeo ancre þet wernde an oðer a cwaer uorto lenen* 248 ' the recluse who refused to lend a book to another ') ; RECORD vb. ; ROLL n. ; **sarmun** ' Sermon ' ; **salut** (*wrot mid his owune blode saluz to his leofmon* 388) ; **scrowe** ' scroll ' (O.Fr. *escroue* ; *scrowe oðer quaer, holi monne uroure* 282 ' scroll or book, the consolation of a holy man ') ; **storie** ' STORY '.

(N) Medical : **akoueren** ' recover ' ; **cancre** ' CANKER ' ; **letuarie** ' electuary ' (*he haueð so monie bustes ful of his letuaries* 226) ; MEDICINE ; REMEDY ; **sabraz** (*drinkeð bitter sabraz uorto akoueren his heule* 364) ; SALVE ; **spitel-**(uvel) ' loprosy '.

(O) Hunting : **tristre** ' TRYST ' ; station ' (*þeos two undeawes, untrust and ouertrust, beoð þes deofles tristren ; tristre is þer me sit mid þe greahundes forte kepen þe hearde* [= to intercept the game] 332).

(X) Miscellaneous : **continuelement, sulement** (note the French adverbial ending ; *sulement etstondeð sikerliche* 266 ' only stand firmly ') ; DOUBLE ; as interjection, **Deuleset** ' God knows ' (cf. O.E. *Crist hit wāt*) 268.

Sawles Warde (see p. 86), which is only a short text, has a fair number of French words, most of them occurring also in the *Ancrene Riwle*. The following, however, may be specially mentioned : **cunffessur** ' CONFESSOR ' ; **cunestable** ' CONSTABLE ' (*Wit þe husbonde, godes cunestable* 247) ; **lettre** ' graphic symbol ' (*a gret boc of sunnen iwriten wið swarte smeale leattres* 249 ' a great book of sins, written with small black letters ') ; **mall** ' hammer ' (*duntes wið mealles istelet* 253 ' blows with hammers headed with steel ') ; ORDER vb. (*i-ordret ant isette sunderliche, þe an buue þe oðre* 261 ' ordered and established separately, one above the other ').

King Horn (see p. 86), one of the earliest English romances, has the following not very long list of French words ; perhaps the most interesting are to be found under (A), (G), and (J).

(A) People : **admirad** ' emir ' 89 ; BARONAGE ; **cosin** ' COUSIN ' ; **damesele** ' DAMSEL ' ; **geaunt** ' giant ' ; **gigours** ' players on the

gigue ' ; **maisteres** ; PALMER ; PILGRIM ; SAINT ; SIRE (as form
of address) ; **spuse ; squiere** ' SQUIRE ' ; **preie** ' company,
troop ' ; **compaynye ; curt.** Finally **mestere** ' office, profession '
(*Steward, tak nu here / Mi fundlyng for to lere / Of pine mestere* 229).

(B) Finance : RENT ; RICH ; **trewage** ' tribute '.

(C) Buildings : CASTLE ; CHAPEL ; **palais** ' PALACE ' ; STABLE ;
ture.

(D) Social : **crune ; dubbing** (O.Fr. *adober* ' to dub a knight ') ;
GRANT ; HEIR ; HERITAGE ; HOMAGE ; **rengne** ' kingdom ' ;
SERVE, SERVICE.

(E) Religion : **crois ;** GRACE ; PRIME ; **preie** ' PRAY '.

(F) Military : ARMS ; ASSAIL ; **banere** ' BANNER ' ; **bataille**
' BATTLE ' ; **enemis** ' ENEMIES '.

(G) Nature : GRAVEL ; **ille** ' isle ' ; PASSAGE ' pass, narrow
way ' ; RIVER ; **roche** ' rock ' (Mod. Eng. *rock* is from the A.-N.
form) ; **flur** ' flower ' ; ROSE.

(H) Clothes, etc. : **sclauyne** ' pilgrim's robe ' ;   also **burdon**
' pilgrim's staff ' ; LACE vb.

(J) Household, etc. : **chaere** ' CHAIR ' ; **couerture ; cupe** ' cup' ;
galun ' GALLON ' ; TABLE.

(K) Physical : AGE ; **ariue** ' ARRIVE ' ; **chaungi** ' CHANGE ' ;
chere ; colur ' COLOUR ' ; **faille** ' FAIL ' (of sword) ; **fine** ' to end ' ;
HASTE ; PLACE ; **scapede** ' escaped '.

(L) Food : **feste** ' FEAST '.

(M) Moral and intellectual quality and action, etc. : **auenture,
mesauentur ; bigile** ' BEGUILE ' ; **bitraie** ' BETRAY ' ; BLAME ; **dol**
' sorrow ' ; DEVISE vb. ; **dute** ' fear ' (DOUBT) ; ENVY ; FOLLY ;
ginne ' device ' ; **glotoun** ' GLUTTON ' ; **ioie** ' JOY ' ; **manere**
' MANNER ' ; **pris ;** PROVE ; **pruesse** ' prowess ' ; STRIFE.

(P) Shipping :   **galeie** ' GALLEY ' :   *Vs he dude lede / In to
a galeie, / wiþ þe se to pleie* 185.

As has already been indicated, the *Owl and the Nightingale*
(see p. 87) contains but few French words ; nor are these of
great interest : (A) CLERK ; CANON ; **maister ; spuse ; meoster**
' trade '.   (B) **poure** ' poor ' ;   RENT.   (C) STABLE (*vor hors a
stable, & oxe a stalle* 629).   (D) GRANT ; **plaid** ' debate ', **plaidi**
' argue '.   (E) **cundut** ' motet sung as the priest goes to the altar '
(O.Fr. *cunduit*).   (F) **bataile ; schirme** ' to fight ' ;   **worre** ' war '.
(G) **best** ' BEAST ' ; **faucun** ' falcon ' ; **flores** ' flowers ' ; **pie**

'magpie' ; **waste** ' WASTE, solitary' (*on ore waste picke hegge* 17). (J) PURSE. (K) **crei** ' crying ' ; **cwesse** ' squash, destroy ' ; **falt** ' falters ' (*min horte at-flip, & falt mi tonge* 37) ; (ouer)**quatie** ' satiate ' ; **siueþ** ' follows ' ; **sure** ' safe, secure, SURE '. (M) **acorde** n. ; **a-foled** ' befooled ' ; **dahet** ' misfortune ' (often used as an expletive) ; **disputing, sputing** ; **foliot** (?) ' foolish matter, trifle ' (*Ne singe ich hom no foliot* 868) ; **gelus** ' JEALOUS ' ; **ginne** ; **grucching** ; **ipeint** ' painted ' ; **merci** ; **pēs** ; **sot** adj., **sottes** n., **sot**(hede) n. (X) **certes** ' certainly ' adv.

The East Midland *Genesis and Exodus* and the *Bestiary* (see p. 87) have a smaller proportion of French than of Scandinavian words ; in neither are they of a specialized type. The first has :

(A) People : **buteler** ' BUTLER ' ; CLERK ; **meister** ; **mester** ' office ' ; **offiz** ' OFFICE ' (*ðu salt ben ut of prisun numen, / And on ðin offiz set ayen* 2071), SPIES ; **tribu** ' tribe '.

(B) Finance : RICH (*richere he it leet ðan he it fand* 1280).

(C) Buildings : **scite** ' CITY ' ; **(h)ostel** (*and bead hem hom to is ostel* 1056 ' asked them home to his house ' ; *And fond good grip and good hostel* 1397) ; **piler** ' PILLAR ' (*a fair piler son hem on o nigt* 3293 ' a fair pillar shone on them by night ') ; PRISON ; TABERNACLE ; **tur.**

(D) Social : BIGAMY (*Bigamie is unkinde ðing, / On engleis tale twie-wifing* 449 ' bigamy is an unnatural thing, in English speech twice marrying ') ; **crune** ; GRANT ; SERVE.

(E) Religion : **auter** ' altar ' (also *alter*, probably O.E.) ; CANTICLE ; CIRCUMCISE ; **sacren** (*wiðuten ilc seuend clene der, / ðe he sacrede on an aucter* 612 ' except for every seventh clean beast, which he sacrificed on an altar ') ; IDOL, IDOLATRY.

(F) Military : **gisarme.**

(G) Nature : CAVE ; FIRMAMENT (*ðo god bad ben ðe firmament / Al abuten ðis walkne sent* 95 ' then God ordered the firmament to be spread all about the sky ') ; **flum** ' river ' (*ðe flum iurdan* 806 ; also *ðe swarte flum, ðe dede se* 1123) ; **munt, mount** ' MOUNT ' ; **roche** (*in a caue[n] / ðe was ðor in roche grauen* 1138 ' in a cave which was there dug in the rock ') ; CAMEL (*him, and hise men, and hise kamel* 1398) ; DESERT ; **dragun** ' DRAGON ' (*fro euerilc ðor crep a dragun* 2924 (of the sorcerers' rods) ' from every one there crept a dragon ' ; also the O.E. *draca* : *ðo wurð he drake ðat ear was knigt* 283, of

Lucifer) ; **leun** ; **flur** ' FLOUR ' ; FRUIT ; LENTIL ; **olie** ' oil '
(*get on olige for tokning* 1624 ' poured on oil for a symbol ' ;
OLIVE ; SPICE.

(H) Clothes : **mentel.**

(J) Household, etc. : **male** ' coffer ' (*and held hem sperd in
helles male* 22) ; PLATE (*ðre hundred plates of siluer fin* 2370) ;
PRESENT (*and bedden him riche present* 2273 ' and offered him
a rich present ' ; TABLE (*tables of ston* 3535).

(K) Physical : **feble** ; FIGURE (*sag abraham figures ðre /
sondes semlike kumen fro gode* 1006 ' Abraham saw three figures,
messengers, apparently, come from God ') ; FINE ; **fin** ' end,
death ' ; **iurne** ' JOURNEY, ' day's journey ' ; **plenteð** ' PLENTY ' ;
SOLSTICE ; SOJOURN (*ðog was him ðat surgerun ful loð* 2696
' though that sojourn was full loath to him ').

(L) Food : FEAST.

(M) Moral, etc. : CHARITY ; **chast**(hed) ; FAITH (*Nu, bi ðe
feið ic og to king pharaon* 2187 ' now, by the faith I owe King
Pharaoh ') ; **gelus** (*for ic am god, gelus and strong* 3495) ; **greuen**
' GRIEVE ' ; **grucchen** ' grumble ' (*here gruching ðo god was loð*
3318 ' their grumbling was hateful to God ') ; **hardi** ; **lecherie** ;
merci ; **orgel** ' pride ' ; **pais** ; **pert** ' knowing, clever ' ; **pris** ;
SPIRIT (*a spirit ful of wit and sckil* 203). **Arsmetike**
' arithmetic ' ; **astronomige** ; MUSIC (*Iobal is broðer song and
glew, / Wit of musike, wel he knew* 460).

(N) Medical : **lepre** ' leprosy ' ; **squinacy** ' quinsy ' (*ða ðe
swinacie gan him nun mor deren* [= injure] 1188).

The *Bestiary* has only eighteen French words : (A) PROPHET ;
spuse. (B) **poure.** (D) MARKET. (G) **bec** ' beak ' ; **capun**
' CAPON ' ; CAVE (*caue ge haueð to crepen in / ðat winter hire ne
derie* 186 ' a cave she (the ant) has to creep into, that the winter
may not harm her ') ; **cete** ' whale ' (*ðis cete ðanne hise chaueles
lukeð / ðise fisses alle in sukeð* 397 ' when this whale locks his
jaws, he sucks in all the fishes ') ; **cul** ' rump ' ; DRAGON
(*ðe dragunes one ne stiren nout wiles te panter remeð ogt* 622 ' the
dragons alone do not stir while the panther roars ') ; **leun** ;
panter ' panther ' (*panter is an wilde der / Is non fairere on werlde
her* 596) ; **turtre** ' turtle-dove ' ; **venim** ' venom '.

(K) ROB. (M) **gin** ' device ' ; GRACE ; SIMPLE (*simple & softe
beo we all* 655 '.let us all be simple and gentle ').

1250–1300

The romance of *Havelok the Dane* shows that French influence was strong in the North-East Midlands by the middle of the thirteenth century. It has already been pointed out that *Havelok* has a large proportion of Scandinavian words, so that its foreign element is altogether very considerable. The names of fishes (under G) and of articles of food, wine,. etc. (L), should be observed ; there are also new words under (A) :—

(A) People : **barun** (*erl and barun, dreng and swain* 31) and **barnage** (*his barnage ðat was un-ride* 2947 ' his company of barons, which was very large ') ; **burgeys** ' BURGESS ' ; **caynard** ' rascal ' (as form of address ; O.Fr. *cagnard*) ; CHAMPION (*with hem com mani champioun, / mani wiht ladde, blac and brown* 1007) ; **chanoun ;** CLERK ; CONSTABLE ; **dam** ' sir ' (O.Fr. *dam, dans,* Lat. *dominus*) ; DAME ; HERMIT ; **iustise** ' JUSTICE ' ; **mayster ;** PAGE ; PATRIARCH ; **sergaunz** ' retainers, SERGEANTS ' ; SIRE ; **strie** ' hag, witch '. COURT ; **meyne** ' household ' ; **mester** ' office ' ; **parlement** ' parliament '.

(B) Finance : **catel** (*For al was youen* [= given], *faire and wel, / þat him was leued* [= left] *no catel* 225) ; **pouere, poure** ' poor ' ; **riche.**

(C) Buildings, etc. : BAR (*And þe barre sone vt-drow / And caste þe dore open wide* 1794) ; CASTLE ; **gronge** ' farm, GRANGE ' ; PRIORY ; TOWER.

(D) Legal and social : CHARTER (*and with þi chartre make us fre* 676) ; **eir** ' HEIR ', **eritage, desheriten** (*Hwat wenden he desherite me ?* 2547 ' why do they think to disinherit me ?) ; **pēr** ' PEER ' (but here in the sense of ' equal ' physically : *In Engelond was none hise per / Of strengþe* 990) ; GRANT ; REIGN ; **saisen** ' seize, give possession ' (*her ich sayse þe / In al þe lond, in al þe fe* [= property] 2518) ; SERVE ; **spusen ; trone** ' THRONE ' ; **warant** ' surety '.

(E) Religion : **aungel** ' ANGEL ' ; **auter** ' alter ' ; **beneisun** ' BENISON ' (*þanne he were set and bord leyd / And þe beneysun was seyd* 1723), also **malisun** ' MALISON ' ; **caliz ; corporaus** (pl.) ' altar-cloth, corporal ' ; **croiz** ' cross ' (also the native *rōd*) ; MIRACLE ; **pateyn** ' PATEN ' ; **preie** ' PRAY ' ; **sauteres.**

(F) Military : ARMS (*And with his hond he made him kniht, /*

And yaf him armes, for þat was riht 2925) ; ASSAIL (*Asayleden him with grete dintes* 1862) ; ANLACE (*Hand-ax, syþe, gisarm or spere, / Or aunlaz, and god long knif* 2554) ; **baret** ' strife ' ; **gisarm** ; **gleiue** ' sword ' ; **skirming** ; **talevas** ' large shield '.

(G) Nature : **bise** (*gan a wind to rise / Out of þe north, men calleth bise* 724) ; BEAST ; **grip** ' griffin ' ; **leoun** ; PALFREY ; **runci** ' horse ' (O.Fr. *roncin*) ; **laumprei** ' LAMPREY ' ; **makerel** ' MACKEREL ' ; **playce** ; **segges** (?) ' cuttlefish ' (O.Fr. *seche*) ; **sturgiun** ' STURGEON ' ; **tumberel** ' porpoise ' ; **turbut** ; **flour** ' FLOWER ' ; **rose** ; **roser** (' rose-tree ' (*þe heu is swilk in here ler / So is þe rose in roser* 2919 ' the colour in her face is like that of the rose on the rose-tree ').

(H) Clothes, etc. : **charbucle** ' carbuncle ' ; **ioupe** ' loose jacket ' (O.Fr. **jupe**).

(J) Household, etc. : **cerge** ' wax-candle ' ; **male** ' bag ' ; **panier** ; **tabour** ' TABOR '.

(K) Physical : **aise** ' ease ' (*þanne was Englond at ayse* 59) ; **bout** ' throw ' (of putting the stone ; O.Fr. *bout*) ; **closen** ' enCLOSE ' (*And þat ich kom til Engelond, / Al closede it intil min hond* 1310) ; **corune, croune** ' CROWN ' (of head) ; **couere** ' reCOVER ' ; **cri, crien** ; FEEBLE ; **formen** ' FORM ' vb. ; **fyn** ' end ' ; **giuelen** ' to heap up ' (O.Fr. **geveler* ; *With fish giueled als a stac* 814) ; PARTED ; PASS ; PLACE ; **plente** ' PLENTY ' ; ROB ; ROBBER ; **saue** ' safe ' ; **sembl**(ing) ; STRANGLE ; STRIVE ; **trusse** vb. ; **uoyz** ' VOICE ' ; **utrage** ' OUTRAGE ' (O.Fr. *out-, ultrage*) ; WAIT.

(L) Food, etc. : **broys** ' broth, BROSE ' (O.Fr. *brouez, -ets* ; *And y schal yeue þe ful fair bred, / And make þe broys in þe led* [= cauldron] 924) ; **claré** ' claret ' ; FEAST ; **flaun** ' pancake ' (O.Fr. *flaon*) ; **pastees** ; **piment** ' sweet spiced wine ' (*Pyment to drinke, and god clare* 1728) ; **simenels** ' bread of fine flour ' ; **super** ' SUPPER ' ; **ueneysun** ' VENISON ' ; **wastel** ' bread of the finest flour '.

(M) Moral and intellectual, etc. : **anuien** ' to weary ' (*þat is þe storie for to lenge* [= lengthen] / *It wold anuye þis fayre genge* 1735) ; BLAME n. ; **chiche** ' mean ' (*And dide greyþe a super riche, / Also he was no wiht chiche* 1763 ' and did prepare a rich supper, as he was by no means niggardly ') ; **conseyl** ' COUNSEL ' ; **curteys** ' of the court, courteous ' (*Hire semes curteys*

forto be, / *For she is fayr so flour on tre* 2917), **curteysye ; doute**
'fear' ; FALSE ; **feith** 'FAITH', **fey ;** FELONY ; **fōl** n., **fōl** adj.
'fool(ish)' ; **gent** 'fair, noble' ; **glotun ; greue** 'GRIEVE'; **ioie ;**
LARGE 'liberal' ; MERCY ; NOBLE ; **payed** 'pleased' ; **pleinte**
'complaint' ; **preyse ; pris** 'worth' ; **tendre** 'TENDER' ;
traysoun, traytour, trecherie. Gest (*Nu haue ye herd þe gest al
poru* / *Of Hauelok and of Goldeborw* 2984) ; **romanz** (*Romanz-
reding on þe bok*) ; **storie ; leteres** (inscribed).

(N) Medical : **salue** 'SALVE'.

(P) Shipping : CABLE (*stronge cables and ful fast* 710).

(X) Miscellaneous : **allas ; daþeit** 'misfortune' (as
expletive) ; **maugre** 'in spite of' (*We sholen at þis dore gonge,* /
Maugre þin, carl, or ouht longe 1789 'we shall go in at this door
in spite of you, fellow, before very long') ; **marz** 'March' ;
hasard, mine, games at dice.

The more courtly *Floris and Blauncheflur* has hardly a larger
or more interesting French element than *Havelok.* Attention
may be drawn to some of the entries under (C), and the list of
precious stones under (G).

(A) Persons : ADMIRAL 'emir' ; **baruns, barnage ; belamy**
(as form of address) ; **burgeis ; chaumberlein ; dame ; duc ;
marchaunt** 'MERCHANT' ; **mariner** (*He hadde wind and weder ful
god,* / *þe Mariner he ȝaf largeliche* 71) ; **mascun** 'MASON' ; **oste**
'HOST' (*And for his niȝtes gestinge* / *He ȝaf his oste an hundred
schillinge* 126) ; PORTER ; **seriauns ;** SIRE (as address) ; SPY ;
compaygnie ; mein 'household, retinue'.

(B) Finance : **marchaundise** 'MERCHANDISE' ; **riche.**

(C) Building : BARBICAN ; **chaumbre** 'CHAMBER' ; CITY ;
paleis 'fine house' (*Uaire hi habbeþ here in inome* / *At one paleis
supe riche* 87 'they have taken rooms at a good hotel') ; **piler**
'PILLAR'; PRISON; **squere** '(carpenter's) square' ; **schauntillon**
'mason's rule ; SCANTLING' (*Ber wiþ þe squire and schauntillun,* /
Also þu were a gud Mascun 325) ; **stage** 'floor, stage' ; **tūr.**

(D) Social and legal : **acupement** 'accusation' ; GRANT ;
honur (*haue þis* [a gift] *to þin honur* 111), **deshoneur ; iugement**
'JUDGMENT' ; **parage** 'high birth' (*þer buþ seriauns in þe stage* /
þat serueþ þe maidenes of parage 256) ; SERVE ; **spusen.**

(E) Religion : **oresun ; parais ; passiun ; preie.**

(G) (Nature) MARBLE (*þe porter he fond anone þerate,* /

Sittende one a marbel ston 155) ;   **cassidoines** ' chalcedonies ' ;
charbugle ' carbuncle ' ;   **crestel** ' crystal ' ;   **jacinctes ;   oniche**
' onyx ' ;   **saphirs ;   sardonies** ' sardonix ' ;   **topaces ;   flur.**

(H) Clothes, etc. :   **meniver** ' MINIVER ' ;   **pane** ' robe ' (*He lat
bringe a cupe of seluer / And eke a pane of meniuier* 110).

(J) Household, etc. :   **bacin ;**   LAMP ;   TORCH ;   **towaille** ' TOWEL '.

(K) Physical :   **aquiten** ' deprive ' ;   **chaungeþ ;   chere ;   cler**
' CLEAR ' (*In þe tur þer is a welle / Supe cler hit is wiþ alle* 224) ;
crie ;   cuntenaunce ;   demure ' delay ' ;   **departen** ' DEPART,
part ' (*He custe hem wiþ softe muþe, / Al wepinge hi departeþ
nuþe* 12) ;   **dureþ** ' endures ' ;   **entermeten** ' to meddle with, take
part in ' ;   **failli** ' FAIL ' ;   **fin** ' death ' ;   **parte** ' share ' ;   **peire**
' PAIR ' ;   PLACE ;   **plenere** ' in full ' (*Eche day in al þe ȝere / þe feire
is iliche plenere* 216) ;   **semblaunt ;**   TENDER (*Of fless of fiss of
tendre bred* 27) ;   **sucur** ' SUCCOUR ' ;   SUFFER.

(L) Food :   **soper** ' supper ' (*Riche soper þer was idiȝt* 23 ;
Me pincheþ bi þine chire / þu nert noȝt glad of þi sopere 169).

(M) Moral and intellectual :   **amur** ' love ' ;   **angussus**
' painful ' ;   **chantement** ' enchantment ' ;   **coniureson** ' con-
juration ' ;   **couetus** ' COVETOUS ' ;   **culvert** ' villainous ' (*þe porter
is culuart and felun* 247) ;   **cunsail ;   curtais** (*þe burgeis / þat was
wel hende and curtais* 116) ;   **dute** ' to fear ' ;   **druerie** ' friendship ' ;
felun, felonie ;   enuius ' ENVIOUS ' ;   **fōl ;   ginne, engin** ' device '
(ENGINE) ;   GRACE ;   **gref** ' GRIEF ' ;   HARDY ;   **ioie ;   large**(liche)
' generously ' ;   MERCY ;   **pite** ' PITY ' ;   **pris** ' worth '.

(X) Miscellaneous :   **escheker** ' chess-board ' (EXCHEQUER) (*and
bidde þe pleie at þe escheker* 344).

The two texts which will be taken next, to conclude this half
century, are both of a religious character. The first is a group of
homilies, the *Kentish Homilies* (E.E.T.S., 49), the second a verse
treatment of the story of *Iacob and Iosep* (see p. 94). The French
vocabulary in each of these is of a very ordinary type ; the
homilies have a larger proportion of French words than the other.
Only the less common words in each are given here.

Kentish Homilies :   (A) **sergant** ' servant ' (*þo serganz þet
seruede of þo wyne* 29) ;   (B) MARKET (*so ha kam into þe Marcatte
so he fond werkmen* 33) ;   SUMMON (*þo dede he somoni alle þo
wyse clerekes* 26) ;   (G) TEMPEST (*a great tempeste of winde* 32) ;
(K) **amunten** ' to mount up, rise ' (*swo amuntet si gode biddinge*

to gode 28 'so a good prayer mounts up to God') ;   **aparailen**
'to prepare' (APPAREL) (*hi hedden aparailed here offrendes* 26
'they had prepared their offerings') ;   APPEAR (*apierede te þo
prie kinges* 26) ;   COMMENCEMENT (*þis was þe commencement of
þo miracles of ure louerde* 30) ;   **cors** 'corpse' ;   **defenden**
'preserve' (DEFEND) (*Mirre . . . defendet þet Cors þet is mide
i-smered* 28) ;   DELIVER (*þet he us deliuri of alle eueles* 33) ;
DISSEVER 'separate' (*nis noon deseuerd pardurabliche fram
gode* 31 'no one is separated from God eternally') ;   MOVE ;
NATURE (*þe nature of Man* 35 ;   *al-so þet water is natureliche
schald* [= cold] 30) ;   **pardurably ; pelrinage ;**   PERIL ;   PERISH
(*lord saue us for we perisset* 32) ;   SUCCOUR (*se þe sucurede hem
ine þa peril* 32) ;   **travail** 'work' (*clepe þo werkmen and yeld hem
here trauail* 33 'call the workmen and pay them for their work') ;
VISIT (*go ine pelrinage, uisiti þe pouie* 28) ;   (M) **aoumbren**
'perplex, ENCUMBER' (*yef se deuel us wille a-cumbri puich senne*
[= sin] 33) ;   **amonestment** 'admonishing' ;   ASSOIL (*for-
leted* [= leave] *yure sennen and per of bieþ a-soiled* 32) ;   **auenture**
'chance ;   chance happening' (*so iuel auenture þet wyn failede*
29 'by ill chance the wine was exhausted') ;   **anuien** 'ANNOY'
(*herodes . . . was michel anud* 26) ;   **a-resun** (O.Fr. *araisonner*)
'to call to account' (*þo a-resunede ure lord þe paens* [= pagans]
35) ;   **bunte** 'BOUNTY, bounteous gift' ;   CONTRARY ;   **cuuenable**
'suitable' (*gold, þet is cuuenable yefte* [= gift] *to kinge* 27) ;
DIVERS (*as we habeþ i-seid of diuers wordles* [= worlds] 35) ;
orgeilus 'proud' (*of þo euele manne good man, of þe orgeilus
umble* 30) ;   SERMON (*þet formeste sarmun þet euerte made in
erþe* 31) ;   **umble** 'HUMBLE' ;   (N) **leprus** 'LEPROUS' ;   MALADY ;
verray 'true' (*scawede þet he was verray prest* 27).

Iacob and Iosep :   (A) **botiler** 'BUTLER' ;   **menestral**
'MINSTREL' (*hem oftok a menestral, his harpe he bar arugge*
366 'a minstrel overtook them ;   he carried his harp on his back) ;
SIR (*þou ssalt, sir baxtere* [= baker], *anhonged be ful heye* 266 ;
(D) **quiten** 'free' (*al his gult ich him forȝiue & quite of bende*
[= bonds] 303) ;   **contre** 'COUNTRY' ;   GRAPE (*wrong hit of þe
grapes ful of win cler* 257 'wrung it (a cup) full of clear wine from
the grapes') ;   SCARLET ;   **sabelin** 'sable' (*Clopes of skarlet & of
sabelin* 505) ;   **gris** 'grey fur' ;   **fer** (O.Fr. *vair*, Lat. *varius*),
a kind of fur ;   **cofre** 'COFFER' ;   PURSE.

K

FOURTEENTH CENTURY

At the beginning of the fourteenth century many hundreds of French words, which still survive, are already in use, besides others which have now disappeared. They are not limited to special parts of the country, but are apparently used as freely in the north and west as in the east and south. It would seem that to the fourteenth century itself we owe that vast number of abstract French derivative words, most of which are still common, with the suffixes *-ance, -ence* ; *-ant, -ent* ; *-tion* ; *-ity* ; *-ment* ; and the prefixes *con-, de-, dis-, en-, ex-, pre-, pro-, trans-,* and so on. Many of these are recorded first between 1350 and 1400, though some are in use before, and others do not appear until the fifteenth century or later. There is a considerable difference between the number of such words used in an early fourteenth-century work, and in, for instance, the writings of Chaucer.

The *Cursor Mundi,* which dates from about 1300, and is a distinctly Northern work, contains slightly over 6 per cent of French words. Without attempting to give all the French forms, of which the author makes use, we may give a number of examples of words which still survive (these are in the majority), to show that the vocabulary is by no means obscure or exotic, or specializing in technical terms of any kind. (The classification is as before.) The words are given in their modern forms.

(A) Abbot, advocate, ancestors, aunt, bachelor, caitiff, clergy, enchanter, friar, juggler, mayor, master, merchant, mariner, marshall, messenger, nation, nephew, official, page, person, parson, pilgrim, prince, people, rebel, squire, virago.

(B) Bargain, debt, extortion, payment, profit, purchase, ransom.

(C) Abbey, dungeon, grange, lodge, parlour, pavilion, tavern.

(D) Assize, sceptre, common, concord, diadem, empire, evidence, exile, franchise, gibbet, govern(or), grant, heritage, homage, judge, jurisdiction, justice, majesty, marriage, ordain, order, pardon, reign, warrant.

(E) Baptism, baptist, penance, pray, repent, sacrifice, sermon, trespass.

(F) Archer, challenge, conquer, victory, war.

(G) Abysm, air, branch, cedar, channel, cypress, fruit, lion, lioness, leopard, marble, metal, mountain, mule, ocean, oil, olive, pasture, plant, scorpion, tempest, valley, venom, venison.

(H) Collar, kerchief, mantle.

(J) Basket, chain, curtain, faggot, lamp, mirror, table, vessel.

(K) Assemble, avail, avoid, boil, circle, chase, close, cover, element, entry, faint, front, genealogy, generation, hasten, haunt, interval, irregularity, journey, join, labour, melody, member, morsel, music, nature, noise, nourish, offer, odour, pain, pale, pass, perceive, peril, plain, presence, pursue, rage, receive, respond, restore, save, succour, stable, stature, substance, suffer, tender, touch, vanish, visit, wait.

(L) Cider, dinner, liquor, supper, vinegar.

(M) Account, affair, allow, argue, assay, assent, avow, certain, despite, error, fierce, fortune, generally, gentle, gracious, grief, honest, honour, humility, idiot, impossible, jealous, joy, lesson, manner, matter, mercy, marvel, noble, opinion, parchment, peace, piteous, positive, praise, preach, precious, prologue, proper, prove, purpose, reason, romance, solace, treason, vengeance, virtue, villainy.

(N) Gout, medicine, ointment, remedy.

The *Handlyng Synne* of Robert of Brunne (see p. 100) has a fairly commonplace French vocabulary, in which abstract words play the greatest part. The following analysis gives the French words of the first thousand lines only, but they are typical of the whole :—

(A) People :   caytyfe, clerkys, cumpanye, dan ' sir ' (*In þe tyme of gode dane Ione / Of Camelton* 67), disciple, ermyte, felun, frere ' friar ', maister, profyte, seyntes (the native *halwes* is also used), termagaunt, vyrgyne.

(B) Finance :   payde, pore, profyt, ryche.

(C) Buildings :   celle, cyte, pryorye.

(D) Social and legal :   asyse, auctoryte, bobaunce ' pomp ', commaundementys, comaundyd, commune ' COMMON ', coroune, cunnant ' covenant ', custome, gouerne, granted, maystry, omage, powere, seruyþ, somoune.

(E) Religion :   bapteme, bybie, chastyed, lay ' law ', matyns, maumette ' idol ', maumetry, orysouns, passyun, penaunce,

preyers, preyden, relygyoun, rependyd, repentaunce, sacra-
mentys, sacryfyse, sacrylege, seruyse, solemnyte ' solemn feast ',
trespas.

(F) Military : cuntek ' contest '.

(G) Nature :   cristal (for ' scrying '), cuntre, flour-gerland,
frutys, fyrmament, menbre, oure ' HOUR ', pasture, pyy (*beleue
nouʒt yn þe pyys cheteryng* 355), tempest, vynys.

(H) Household, etc. :   bacyn, barre (in the compound *for-
barre* ' to shut out '), ' pick-axe ' (*Mattok is a pykeys* ; the Mod.
Eng. form is from this, with the ending assimilated to *axe*).

(K) Physical : a-party ' apart ', apertly ' openly ', auaunsed,
auayle, ·chaunge, crye, delayde, dyspende ' spend ', destroyed,
dysmembre, fayleþ, febylnesse, florysyngge, fyn (n.), hastyly,
hauntes (vb.), karol, leysere ' LEISURE ', parceyued, peyn, plente,
pryuyte, quyte ' QUIT ', receyue, saueþ, secede ' CEASED ',
stable (adj.), strangled, suffryd, surfeture, toucheþ, trauayle,
troteuale ' idle talk ', turment, turmentours, vengaunce, vse,
weyte.

(L) Food : festys.

(M) Moral and intellectual, etc. :   acorde, afflyccyouns,
affyaunce, anoyd, amende, blame, certeyn, charge ' importance ',
charme, chaunce, corage, coueytyd, cunsel, curteys(y), damp-
nacyun, defaute, deseyue, deseuable, doute, enchesoun ' cause ',
ensample, entent, erre, feyþ, folehardy, folye, gentry ' gentility ',
gentyl(men), gracys, greue, greues(nesse), gyle (n.), gylys (vb.),
ioye, kas, lecherye, lessun, manere, manteyne, mercy, meruelys,
mesure, mysauenture, noy, nygromancy, ordeyned, outrage,
point (*þe twelue poyntes of shryfte* 25), preuyd, prow, pyte,
quentyse ' dexterity, clever action ', resun, reuelacyun, scorne
(vb.), speciali, spice ' species ' (*dedly synne, / In any spyce þat
we falle ynne* 28), spyryte, stody, temptacyoun, temptyd, tent,
tysyn ' entice ', tresoun, tycement, vanyte, veyn, vylanye.

(X) Miscellaneous : certys (adv.), verement (adv.).

To compare with this we may take a fairly typical fourteenth-
century romance, *Sir Beves of Hamton*. The French element in
this is perhaps of a slightly more picturesque character than that
of the *Handlyng Synne* or the *Cursor Mundi*, but this is largely
due to the fact that a higher proportion of the words are obsolete
or archaic and many of them have become known to us with the

atmosphere of the Middle English romance surrounding them. It must not be forgotten, either, that many of the romances were translated from, or based on, French originals, which must have affected the English writer's vocabulary, and induced a tendency to use foreign words especially in such phrases and contexts as became the romance-writer's stock-in-trade. Sir Beves was in origin an English hero, and a very popular one ; but the versions of his story which are extant in English all derive from French. The work is, however, a good specimen of its type, and the author, in his use of French terms, does not give the impression of dealing in *clichés*. The largest groups of French words, as will be seen, occur under (A) People, a remarkable collection of mediaeval personalities, (K) Physical, a very miscellaneous group, (M) Moral and intellectual (as usual a long list); but the lists under (F), including terms for arms and armour, under (C) Buildings, etc., and (J) Household, etc., are all of interest.   Illustrations are given here freely, since this is the only fourteenth-century romance which will be dealt with in detail.

(A) People : **amy** ' friend, lover ' (*þow schelt after her wedde to spouse / To þin amy* 144) ; **amiral** ' emir ' ; **bacheler** (*What dones man ertow, bacheler?* 3731 ' what kind of man are you, young man ? ') ; **baroun ; borgeis ; chaumberlain ; chaumpioun ; clerk** (*Icham a clerk and to scole ʒede* 1325 ' I am a clerk and went to school ') ; **cuntasse ; cosin** (*Wolkome, leue cosin* 2577 ' welcome, dear cousin ') ; **dam** ' mother ' (*Damme, for-ʒeue me þis gilt* 3465) ; **dame, madame** (the latter only as form of address) ; **damesele ; dekne** ' deacon ' ; **doce-amur** ' sweet love ' (*he hire clepede doceamur* 161) ; **duke ; emperur ; ermite ; forster ; feloun ; gailer ; garsoun** ' boy ' (*His sone, þat was a proud garsoun* 2991) ; **geaunt ; losenger** ' flatterer ' ; **mariner ; marchal** (*Gii, is fader, was me marchal* 3507) ; **marchaund** (*Marchaundes þai fonde . . . / And solde þat child* 506) ; **meister ; masager** ' messenger ' ; **menstral** (*bouʒte a fiþele, so saiþ þe tale, / For fourti panes, of one menstrale* 3912) ; **ostesse** (of an inn) ; **page ; painim ; palmer ; patriark** (of Jerusalem) ; **pautener** ' vagabond ' ; **pilgrim ; porter ; prinse ; priour** (not *prior* in the monastic sense, but ' one who presides ' : *þow schelt þis dai be priour / And beginne oure deis* 2122) ; **recreant** (*ich me ʒelde, /*

Recreaunt, to þe, in þis felde 1042) ; **roboun** (*A roboun hit stal* 4059 'a robber stole it') ; **seint** ; **sauagene** 'savage' (*I haue herde of sauagenes* 2363) ; **seruaunt** ; **sire** (*Sire Gii : of Hamtoun he was sire* 9) ; **soudan** ' sultan ' ; **spouse** ; **squier** ; **tauarnere** ; **treitour** ; **truant** ('*go hom, truant*', *þe porter sede*) ; **virgine** ; **wardaine. Baronage** ; **meini** ; **ost** (*a prikede out before is ost* 214) ; **parlement** (*be comin acent / þar was comin parlement* 1715) ; **peple** (*ʒour stiward gret peple hadde* 943) ; **route** (*his kniʒtes stoute, / Foure and twenti in a route* 842).

(B) Finance : **catel** (*Wiþ þat and wiþ more catel / He made þe castel of Arondel* 3542) ; **pouer** ' poor ' ; **pouerte** (*whan a man is in pouerte falle, / He haþ fewe frendes wiþ alle* 2594) ; **ransoun** ; **stor** ' STORE ' treasure ' (O.Fr. *estor*, Lat. *staurum* : *þe palmer nas nouʒt wiþouten store* 1295) ; **tresor** ; **wage** (*for þow bringest fro hire mesage, / I schal þe ʒeue to þe wage / A mantel* 1156) ; **warisoun** (of Germanic origin ; related to the Norse loan-word *garsum* : *Wide whar ichaue iwent / And me warisoun ispent* 2142).

(C) Building : **barre** (*þai schette anon eueri gate / Wiþ þe barres* 4344) ; **barbican** ; **castel** ; **chapel** ; **chaumber** ; **cite** (*toward þe cite of London toun* 4479) ; **des** ' dais ' ; **garite** ' watch-tower ; upper floor ; GARRET ' ; **logge,** a temporary shelter ; **pauiment** (*ded a fel on þe pauiment*, in Tower Street) ; **palais** ; **pavilon** (*þai piʒte pauilouns*, before a castle to be besieged, 3356) ; **prisoun** ; **solere** ' sun room, balcony ' ; **stable** ; **tour** ; **touret** (*a touret / þat was in þe castel iset* 2100).

(D) Legal and social : **bandoun** ' authority ' (*Ich do me alle in þe bandoun* 1044) ; **banist** 'banished' (*þis forbanniiste man / Is come to þe land aʒan* 4309) ; **barony** (*Of Almaine, is owene barouny* 3331) ; **cheualrie** (*wiþ wonder-gret cheualrie* ' company of knights ' 2217) ; **cleimen** (*a cleimede his eritage* 1344) ; **comaundement** ; **comin** ' common ' ; **cordement** ; **croun** ; **daunger** (*I nel namore of þe daunger* 1132 ' I will have no more of your domineering ') ; **desereten** (*desereteþ Robaunt, þin eir* 4265 ' disinherit Robaunt, your heir ') ; **eir** ; **eritage** ; **empire** ; **feute** ' fealty ' (*dede him feute & omage* 3469) ; **graunte** ; **lay** ' law ' ; **meistre** ' mastery ' ; **office** ; **omage** ; **parage** ' high birth ' ; **riale** ' royal ' ; **seinori** (*ich hatte Beuoun / & cleymeþ þe seinori of Hamtoun* 3070) ; **sele** ' seal ' (*þe prente of ure sele* 1244) ; **serven, seruise** ; **spusaille** ; **usage** (*Ase hit was*

lawe & riȝt vsage 3470) ; **waraunt** (*And ich wile ȝour waraunt
be* 704).

(E) Religion : **benison** (*God ȝeue vs alle is benesoun* 4620 ;
also : *And on here knes set hem doun / And bad her moder benesoun*
4474 ; also **malisoun :** *I praie Mahoun / par fore ȝeue þe is
malison* 3696) ; **crois ; mamerie** (? for **maumetry,** in the sense
of ' heathen temple ' : *Out of a mameri a sai / Sarasins come
gret foisoun / þat hadde anoured here Mahoun* 1350) ; **praie,
praier ; prosessioun ; riligioun** (*an house he made of riligioun*
4613) ; **sauiour ; trinite.**

(F) Military : **actoun** ' a quilted jacket, worn under the
armour ' (O.Fr. *aqueton*) ; **armen** (*al iarmede to þe teþ* 3644
' armed to the teeth ') ; **armur ; asaut ; bacinet ; baner ;
be-seged ; bataile ; champe** ' field ', in heraldry (*And ȝaf him
a scheld gode & sur / Wiþ þre eglen of asur, / þe champe of gold
ful wel i-diȝt / Wiþ fif lables of seluer briȝt* 974), also **asur,** and
lables ; crestel ' crest ' (*þat sercle of gold & is crestel* 4175) ;
dart ; defendaunt ' defending ' (*Boute hit were him self defendaunt*
660) ; **fauchon** (*Beues smot doun / Grander is scheld wiþ is
fachoun* 1768) ; **gonfanoun** (borrowed in O.Fr. from O.H.G.
gund-fano) ' banner ' (*A gonfanoun wel stout and gay / Josian
him brouȝte for to bere* 976 ; *baner* is used of the same flag, 966) ;
hauberk ; just ' joust ' (*And to þe iustes þai gonne ride* 3961) ;
lance (*Wiþ here launces þei gonne mete* 1748) ; **mace** ' club ' ;
masnel (*þouȝte haue slawe sire Beuoun / Wiþ an vge masnel* 4503) ;
plate (*Hauberk, plate and aktoun* 1761) ; **scomfit** ' defeat '
(*Josian lay in a castel / & seȝ þat scomfit euerich del* 890) ; **springal,**
a machine for hurling stones (*Wiþ bowes and wiþ springal* 4346) ;
stŏr (O.Fr. *estor, estour,* from O.H.G. (*ki*)*stŏr* ' battle ') (*Beues
toulde vnto him þan / How þat stour ended & gan* 722) ; **talevas,**
a kind of shield (*þe children* [= young men] *pleide at þe taluas, /
And to þe iustes þai gonne ride* 3960) ; **targe** ' shield ' (of Germanic
origin ; cf. the Norse loan in O.E., *targa* ; *he kepte his strokes
wiþ is targe* 4214) ; **tornement, torneien** vb. (*mani a gentil kniȝt /
Torneande riȝt in þe feld* 611 ; *Wile we tornaie for þat leuedy*
[= lady] ? 3774) ; **tronson** ' shaft, staff, TRUNCHEON ' (*And
on a tronsoun of is spere / þat heued a stikede for to bere*
827) ; **ventail,** part of the front of the helmet (*Al to-brosten is
ventaile* 2835) ; **venue** ' meeting ; combat ' (*Beues in þat ilche*

veneu, / pourʒ godes grace & is vertu ... 811) ; **vintaine** (*her comeþ a vintaine / Al prest an hondred kniʒte* 2962) ; **visor** (*doun riʒt þe viser wiþ is swerd* 4179) ; **werre** (*brused in werre & fiʒt* 62).

(G) Nature :   **caue** ' cave ' ;   **contre(i)** ;   **cost** ' coast ' (*Ase he com ride be a cost* 1023) ; **forest ; yle** ' isle ' ; **pleine ; riuere. Marbel** (*A faire chapel of marbel fin* 4609). **Best** (*hert and hinde / And other bestes* 2366) ; **deistrer** ' war-horse ' ; **dragoun** (also *drake*, a Latin loan in O.E. : *Swich bataile dede neuer non* ... *Of a dragoun þer beside, / þat Beues slouʒ þer in þat tide, / Saue sire Launcelet de Lake, / He fauʒt wiþ a fur drake* 2599–604) ; **dromedary ; egle ; faucoun** (*ase fresch to fiʒt / So was þe faukoun to þe fliʒt* 736) ; **groin** (O.Fr. *groing*) ' snout ' (*A spanne of þe groin be-forn / Wiþ is swerd he haþ of schoren* 815) ; **hakenai** ' hackney ' (*Ac nim a liʒter hakenai* 1255) ; **lyoun ;   mule ; palfrei ;   rabit** (O.Fr. *arabi, arabiz* ' Arab horse ' ; *Sire Gii lep on a rabit* ... *And sire Miles wiþ gret randoun / Lep vpon a dromedary* 4481) ; **rounsi** (*Beues let sadlen is ronsi* 757) ; **somer** ' pack-horses ' (*Men graipede cartes & somers* ; cf. O.E. *sēamere*, also from Lat. *sagmārius*). **Herbe** (*I know an Erbe in þe forest* 2301) ; **chesteine** ' chestnut ' (*he reinede his hors to a chesteine* 1699 ; cf. O.E. *ćesten-bēam*) ; **medle** ' medlar ' (O.Fr. *mesle(r)* ; *Vnder a faire medle tre* 1287).

(H) Clothes, etc. :   **bordon** ' pilgrim's staff ' (*ʒaf him is hors* ... / *For is bordon and is sklauin* 2066) ; **ermin** (*þei kottede here forers of ermin* 3721) ; **forers** ' fur coats ' ; **keuerchef ; mantel** (*A mantel whit so melk* ; / *þe broider is of tuli selk / Beten abouten wiþ rede golde* 1157) ; **quilte** (O.Fr. *cuilte*, Lat. *culcitra* ; *Foure hondred beddes of selk echon / Quiltes of gold þar vpon* 3996) ; **sklauin** ' pilgrim's cloak ' ;   (vn)**lacen** (*And vnlacede his ventail* 4236).

(J) Household, etc. :   **arsoun** ' saddle-bow ' ;   **boiste** ' box ' ; **boute** ' button ' (*Ne vailede him nouʒt worþ a boute* 100) ; **chaine ; chare** (*Josian wiþ meche care / þeder was brouʒt in hire chare* 1490) ; **cord** (*be a kord of a solere* 1532 ' by a rope from a balcony ') ; **couertine** ' curtain ' ; **couertour ; flaket** ' flagon ' (*Bred and flesc out of is male / And of his flaketes win & ale* 1298) ; **galon** (*And of is helm a drank þore / A large galon oþer more* 2816) ; **lamp ; levour** ' lever ' (*He took a leuour in is hond* 1861) ; **male ; tabour** (*Trompes he herde and tabour* 383) ; **torge**

'torch'; **towaile** (*on a towaile ʒhe made knotte riding* 3220);
trompe 'trumpet'.

(K) Physical: **afin** 'in the end'; **age**; **anguysse**; **arive**
(*par þe dragoun gan ariue / At Cologne* 2659 'when the dragon
arrived at Cologne'), also **riuen**; **asaile**; **ascapen**; **aspien**;
balaunce (*Almest is lif was in balaunce* 1562); **cacchen** ' CATCH ',
chace ' CHASE ' (the first from A.-N. *cachier*, the second from
O.(Centr.)Fr. *chacier*, both from Late Lat. *captiāre*); **chargen**
(*An hors icharged wiþ golde rede* 152); **cercle**; **cler** (*A morwe,
whan hit was dai cler* 755); **contenaunse**; **coulour**; **companie**
(*hadde bore him gode companie* 1988); **cornere**; **craue**; **crie**;
damage; **defende**; **delai**; **delivren**; **demeinen** ' behave ';
demere ' delay '; **discure** ' reveal '; **destruʒen**; **discriue**;
ensemlen ' assemble '; **face**; **faile** (*wiþouten faile*; also the
Fr. phrase *saunfaile*); **failen** (*whan þe rop failede in is hond*
1631); **fasoun** ' appearance, fashion '; **feble** (*Man, whan he
falleþ in to elde / Feble a wexeþ* 47); **feint**; **fin** (*And þat I wet
finliche wel* 4052); **foisoun** (*whan Beues hadde eten gret foisoun*
1299); **fors**; **front** ' forehead ' (*His frount be-fore hard & strong*
2662); **gay**; **glacen** ' slip ' (*doun of þe helm þe swerd gan glace*
4177); **hast, -eli**; **jurne** ' day's journey ' (*þat is henne four
iurne* 2227); **keuere** ' recover '; **kors**; **kours** (*Whan kniʒtes
mest an hors ride, / A gret kours þar was do grede* [= announced] /
For to saien here alþer stede 3514); **language**; **large**; **miseise**;
noise; **nombre**; **pairen** ' impair '; **parten**; **parti** (*be fele parti*
2048 ' in many regions '); **pas** ' pace ' (*In is wei he rit pas for
pas* 847); **pase** ' pass '; **pawe** (*Wiþ his pawes he rent adoun /
His armour* 2439); **pein**; **perseven**; **peril**; **plein** (*I schal winne
hire in plein bataile* 920); **pise** ' piece ' (*His spere burst to pises
þore* 790); **place**; **pleint**; **plente**; **poynt** (*And to his hert þe
poynt þrast* 2463); **pray** ' prey '; **presenten** vb.; **prest** ' ready ';
priuite ' privacy ', **priue**(liche); **quarter** (*ech a dai quarter of
a lof bred* 1420); **ragen**; **rampen** (*Two lyouns þer com yn pare /
Grennand and rampand with her feet* 2379); **randoun** ' rush,
force '; **reseven**; **retret** ' backward step '; **riot** ' riot, revel ';
ronde (*God þat made þis world al ronde* 1373); **saien** " assay,
try '; **saven**; **semlaunt**; **sewen** ' follow '; **sokour**; **sojurnen**;
squachen ' squash ' (*þe medwe squauʒte of her dentes* 1753);
stat ' state, condition '; **stout** (O.Fr. *estout*, from M.Dutch;

Beues stoutliche . . . *Haf vp is heued fro þe ground* 683) ; **sofren ; sur** ' sure ', **surte ; sostenaunse ; teise** ' fathom ' (*Vnder þerþe twenti teise* 1417) ; **tempest** ' attack ' ; **trossen** ' pack up ' ; **vailen ; vge** ' huge ' ; **visage** (*Who is þis wiþ þe grete visage* ? 2585 ; the giant Ascopard).

(L) Food, etc. : **brochen** ' broach ' (*let brochen reynessh wyne* 2303) ; **diner, dinen ; piment ; sause ; sopere ; spisorie ; vitaile.**

(M) Moral and intellectual, etc. : (i) States of mind, qualities, etc. : **bounte ; corteis, corteisie ; delit ; distresse ; doul** ' sorrow ' ; **doute ; egre ; enui ; errur ; gent** (*Lemman, ʒhe seide, gent and fre* 707) ; **gentil ; glori ; gile ; glotoun ; grace ; ioie ; lēl** ' faithful ' (*Beues rod on Arondel / þat was a stede gode and lel* (590) ; **mautalent** (*for-ʒaf him alle is mautalent* 3978) ; **merci ; nice** ' foolish ' ; **onour ; pēs ; pite ; prowesse ; semple ; vertu ; vile ; vileinie ;** (ii) Mental action, etc. : **agreued ; amende ; anuie ; apaien ; asaien ; avengen ; asent ; betrayen ; blame ; bost ; cas ; certaine ; charme ; confort ; consaile ; defaut ; desmeien ; despit** ' scorn ' ; **disiren ;. divis** ' device ' ; **ensoin** ' excuse ' ; **engyn** ' guile ' ; **entent ; gien** ' guide, direct ' (*To riche erl, þat schel þe gie / And teche þe of corteisie / In þe ʒouþe* 364) ; **greven ; hardi ; meintene ; manere ; mervaile ; paramur** adv. ; **preisen ; pris ; proven ; queint** ' clever, cunning ' ; **queintise ; renable** ' reasonable ' (*þat renabliche kouþe frensch speke* 2974) ; **renoun ; resoun ; scornen ; solas, solacen ; tresoun ; vengen ; viktori ;** (iii) Writing and other arts : **fable ; letter ; mesage ; minstralcie** (*Ʒhe hadde lerned of minstralcie, / Vpon a fiþele for to play / Staumpes, notes, garibles gay* 3906–8) ; **nygremancy ; parchemin** (*Lo her, þe king Ermin / þe sente þis letter in parchemin* 1384) ; **portraien** (*Portraid al wiþ rosen rede* 3786, of a shield) ; **prent** ' imprint ' ; **romance.**

(N) Medical : **caudel** (*Dame, let make him a caudel* 3248) ; **fysik ; maladie ; oyniment ; poisoun ; venim ; sirgirie.**

(X) Miscellaneous : **allas ; doble ; aviroun** (*In þis contre aviroun* 2709) ; **saundoute ; sertes ; verament.**

Not infrequently there are passages in the romances where the French words appear in great numbers, one after another, over-shadowing the native element almost entirely. This happens most frequently in descriptions of a more or less technical character, such as the list of precious stones in *Ipomadon* :—

At the laste was browght forthe for þe nonys
A *cupe*, sett wyth *precyous* stonys,
Wyth *cassidoins*, þat were *clere* ;
The *cupe* was good and *precyous*,
The stonys good and *vertuous*,
And *dyamovndes*, þat were dere,
The *crapet* and the *sersolitte*,
The *emeraud* and the *ametite*,
The *ruby* and the *safere*,
Perle, *topyas*, and mony claspys,
And on fowre sydes were *dyueres* haspis,
That *queynte* and *sotell* were, etc. (ll. 2648–59) ;

or descriptions of hunting scenes, as in the *Anturs of Arther* :—

Thay kest of hor *cowpullus*, in cliffes so cold,
Cumfordun hor *kenettes*, to kele hom of care ;
Thay felle to the *female dure*, feyful thyk fold ;

> *   *   *   *   *   *

The king blue a *rechase*,
Folut fast on the *trase*,
With mony *seriandys* of *mase*,
That *solas* to see ;

or the well-known passages in *Sir Gawayne and the Grene Knight* ;
or descriptions of clothes or armour :—

Her *gide* that was *glorius*, was of a gresse-grene ;
Her belte was of *blenket*, with briddus ful bold,
Beten with *besandus*, and *bocult* ful bene :
Her fax in *fyne perré*, was frettut and fold,
Her *countur-felit* and hur *kelle* were *colurt* ful clene
With a *croune* cumly, was *clure* to be-hold ;
Hur *kerchefes* were *curiouse*, with mony a *proud* prene
Hur *enparel* was *a-praysut*, with *princes* of myȝte ;

> *   *   *   *   *   *

Than the knyȝte in his *colurs* was *armit* ful clene,
With a *crest* comely, was *clure* to be-hold,
His brene, and his *basnet* was busket ful bene,
With a *bordur* a-boute, alle fo brent gold ;

His *mayles* were mylke quyte, *enclawet* full clene,
His stede *trapput* with that ilke, os true men me told ;
With a schild on his shildur, of siluer so schene,
With bore-heddis of blakke, and brees full bold ;
His stede with *sandelle* of *Trise* was *trapput* to the hele.
   Opon his *cheueronne* be-forn,
   Stode as a *vnicorn*,
   Als scharpe as a thorn,
   An *nanlas* of stele.
In stele was he *stuffut*, that sterne on his stede,
With his sternes of gold, *stanseld* on *stray* ;
His gloues and his *gamesuns* gloet as the gledes,
A-rayet aure with *rebans*, *rychist* of *raye* ;
With his schene schinbandes, scharpest in schredus.
His *polans* with his *pelidoddes* were *poudert* to *pay*,
Thus *launce* opon lofte that louely he ledus.
        Anturs of Arther, xxix–xxxi.

Romances of the fifteenth century still display a similar
tendency to descriptive passages containing a large proportion
of French words ; the following rather long extract from *The
Squyr of Lowe Degre* includes a considerable vocabulary of dress,
food, wine, hunting, sailing, music, etc. The king of Hungary
is speaking to his daughter, wishing to comfort her for the
(supposed) death of her lover :—

   ‘ To-morowe ye shall on hunting fare,
   And ryde, my doughter, in a *chare*,
   It shal be *covered* with *velvet* reede,
   And clothes of *fyne* golde al about your hed,
   With *damaske* white, and *asure* blewe,
   Wel *dyapred* with *lyllyes* newe ;
   Your *pomelles* shal be ended with gold,
   Your *chaynes enameled* many a folde ;
   Your *mantel* of *ryche degre*,
   Purpyl palle, and *armyne* fre ;
   Jennettes of *Spayne*, that ben so wyght,
   Trapped to the ground with *velvet* bright ;
   Ye shall have harp, *sautry* and songe,
   And other myrthes you amonge ;

You shall have *rumney* and *malmesyne.*
Both *ypocrasse,* and *vernage* wyne,
Mount rose and wyne of *Greke,*
Both *algrade,* and *respice* eke,
Antioche, and *bastarde,*
Pyment, also, and *garnarde* ;
Wyne of *Greke,* and *muscadell,*
Both *clare, pyment,* and *Rochell.*
The reed your *stomake* to *defye,*
And pottes of *osey* set you by,
You shall have *venison* ybake,
The best wylde foule that may be take.
A *lese* of grehound with you to stryke,
And hert and hynde and other lyke,
Ye shal be set at such a *tryst*
That herte and hynde shall come to your fyst.
Your *dysease* to dryue you fro,
To here the *bugles* there yblow,
With theyr *begles* in that place,
And sevenscore *raches* at his *rechase.*
Homward thus shall ye ryde,
On haukyng by the *ryvers* syde,
With goshauke, and with *gentyll fawcon,*
With *eglehorne* and *merlyon.*
Whan you come home, your men amonge,
Ye shall have *revell, daunces,* and songe ;
Lytle chyldren, great and smale,
Shall syng, as doth the nyghtyngale.
Than shall ye go to your evensong,
With *tenours* and *trebles* among ;
Threscore of copes, of *damaske* bryght ;
Full of *perles* they shal be pyght ;
Your *aulter* clothes of *taffata,*
And your sicles all of *taffetra.*
Your *sensours* shal be of golde,
Endent with *asure* many a folde.
Your *quere* nor organ songe shall wante,
With *countre note,* and *dyscant,*
The other halfe on *orgayns* playeng,

With yonge chyldren full fare syngyng,
Than shall ye go to your *suppere*,
And sytte in *tentes* in grene *arbere*,
Wyth clothes of *aras* pyght to the grounde,
With *saphyres* set and *dyamonde*.
A cloth of golde abought your heade,
With *popinjayes* pyght with *pery* reed,
And *offycers* all at your wyll,
All *maner delightes* to bryng you till.
The nightingale sitting on a thorne,
Shall synge you *notes* both even and morne.
An hundreth knightes, truly tolde,
Shall play with *bowles* in *alayes* colde,
Your *disease* to drive awaie,
To se the *fisshes* in poles plaie ;
And then walke in *arbere* up and downe,
To se the *floures* of great *renowne*,
To a drawbrydge than shall ye,
The one halfe of stone, the other of tre ;
A *barge* shall mete you, full ryght,
With twenty-four ores full bryght,
With *trompettes* and with *claryowne*,
The fresshe water to rowe up and downe.
Than shall ye go to the salte fome,
Your *maner* to se, or ye come home,
With eighty shyppes of *large towre*,
With *dromedaryes* of great *honour*,
And *carackes* with sayles two,
The swetest that on water may goo,
With *galyes* good upon the haven,
With eighty ores at the fore staven.
Your *maryners* shall synge arowe
Hey how and rumby lowe.
Than shall ye, doughter, aske the wyne,
With *spices* that be good and *fyne*,
Gentyll pottes with *genger* grene,
With *dates* and *deynties* you betwene.
Forty *torches*, brenynge bryght,
At your brydges to brynge you lyght.

Into your *chambre* they shall you brynge,
With muche myrthe and more lykyng.
Your *costerdes covered* with whyte and blewe,
And *dyapred* with lyles newe.
Your *curtaines* of *camaca*, all in folde,
Your *felyoles* all of golde.
Your *fester pery* at your heed,
Curtaines with *popinjayes* white and reed.
Your hyllynges with *furres* of *armyne*,
Powdred with golde of hew full *fyne*.
Your *blankettes* shall be of *fustyane*,
Your shetes shall be of clothe of *rayne*.
Your head-shete shall be of *pery* pyght,
With *dyamondes* set and *rubyes* bryght.
Whan you are layde in bedde so softe,
A *cage* of golde shall hange alofte,
With longe-peper fayre burnning,
And *cloves* that be swete smellyng,
Frankensence, and *olibanum*,
That whan ye slepe the *taste* may come.
And yf ye no rest may take,
All night *minstrelles* for you shall wake.'
' *Gramercy*, father, so mote i the,
For all these thinges lyketh not me.'

Obviously no form of recreation was possible without the help of the French language.

But for the best examples of French terms for food, we have to go to the fifteenth-century cookery books (E.E.T.S., 91). Here are two or three recipes chosen at random :—

(i) *Oystres* in *grauey* : Take *almondes*, and *blanche* hem, and grinde hem, and drawe hem þorgh a *streynour* with wyne, and with goode fressh broth into gode mylke, and sette hit on þe fire and lete *boyle* ; and cast þereto *Maces*, *clowes*, *Sugur*, *pouder* of *Ginger*, and faire *parboyled oynons my[n]ced* ; And þen take faire *oystres*, and *parboile* hem togidre in faire water ; And then caste hem there-to, And lete hem *boyle* togidre til þey ben ynowe ; and *serue* hem forth for gode *potage*.

(ii) Pike in *galentyne* : Take a pike and seth him ynowe in gode *sauce* ; And *couche* him in a *vessell*, that he may be y-*caried* yn, if þou wilt. And what tyme he is colde, take brede, and stepe hit in wyne and *vinegre*, and cast there-to *canell*, and drawe hit þorgh a *streynour*, And do hit in a potte, And caste there-to *pouder* peper ; And take smale *oynons*, and *my[n]ce* hem, And *fry* hem in *oyle*, and cast there-to a fewe *saundres*, and lete *boyle* awhile ; And cast all this hote vppon þe pike, and *cary* him forth.

(iii) *Cryspes* [1] : Take white of eyren, Milke, and *fyne floure*, and bete hit togidre, and drawe hit thorgh a *streynour*, so that hit be rennyng, and noght to stiff ; and caste there-to *sugur* and salt, And then take a *chaffur* ful of fressh *grece boyling* ; and þen put thi honde in the *batur* and lete the *bater* ren thorgh thi fingers into þe *chaffur* ; And when it is ren togidre in the *chaffre*, and is ynowe, take a *Skymour*, and take hit oute of the *chaffur*, and putte oute al the *grece*, And lete ren ; And putte hit in a faire dissh, and cast *sugur* thereon ynow, and *serue* it forth.

And finally, a dish on a somewhat lavish scale, called, with reason, (iv) Grete *pyes* : Take faire yonge *beef*, And *suet* of a fatte *beste*, or of *Motton*, and hak all this on a borde small ; And caste thereto *pouder* of peper and salt ; And whon it is small hewen, put hit in a bolle, And *medle* hem well ; then make a faire *large Cofyn*, and *couche* som of this *stuffur* in. Then take *Capons*, Hennes, *Mallards*, *Connynges*, and *parboile* hem clene ; take wodekokkes, *teles*, grete briddes, and *plom* hem in a *boiling* potte ; And then *couche* al þis fowle in þe *Coffyn*, And put in euerych of hem a *quantite* of *pouder* of peper and salt. Then take *mary*, harde yolkes of egges, *Dates* cutte in ij. *peces*, *reisons* of *coraunce*, *prunes*, hole *clowes*, hole *maces*, *Canell*, and *saffron*. But first, whan thou hast *cowched* all thi foule, ley the *remenaunt* of thyne other *stuffur* of *beef* a-bought hem, as þou thenkest goode ; and then strawe on hem this : *dates*, *mary*, and *reysons*, etc., And then *close* thi *Coffyn* with a lydde of the same *paast*, And put hit in þe oven, And late hit bake ynogh.

This reminds us of Chaucer's cook, with his ' *poudre-marchaunt tart and galyngale* ', and it is time that we turned our attention to Chaucer and his French element.

The proportion of French words used by Chaucer varies,

---

[1] i.e. *Crêpes*, pancakes.

sometimes being ten or eleven per cent, and sometimes rising as high as fifteen per cent. In some of his writings, as in the more philosophical parts of his translation of Boethius, and in his *Treatise on the Astrolabe*, many of the words used are of a learned type which can never have been current in the ordinary colloquial language ; the *Astrolabe* in particular, written for his ' litel sone ', must indeed have been ' harde ' for Lowys's ' tendir age of x yere to conceyve '.[1] Here are four passages, one from the Canterbury Tales, being the beginning of the Nun's Priest's tale ; the second from *Boece* ; the third the *Balade to Rosemounde* ; the last, seven stanzas from the concluding part of *Troilus and Criseyde*.

(i) A *poure* wydwe, somdel stape in *age*,
Was whilom dwellyng in a narwe *cotage*
Beside a greve, stondynge in a dale.
This wydwe, of which I telle yow my tale,
Syn thilke day that she was last a wyf,
In *pacience* ladde a ful *symple* lyf,
For litel was hir *catel* and hir *rente*.
By housbondrie of swich as God hire sente
She foond hirself, and eek hire doghtren two.
Thre *large* sowes hadde she, and namo ;
Three keen and eek a sheep that highte Malle.
Ful sooty was hir bour, and eek hire halle,
In which she eet ful many a sklendre meel ;
Of *poynaunt sauce* hir neded never a deel.
No *deyntee morsel passed* thurgh hir throte,
Hir *diete* was *accordant* to hir cote ;
Repleccioun ne made hir never sik,
Attempree diete was al hir *phisik*,
And *exercise*, and hertes *suffisaunce*.
The *goute* lette hire no-thyng for to *daunce*,
Napoplexie shente nat hir heed ;
No wyn ne drank she, neither whit ne reed ;

---

[1] e.g. ' Further over thei seyn that the *infortunyng* of an *ascendent* is the *contrarie* of these forseide thinges. The Lord of the *Ascendent* sey thei that he is *fortunat* whan he is in gode *place* fro the *ascendent*, as in an *angle*, or in a *succident* where as he is in hys *dignite* and *comfortid* with frendly *aspectes* of *planetes* and wel *resceyved* ; and eke that he may seen the *ascendent* ; and that he be not *retrograd* ne *combust* ne *joyned* with no shrewe in the same *signe* ; ne that he be not in his *discencioun*,' etc.

Hir bord was *served* moost with whit and blak, —
Milk and broun breed, — in which she foond no lak ;
Seind *bacoun* and somtyme an ey or tweye,
For she was, as it were, a *maner* deye.
A yeerd she hadde, *enclosed* al aboute
With stikkes, and a drye dych withoute,
In which she hadde a cok, heet *Chauntecleer*.
In al the land of crowyng nas his *peer*.
His *voys* was murier than the murie orgon
On messe dayes that in the chirche gon ;
Wel sikerer was his crowyng in his *logge*
Than is a clokke, or an *abbey orlogge*.
By *nature* knew he eche *ascencioun*
Of the *equynoxial* in thilke toun ;
For whan *degrees* fiftene weren *ascended*,
Thanne crew he that he myghte nat been *amended*.
His coomb was redder than the *fyn coral*,
And *batailled* as it were a *castel* wal ;
His byle was blak, and as the *jeet* it shone ;
Lyk *asure* were his legges and his toon ;
His nayles whiter than the lylye *flour*,
And lyk the burned gold was his *colour*.

(Nun's Priest's Tale, 4011–54.)

(ii) (*Fortune* is speaking) :   I *envyrounde* the with al the *habundance* and schynynge of alle goodes that ben in my ryght. Now it liketh me to with draw myn hand. Thow hast had *grace* as he that hath used of *foreyne* goodes ; thow hast no ryght to *pleyne* the, as though thou haddest outrely forlorn alle thy thynges. Why *pleyne*stow thanne ? I have doon the no wrong. *Richesses, honours,* and swiche othere thinges ben of my right. My *servauntes* knowen me for hir lady ; they comen with me, and *departen* whan I wende. I dar wel *affermen hardely* that, yif tho thynges of whiche thow *pleyn*est that thou hast for-lorn hadden ben thyne, thow ne haddest nat lorn hem. Schal I thanne, oonly be *defended* to *usen* my ryght ? *Certes* it is leueful to the hevene to maken *clere* dayes, and after that to *coveren* the same dayes with dirke nyghtes. The yeer hath eek leve to *apparaylen* the *visage* of the erthe, now with *floures,* and now with *fruyt*, and to *confownden* hem som-tyme with reynes and with coldes. The see hath eek his ryght to ben som-tyme *calm* and *blaundysschyng* with smothe watir, and som-tyme to ben *horrible* with wawes and with *tempestes*. But the *covetise* of men, that maĵ nat be *stawnched*, — schal it bynde me to ben stidfast, syn that stidfastnesse is uncouth to my *maneris*? Swiche is my strengthe, and this pley I pleye *continuely*. I torne the whirlynge wheel, with the turnynge *sercle*; I am glad to *chaungen* the loweste to the heyeste, and the heyeste to the loweste.

(Boece, Book ii, Prosa 2.)

(iii) To Rosemounde

Madame, ye ben of al *beaute* [the] shryne
As fer as *cercled* is the *mappemounde*,
For as the *cristal glorious* ye shyne
And lyke *ruby* ben your chekes *rounde*.
Therwith ye ben so mery and so *jocounde*
That at a *revel* whan that I see you *daunce*,
It is an *oynement* unto my wounde,
Though ye to me ne do no *daliaunce*.

For though I wepe of teres ful a tyne,
Yet may that wo myn herte nat *confounde*;
Your seemly *voys* that ye so smal out-twyne
Maketh my thoght in joye and blis *habounde*.
So *curteisly* I go, with love bounde,
That to myself I sey, in my *penaunce*,
Suffyseth me to love you Rosemòunde,
Though ye to me ne do no *daliaunce*.

Nas never pyk walwed in *galauntyne* [1]
As I in love am walwed and y-wounde,
For which ful ofte I of my-self *dyvyne*
That I am trewe Tristam the *secounde*,
My love may not *refreyd* be nor *afounde*;
I brenne ay in an *amorous plesaunce*.
Do what you lyst, I wyl your thral be founde
Though ye to me ne do no *daliaunce*.

[1] See p. 149.

(iv) Go litel book ! Go, litel myn *tragedie* !
    Ther God thy maker yit, or-that he he dye,
    So sende might to make in som *comedie* !
    But, litel book, no making thou n'*envye*,
    But *subgit* be to alle *poesye* !
    And kis the steppes wher-as thou seest *pace*
    Virgile, Ovide, Omer, Lucan and Stace !

    And for ther is so gret *diversite*
    In Englissh and in writing of our tonge,
    So *prey* to God that non miswrite thee,
    Ne thee *mismetre* for *defaute* of tonge !
    And, red wher-so thou be or elles songe,
    That thou be understonde God biseche !
    But yet to *purpos* of my rather speche.

    The wraththe, as I began you for to seye,
    Of Troilus the Grekes boughten dere ;
    For thousandes his hondes maden deye,
    As he that was withouten any *pere*
    Save Ector in his time, as I can here,
    But weylawey, *save* only Goddes wille,
    Ful *pitously* him slough the *fierse* Achille.

    And whan that he was slayn in this *manere*
    His lighte goost ful blisfully is went
    Up to the holwnesse of the eighte *spere*,
    In *convers* leting everich *element* ;
    And ther he saugh with ful *avisement*
    Th'*erratik* sterres, herkning *armonye*
    With *sounes* fulle of hevenissh *melodye*.

    And down from thennes faste he gan *avise*
    This litel spot of erthe that with the see
    Embraced is, and fully gan *despise*
    This wrecched world, and held al *vanite*
    To *respect* of the *pleyne felicite*
    That is in hevene above. And at the laste,
    Ther he was slayn his loking down he caste,

And in himself he lough right at the wo
Of hem that wepen for his deth so faste,
And *dampned* al our werk, that folwen so
The blinde lust the whiche that may not laste,
And sholden al our herte on hevene caste.
And forthe he wente, shortly for to telle,
Ther-as Mercurie *sorted* him to dwelle.

Swich *fyn* hath tho this Troilus for love !
Swich *fyn* hath al his grete worthinesse !
Swich *fyn* hath his *estat real* above !
Swich *fyn* his lust, swich *fyn* hath his *noblesse* !
Swich *fyn*, this *false* worldes brotelnesse !
And thus bigan his loving of Criseyde
As I have told, and in this wise he deyde.

(*Troilus and Criseyde*, v, 1786–1834.)

In these extracts, the proportion of French words is respectively
(i) 13·5 per cent ; (ii) 12·3 per cent ; (iii) 15·6 per cent ; (iv)
11·6 per cent. This makes an average of 13·2 per cent. Possibly
a little less should be taken as Chaucer's real average, since the
proportion in *Rosemounde* seems to be rather unusual. Chaucer
is not, however, the writer with the highest proportion of French
loans ; both Langland and Lydgate, for instance, have slightly
higher averages. Nor is it true, as has sometimes been said, that
Chaucer himself introduced large numbers of French words into
English. The majority of his words were already in use well
before his time. Lydgate is probably more of an innovator than
Chaucer ; but his introductions are very much of a rather
exaggeratedly ' learned ' type, or can be ascribed to a rather
strained poetic diction, and many of them were never established
in English, either literary or colloquial.

In dealing with the French loans of the later period of English
we shall be limiting ourselves for the most part to such words as
have survived in ordinary spoken or written English. But the
Middle English period, as well as other centuries, introduced
also very many words of a technical character, connected with the
law, with heraldry, with arts and crafts, such as jewel-work,
etc., and these technical vocabularies still survive. Hundreds

of legal words of French origin (chiefly Anglo-Norman) were adopted into English after English became officially the language of the courts, and the influence of Anglo-Norman remained strong long after this, as it was still used for many legal affairs for several centuries. Some of these legal terms made their way into the non-technical language, and everyone is familiar with such words as *remainder, rejoinder, assets, entail,* while of course very many were never exclusively legal, though perhaps have always been most frequent in a legal connexion, e.g. *try, judge, examine, prove, issue, demur,* etc. Many heraldic terms are now unfamiliar to most people, though some are fairly widely current, e.g. *azure, quatrefoil, cinquefoil, chevron* ; others are used commonly in non-heraldic senses, e.g. *bend, chief, displayed, label, lozenge, proper* ; some are fairly easy to guess, e.g. *rampant, roundel, argent, sable* ; but many people would find it impossible to say what was meant by *mullet, saltire, caltrap, garb, fess, mascle, flaunch, maunch, gules, passant, guardant, formée, pattée, paly, semé, ragulée, gemel, gorged, segreant, engrailed.*

Modern French Words in English

Naturally, the French language did not remain static during the whole period from the Norman Conquest of England down to the fifteenth century. By about 1500 many of the changes typical of Modern French had taken place, and words borrowed after this reached English speakers in a different form from that which they would have had if they had been adopted, say, three hundred years earlier. For instance, in early Middle English words were borrowed from French containing the sound-group *ch* [tʃ] (as in Eng. *child*), e.g. *chief, chivalry, duchess, chase, torch* ; and [dž] (as in *gem*), e.g. *judge* (both consonants), *just, journey, large* ; these consonant-groups became respectively [ʃ] and [ž] in later French, and words borrowed after the period of this development came into English with these sounds, e.g. *champagne, chef, chaperon, sachet* (cf. *satchel*) ; *négligé, garage.* Again, O.Fr. *oi* (in some cases from earlier *ei*) became first *ué,* and then, perhaps by the sixteenth century, *ua* (*wa*), e.g. Mod. Fr. *loi, roi, poids, joie* (earlier *lei, rei, peids* ; *joi*) ; Middle English loans have the diphthongs *ei, oi* (e.g. M.E. *lei* ' law ',

preie ' PREY ', *ioie* ' JOY ', POISE, NOISE) ; but with such
forms should be compared *soirée, noisette, moiré,* all of recent
introduction, and also *turquoise,* as compared with the early
modern *turkis,* a Middle English loan where the -*i*- represents
the usual English development of unstressed *oi.* (This word,
however, often has now a spelling pronunciation with *oi.* Similar
spelling pronunciations may occasionally be heard in the words
porpoise, tortoise, though the historical [pɔ̄pəs, tɔ̄təs] are still
the normal forms ; these have an alternative development of
M.E. unstressed *oi,* but *porpis* and *tortis,* like *turkis,* may be
found in Early Modern English, just as *turkis* sometimes has
[-əs], e.g. in Milton's *turkas.*)

Further, by the end of the fifteenth century, the majority of
the changes which distinguished Modern from Middle English
had taken place, so that, whereas French words borrowed before
1450 or so had to undergo, with native words, sound-changes
which transformed them completely from what they had been
in their parent language, words adopted after this were too late
for these developments, or most of them, and were less completely divorced from their original forms, such differences as
there are being due more to sound-substitution than to sound-
change. For example, the words *fine, nice, guile,* which had the
vowel [ī] (as in Mod. Eng. *feed*) in M.E., now have developed
a diphthong [*ai*] along with the native *find, mine, write,* etc. ;
but words like *machine, clique, pique, élite* did not become liable
to this change, since when they were borrowed the English
tendency to diphthongize [ī] to [*ai*] had passed. As has been
pointed out in the introduction, the closeness of the pronunciation
of a borrowed word to that of its own language depends upon the
presence in the borrowing language of the native sounds of
the word, or upon the acquaintance of the speaker with the
language borrowed from ; also to some extent upon the
popularization of the word. Thus Modern Standard English
does not normally have nasalized vowels, so when a word such
as *confrère,* or *coupon,* or *envelope,* is adopted, the English
speaker may substitute for the nasalized vowel the nearest
English equivalent, probably *on* ; if he does, however, speak
French, he may retain the French vowel. Again, Mod. English
does not contain an exact equivalent of the French short *a,*

and the English speaker will usually substitute for it the Standard English [æ] ; even one who speaks French fairly accurately will use this vowel instead of the French one in a word which has become very common, such as *garage* (first syllable), *camouflage*. Similarly, where French has *é*, an English speaker will replace it by his nearest sound, the diphthong [ei], e.g. *glacé, éclat, café, papier mâché*, and so on ; the same diphthong does duty also for French *ê* in *fête*, etc.

Almost all borrowings from French are, as we have already found, either from Northern French,[1] or from the Central French dialect which became the standard dialect of France, but English has a few words from other French dialects, most of them, however, coming into this language by way of Central French. The most important of these are from the southern type of French known as Provençal. The earliest seems to be **marque** (in the phrase 'letters of marque', licence given to a privateer), which dates from 1419 ; this is from Prov. *marca*, from the verb *marcar* 'to seize as a pledge'. The importance of Southern France as a wine-growing country is reflected in the three words **spigot** (Prov. **spigot*, cf. *espiga* 'spike'), which appears in Late Middle English ; **rack** 'to draw off (wine) from the lees' (especially a Gascon word, and apparently the only word now surviving to indicate our connexion with Gascony ; the original form was *arracar*, from *raca* 'husks of grapes'), recorded first in English in 1460 ; and **ullage,** the difference between the capacity of a cask or bottle and the amount of liquor which it contains ; this is much later than the first two, not being found till 1749 ; the Provençal word is *ulhage*, from the verb *ulha* 'to fill up to the bung'. The word **mistral,** first met with in English in 1604, is still restricted in sense to the Mediterranean coast of France, and has not been extended in use to other types of wind ; but **lucerne** (Prov. *luzerno*) has become fairly widespread ; it dates from 1626. **Lingo** is apparently Prov. *lingo, lengo* 'language' ; it appears first in 1660. **Gavotte** came over with numerous other French terms of society in the second half of the seventeenth century ; it represents Prov. *gavoto*, which is from *gavot*, a name used for an inhabitant of the Alpine districts ; it is recorded

---

[1] A few Northern forms were borrowed in Late Middle English, e.g. *task*, and *tuck* (of drum).

first in 1696. Although the minstrels and poets of Southern France exerted indirectly a considerable influence on the English literature of the Middle Ages, we do not find any influence on the vocabulary from these regions until the eighteenth century, but then with reference to the earlier period ; **troubadour** dates from 1727 (the French *trouvère* is even later, 1795), the Provençal form being *trobador*. Connected with this is the less familiar **sirvente,** a form of verse used by the troubadours, dating from 1819. Another eighteenth-century loan is **charade** (Prov. *charrada* ' chatter '), 1776 ; and to the nineteenth century belong **nougat** (1827 ; see other French words of this period), the rare **picayune** (Prov. *picaion*), at one time the name for a small coin in the French-speaking district of Louisiana, and later (chiefly American slang) used to denote something mean or worthless ; this is found first in 1852. Finally, there is one more reflection of an industry of Provence ; this is **pébrine,** hardly naturalized in English, from French, from Prov. *pebrino*, the name of a silk-worm disease (1870).

Swiss-French dialects have given us **chamois,** as early as 1560 ; **chalet,** not till 1817 ; and **crétin** (French, from Swiss *crestin*), from 1779. The first word has been completely naturalized (in pronunciation and sometimes also in spelling) in *shammy leather*, though for the animal itself a pseudo-French pronunciation [ʃæmwa] is generally used. (The word is ultimately of Germanic origin, and is related to the German *Gemse* ; it is probably from a Gmc. dialect of that part of the Alpine district to which Romance dialects afterwards spread.)

In spite of our long connexion with the Channel Islands, only one English word can be definitely ascribed to the French dialect spoken there. This is **ormer** (1672), applied to a special kind of shell-fish found on the coasts of the islands.

It has already been indicated that Old French borrowed a fairly large number of words from Germanic, especially from Old High German, and many have been pointed out as having passed on into English during the Middle English period. Such words are still being borrowed in the Modern period, and we may give as examples **harangue, spavin, skirmish, stallion, tack** n. (all from the fifteenth century) ; **vogue** (sixteenth century) ; **ratchet, soup, stockade** (seventeenth century), and so forth. In the same

way many other words which came into English from French
are ultimately from languages more remote, showing by their
passage through French what great influence the knowledge,
arts, and commerce of France have had on this country. Most
of these words will be dealt with under the languages from which
they came.

A point which must be insisted on before we consider in detail
the later loans from French, is that a word may be borrowed, lost,
and borrowed again, or, if not lost, borrowed again in a different
form and perhaps with a slightly different sense. For instance,
the words **potage** and **pottage** represent two different periods of
borrowing, the latter dating from Middle English. The same is
true of **valet**, with its two pronunciations : that with final *-t*,
from the M.E. period, and that with a final vowel, approximating
more or less to the Modern French. **Corsage** in the later fifteenth
century (pronounced with final *-idge*) meant ' the shape of the
body ', but when borrowed afresh in 1857 had the sense of part
of a woman's dress.

Before starting on the sixteenth century we may mention a few
words from the late fifteenth century, which seem to have been
in continuous use since then in approximately their modern forms,
and which give no impression of archaism. Such are **serviette,
redeem** (Fr. *redimer*), **mademoiselle** (cf. M.E. *damesel*, etc. ;
demoiselle is sixteenth century) ; **serge ; tapis** (though this may
have been reborrowed later).

In the sixteenth century, the most important loans are military
and naval. To this period belong **trophy** 1513 ; **pioneer** (originally
' foot-soldier ') 1523 ;   **jacquerie** (used chiefly historically with
reference to the peasants' revolt in France in 1357, but also in
transferred sense) 1523 ;   **brigantine** 1525 ;   **pilot** (ultimately
Greek, passing through Italian into French) 1530 ; **sally** 1542 ;
colonel 1548 (another form, *coronel*, borrowed in the following
century ; from this comes the modern pronunciation) ; **guidon,**
a type of flag (orig. Italian) 1548 ; **corsair** 1549 ; **volley** 1573 ;
cartridge 1579 ; **perdu** (orig. of a sentry placed in a dangerous
position) 1591 ; **rendezvous** 1591 ; **apeak** (from the French
nautical phrase *à pic*) 1596. Terms which may be related to
trade are **palliasse** 1506 ; **livre** 1553 ; **indigo** 1555 ; **sou** 1556 ;
gauze 1561 ; **grogram** 1562 ; **vase** 1563 ; **cabochon** 1578 ; **cordon**

1578 (in the sense of 'braid'); the more usual modern sense does not appear till 1758); **portmanteau** 1584. The following may be considered 'social' terms : **demoiselle** 1520 (it was borrowed again, with a different application, in 1687, as a zoological name for a certain kind of crane); **viceroy** 1524 ; **sirrah** (now obsolete) 1526 ; **partisan** 'supporter' (from an Italian dialect) 1555 ; **minion,** orig. 'small, delicate', or as noun 'darling'; also **mignon** 1556, perhaps with the French pronunciation ; the former is anglicized as [mínjən] ; **bourgeois** 1564 ; **vogue** 1571 ; **esprit** 1591 ; **genteel** 1599 (cf. *gentle,* borrowed in M.E. from O.Fr. *gentil* ; the *-ee-* of *genteel* represents Fr. *-i-*) ; **madame** 1599 (*madam*, with the stress on the first syllable, is a M.E. loan) ; and perhaps we may include here **racket** 1500, possibly Arabian in origin. **Potage** 1567 (cf. the M.E. loan **pottage**), **fricassee** 1568, and **rennet** (a kind of apple, Fr. *reinette*) 1568, are all Tudor borrowings. Words relating to art and literature are **rondeau** 1525 (cf. the earlier *roundel* ; **scene** 1540 (first with the meaning 'scenery') ; **grotesque** 1561 ; **hautboy** 1575 (the spelling *oboe* is an Italian representation of the French pronunciation ; this is not found till 1700) ; **quatorzain** 1583. Finally a few miscellaneous words : **piquant** 1521, and **pique** (in the sense of 'quarrel') 1532 ; **promenade** 1567 (in the sense of 'walking' ; as 'place for walking' it is recorded in 1648) ; **cache** 'hiding-place' 1595 ; **moustache** 1585 (this is a French version of an Italian *mostaccio*, which also appears in Tudor English as *mustachio* 1585 ; O.E. has a Gmc. word *cenep*) ; **machine** 1549 ; and the anatomical term **fontanelle** 1541.

During the seventeenth century, social, literary, and commercial relations with France were very close ; English writers imitated French writers, and, particularly after the Restoration there was a widespread fashion for introducing French words and phrases into ordinary conversation ; something of this can be seen in the drama of the time, and it appears also in the dates of introduction of many French words, from the latter part of the reign of Charles I, and from the last forty years of the century. The number of words recorded for the first time between 1600 and 1640 is not very large ; again the most important are the military, naval, and diplomatic : **fanfare** 1605 ; **pratique** 1609 ;

cartouche 1611 ; **stockade** 1614 ; **parole** 1616 ; **rencontre** 1619 (the form *rencounter* is earlier, 1523) ; **dragoon** 1622 ; **brigade** 1637 ; **platoon** 1637 ; besides **cachet** 1639. Social terms include : **monseigneur** 1600 (*monsieur* dates from 1500) ; **spa,** in a general sense, 1610 (it is used with reference to Spa, in Belgium, in 1565) ; **coquette** 1611 ; **étui** 1611 ; **table-d'hôte** 1617 ; **fainéant** 1619 ; **accolade** 1623 ; **hauteur** 1628 ; **flambeau** 1632 ; **reprimand** 1636. Art, literature, etc. : **rôle** 1606 (also spelt *roll*) ; **paysage** 1611 ; **parterre** 1639 (for a garden-bed ; as part of a theatre, not till 1711). Miscellaneous : **unique** 1602 ; **sabot** 1607 ; **absinthe** 1612 (as name of plant ; as a liqueur, not till 1854).

1644–1700 : Military, naval, and diplomatic : **carbine** 1605 ; **reveillé** 1644 ; **mêlée** 1648 ; **envoy** 1666 ; **aide-de-camp** 1670 ; **carabineer** 1672 ; **glacis** 1678 ; **redan** 1684 ; **commandant** 1687 (chiefly of foreign commanders) ; **cheval-de-frise** 1688. People and things : **concierge** ' custodian ' 1646 ; **pastille** 1648 ; **cabaret** 1655 (the sense of ' entertainment ', etc., is not recorded till 1915) ; **curé** 1655 ; **plafond** 1664 ; **tourniquet** 1695 ; **attic** 1696 ; **fiacre** 1699 (named from the Hôtel St. Fiacre in Paris ; St. Fiachra was a Celtic saint of the eighth century, so the word is ultimately Celtic) ; **vinaigrette** 1698. Games and dancing : **capot** (a term in piquet) 1651 ; **ballet** 1667 ; **quart** (as a term at cards, 1672 ; in fencing, 1692 ; Mod. *quart*, the measure, is a M.E. loan) ; **loo** (abbreviated from *lanterloo*) 1675 ; **chicane** 1676 ; **rigadoon** 1691 ; **pool** 1693. Art and literature : **crayon** 1644 ; **arabesque** 1656 ; **burlesque** 1656 (orig. Italian) ; **memoirs** 1659 ; **bas-relief** 1667 ; **aubade** 1678 (orig. Spanish) ; **nom-de-plume** 1679 ; **group** 1686 ; **tableau** ' picture ' 1699. Natural products : **aigrette** 1645 ; **manganese** 1676 ; **varec** 1676 ; **guillemot** 1678 ; **jargonelle** 1693. Dress, textiles, etc. : **cravat** 1656 (orig. ' a Croat ') ; **chagrin, shagreen** 1656 (in the figurative sense, 1847) ; **moire** ' mohair ' 1660 ; **paduasoy** 1663 ; **shalloon** (from the place-name *Chalons*) 1678 ; **ratteen** 1685 ; **surtout** 1686 ; **denim** (= serge de Nîmes) 1695 ; **mousseline** 1696 (but the anglicized **muslin** in 1609) ; **batiste** (from a personal name) 1697. Food and drink : **bisque** 1647 ; **soup** 1653 ; **haricot** (= ragout) 1653 ; **bouillon** 1656 ; **champagne** 1664 ; **salmagundi** 1674 ; **compote** 1693. Fashionable social terms : **invalid** n. 1642 (the adj. *inválid*, 1635, is direct from Latin) ; **repartee** 1645 ; **forte** n.

1648 ; **liaison** 1648 ; **complaisance** 1651 ; **mélange** 1653 ; **reverie** 1653 (already in M.E., but now reborrowed) ; **naïve** 1654 ; **décor** ' ornament ' 1656 (as a term of the theatre, not till 1927) ; **démarche** 1658 ; **façade** 1656 ; **rapport** ' relationship ' 1661 (the phrase *en rapport* appears in 1818) ; **contour** 1662 ; **en passant** 1665 ; **malapropos** 1668 ; **doyen** 1670 ; **penchant** 1672 ; **dishabille** 1673 ; **double entendre** 1673 ; **spirituelle** 1673 ; **suite** 1673 (= train of followers ; of rooms, 1716 ; of furniture, not till 1851) ; **métier** 1674 ; **canaille** 1676 ; **faux pas** 1676 ; **pis aller** 1676 ; **routine** 1676 ; **nonchalance** 1678 (the adj. in 1734) ; **cortège** 1679 ; **contretemps** 1684 ; **beau** n. 1687 ; **reservoir** 1690 ; **rouleau** (of coins) 1693 ; **par excellence** 1695 ; **tête-à-tête** 1697 ; **verve** 1697 ; **ménage** 1698. Miscellaneous : **patois** 1643 ; **ratchet** 1659 ; **louis** 1689.

In the eighteenth century, the French words on the whole tend to belong to the first quarter or the last quarter. In the last decade there appear a number of words having special reference to the French Revolution, such as **émigré** 1792, **guillotine** 1793, **carmagnole** 1796 (as nickname for a French soldier ; in its first sense, of a song and dance of this period, it is recorded first in 1827), **régime** 1789 (in the phrase *the ancient régime*, representing French *l'ancien régime* ; for ' regimen ' it had already appeared in 1776), and **noyade** (first in 1819). Many of the military terms are to be associated either with the wars of the reign of Queen Anne, or with the Napoleonic wars, fewer to the Seven Years' War. In this century terms for food and cooking, for clothes and textiles, are specially noticeable ; there are also a considerable number of ' social ' terms, and we also find the beginning of the mountaineering terms of French origin, which become more numerous in the next century.

Military : **caisson** 1704 ; **pas** 1704 (as a term in fortification ; in the sense of ' precedence ' it is used in 1707) ; **enfilade** 1706 ; **bivouac** 1706 (this is ultimately from Swiss-German *Beiwacht*) ; **pâté** (fortifications ; the sense of ' pasty ' is later) ; **enceinte** 1708 ; **corps** 1711 ; **lateen** (sail ; Fr. *voile latine*) 1727 ; **terrain** 1727 ; **manœuvre** 1758 ; **abattis** 1766 ; **ricochet** n. 1769 ; **barbette** 1772 ; **echelon** 1793 ; **espionage** 1793 ; **tirailleur** 1796 ; **depôt** 1794 ; **sortie** 1795 ; **chasseur** 1796 ; **tricolor** 1798 (first as revolutionary flag) ; then, at the beginning of the nineteenth century, **feu de joie** 1801 ; **fusillade** 1801 ; **revet** 1812 ; **razee** (of warship) 1803 ; **chaussée** (high-road in France, etc.) 1817.

People : **clique** 1711 ; **solitaire** ' recluse ' 1716 ; **savant** 1719 ; **chaperon** 1720 (it had been borrowed earlier in the sense of ' hood ') ; **précieuse** 1727 ; **pierrot** 1741 (*pierrette* not till 1888) ; **confrère** 1753 (a re-borrowing; it had already been used in M.E.) ; **soubrette** 1753 ; **femme de chambre** ' lady's maid ' 1762 ; **protégé** 1778 ; **martinet** 1779 ; **abbé** 1780 ; **colporteur** 1796.

Buildings, furniture and other objects : **chaise** 1701 ; **escritoire** 1706 ; **envelope** 1707 ; **entresol** 1711 ; **salon** 1715 (French from Italian ; **saloon,** which is probably directly from Italian, is found in 1728 ; **salle** in 1762) ; **bouquet** 1716 ; **gadroon,** a pattern used in architecture, 1723 ; **bureau** 1720 (' office ' ; as ' desk ' in 1742) ; **mansard** 1734 ; **canteen** 1737 ; **diligence** (' coach ') 1742 ; **fauteuil** 1744 ; **épergne** 1761 ; **pavé** 1764 ; **ormolu** 1765 ; **boulevard** 1772 ; **château** 1789 ; **pisé** 1797.

Dancing and games : **pirouette** 1706 ; **carte, quarte** (fencing) 1707 ; **croupier** 1707 ; **roulette** 1734 ; **cotillion** 1766 ; **figurant(e)** (ballet-dancer) 1790 ; **valse** 1796.

Literature, art, music : **critique** 1702 ; **roulade** 1706 ; **belles-lettres** 1710 ; **bouts rimés** 1711 ; **connoisseur** 1714 ; **faience** 1714 ; **coterie** 1738 ; **vaudeville** (' a popular, topical song ') 1739 ; **morceau** 1751 ; **vignette** 1751 ; **dénouement** 1752 ; **papier maché** 1753 ; **précis** 1760 ; **brochure** 1765 ; **conservatoire** 1771 ; **jongleur** 1779 (historical, with reference to mediaeval literature) ; **nuance** 1781 ; **raisonné** 1777 ; **trouvère** 1795 (cf. *jongleur* ; also *troubadour*, among words from Provençal) ; **silhouette** 1798.

Geographical, rivers, mountains, mountaineering, etc. : **débris** 1708 ; **cul-de-sac** 1738 ; **glacier** 1744 ; **avalanche, crampon, moraine** (all in Coxe's *Travels in Switzerland*) 1789 ; **embouchure** 1760 ; **plateau** 1796.

Animals and plants : **chevrotain** (a small musk-deer), **loris** 1774 (both in Goldsmith's *Natural History*) ; **grison** 1796. **cachou** 1708 (cf. *cashew*) ; **beurré** (pear) 1741 ; **aubergine** 1794 (in a book on Surinam).

Dress, textiles, etc. : **grisette** (grey fabric) 1700 ; **velours** 1706 ; **pelisse** 1718 ; **tarlatan** 1727 ; **toupee** 1727 ; **chenille** 1738 ; **pompon** 1748 ; **rouge** 1753 (earlier with reference to Heraldry) ;

moquette 1762 ; **polonaise** 1773 ; **chignon** 1783 ; **epaulette** 1783 ; **corduroy** 1787 ; **bandeau** 1790.

Food and cooking : **casserole, croquette, fricandeau, méringue, ramekin, rissole, tureen** 1706 ; **ragout** 1710 ; **praline** 1727 ; **matelote** 1730 ; **liqueur** 1742 ; **salmi** 1759 ; **plat** 1763 ; **blomange** 1769 (this is the form on which our modern pronunciation depends ; it is a shortened form, either from French or from the M.E. loan **blancmanger**) ; **cuisine** 1786 ; **déjeuner** 1787 ; **aspic** 1789 ; **bechamel** 1796 ; **noyau** 1797.

Colours, etc. : **brunette** 1712 ; **bistre** 1727 ; **celadon** 1768 ; **chatoyant** 1798.

Medical, etc. : **sac** 1741 ; **curette** 1753 ; **grippe** (' influenza ') 1776 ; **migraine** 1777.

Social : **picnic** 1748 ; **etiquette** 1750 ; **début** 1751 ; **fête** 1754 ; **entrée** 1782 ; **monde** (society) 1765.

Personal qualities, behaviour, etc. : **sang-froid** 1712 ; **outré** 1722 ; **récherché** 1722 ; **éclat** 1741 ; **distrait** 1748 (Lord Chesterfield) ; **empressement** 1749 ; **diablerie** 1751 ; **gauche** 1751 ; **morale** 1753 (' moral principles ' ; first used of troops in 1831) ; **persiflage** 1757 ; **ennui** 1758 ; **farouche** 1765 ; **passé** 1775 ; **intriguant** 1781 ; **insouciance** 1799.

Miscellaneous : **ensemble** 1703 ; **écu** 1704 ; **goffer** 1706 ; **carte blanche** 1707 (figuratively, in 1766) ; **encore** 1712 ; **menagerie** 1712 ; **hors d'œuvre** (adv. ' out of the ordinary ', Addison) 1714 (with reference to meal, 1742) ; **police** 1730 (civil administration ; in modern sense, 1800) ; **entrepôt** (commercial depôt) 1721 ; **détour** 1738 ; **hors de combat** 1745 ; **potpourri** (of flowers) 1749 ; **embonpoint** 1751 ; **soi-disant** 1752 ; **vis-à-vis** 1753 ; **piaffe** 1761 (of horse) ; **chef-d'œuvre** 1762 ; **douceur** 1763 ; **soupçon** 1766 ; **poste restante** 1768 ; **souvenir** 1775 ; **route** 1779 (cf. the earlier *rout*) ; **coup** 1791 ; **gramme** 1797.

The nineteenth century introduced more French words into this country than any period since Middle English. The most numerous are those under the headings of Art and Literature, etc., Dress and Textiles, etc., the latter group, with Furniture, etc., are perhaps the most typical of the century ; it may be observed that the majority of the words in these two groups belong to the period between 1830 and 1860. Food and Cooking are well represented, and there is a fair number of general political terms.

Military : **matériel** 1814 ; **parados** 1834 ; **sabreur** 1845 ; **barrage** 1859 ; **fourgon** (baggage-wagon) 1848 ; **communiqué** 1852 ; **chassis** 1869 (part of gun-carriage ; as part of a motorcar, it is found first in 1903) ; **franctireur** 1870 ; **mitrailleuse** 1870 ; **melinite** 1886.

People : **roué** 1800 ; **habitué** 1818 ; **troupe** 1825 (*troop* is an older loan) ; **raconteur** 1829 ; **attaché** 1835 (the compound *attaché-case* appears in 1904) ; **garçon** 1839 (waiter) ; **gamin** 1840 ; **chargé d'affaires** 1850 ; **clientèle** 1860 ; **chauffeur** 1899.

Buildings, institutions, etc. : **morgue** 1821 ; **oubliette** 1819 ; **abattoir** 1840 ; **lycée** 1865 ; **crèche** 1882.

Furniture, and other things of Use and Ornament : **chiffonier** 1806 ; **aventurine** (a kind of glass) 1811 ; **parquet** 1816 ; **secretaire** 1818 ; **jalousie** 1824 ; **reticule** 1824 ; **sachet** 1838 ; **bric-à-brac** 1840 ; **jardinière** 1841 ; **persiennes** 1842 ; **châtelaine** 1851 ; **cheval-**(glass) 1855 ; **portière** 1855 ; **étagère** 1858 ; **carte de visite** 1861 ; **passe-partout** 1867.

Dancing and games : **chassé** vb. 1803 ; **écarté** 1824 ; **acrobat** 1825 ; **misère** 1830 ; **glissade** 1843 ; **can-can** 1848 ; **croquet** 1858 (a Northern French word, corresponding to *crochet*) ; **planchette** 1860 ; **bézique** 1861 ; **écossaise** 1863 ; **baccarat** 1866 ; **coryphée** 1866 ; **lacrosse** 1867.

Literature, art, music, and architecture : **carillon** 1803 ; **fabliau** 1804 (historical) ; **résumé** 1804 ; **littérateur** 1806 ; **chevet** 1809 ; **sanserif** 1830 ; **cliché** 1832 (metal stereotype used in wood-engraving ; in the figurative sense, first in 1892) ; **flamboyant** 1832 ; **rococo** 1836 ; **atelier** 1840 ; **format** 1840 ; **renaissance** 1840 ; **guilloche** 1842 ; **repertoire** 1847 ; **grisaille** 1848 ; **motif** 1848 (as trimming for dress, 1882) ; **baroque** 1851 ; **repoussé** 1851 ; **hachures** (map-making) 1858 ; **foyer** 1859 ; **nocturne** 1862 ; **cloisonné** 1863 ; **dinanderie** 1863 ; **entr'acte** 1863 ; **baton** 1867 ; **aquarelle** 1869 ; **cor anglais** 1870 ; **matinée** 1880 ; **aperçu** 1882 ; **macabre** 1889 (M.E. has this word in the phrase *danse macabre*) ; **fin de siècle** 1890 ; **première** 1895.

Mountaineering : **ravine** 1802 ; **aiguille** 1816 ; **crevasse** 1819 (cf. the M.E. loan *crevice*) ; **couloir** 1855 ; **moulin** 1860 ; **sérac**

1860 ; **gendarme** 1883 (in the sense of ' policeman ' this appears in 1796) ; **névé** (field of snow) 1884 ; **massif** 1885.

Animals and plants : **bêche-de-mer** 1814 ; **guenon** 1838 ; **grivet** 1859 ; **fer-de-lance** 1880 ; **griffon** 1882. **Immortelle** 1832 ; **marguerite** 1866.

Dress, textiles, etc. : **rosette** 1802 ; **fichu** 1803 ; **chemisette** 1807 ; **pouffe** 1817 (a head-dress ; as a cushion, 1884) ; **moiré** 1818 ; **lorgnette** 1820 **(lorgnon** 1846) ; **jabot** 1823 (shirt-frill ; for women, 1881) ; **crêpe** 1825 ; **blouse** 1828 ; **crinoline** 1830 ; **costumier** 1831 ; **décolleté** 1831 ; **trousseau** 1833 ; **lingerie** 1835 ; **négligé** 1835 ; **peignoir** 1835 ; **redingote** 1835 (but first borrowed by French from English *riding-coat*) ; **bijou** 1838 ; **revers** 1838 ; **delaine** 1840 ; **appliqué** 1841 ; **guipure** 1843 ; **paillette** 1843 ; **crochet** 1848 ; **béret** 1850 (Basque cap) ; **passementerie** 1851 ; **modiste** 1852 ; **piqué** 1852 ; **postiche** 1854 ; **corsage** 1857 ; **beige** 1858 ; **genappe** (Belgian place name) 1858 ; **écru** 1869 ; **picot** 1869 ; **brassard** 1870 ; **cretonne** (Normandy place-name, *Creton*) 1870 ; **frou-frou** 1870 ; **tricot** 1872 ; **layette** 1874 ; **chiffon** (first in the plural, ' frills,' etc. ; as material, in 1890) ; **torchon** 1879 ; **pince-nez** 1880 ; **rivière** 1880 ; **ficelle** 1882 ; **suède** 1884 ; **crépon** 1887 ; **voile** 1889.

Food and Cooking : **café** 1816 (coffee-house) ; **gourmet** 1820 ; **à la carte** 1826 ; **restaurant** 1827 ; **menu** 1837 ; **chef** 1842. **Chasse-(café)** 1800 ; **réchauffé** 1805 (first in the figurative sense) ; **sauté** 1813 ; **soufflé** 1813 ; **bonbon** 1818 ; **bain-marie** 1822 ; **consommé** 1824 ; **purée** 1824 ; **vol-au-vent** 1828 ; **mayonnaise** 1841 ; **gratin** 1846 ; **quenelle** 1846 ; **frappé** 1848 ; **charlotte** 1855 ; **sorbet** 1865 (1585 in the sense of ' sherbet ', which has ultimately the same etymology) ; **chartreuse** 1800 ; **fondant** 1877 ; **glacé** 1882 ; **noisette** 1891 ; **mousse** 1892.

Vehicles : **cabriolet** 1823 ; **char-à-banc** 1832 ; **coupé** 1834 ; now transferred to motor-vehicles.

Colours : **ponceau** (a bright red) 1835 ; **cerise** 1858 ; **celeste** 1881 ; **sang-de-bœuf** 1886 (especially of a deep red found in Chinese porcelain).

Physical : **svelte** 1817 ; **physique** 1826 ; **retroussé** 1837 ; **timbre** 1849.

Medical : **râle** 1829 ; **glycerine** 1838 ; **pipette** 1839.

Social : **parvenu** 1802 ; **surveillance** 1802 ; **séance** 1803

M

(of spiritualism, 1845) ; **luxe** 1819 (later, *train-de-luxe*, etc.) ;
soirée 1820 ; **élite** 1823 ; **débutant** 1824 (the feminine form in
1837) ; **née** 1835 ; **pourboire** 1836 ; **convenances** 1847 ;
fiancé 1853 ; **demi-monde** 1855 ; **chic** 1856 ; **rente, rentier**
1881 (with French pronunciation ; cf. *rent*, borrowed in M.E.) ;
déclassé 1887.

Qualities, behaviour, etc. : **bonhomie** 1803 ; **exigeant** 1803 ;
distingué 1813 ; **mot** 1813 ; **savoir faire** 1815 ; **blasé** 1819 ;
volte-face 1819 ; **aplomb** 1828 ; **prestige** 1829 (in modern sense ;
it had been borrowed earlier with the meaning of 'illusion,
conjuring trick'); **camaraderie** 1840; **claque** 1863; **flâneur** 1872 ;
élan 1880 ; **flair** 1881 ; **réclame** 1883 ; **risqué** 1883.

Political and diplomatic : **rapprochement** 1809 ; **secretariat**
1811 ; **laissez-faire** 1825 ; **communism** 1843 ; **entente** 1844 (in
the phrase *entente cordiale*) ; **débacle** 1848 (earlier in this century
in physical sense) ; **impasse** 1851 ; **canard** 1856 ; **visé** 1858 ;
octroi 1861 ; **émeute** 1862 ; **raison d'être** 1867 ; **enclave** 1868 ;
chauvinism 1870 (with reference to the First Empire) ;
dossier 1880.

Miscellaneous : **en masse** 1802 ; **litre** 1810 (the word came into
use in France in 1793) ; **hectare** 1810 ; **mirage** (used by Southey
in figurative sense) 1812 ; in the physical sense, 1837 (Carlyle) ;
battue (of driving game) 1816 ; **genre** 1816 ; **revenant** 1828 ;
cabotage (coasting and coasting-trade) 1831 ; **chute** 1847 ;
clairvoyance 1847 ; **bête noire** 1850 ; **caporal** (tobacco) 1850 ;
savate 1862 ; **coupon** 1864 ; **cloche** (in gardening) 1882 ; **wagon-
lit** 1884.

In the twentieth century words are still being borrowed from
France, though as in the nineteenth century the amount of
naturalization, anglicizing, and popularization which they
undergo varies very much.   Even some quite recent loans are
on everyone's lips, while others, usually of a technical character,
have a restricted use.   They are most frequent now in the
vocabulary of art, literature, the theatre (e.g. **revue, vers libre,
montage**), of dress (**georgette, marocain, rayon,** etc.), and of
mechanics, especially motoring and aviation (**fuselage ; garage**
1902 ; **hangar ; limousine ; longeron ; nacelle**).

These do not complete the whole list of recent borrowings or
occasional borrowings from French.   The reader will be able to

add many more, chiefly of an abstract character, both from this century, and from the latter part of the nineteenth. We may conclude with a few miscellaneous ones : *camouflage* (1917) ; *pension* (with French pronunciation) ; *ballon d'essai* ; *borné* ; *causerie* ; *champlevé* ; *cire-perdue* ; *crême-de-menthe* ; *de trop* ; *éclair* ; *enfant terrible* ; *entre nous* ; *idée fixe* ; *pied à terre.*

And so we leave these French loans, with an acknowledgement of our great debt to a neighbour nation, even if some of the loans are rather unwillingly accepted. The question of repayment does not arise.

Chapter VI

LOW GERMAN AND HIGH GERMAN

A. Low German

Under the term Low German we include the dialects of Dutch (sometimes called Low Franconian), Flemish, and continental Saxon. The last-named includes the local dialects of North Germany, and the term Low German (or *Plattdeutsch*) is sometimes applied specifically to these. The Low German dialects are in many respects nearer in form to English than to High German ; in Old and Middle English particularly the resemblance was very close, and it is indeed sometimes impossible to decide whether a word which is recorded perhaps first in the fourteenth century, and which *may* be a Low German loan, is actually foreign or is really a native word which has until then escaped being recorded in writing.

Already in pre-Conquest times there were connexions between England and the coasts of the Baltic. The racial tie between the peoples of these countries was not entirely broken when the Angles and Saxons left their continental homes. English missionaries travelled and taught in North Germany ; and the literature of that region (the most important extant specimen of which is a poem on the Gospels, called the *Hēliand*, dating from the ninth century) certainly became known to Englishmen, for we possess part of a poem on the Fall of the Angels, translated from Old Saxon, of which fragments of the original still survive. This poem shows certain usages and certain words which reflect the Old Saxon original, though they did not become established in English and can hardly be considered as loan-words.

There is ample historical evidence [1] of the close relations which existed between England and the Dutch and Flemish-speaking countries from the time of the Norman Conquest. The common

[1] See especially J. F. Bense, *Anglo-Dutch Relations from the Earliest Times to the Death of William III*, 1926. Also the same writer's *Dictionary of the Low-Dutch Element in the English Vocabulary*, O.U.P., 1926, etc.

170

commercial interests of these countries in the Middle Ages are well known. Dutch and Flemish immigrants, often skilled workmen in various handicrafts, were constantly settling in England, and their names are to be found in considerable numbers in records from the beginning of the twelfth century down to the present day. English merchants travelled, and sometimes settled, in the Low Countries. English sheep produced the finest wool ; Flemish weavers of the thirteenth century and later were the best of their profession ; not only was English wool sold in large quantities to Flanders, but Flemish workmen came to this country to teach as well as to ply their trade. Nor was this limited to those parts of England which were nearest to the Continent. Wool-growing and weaving centres are known to have existed in all parts of the country, many of the great monastic houses, in particular, maintaining large flocks of sheep. Hence the early Dutch and Flemish words may be found in any part of England ; although far fewer in number, they are less restricted in distribution than the Scandinavian loans of an earlier period.

At the same time, trade was constant between the English ports and those of the Hanseatic League, and this provided at least one route by which Low German words could reach England from the Baltic coast. English sailors and English fishermen were constantly in touch with their Dutch neighbours ; and in Tudor times particularly, English soldiers fought side by side with Dutch and Flemish in the wars in the Low Countries.

Then, too, religion and art both played their part as links across the North Sea, and the honoured position of Dutch painting in the sixteenth and seventeenth centuries led to the introduction into Early Modern English of a number of Dutch words from the vocabulary of art.

It is rather curious that there seems to be no special introduction of Dutch words into English after the coming of a Dutch prince, William III, to this country. But the lists given below show no striking additions in the late seventeenth century which could be ascribed to the influence of the new sovereign or his court.

During the Early Modern and later periods English and Dutch have come into contact or conflict in their colonies. Not many words seem to have been introduced into English as a result of the long struggle between these two nations in the East Indies. The few exceptions are eastern words which entered English through Dutch (e.g. *bamboo* ; see the chapter on Malay-Polynesian). A more important contribution from Dutch to English was made in South Africa. Parts of this area had been Dutch-speaking since the seventeenth century, and when the English at length established themselves at the Cape and elsewhere, they adopted a number of words from Dutch settlers. Some of these at least have become familiar in this country, though most, as will be seen, are used with purely local reference.

Low German words came into English in the greatest numbers in the sixteenth century, even if one considers only those which are still in use. But a few Dutch words can be traced back as early as the beginning of the thirteenth century.

Perhaps the earliest are **poll** ' POLL, head ' and **drivel** ' servant ' (M.Du. *polle*, and M.Flem. *drevel*), which occur in the legend of *St. Margaret*, *c.* 1200 ; *drivel* is found again in the sister-legend of *St. Katherine*, which has also another Low German word : **doten** ' to be foolish, rave ; DOTE ' (M.L.G. *doten*) ; this is to be found also in the earlier manuscript of *Laʒamon* (*c.* 1200) : *me punched þe alde mon wole dotie nou nan* I, 140 ; and as a noun in *Sir Beves of Hamton* : *Aʒilt þe, treitour, þow olde dote!* 217 ; the noun **dotard,** with a French suffix, appears first in the late fourteenth century. The earliest nautical word of Dutch origin which we have is **luff,** from O.Du. *loef*, perhaps through Old French. This occurs in *Laʒamon*, in reference to some device for steering, though the exact meaning is uncertain ; other senses developed later. **Bounce,** in the form **bunsen** (L.G. *bumsen*) is used in the *Ancrene Riwle* (*c.* 1225) ; *Ðer ʒe schulen iseon bunsen ham mit tes deofles bettles* [= clubs] 188 ; here the sense is ' to beat ' ; the intransitive use is not recorded till 1519. The same text has also **snecchen** ' SNATCH ', which seems to be from M.Du. *snacken*, influenced by Eng. *lacchen* and *cacchen*. The North-East Midland writer Orm (*c.* 1200) seems to have only one Low German word, **hucster** ' HUCKSTER ' in the phrase *hucsteres boþe*. Another East Midland poem, the paraphrase of *Genesis and Exodus* (*c.* 1250) has the word **takel** ' TACKLE ' (L.G. *takel*, a Scandinavian loan), in the sense of ' gear, implements '.

The word BOY, whose origin is quite uncertain, but which may be Low German, seems to correspond most closely in form and meaning to East Frisian *boi* ' young gentleman ' ; it is found first in the legend of Beket (MS. Cotton Harley 2277, *c.* 1300) : ʒunge *childerne and wylde boyes also* ; and a little later in the romance of *Havelok*, which has also **ling** (fish ; Du. *lenge*). The word **bouse** ' BOOZE, drink deeply ' also appears during the fourteenth century ; and another Dutch word to do with drinking, or rather brewing, is **gyle** ' quantity of ale brewed at one time ' (besides other technical senses) ; this occurs first in a Yorkshire will of 1341, in the compound *gyle-fatt* (gyle-vat), and later, in the form *gyylde*, in the *Promptorium Parvulorum*, an English–Latin dictionary of about 1440. The fourteenth century also adopted **waynscot** ' WAINSCOT ', originally of a fine oak imported from Holland and used for panelling (*Ely Sacr. Rolls*, 1352) ; **hobble** (M.Du. *hobbelen* ' to rock from side to side ' ; *out of heuene into helle hobleden faste* Piers Plowman A I, 113 ; *c.* 1362) ; **splint,** first in the sense of a metal plate or peg (M.Du. *splente* ; *He was armyd in splentes of steel* Richard Coer de Lyon 4979) ; **kit** (M.Du. *kitte*), first in the sense of ' tub ', 1375 ; **flue,** a kind of fishing-net (M.Du. *vlouwe* ; *j rete vocatum wade et j flowe* Accounts of Abingdon Abbey, Camden Soc., 1388–9) ; **kilderkin** ' cask, half a barrel ' (M.Du. *kindekyn*), 1390 ; **skipper** (M.Du. *schipper*, master of a ship) 1390 ; and finally **Lollard,** which is from M.Du. *Lollaerd*, formed from the verb *lollen* ' to hum ' ; the Dutch word was applied first, about 1300, to members of a fraternity who cared for the sick, and arranged funerals for the poor ; they had achieved a reputation for exaggerated piety and humility.

The fifteenth-century Dutch loans are nearly all nautical, commercial, and industrial. The chief source is the *Promptorium Parvulorum* (mentioned above) from East Anglia. (Words dated 1440 are from this work, which also contains a number of other Low German words which do not occur here for the first time.)

Commercial : **firkin** 1423 in one of the Acts of Henry VI ; probably from a M.Du. *verdelkijn*) ; **mart** 1437 (M.Du. *marct,* like *market*, from Lat. *mercatus* ; in the first instances referring to the markets of Antwerp and Bruges) ; **hop** (plant) 1440

(O.Du. *hoppe* ; England had a native *humulus*, but the
variety used in brewing was perhaps introduced from Flanders,
together with other things used in the brewing industry) ;
pickle (M.Du. *pekel*) 1440 ;   **spool** (M.Du. *spoele*) 1440 ;
rack n. 1440 (L.Germ. *rakk* ;   the *Prompt. Parv.* has
rakke as equivalent to *praesepe* 422 ;   Wyclif (and other
writers) associates it with ' manger ' :   *at racke and at manger*,
etc.) ;   **sled** (M.Du. *sledde*) 1440 ;   **selvedge** (E.Mod.Du. *selfegghe*,
but assimilated to *self* + *edge* ;   first in the *Boke of Curtasye*
1460, with reference to the selvedge of the ' dowbull napere '
on the table) ;   **guilder,** apparently from the Flemish *gulden*,
1481 (Caxton) ;   **corf,** a kind of basket of fish, etc., 1483 (Caxton) ;
Mechlin (lace) 1483 ;   **excise** (M.Du. *excijs*, from Lat.) 1494.

Nautical :   **marline** (Du. *marlijn*) 1417 :   **buoy** (M.Du. *boje,
boei*) 1466 ;   **deck** (Du. *dec* ' roof, covering ' ;   the nautical sense
seems to be a development in English of the sense ' roof ' etc.
(also found in English) ;   this meaning does not appear in Dutch
till the seventeenth century) 1466 ;   **orlop** (M.L.G. *overlōp*)
1467 ;   **hoist,** variant of **hoise** (Du. *hijschen*) 1490 (Caxton) ;
hoy (*An hoye of Dorderyght*, Paston Letters 1495 ;   M.Du. *hoy*) ;
hose (M.Du. *hoos*, the same word as Eng. *hose* ' stocking ' ;
makyng of hoses for the pompes of the seid ship Naval Accounts,
Henry VII, 1495).

Military :   **bulwark** 1430 (Lydgate) ;   M.Du. has *bolwerk*,
probably from M.H.G. *bolewerc* ;   it is used first of a rampart,
earthwork, etc. (cf. Fr. *boulevard*, also from Dutch) ;   the nautical
sense is not found till 1804.

Miscellaneous :   **pip** (M.Du. *pip* ;   *Other while an hen wul ha
the pippe, / A whit pilet that wul the tonge enrounde*) c. 1420
(*Palladius on Hosebondrie*); **brake,** in three senses all perhaps from
Du. or L.G. :   ' thicket ' (M.L.G. *brake*) 1440 ;   ' instrument for
beating flax ' 1440, but the verb a little earlier, 1398 ;   for
vehicle (M.Du. *braeke*) 1430 ;   **boor** ' peasant ' (Du. *boer*, whence
the later *Boer* ;   M.L.G. *būr* ;   *Of tilthe of lande treteth the boueer*
Lydgate) 1430 ;   **loiter** (probably M.Du. *leuteren* ;   1440, unless
the emendation of *loltrande* to *loitrande* (Pres. Part.) in the
alliterative poem of *Patience* 458 be accepted) ;   **placard** 1481,
but through French *plaque* (cf. Mod. *plaque*), which formed the
noun from the M.Du. verb *placken* ' to stick ' ;   it was used of a

formal document with a seal stuck on to it ; the suffix -*ard* is
French ; **bruin** 1481 (Caxton's translation of the popular epic
Reynard the Fox) ; **snap** n. (Du. *snap*) 1495 ; the verb (Du.
snappen) appears in 1530 ; **groove** (M.Du. *groeve* ' trench,
groove ' ; *Wars of Alexander*, fifteenth century, in the sense of
' cave ' ; later it means ' channel, hollow ; mine, pit ') ; **luck**
(M.Du. *luc* ; *Wher-for lucke and good hanselle my hert y sende you*
Political, Religious, and Love Poems of the XV Century).

The sixteenth century introduced a number of military words
from the Low Countries, and its close also brought us the first
of the Dutch words relating to art, most of which are recorded
first in the following century. Nautical words are still to the fore.

Commercial and industrial : **gulden** (early sixteenth century) ;
stiver (Du. *stuiver*) 1502 ; **hawker** (from M.L.G. *hoker*, or perhaps
from *hac* ' retail dealer ') 1510 ; **scone** (probably shortened from
L.G. *schonbrod*) 1513 ; **isinglass** (O.Du. *huizenblas* ' sturgeon's
bladder ', assimilated to *glass*) 1528 ; **cambric** (from the Flemish
place-name *Kamerijk* = Cambrai) 1530 ; **muff** (Du. *mof*)
1579 (Ben Jonson) ; **flue,** earlier **floow** ' woolly fluff ' (M.Du.
vloe, or W.Flem. *vluwe*) 1589 ; **doit** (M.Du. *duit*) 1594 ; **anker,**
a liquid measure, 1597 ; **rix-dollar** (Du. *rijksdaler*) 1598.

Nautical : **dock** (M.Du. *docke*) 1513 ; **splice** (M.Du. *splissen* ;
recorded in England first of bell-ropes : *Paid for Splisyng of
v bell ropis vd* Records of St. Mary at Hill) 1524 ; **rove,** originally
' to practise piracy ' (Du. *rooven*) 1536 ; **train-**(oil) 1553
(Chancelour, in Hakluyt's *Voyages*, with reference to whaling) ;
yacht (Du. *jacht*) 1557 ; **freebooter** (M.Du. *vribueter* ' pirate ')
1570 ; **shallop** 1578 (Du. *sloep*, through Fr. *chaloupe* ; cf. *sloop*
in the seventeenth century) ; **monsoon** 1684 (originally Arabic ;
came into Dutch through Portuguese) ; **reef** ' ridge of rock ',
earlier **riff** (Du. *ref, rif*) 1584 ; **filibuster** (like *freebooter*, from
Du. *vribueter* ; the *l* is perhaps due to Du. *vlieboot*, Eng. **flyboat**
1577) 1587 ; **swabber** (Du. *zwabber*) 1592, of part of crew.

Military : **sutler** (Du. *zootelaer*) 1500 ; **wag(g)on** 1523 (Berners,
Froissart ; Du. *wagen*) ; **uproar** ' insurrection ' (Du. *oproer*)
1526 ; **snaffle** (Du. *snavel*) 1533 ; **snaphance,** of the cock of a gun
(Du. *snaphaan*), 1538 in a transferred sense, of an armed robber ;
forlorn hope, originally a picked detachment leading an attack
(Du. *verloren hoop* ' lost troop '), 1539 ; the abstract sense is

found already in 1572 ; **hackbut** (through Fr. *haquebut*, from Du. *haakbus*) 1541 ; **linstock** 1560 (Du. *lontstok* 'match stick' ; it has been influenced in English by *lint*, i.e. flax used as tinder) ; **beleaguer** (Du. *belegeren*) 1589 ; (land)**loper** (Du. *looper* 'runner '), before 1583.

People : **younker** 'young man' (Du. *jonker*) 1505 ; **minikin** 'darling ' (M.Du. *minnekijn*) 1541 ; **minx** (E.Mod.Du. *mensch*, of woman in depreciatory sense in neuter) 1542 ; **palsgrave** 'Count Palatine' 1548 ; **margrave** (M.Du. *marcgrave* ; *The marcgraue as thei call him of Bruges*, Robinson's translation of More's *Utopia*) 1551 ; **burgher** 1568 ; **quacksalver** (Du. *kwak-zalver*), Gosson's *School of Abuse* 1579 ; **burgomaster** (Du. *burgemeester*, with assimilation of the second element to *master*) 1592 ; **wiseacre** (M.Du. *wijs-segger*, from M.H.G. *weis-sager*) 1595.

Art : **manikin** 1570 (E.Mod.Du. *manneken* ; *Thus, of a Manneken, (as the Dutch painters terme it)* . . . *may a Giant be made* ; cf. Fr. *mannequin*, also from Dutch ; this appears in English in 1911) ; (land)**scape** (M.Du. *lantscap*) 1598.

Miscellaneous : (i) Verbs : **mum** 'to act in dumb-show' (Mod.Du. *mommen* 'to mask, masquerade ') 1530, but the noun *mumming, c.* 1465 ; **foist** (M.Du. *vuysten* 'to take in the fist' ; perhaps introduced first as a gambling term) 1545 ; **snip** (Du. *snippen* 'to cut in small pieces ') 1558 ; **spatter** (apparently a frequentative from Du. *spatten* 'to burst, spout ') 1582 (Stanyhurst's *Æneis*) ; **ravel** (M.Du. *ravelen*) 1582 ; **domineer** (Du. *domineeren*, which is from French) 1588 ; **split** (M.Du. *splitten*) 1590 ; **rant** (M.Du. *ranten*) 1598. (ii) Other words : **litmus** (M.Du. *leecmoes*) 1502, spelt *lyʒtmose* ; **fitch** 'pole-cat ' (M.Du. *vitsche*) 1502 ; **spit** n., of earth in digging, 1507–8 ; **frolic** adj. (M.Du. *vrolyc* ; *And make frowlyke chere*, Bale's *Thre Lawes*) 1538 ; the verb in 1583 ; **pad** 'path, track ', 1554, originally a slang term (Du. *pad*) ; **siskin** 1562 (M.Du. *sijsken*, from L.G. *zieske*, from Slav. *czyżik*) ; **kermess** (Du. *kermis*, from M.Du. *kerk-misse*) 1577.

The seventeenth century brought in rather fewer words than the sixteenth ; they belong for the most part to the sea, to warfare, and to art.

Commercial and industrial : **coper** (M.Du. *coper* 'merchant ') 1609 ; **brandy,** earlier **brandewine** (Du. *brandewijn* 'vinum ardens') 1622 ; **stoker** 1660 (of brewer's furnace) ; **stum,** unfermented grape-juice, 1662 (Du. *stom*) ; **duffel** (from name of town in Brabant) 1677 ; **smuggle** (L.G. *smuggeln*) 1687.

Nautical : **smack** (M.Du. *smacke*) 1611 ; **keelhaul** (E.Mod.Du. *kielhalen*) 1626 ; **garboard** (Du. *gaarboord*) 1626 ; **sloop** (Du. *sloep*) 1629 ; **hooker** (E.Mod.Du. *hoeck-boot*) 1641 ; **cruise** (Du. *kruisen* ; this loan belongs to the time of the first Anglo-Dutch war) 1651 ; **walrus** (Du., from Swed. *vallross*) 1655 ; **jib** 1661 (this seems to be a variant of **gybe** 1693 ; Du. *gijben*) ; **patroon** ' master of a ship ', etc. (Du. *patroon*) 1662 ; **yawl** (Du. *jol*) 1670.

Military : **knapsack** (Du. *knapzak*) 1603 ; **onslaught** (Du. *aanslag* ; influenced by *slaughter*) 1625 ; **furlough** (Du. *verlof*) 1625 ; **tattoo** (Du. *taptoe*) 1644 ; **blunderbuss** (an altered form of Du. *dunderbus*) 1654.

Art : **easel** (Du. *ezel*) 1654 ; **maulstick** (Du. *maalstok*, re-formed with Eng. second element) 1658 ; **sketch** (Du. *schets*, a loan from Ital. *schizzo* ; the Latin word from which this comes is used in a literary sense, and is itself a loan-word from Greek) 1668 ; **stipple** (Du. *stippelen*) 1669 ; **lay-**(man) ' lay-figure ' (Du. *leeman*) 1688 ; *lay-figure* in 1795.

Agriculture, etc. : **decoy,** also **coy,** 1618 (Du. *kooi* ' cage ' ; the source of the *de-* is doubtful ; it may be the Dutch definite article) ; **morass** (Du. *moeras*, from French ; in the earlier part of the seventeenth century many Dutchmen were employed on the drainage of the fens) 1655.

People : **outlander** 1605 (Verstegan ; English in form, but suggested by Du. *uitlander*) ; **Dopper** ' Baptist ' (E.Mod.Du. *dooper* ; later from S. African Dutch = member of the Dutch Reformed Church of S. Africa) 1620.

Miscellaneous : (i) Verbs : **hanker** (Flem. *hankeren*) 1601 ; **slur** (M.Du. *sleuren* ' to draggle ') 1609 ; **drill** vb. ' to bore ' (E.Mod.Du. *drillen*) 1611 ; other senses from this or directly from Dutch ; **snort** (L.G. *snorten*) 1619 ; **shamble** (M.Du. *schampelen*) 1681 ; **snuff** (M.Du. *snuffen* ' to clear the nose ') 1683 ; the noun is from the verb ; **hustle** (Du. *hutselen*) 1684 (Otway). (ii) Other words : **spancel** (M.Du. *spansel*) 1610 ; **skate** (Du. *schaatz*, from Fr. *eschace* ' stilt ', from L.G. *shake* ' leg ' ; so the word is, as it were, doubly from Low German)

1656 ; **slim** 1657 ; **spelter** (L.G. *spialter*) 1661 (Boyle) ; **abele** (Du., from Fr. ; *a finer sort of white Poplar, which the Dutch call abele* 1681) ; **mallemuck,** the fulmar (Du. *mallemok*) 1694.

The eighteenth century is specially remarkable for the beginning of the introduction of words from South African Dutch ; the earliest is from 1731. These are due partly to political contacts between the two races in the Cape of Good Hope, but mostly to the writings of travellers.

Commercial : **geneva** (Du. *jenever*, from O.Fr. *genevre* from Lat. *juniperus* ; the word was wrongly associated in English with the Place-Name Geneva) 1706 ; the shortened form **gin** appears in 1714 ; **colza** (Du. *koolzaad* = coleseed, through French *colsat, colza*) 1712 ; **lambrequin** (Du. *lamperkin*, again through French) 1725.

Nautical : **schooner** (this is Du. *schooner*, apparently borrowed first from Eng. *scoon* ' to skim over the water ' ; reborrowed by English from Dutch in America) 1716 ; **pea-jacket** (probably from Frisian *pijekkat* ; again found first in America) 1725 *New Jersey Archives* ; **drogher,** a vessel used in the coasting-trade of the West Indies, 1756 ; **caboose** (M.Du. *kabuse*) 1769 ; **vang** 1769 ; **scow** (Du. *schouw*) 1775.

Military : **roster** (Du. *rooster*) 1727.

Miscellaneous : **spillikin** (M.Du. diminutive of *spille* ' pin, peg ') 1734 ; **wentletrap** (Du. *wenteltrap* ; earlier ' spiral stair ') 1758 ; **mangle** n. (Du. *mangel* ; ultimately from Greek *magganon*) 1774 ; **dune** (M.Du. *duun*, but through French ; ultimately the same word as *down*) 1790 ; **moss-bunker** ' menhaden ' (Du. *marsbunker*) 1792 ; **trass,** a volcanic earth used as cement, (Du. *tras*, from Ital. *terrazza*) 1796.

South African : **kloof** 1731 (Medley's translation of Kolben's *Cape of Good Hope* : *kloof, as the Dutch call it* ; so not really accepted as a loan-word) ; **steenbok, springbok** (Masson, *journey to the Cape*) 1775 ; **duiker, gemsbok** (Forster, *Voyage Round the World*) 1777 ; **ratel** 1777 ; **klipspringer** 1785 ; **eland, hartebeest, grysbok** (Sparrman, *Voyage to the Cape of Good Hope*) 1786 ; **krantz,** earlier **krants** 1798.

In the nineteenth century the greater number of Dutch loans are from South Africa, several appearing first in newspaper reports. A few words come first into American English.

Nautical : **taffrail** (Du. *tafereel*) 1814 ; **flench, flense,** a whaling term, 1814 (the whaling industry was mainly in the hands of the Dutch until the late eighteenth century, after which the English interest in it increased largely) ; **specktioneer,** the chief harpooner in a whaler, (Du. *spek-snijer*, from *spek* ' blubber ' + *snijden* ' to cut ') 1820.

Miscellaneous : **sprue,** a tropical disease (Du. *spruw*) 1825 ; **plaque** (French from Flemish) 1848 ; **schipperke** 1887.

Words borrowed by American English : **spook** 1801 (in an American journal) ; **waffle** (Du. *wafel*) 1808 ; **boss** (Du. *baas*) 1822 ; **dope** 1880.

South African : **meerkat** 1801 (Barrow, *Travels in South Africa*) ; **aardvark, aardwolf** 1833 ; **wildebeest** 1838. **Veldt** 1801 ; **sjambok** 1804 (Dutch from Malay—a reflection of the Dutch power in the East Indies—originally Persian : *chabūq* ' whip ') ; **biltong** 1815 ; **stoep, outspan** (Burchell's *Travels*) 1822 ; **commando,** military party, 1834 ; **knobkerrie** (the second element is Hottentot), **trek** 1849 (Napier, *Excursions in S. Africa*) ; **predikant** (*Daily News*) 1849 ; **laager** 1850 ; **inspan** 1850 ; **spoor** (Cumming, *A Hunter's Life in S. Africa*) 1850 ; **mealie** 1853 (Du. from Portuguese) ; **commandeer** (*The Times*, with reference to the Boers) 1881 ; **kopje** (*Contemporary Review*) 1881 ; **banket,** a gold-mining term, 1886 ; **taal** 1898.

B. High German

There was less direct influence of High German on English in the earlier stages of the language than we have found in the case of French, Dutch, or Scandinavian. It has already been indicated that French possessed a number of words which came originally from Germanic or High German, and some at least of these came into English during the Middle English period ; but until the sixteenth century the only word which appears to have reached this country directly from Southern Germany is the Old English word for the Greeks : *Crēacas*, which comes, it has been maintained, from O.H.G. *Kriaha* (from Lat. *Graec-*), in which the initial consonant represents the regular change of *g* to *k* in the South German dialects ; this explanation of the Old English form is, however, doubtful.

The most distinctive contribution of German to English has been in the domain of mineralogy, and though many of these words have remained only in technical use, some are in universal use, e.g. *zinc*, *nickel*. The Germans were noted for their skill in mining and metal-work as early as the fifteenth century, and in the late sixteenth century German workmen (*certayn Almaynes*) were brought into England for working the copper and other ores in Cumberland and elsewhere. Elizabeth incorporated two companies for working the English mines, and many Germans were employed by them.[1]

Beginning in the sixteenth century, the first German loan-words which can be certainly traced are the following : **landgrave** 1516 ; **junker,** a young German noble (cf. Dutch *jonker*, adopted in English as *younker*), 1554 ; **kreutzer** 1547 ; **lobby** 1553 ; originally a monastic term, coming into English from Mediaeval Latin *laubia*, *lobia* (from O.H.G. **laubja*) rather than directly from German ; from the same Latin form the French *loge* is derived, borrowed in Middle English as *lodge* ;. **kinchin** ' child ', a cant term, from Germ. *kindchen*, 1561 ; **carouse** n. and vb., through French from Germ. (*trinken*) *gar aus* ' drink to the last drop ', 1567.

Seventeenth century loans are only slightly more numerous : Commercial : **groschen** 1617 ; **drill** (fabric, Germ. *drillich*) is abbreviated from the earlier *drilling*, which is found in 1640 ; **silesia,** a fine linen or cotton fabric (made originally in *Silesia*, which is the Latinized form of *Schlesien*) 1674.   Military : **lansquenet,** a mercenary soldier, 1607 (Germ. *landsknecht*, through French) ; **plunder** (Germ. *plündern*) 1632 ; **shabrach,** a saddle-cloth (originally a Turkish word) 1667 ; **sabre** (through French from Germ. *sabel*, but Slavonic in origin) 1680. Mineralogical : **zinc** 1651 ; **guhr** (from a Germ. dialect) 1686. Products of, and things specially associated with, Germany : **hamster,** a .kind of rodent, 1607 ; **sauerkraut** 1617 ; **morgen,** a measure of land, 1674 ; **krummhorn,** a musical instrument, 1694 ; a French version of this word appears also in the same year (**cromorne**) ; and finally the German word for a water-nymph, **undine,** fairly well known, though hardly naturalized

---

[1] See the Charter of the Mines Royal, 1568, and letters concerning English and Welsh mines and German miners, in R. H. Tawney and E. Power, *Tudor Economic Documents,* vol. i, London, 1924.

(the word in German was formed from the Mod. Lat. *Undina*, coined by Paracelsus).

Mineralogical and geological terms become more numerous in the eighteenth century, forming indeed more than half of this century's contribution. We find in addition such familiar words as *iceberg* and *waltz.*

Military : **hetman** 1710 (this is actually a Polish form of the German *hauptmann*, and was used for a captain or military commander in Poland) ; **uhlan** 1753 (this came to us from German, but that language borrowed it from Polish, in which it was a loan-word from Turkish *ughlān* ' son, youth, servant ') ; **jaeger** ' rifleman ' (Germ. *jäger*, originally ' hunter ') 1776.

Mineralogical, etc. : **cobalt** 1728 (Germ. *kobalt*, probably the same word as *kobold*) ; **seltzer** (Germ. *Selterser*, from *Selters*, a village in Prussia) 1741 ; **shale,** a laminated rock (Germ *schale* ' scale ') 1747 ; **quartz** 1756 ; **spath(ic)** 1763 ; **fel(d)spar** (Germ. *feldspar*) 1757 (Costa, *Natural History of Fossils*) ; **sinter** 1757 ; **gneiss, wolfram** (Henckel's *Pyritology*) 1757 ; **hornblende** 1770 ; **nickel** 1775 ; **schorl** 1779 ; **meerschaum** 1784 ; **nephrite** 1794 ; **speiss** 1796 ; **wacke** 1796.

Products of Germany : **maw**(seed), seed of the opium poppy, 1730 (Germ. dial. *mahsaat*, cf. Germ. *mohn* ' poppy ') ; **landau** 1743 (Place-Name) ; **pumpernickel** 1756 ; **zinke,** a musical instrument, 1776 ; **mangel-wurzel** (Germ. *mangold-wurzel* ' beet + root ') 1779 ; **waltz** 1781 (the French form of this, *valse*, appears in English in 1796).

Miscellaneous : **zigzag** (through French from Germ. *zickzack*) 1712 ; **veneer** n. 1702, vb. 1728 (a curious example of borrowing and re-borrowing ; Germ. *furnieren*, which became Eng. *veneer*, is from French *fourner*, from an O.H.G. form) ; **iceberg** 1774 (Germ. *eisberg*).

Nineteenth century : Military : **fugleman** (Germ. *flügelmann*) 1804 ; **landsturm** 1814 ; **landwehr** 1815 ; and here might be included the French **kepi** 1861, which is from German-Swiss *käppi*.

Mineralogy : **gangue** (through French, from Germ. *gang*) 1809 ; **loess** 1835 ; **spiegeleisen** 1868 ; **kainite** 1868 ; **kieselguhr** 1875.

Birds and animals : **lammergeier** 1817 ; **poodle** 1825 (Germ.

pudel(*hund*), from L.G. *pudeln* ' to splash ') ;   **spitz** 1845 ; **dachshund** 1881.

Food and drink :   **vermouth** (French *vermout*, from Germ. *wermuth*) 1806 ;   **schnapps** 1818 ;   **lager** 1853 ;   **kirsch** 1869 ; **kümmel** 1882 ;   **marzipan** 1891 (the origin of this German word is unknown ;   corresponding forms occur in many European languages, including English, which has *marchpane*, found first in the fifteenth century, now quite superseded by the German form).

Music :   **kapellmeister** 1838 ;   **zither** 1850 ;   **leitmotiv** 1876 (with reference to the operas of Wagner) ;   **humoresque** (Germ. *humoreske*) 1889.

Words relating to Switzerland :   **alpenstock** 1829 ;   **yodel** (Germ. *jodeln*) 1830 ;   **edelweiss** 1862.

Educational :   **semester** (Germ. from Latin) 1827 ;   **kindergarten** 1852, type of school devised by Friedrich Fröbel (1782– 1852) ;   **seminar** 1889.

Scientific :   **paraffin** (Germ. name invented by Reichenbach in 1830) 1835 ;   **protein** (Germ. from Greek) 1869 ;   **ohm** 1870 (from the name of a German physicist) ;   and we may include here **veronal** 1903.

Miscellaneous :   **kohl-rabi** (Germ. from Ital. *cavoli rape* ' colerape ') 1807 ;   **deckle** (Germ. *deckel*) 1810 ;   **barouche** (Germ. dial. *barutsche*, from Ital. *barrocio*) 1813 ;   **buhl** (Germ. adaptation of the French name *Boule*) 1823 ;   **kobold** 1830 ;   **nix,** a water-sprite, 1833 ;   **poltergeist** 1838 ;   **philippine** 1848 (through French from Germ. *vielliebchen,* approximated to the personal name *Philippe*) ; **kursaal** 1849 ;   **schottische** (Germ. *schottische tanz* ' Scottish dance ') 1854 ;   **rinderpest,** a disease of cattle, 1865 ;   **coburg** a fabric, 1882 ;   **hinterland** 1890 ;   **zeitgeist** 1893 ;   **rucksack** 1895.

CHAPTER VII

THE ITALIAN ELEMENT

Next [1] to Latin, French, and Scandinavian, the language to which English owes the greatest number of foreign words is Italian. Its influence, however, extends over a shorter period, while it must be remembered that a good many Italian loans have come to us, not directly, but through French, and that a good many also are not naturalized here, but retain in some measure an Italian form or application, or both (e.g. *gondola, doge, camorra, condottiere*), even though some have settled down entirely as English words (e.g. *race* 'stock', *traffic, umbrella, artichoke*, and even *volcano* and *macaroni*). It is the vocabularies of art, music, and literature that have acquired most from Italian during the last three centuries, but the earliest Italian loans were of a commercial or military character.

Of loans before the sixteenth century there are very few, and all came through French. Even diplomatic relations in the Middle Ages, and a slowly increasing acquaintance with contemporary Italian literature during the fourteenth century (culminating in Chaucer's translations from the Italian) seem to have brought to this country few or no Italian terms to add to the common stock. But when the Tudor period begins there is an inrush of new terms from Italy, and Italian borrowing reaches its peak in the second half of the sixteenth century. During the fifteenth and sixteenth centuries (and even in the fourteenth) there was a direct connexion between England and Italy through the Flanders galleys, which carried the Flemish trade ; these sailed to Venice regularly every year, and part of the fleet touched as regularly at three English ports on their return from Italy.

It has just been said that trade terms owe much to Italy, and it is in these words of Tudor times that to us nowadays commerce seems to wear its aspect of highest romance. Perhaps there is

---

[1] See especially Mario Praz, *The Italian Element in English,* in *Essays and Studies by Members of the English Association,* vol. xv, 1929.

N

some magic in the Italian words themselves, or perhaps it is
partly literary associations that stir the mind when we read of
caravel, of frigate, of galleass, or of the ocean where—

> argosies with portly sail
> Like signiors and rich burghers on the flood
> Or, as it were, the pageants of the sea,
> Do overpeer the petty traffickers,
> That curtsy to them, do them reverence,
> As they fly by them with their woven wings.

But even as the commerce of England was preparing to carry
the words of Italy farther and farther afield, the strength of
Italian trade was beginning to decline. From the early sixteenth
century Spain and Portugal led the way across the oceans, while
Italy's scope remained within the confines of the Mediterranean
coasts. However, while Italian commercial terms in English
increase little in number after the end of the sixteenth century,
words relating to the arts, which have by then begun to make
their appearance, accumulate fast in succeeding periods. Names
of musical instruments and types of music (beginning with the
madrigal), terms of art and of literature (beginning with the
sonnet on the one hand, and with the *buffoon* of Italian comedy
on the other), are as common as words of trade by the end of
the century.

But we must turn back to the Middle English period to consider
those words which can be traced back to Italian, even though
they came to us indirectly. To the fourteenth century belong
florin (Ital. *fiorino*, through French, and influenced by Latin ;
it owes its name to the fact that when first minted at Florence
it bore the city's badge, a lily), earliest in 1303, and thereafter
several times in that century ; the military **alarm** (from French,
from Ital. *allarme* = *all' arme* ' to arms ! ') from 1325 ; **million**
(Chaucer, *milioun* ; Ital. *millione*) 1362 ; commercial again in
ducat 1384 (Ital. *ducato*). The word **Lombard** reminds us of the
connexion in this country between Italians and banking ; it
acquired the general sense of ' financial agent, banker ' in Old
French ; the same development of sense took place in English,
and already in the fourteenth century Langland uses *Lumbardes*
without geographical implication.

In the fifteenth century **brigand** (Chaucer, *brigaunt* 1400) brings to our minds a danger to commerce, while **mizzen** (Fr., from Ital. *mezzana*) 1465, and **bark** (Fr. *barque*, Ital. *barca*) 1475, carry trade to sea. One article of trade is to be found in the fish-name **tunny** 1480 which is (through French) from Ital. *tonno* (from Latin, but before that Greek, and probably ultimately from a pre-Hellenic Mediterranean language).

During the sixteenth century words came to us directly from Italy, and not only by way of France. This is partly due to the growing fashion of travel in Italy, whence many travellers returned imbued with Italian manners and customs, as well as with a knowledge of the language, and partly to a far closer acquaintance with Italian literature than there had been before. Translations from Italian became numerous, and the popularity of Italian plots, characters, and scenes may be seen by a glance at Shakespeare alone, to say nothing of Jonson, Massinger, Beaumont, and Fletcher, and others of his successors. Poets such as Wyatt and Surrey brought us Italian forms of verse, and Spenser and lesser writers after him owe much to Ariosto in characters, in episodes, in turns of phrase, if not in temper.[1] Ariosto has indeed given us the word *rodomontade* (see below), and it has been suggested that the popularity of the word *paladin* at one time is due to his influence.

Let us now consider the individual loans which belong to this century, and make an attempt at classifying them. First, words indicating rank and office and people in general : **race** (Fr., from Ital. *razza*) 1500 is now used universally ; **nuncio** 1528 is chiefly used now, as in the sixteenth century, of a Papal ambassador, but it will be remembered that Shakespeare could use it as a general term for ' messenger '[2] ; **poltroon** 1529 is interesting in form, since it is the first of a number of loans in which *-oon* represents an Anglicizing of French *-on* from Ital. *-one* (cf. *balloon* ; *bassoon* ; *maroon* ; *pantaloon*, etc.) ; **artisan** (Fr. from Ital. *artigiano*, cf. *partisan* for the form) 1538 is now thoroughly English ; **podesta** 1548 was known first, as it was used in Italy, for the governor, under the Empire, of a city of

---

[1] See especially B. E. C. Davis, *Edmund Spenser*, pp. 84 ff.

[2] ' She will attend it better in thy youth / Than in a nuncio of more grave aspect '—*Twelfth Night,* I, iv.

Lombardy, but its use was extended later to the chief magistrate of other cities, though it is still confined to Italy, as is also **doge** 1549 (Venetian) ; **partisan** ' supporter ' appears in 1555, and **populace** (Fr., from Ital. *popolaccio*), another word of general application, in 1572 ; **magnifico** 1573 and **signor** 1577 were applied to Italian noblemen and gentlemen. Other aspects of Italian life are reflected in **mountebank** 1577 (Ital. *montambanco*) and **bravo** ' villain ' 1597, the former now having the wider use. **Madonna** is used as a form of address to a lady, in Shakespeare and elsewhere (first in 1584) ; as a term of art, signifying a picture of the Madonna, it is found first in 1644. **Pedant** is also used by Shakespeare in the sense of ' schoolmaster, tutor '.

Social activities, customs, clothes, etc. : **gambol** 1503 ; **scope** 1534, now a word of very wide application, came into English with the sense of ' space for free exercise of movement ', though its original meaning had been ' target, mark, thing aimed at ' ; **peruke** (Fr. from Ital. *perruca*) 1547 ; **disgrace** (Fr. *disgracier*, Ital. *disgraziare*) 1549 ; **ballot,** with reference to voting, 1549 ; **gondola** 1549 ; **carnival** 1549 ; **lazaretto** 1549 ; (these last four from Thomas's *History of Italie*) ; **cassock** 1550 was not always a term of clerical dress, but was used earlier for a long, loose gown which might be either civil or military ; as applied to the dress of an Anglican clergyman it is used first in 1663 ; **mustachio** has been referred to already under its French form *moustache* (Ital. *mostaccio*) ; the (more or less) Italian form is still occasionally used ; it appears in 1551 ; **strappado** 1560 (Ital. *strappata*) has had its suffix re-formed, perhaps on the analogy of Spanish words in *-ado* ; most of the Italian words in *-ata* have come to us with the French form of the suffix : *-ade* (e.g. *arcade*) ; **lottery** 1567 (this is ultimately a Gmc. word) ; **pall-mall** 1568 (Fr. *pallemaille*, from Ital. *pallamaglio*) ; this game is now obsolete, but its name, used also for the type of alley in which it was played, has survived in the London street-name *Pall-Mall*, which dates from 1656 ; **galligaskins,** still occasionally used for a kind of breeches, or gaiters, is an irregular form from Fr. *garguesque* from Ital. *grechesca*, a feminine adjectival form meaning ' in the Greek fashion, *à la grecque* ' ; it is found first in 1577 ; **seraglio** (Ital. *serr-*) 1581, referring originally to the palace of the Sultan at Constantinople ; **garb**

1591 has the general sense of ' fashion, style, manner ' ; Ital. *garbo* meant rather ' grace, elegance ' ; **concert** 1598 is found first as a verb, ' to bring to accord, bring into agreement ' ; the noun does not appear till 1656, in a musical sense in 1689 ; **biretta** 1598, and the now obsolete card-playing term **taroc, tarot** (Ital. *tarocca*) 1598, close this century.

Italian products, plants, etc., give us very few words at this period : **rocket** (the herb), Fr. *roquette*, from Ital. *ruchetta*, 1530 ; **tarantula** (Ital. *-ola*) 1561 ; **belladonna** 1597 ; **macaroni** (Ital. *maccaroni*, later *maccheroni*) 1599.

Terms relating to military matters, or to horsemanship, for which the Italian was celebrated, are fairly numerous, and many have survived, often with changed or generalized meanings. **Plastron** 1506, through French, representing Ital. *piastrone* ; **post** 1506 (Fr. from Ital. *posta*) was applied first to the relays of mail-carriers who bore royal despatches ; **pistol** 1550 is shortened from **pistolet,** a French derivative of Ital. *pistol-ese*, from the Place-Name *Pistoia* (Tuscany) ; **panache** 1553 (Fr., from Ital. *pennacchio*) ; **partisan,** a kind of pike, 1566 (Ital. *partesana*) ; this seems to have become obsolete at the end of the seventeenth century, but was revived by Scott ; **cartel** 1560 (Ital. *cartello*) was a written challenge ; **cavalier** 1560 now has several specialized meanings, but was in origin simply a horse-soldier ; **manage** 1561 has now acquired a very wide application, but was once a term of horsemanship, Ital. *maneggiare*, to control a horse, put it through its paces, etc. ; cf. the French form *manège* n., which retains this sense ; **squadron** (Ital. *squadrone*) 1562 ; **postillion** (Fr., from Ital. *postiglione*) 1565 ; **casemate** 1575, a term in fortification, probably represents Ital. *casa*, but the origin of the second element of the word is unknown ; **curvet** (Ital. *corvetta*) 1575 n. again refers to horses ; **bandolier** 1577 (Ital., from a Gmc. stem) ; **escort** (Fr., from Ital. *scorta*) in a military sense in 1579 ; **gabion** (Ital. *gabione*) 1579 ; **citadel** (Ital. *cittadella*, through French) 1586 ; **musket** (Fr. from Ital. *moschetto*) 1587 ; **duel(lo)** has the two forms already in the sixteenth century, *duello* in 1588, *duel* 1591 ; it may be mentioned that most of the technical fencing-terms now used are from, or through, French, but some appear to be Spanish, and a few, such as *riposte*, are in origin Italian ; **battalion** (Fr., from Ital. *battaglione* 1589) ;

ravelin (Fr. from Ital. *ravellino*) 1589 ;   **parapet** (Ital. *-etto*)
1590 ;   **cavalcade** (Fr., from Ital. *-ata*) 1591 ;   **salvo,** which now
has changed its ending from the earlier *-a* 1591 (Ital. *salva*) ;
paladin (Ital. *paladino*) 1592 ;   **bandit** 1593 (Ital. *bandito*) ;
cavesson, a horse's nose-band, 1598 (Fr. *câveçon*, Ital. *cavezzone*) ;
and finally **post** in the sense of ' military station ' 1598, later
generalized.

Next we come to trade, beginning with the general term
traffic (Ital. *traffico* 1506) ;   **contraband** 1509 ;   **milliner** 1529 was
originally an inhabitant of Milan, but was later restricted to
a maker of the fancy goods from Milan, ribbons, hats, etc. ;
bankrupt has been assimilated to the Lat. past participle *ruptus*,
from which it ultimately comes, but is through French from Ital.
banca rotta (1553) ;   **carat** 1552 is Ital. *carato*, but beyond that is
Arab. *qīrat* ;   **soldo,** a coin, 1599. Six names of vessels now appear :
caravel 1527 ;   **galleass** (Ital. *galeazza*) 1544 ;   **skiff** (Fr. *esquif*,
Ital. *schifo* from O.H.G. *scif*, and thus cognate with *ship*) 1575 ;
argosy 1577 (Ital. *ragusea* ' (ship) of Ragusa ') ;   **frigate** 1585
(Ital. *fregata*) ;   **settee,** a type of vessel used in the Mediterranean,
1587 (from French, from Ital. *saettia*, from Latin *sagitta* ' arrow ').
Then there are a number of words indicating objects of trade :
parmesan (Ital. *parmegiano* ' (cheese) of Parma ') 1519 ;   **citron**
1530 ;   **porcelain** (Fr., from Ital. *porcellano*) 1530 ;   **artichoke**
1531 (this has wandered far, for the North Italian *articiocco*
is borrowed from Old Spanish, which took it from Arabic) ;
majolica 1555 (from the old Italian form of *Majorca*) ;   **smalt,**
a kind of blue glass, 1558 (Ital., but in origin Gmc. and related
to *smelt*) 1558 ;   **ferret,** a kind of silk ribbon, 1576 (Ital. *fioretti*) ;
baldachin, a rich brocaded material, usually of silk and gold
thread, 1598 (Ital. from *Baldacco* = Baghdad, from which the
stuff was imported).

Architectural :   **cupola** 1549 ;   **duomo** 1549 ;   this and *piazza*
are the only words in this group which did not become naturalized
in English ;   **cornice** 1563 ;   **frieze** (Fr. *frise*, Ital. *fregio*) 1563 ;
modillion 1563 ;   **pedestal** (Fr. *piédestal*, Ital. *piedestallo* ;   the
word has been influenced by Lat. *ped-em*) 1563 [1] ;   · **pilaster**
1575 ;   **piazza** 1583 (Ital. *piazza* ;   Lat. *platea*, whence also Fr.
place and Span. *plaza*, both borrowed by English ;   cf. also O.E.

---

[1] All these from Shute's *Architecture*, 1563.

plætse, a rare word, borrowed directly from Latin) ; **belvedei** 1596 ; **stucco** 1598 n.

Words connected with the arts : (i) Music : **madrigal** 1588 ; **sordine** 1591 ; **pandora** 1597 ; **viol da gamba** 1597 (in the title of Dowland's *First Booke of Songes or Ayres*) ; **fugue,** at first spelt **fuge** 1597 (Ital. *fuga* ; the spelling with *-ue* is French). (ii) Painting and sculpture, etc. : **impaste** 1548 ; **cameo** 1561 ; **model** 1575 (Ital. *modello*) ; **pastel,** a dye obtained from woad, 1578 ; later used for a paste made into crayons ; **miniature** 1586 ; **motto** 1589, a word or phrase inscribed on or beneath an emblematic design, on a shield, etc. ; **gesso** 1596 ; **fresco** 1598 ; **mezzo-rilievo** 1598. (iii) Literature : **buffoon** 1549 (Ital. *buffone* ; like the *pantaloon* and the *zany*, a character from Italian comedy) ; **sonnet** 1557 (Ital. *soneto*) ; **villanelle** 1586 (Fr. from Ital. *villanella*) ; **stanza** 1588 ; **zany** (Ital. *zanni*, Venetian form of *Gianni = Giovanni*) 1588 (this, like *stanza*, first in *Love's Labour's Lost*) ; **canto** 1590 ; **pantaloon** 1590 ; **inamorato** 1592 (the feminine *inamorata* is not recorded in English till 1651) ; **canzone** 1590, **canzonet** 1593 ; **tercet** (Fr., from Ital. *terzetta*) 1598.

In the seventeenth century we have an increase in the number of words indicating Italian social customs and products, rather fewer in the military group, and considerable numbers of words relating to art, music, and literature. In the preceding century most of the loans came in during the last fifty years, but here they seem to be fairly evenly distributed throughout the period.

Italian life and society : **capriccio** ' caprice ' 1601 ; **intrigue** vb. 1612 (Ital. *intrigare*) ; **caprice** (the Fr. form of *capriccio*) 1667. **Charlatan** (Fr., from Ital. *ciarlatano*) 1618 ; **gala** 1625, first in the sense of ' gala dress ' ; **monsignor** 1635 ; **incognito** 1638 ; **regatta** (Venetian) 1652 ; **cortège** 1679 (Fr., from Ital. *corteggio*) ; **gazette** (Fr., from Ital. *gazzetta*, a small Venetian coin, and also a news-sheet, costing this amount) 1605, both with reference to the Italian coin, and also for an English news-sheet ; **umbrella** (Ital. *om-*) 1609 ; its restriction to a protection against rain has been gradual ; to begin with it was used either for rain or for sun ; **lagoon** (Ital. *laguna*) 1612 ; it is used in English first with reference to the lagoons of Venice ; **parasol** 1616 (Ital. *parasole*) ; **sirocco** 1617 (Ital. from Arab.) ; **vetturino** 1617 (hardly used except in reference to Italy) ; **valise** (Fr., from Ital. *valigia*) 1633 ; **balloon** (Fr. *ballon*, from Ital. *ballone*) 1634 ; **cascade** (Fr., from Ital. *cascata*) 1641 ; **gambit,** in chess, 1656 ; **espalier** (Fr., from Ital. *spalliere*) 1662 ; **sbirro** 1668.

Words for food were never borrowed in large numbers from Italian : **macaroon** (Ital. *maccarone*) 1611 ; **vermicelli** 1669.

Geological : **volcano** 1613 ; **granite** 1646.

Trade : **piastre** 1611 (Ital. *piastra*, but originally a Spanish coin, used by Italian traders in the Mediterranean) ; **lira** 1617 ; **muslin** (Fr. *mousseline*, later borrowed in a form approximating to the French, from Ital. *mussolina*, from the Place-Name *Mussolo* = Mosul, in Mesopotamia) 1609 ; **felucca** (Ital. from Arabic) 1628 ; **mercantile** 1642 ; **risk** (Fr. *risque*, Ital. *risco*) 1661 n. ; the verb in 1687 ; **scudo** 1644 ; **padrone** 1660 ; **agio** 1682 ; **organzine,** a kind of silk thread, 1699.

Military, mostly through French : **attack** (Ital. *attacare*) 1600 vb. ; **rocket** (Ital. *roccheta*) 1611 ; **stiletto** 1611 ; **generalissimo** 1621 ; **musketoon** 1638 (Ital. *moschettone*) 1638 ; **fuse** (Ital. *fuso*) 1644 ; **barrack** 1686 (Ital. *baracca* ' tent ' or other shelter) ; **vedette** 1690 ; **caserne** 1696.

Political or diplomatic : **internuncio** 1641 ; **manifesto** 1644 ; **bulletin** (Ital. *bulletino*, an official health-certificate) 1651.

Italian birds and plants : **beccafico** 1621 ; **morello** 1648 ; **francolin** 1653 ; **ortolan** 1656 ; **broccoli** 1699.

Architectural : Most of these are now common in English ; English architecture was much affected by Italian at this period, especially through the influence of Inigo Jones, and other architects who had travelled in Italy : **portico** 1605 ; **entablature** 1611 (through Fr., from Ital. *intavolatura*) ; **villa** 1611, but partly direct from Latin *villa*, the source of the Italian word ; in either case the sense has now changed and is changing ; the original sense was ' country residence ' ; in Italian the stress is on the gardens and grounds rather than on the house ; **grotto** 1617 ; **balcony** (Ital. *balcone*) 1618 ; **corridor** 1620 ; **pergola** 1654 ; **catacomb** 1662 (this word, from Latin, is already to be found in O.E., *catacumbas*, but the modern word is certainly a new loan from Italian) ; **dado** 1664 ; **impost** 1664 ; **rotunda** 1687.

Music : (i) Musical instruments, and types of composition, etc. : **opera** 1644 ; **recitative** 1645 ; **serenade** (Fr. *-ade*, from Ital. *-ata*) 1649 ; **ritornello** 1675 ; **sonata** 1694 ; **solo** 1695 ;

theorbo, a kind of lute (Fr., from Ital. *tiorba*) 1605 ; **spinet** 1664 (Fr. *espinette*, apparently from the Italian personal name Spinetti) ; **pedal** (Ital. *pedale*) 1611. (ii) Musical directions : **allegro** 1632 ; **largo** 1683 ; **piano** 1683 (*pianissimo* in 1724) ; **presto** 1683 ; **vivace** 1683 ; all but the first of this group are from Purcell's *Sonnatas in 3 Parts.*

Art : **relief, relievo** (Ital. *rilievo*) 1606 ; **morbidezza** 1624 ; **girandole,** a revolving jet of water, or firework, 1634 ; **catafalque** 1641 ; **intaglio** 1644 ; **pietà** 1644 ; **putti** 1644 [1] ; **virtuoso** 1651 ; **bust** (Ital. *busto*) 1653 ; **profile** 1656 ; **vista,** earlier also *visto* (Ital. *vista*, past part., then ' something seen ') 1657 ; **mezzotint** 1660 ; **attitude** (Ital. *attitudine*) 1668 ; **filigree** 1693 is apparently from **filigreen,* a variant of **filigrane** 1668 (Ital. *filigrana*) ; **cartoon** (Fr. *carton*, Ital. *cartone*) 1671 ; **chiaroscuro** 1686.

Literature ; most of these words appear to have come in with the numerous French words borrowed after the Restoration : **rodomontade** 1612 (from the Ital. *Rodomonte*, the Saracen leader in Ariosto's *Orlando Furioso*) ; **burlesque** (Ital. *burlesco*) 1656 ; **pasquinade** 1658 ; **scaramouch** (Fr., from Ital. *Scaramuccia*, another of the stock characters of Italian farce) 1662 ; **sonnetteer** 1665 ; **Punch,** abbreviated from *Punchinello*, which in the form *Polichinello*, perhaps directly from Neapolitan *Polecenella*, appears in 1666 in reference to the puppet-show in which the character takes part.

Miscellaneous : **ditto** 1625, as adj. ; **gusto** ' zest ' 1629 ; **bagatelle** (Fr., from Ital. *bagatella*) 1637 ; **hippogriff** (Ital. *ippogrifo*) 1656, a fabulous monster ; **parry** vb. 1672.

The eighteenth century loans from Italian are of very much the same character as those of the seventeenth, but it may be pointed out that there are none to come under the head of Military, and that there is a distinct increase in the number of geological terms. A much higher proportion than hitherto comes directly from Italian, instead of through French.

Italian life and society : **cicisbeo** 1718 ; **cicerone** 1726 ; **conversazione** 1740 ; **villegiatura,** residence at a country villa, 1742 ; **alfresco** adj. 1753 ; **poco-curante** adj. and n. 1762 ; **casino** 1789, a public room for social gatherings.

Birds and other Italian products : **avocet** (Fr., from Ital.

---

[1] These three from Evelyn's *Diary.*

avosetta) 1766 ; **pipistrel(le),** a kind of bat, 1771 (Ital. *pipistrello*) ; **maraschino** 1791 ; **semolina** 1797.

Medical : **malaria** 1740 (Ital. from *mal'aria* ' bad air ') ; **influenza** 1743 (there was a serious epidemic of influenza in this year ; the name had previously had a general sense of ' epidemic disease ' in Italian).

Geological, etc. : **pozz(u)olana** 1706 ; **bronze** 1721 ; **lava** 1750 ; **madrepore** 1751 ; **tufa** (Ital. *tufa* ; cf. *tuff*, from Fr. *tuffe* from Ital.) 1770 ; **breccia** 1774 ; **scaglia** 1774 ; **peperino** 1777 ; **solfatara** 1777 ; **travertine** 1797 ; **cipolin,** a kind of marble, 1798.

Architecture : **merlon** 1704 ; **socle,** a plinth, 1704 (Ital. *zoccolo*) ; **mezzanine** 1711 ; **colonnade** 1718 ; **arcade** 1731 ; **loggia** 1742.

Music : (i) Performers, etc. : **soprano** 1730 ; **impresario** 1746 ; **improvisatore** 1765 ; **maestro** 1797. (ii) Instruments : **mandolin** 1707 ; **trombone** 1724 ; **violoncello** 1724 [1] ; **mandola** 1758 ; **pianoforte** 1767 (the shortened **piano** first in 1803) ; **viola** 1797. (iii) Forms of composition : **cantata** 1724 ; **duetto** 1724 (**duet** in 1740) ; **fantasia, pastorale, saltarello, terzetto, toccata, trio** 1724 ; **oratorio** 1727 ; **concerto** 1730 ; **aria** 1742 ; **arpeggio** 1742 ; **pasticcio** 1752 (the French form *pastiche* not till 1878) ; **appogiatura** 1753 ; **solfeggio** 1774 ; **tarantella** 1782 ; **finale** 1783 ; **quartet** 1790 ; **rondo** 1797 ; **barcarolle** (Fr., from Ital. *barcaruola*) 1799. (iv) Musical directions : **da capo, forte, fortissimo, maestoso, sostenuto, staccato, tutti** 1724 ; **cantabile** 1730 ; **andante** 1742 ; **adagio** 1746 ; **portamento** 1774 ; **diminuendo** 1775 ; **crescendo** 1776 ; **obbligato** 1794. (v) Miscellaneous : **tempo** 1724 ; **libretto** 1742 ; **bravo,** as exclamation of applause, 1761 ; **falsetto** 1774 ; **bravura** 1788.

Art : **picturesque** 1703 (Ital. *pittoresco*, assimilated to *picture*) ; **costume** 1715 ; **portfolio** 1722 ; **terra-cotta** 1722 ; **virtu** 1722 ; **dilettante** 1733 ; **bambino** 1761 ; **impasto** 1784 ; **sienna** 1787 ; **torso** 1797.

Literature : **concetto** 1737 ; **fantoccini** 1771 ; **rifacimento** 1773 ; **extravaganza** 1789 (Ital. *es-* ; the *ex-* is due to the common Latin prefix).

Miscellaneous : **viva !** 1700 n. ; **piston** 1704 (Ital. *pistone*) ;

---

[1] Words dated 1724 are all from a work called *A Short Explication of Foreign Words in Music Books.*

riposte, in fencing (Fr., from Ital. *risposta*) 1707 ; **spontoon,** a kind of halberd, 1708 ; **poplin** (Fr. *popeline*, earlier *papaline*, from Ital. *papalina*, material made at Avignon, which was a Papal town until 1751) 1710 ; **fracas** (Fr. from Ital. *fracasso*) 1727 ; **firm,** trading company, 1744 (Ital. *firma*) ; **imbroglio** 1750 ; **lotto** 1778 ; **condottiere** 1794.

Again in the nineteenth century most of the Italian words are direct borrowings. Considerably more than half represent music, art, and literature.

Italian life and politics : **vendetta** 1855 (especially Corsican) ; **camorra** 1865 ; **mafia** 1875 ; **irredentist** 1882.

Scientific : **gelatine** 1800 ; **mofette** (Fr., from Ital. (Neapolitan) *mofeta*) 1822 ; **nuraghe,** an archaeological term, applied to a round fort of Sardinia (1828) ; **gabbro** 1837 ; **graffito** 1851 ; **magenta** 1860 (a dye discovered shortly after the battle of Magenta in 1859) ; **terramara** 1866.

Food, etc. : **rosolio,** a sweet cordial, 1819 ; **cantaloup** 1839 (from the Place-Name *Cantalupo,* a Papal villa near Rome, where the plant is said to have been grown when introduced from Armenia) ; **salame,** a variety of sausage, 1852 ; **risotto** 1884 ; **gorgonzola** (Place-Name) 1885 ; **spaghetti** 1882.

Medical : **scarlatina** 1803 ; **pellagra** 1811 ; **ptomaine** 1880.

Music : (i) Instruments : **bombardon** 1856 ; **piccolo** 1856 ; **cymbalo** 1879. (ii) Performers : **prima donna** 1812 ; **flautist** 1860 ; **cantatrice** 1866 ; **diva** 1883. (iii) Forms of composition, etc. : **sestet** 1801 ; **sonatina** 1801 ; **mordent** 1806 ; **polacca,** a Polish dance, 1813 ; **scena** 1819 ; **intermezzo** 1834 ; **cadenza** 1836 ; **cavatina** 1836. (iv) Musical directions : **rallentando** 1800 ; **sforzando** 1801 ; **tremolo** 1801 ; **legato** 1811 ; **pizzicato** 1845 ; **vibrato** 1861 ; **scherzo** 1862 ; **allegretto** 1879 ; **rubato** 1887. (v) Miscellaneous : **improvise** 1826 ; **contrapuntal** 1845 ; **furore** 1851 ; **fiasco** 1855 (with reference to musical performances, like the previous word).

Art : **studio** 1819 ; **replica** 1824 ; **tempera** 1832 ; **gradine** 1834 ; **predella** 1848 ; **baroque** 1851 ; **secco** 1852 ; **figurine** 1854 ; **gouache** (Fr., from Ital. *guazzo*) 1882 ; **tondo,** a round painting, etc., 1890.

Literature : **galanty**-show 1821 ; **comedietta** 1836 ; **sestina** 1838 ; **scenario** 1880.

Miscellaneous :   **portolano** 1850, a book of sailing directions ; **garibaldi,** a kind of blouse, etc., 1862 (named from the Italian leader of this name) ; **pallone** 1865 ; **tombola** 1880. **Tirade** 1801 ; **maremma** 1832 ; **inferno** 1834 ; these last three have now a fairly wide application.

Chapter VIII

THE SPANISH ELEMENT

The introduction of Spanish words into English by direct contact, as in the case of Italian, hardly begins until the sixteenth century. Before this time, it is true, French had handed on to us certain terms which they had acquired from Spanish, but which were in origin Arabic. These will be dealt with later. Of real Spanish (Romance) words, the noun **cordewan, cordwain** 'Spanish leather', from the Place-Name Cordova, through French, and **cork,** probably from Spanish *corcha*, seem to be the only examples of loans in Middle English, and even these are not found till about 1440 (in the *Promptorium Parvulorum*).

It is after the middle of the sixteenth century that Spanish words begin to be borrowed with some freedom, though they are never adopted in such numbers as Italian words. A close connexion between the courts of England and Spain obtained for a time under Queen Mary, the daughter of Catherine of Aragon, particularly after her marriage to Philip II of Spain, and Spanish dons and señors and hidalgos became familiar figures in this country. Spanish coins made their appearance, as well as articles of trade, and a small number of military terms were adopted at this period.

But the most interesting Spanish loan-words in this period as well as later came in a different way. From the end of the fifteenth century Spanish merchant-vessels were exploring the ocean westwards from Europe, and by the time of Elizabeth Spanish-speaking settlements were sprinkled along the coasts of the Americas. When the naval power of England began to grow, and Englishmen came into contact, even though this was hostile contact, with Spaniards upon the high seas, in the West Indies and on the coasts of Mexico and South America, they adopted from them the names they used for the inhabitants, animals, plants, etc., some of these being really Spanish words, now used in specialized senses (e.g. *lagarto* ' lizard ', used for—and borrowed as— ' alligator '), while others were taken over by the Spaniards themselves from the natives (e.g. *potato*). English sailors brought back such words to England, and many of them gained currency rapidly as stories and products of the New World spread in this country. Many of them appear for the first time in the tales of voyagers collected and published by Hakluyt ; others in books written specially to describe the lands across the ocean, such as Eden's *Decades of the Newe Worlde or West Indies, conteyning the Navigations and Conquestes of the Spanyardes with particular description of the most ryche and large Landes and Islandes lately found in the West Ocean,* Frampton's *Ioyfulle Newes from the Newe Founde World,* and, in the early part of the next century, *Purchas his Pilgrimes, Purchas his Pilgrimage,* and Captain John Smith's *General History of Virginia, New England, and the Summer Isles.*

Literature, too, shows its share of interest in America, in the use of Spanish words borrowed there, as well as in references such as Shakespeare's to ' the new map with the augmentation of the Indies ', and by direct statement, as when Spenser speaks of the way in which

> through hardy enterprise
> Many great regions are discovered,
> Which to late age were never mentioned.
> Who ever heard of th' Indian Peru ?
> Or who in venturous vessell measured
> The Amazon huge river, now found trew ?
> Or fruitfullest Virginia who did ever vew ?
>
> (*Faerie Queene,* II, Introd.)

The seventeenth century shows the largest number of Spanish borrowings, of which some relate to Spanish life, trade, politics, etc. (*duenna, toreador, junta, cortes, embargo,* etc.), but the most important are again American, and this relative importance holds good through the following centuries.

Of modern English dialects, those from areas on the borders of Spanish-speaking America, or from areas in the southern United States where Spanish was once spoken, have the highest proportion of Spanish words, a good many having been absorbed there which have not penetrated into the more northerly states, or even if they have reached these have remained on that side of the Atlantic, though some may have become known in England through the medium of American books. Such are *chaparral, caballero, arroyo, vaquero, tamale, posada, poncho, hombre.*[1] These as a class are not dealt with here, though some of those which have become most familiar in this country will be found given below ; most of them are farming terms.

Of words adopted by Spanish from American Indian languages, only a few are given here, to illustrate the type of word thus borrowed, chiefly names of plants and animals. The reader is referred for further information to the chapter on American Indian.

Now we must deal in turn with the four centuries from 1500 to 1800, giving the relevant words in order as they appear, arranged under several headings. For the sixteenth century our headings will be (i) Spanish trade and products, (ii) words denoting persons, and titles of rank, (iii) games and dancing, (iv) naval and military, (v) miscellaneous, and finally (vi) words from America.

Spanish trade and products : **peso** 1555 ; **cask** 1557 (the sense of ' barrel ' developed in England from that of ' helmet ', see *casque* below) ; **real,** a Spanish coin (originally an adjective, = royal) 1588 ; **rusk** 1595 (in Drake's *Voyage*, in Hakluyt) ; **panada** (Florio) 1598 ; **anchovy** 1596 (Span. *anchova*, possibly from Basque *anchoa* in the sense of ' dried fish ') ; **sherry,** earlier **sherris,** taken as plural, 1597 (Shakespeare, 2 *Henry VI*) ; *sherry*, or rather *shirry*, appears first in Middleton, 1608 ; it is from a Place-Name, Span. *vino de Xeres.*

Persons and titles of rank : **don** 1523 (Wolsey, *State Papers* : *The Archiduke Don Ferdinando*) ; **infante** 1555 (Eden, *Decades of the Newe Worlde*), the feminine **infanta** in 1601 ; **senora** 1579 (but *senor* not till 1622 ; *senorita* in 1845) ; **renegade** (Span. *renegado*, a form also found in English) 1583 ; **hidalgo** 1594 ; **grandee** 1598 (Span. *grande* ' nobleman ') ; **santon,** a European name for a Mohammedan hermit (Span. *santo* ' holy ') 1599 ; **booby** 1599 (Span. *bobo* ' fool ').

Games and dancing : **primero,** a card-game, 1533 (Span. *primera*) ; **coranto** 1564 (actually French, assimilated to Spanish

---

[1] See Bentley, *Dictionary of Spanish Terms in English*, 1925.

words in -*o*) ; **spade** (on cards) 1598 (Span. *espada*, orig.
' sword ').

Naval and military : **galleon** 1529 (Lyndsay, *Testament and
Complaynt of our Soverane* ; Span. *galeon*) ; **grenade** 1532 (French,
from Span. *granada*, orig. ' promegranate ') ; **armada** 1533 (*The
Turks' armada*, from a letter in Ellis, *Original Letters*) ; **casque**
1580 (Span. *casco*) ; **comrade** 1591 (Span. *camarada* ; Garrard,
Art of Warre : *A Souldier in Camp must make choise of two or
three or more Camerades*) ; **bilbo,** a sword, 1592 (from the Span.
Place-Name *Bilbao*) ; **escalade** 1598 (Span. *escalada*).

Miscellaneous : **tornado,** first as *ternado* 1556 (apparently from
Span. *tronada* ' thunder ', influenced by the Span. verb *tornar*
' to turn ') ; **corral** n. 1582 (the verb not till 1847) ; **cordovan**
(leather) 1591 (cf. the earlier *cordwain*) ; **calenture,** a fever,
1593 ; **sombrero** 1598 (Hakluyt : *With a great Sombrero or
shadow ouer their heads . . . as broad as a great cart wheele*) ;
cedilla (= a little *z*) 1599. **Bastinado** 1577 (Span. *bastonada*) ;
peccadillo 1591 ; **punctilio** 1596 (Span. *puntillo*) ; **bravado** 1599
(Span. -*ada*).

American : (i) Persons : **cannibal** 1553 (Span. *canibales*,
from *Caribes* ; Eden, translation of Munster's *Cosmography* :
Columbus . . . at ye length came to the Ilandes of the Canibals) ;
cacique 1555 (Span. from Haitian ; first in Eden, *Decades*) ;
negro 1555 (Eden, *Decades* ; **neger,** from which **nigger** comes,
1568) ; **mestizo** 1588 ; **mulatto** 1595 (Drake's *Voyage* ; Span.
mulato). (ii) American products : **guaiacum,** a West Indian
tree, 1533 (in a medical work ; a Latinized form of Span.
guayaco, from a Haitian word) ; **iguana** 1555 (Eden, *Decades*) ;
alligator, earlier sometimes **lagarto,** 1568 (Span. *el lagarto* ' the
lizard ' ; Hortop, in 1568, has *lagarto* ; cf. Raleigh, 1614 ; *the
Crocodiles . . . now called Alegattos*) ; **sarsaparilla, armadillo,
sassafras, batata** 1577, all from Fràmpton, *Joyfull Newes from
the Newe Founde Worlde* (note : *The Batatas . . . a common
frute in those countries . . . a victaill of much substance* ; but
potato is a few years earlier, 1565) ; **mosquito** 1583 (Phillips, in
Hakluyt's *Voyages* : *a kinde of flie . . . the Spanyards called them
Musketas*) ; **palmetto** 1583 (Cotton, in Hakluyt's *Voyages*) ;
cochineal 1586 (Span. *cochinilla*, through Fr. *cochenille*) ; **banana**
1597 (Span., from the native name in Guinea ; first in a book

on the Congo) ; **bonito,** the striped tunny, 1599. (iii) Miscellaneous : **manilla** 1556 ; **El Dorado** 1596 (Raleigh (title), *Discoverie of Guiana, with a relation of the Great and Golden Citie of Manoa, which the Spaniards call El Dorado*) ; **machete** 1598 (in the anglicized form *matchet*).

Seventeenth century : Trade : **doubloon** 1622 (Fr. *doublon*, from Span. *doblon*) ; **cargo** 1657. People : **creole** 1604 (Span. *criollo* ' native ', through French) ; **desperado** 1610 ; **toreador** 1618 ; **dona** ' lady ' 1622 (Span. *dona* ; cf. the recent *donah* ' sweetheart ' 1873) ; **picaroon** ' pirate, brigand, rogue ' 1624 (Span. *-on*) ; **duenna** 1668 ; **matador** 1674 (a term in card-playing ; with reference to bull-fighting in 1681).

Products of Spain : **dorado,** a fish, 1604 ; **granadilla** 1613 ; **lime,** fruit, 1622 (Span. *lima*, from Arab. *līmah*).

Political, etc. : **embargo** 1602 ; **gar(r)ot** n. 1622 (Span. *garrote*, method of execution ; the verb first in English in 1851) ; **junta** 1623 ; **cortes** 1668.

Naval and military : **corvette** 1636 (Span. *corbeta*) ; **parade,** a muster of troops, 1656 (Span. *-ada*).

Games and dancing : **saraband** 1616 (French from Span. *zarabanda* from Arabic) ; **guitar** 1629 (Span. *guitarra*) ; **castanet** 1647 (Span. *castañeta*) ; **ombre** 1660 ; **manille** 1674 (Span. *malilla*) ; **chaconne** 1685 (French, from Span. *chacona*, probably from Basque *chucun* ' pretty ').

Miscellaneous : **sierra** 1613 ; **caracole** 1614 ; **olio** 1643 (Span. *olla*) ; **escapade** 1653 ; **siesta** 1655 ; **salver** 1661 (Span. *salva* ; the suffix is English) ; **esplanade,** a level open space, 1681 ; **plaza** 1683.

American : (i) People : **peon,** a labourer, 1609 ; **piccaninny** 1657 (from Span. *pequeño* ' little ' ; first in a book on Barbados). (ii) Animals, plants, etc. : **llama** 1600 ; **chinchilla** 1604 (D'Acosta, *History of the Indies* : *The Chinchilles is another kind of small beasts, like squirrels ; they have a wonderfulle smoothe and soft skinne*) ; **ananas** 1613 (Purchas ; Span. from Peruvian *nanas*) ; **cockroach** 1624 (John Smith, *Virginia* : *A certaine India Bug called by the Spaniards a Cacarootch* ; Span. *cucaracha*) ; **manchineel** 1630 (John Smith, *Travels and Adventures* ; Fr. *mancenille*, from Span. *manzanilla*) ; **turtle** 1657 (French *tortue* from Span. *tortuga*, assimilated to Eng. *turtle* = dove) ; **vanilla**

o

1662 (Span. *vaynilla*) ; **barracouta** 1678 ; **pimento** 1690, ' Cayenne pepper ', later ' allspice ' (Span. *pimienta*) ;   **pulque** 1693 ; **avocado** 1697 (Span. popular substitution for Aztec *ahuacatl*) ; **naseberry** 1698, a West Indian tree (by popular etymology from Span. *nispero*, from Lat. *mespilus* ' medlar '). (iii) Miscellaneous : **llano** 1613 (*Purchas his Pilgrimage*) ; **muscovado**, unrefined sugar, 1619 (Span. *mascabado*) ;   **vega,** a grassy plain, 1645 ;   **rancho,** a hut for the shelter of travellers, 1648 ;   the use of this word and of the anglicized *ranch* in the sense of ' farm ' does not appear till the nineteenth century ; **barbecue,** a wooden framework used as support for a bed or for roasting meat, 1697 (Span. *barbacoa*, from Haitian) ; **maroon** n. 1666 (apparently from Span. *cimarrón* ' wild ' ;   applied first to a fugitive slave in the West Indies ; the verb occurs in 1724) ; **tortilla** 1699.

Eighteenth century :   People :   **quadroon** 1707 (Span. *cuarteron*) ;   **albino** 1777 ;   **stevedore** 1788 (Span. *estivador*) ; **picador** 1797.

Animals, etc. :   **merino** 1781 ;   **galeeny** 1796 (Span. *gallina morisca* ' Moorish hen ').

Games and dancing, etc. :   **fandango** 17 . . . ;   **domino** 1719 (as a game in 1801) ;   **quadrille,** a card-game, 1726 (Span. *cuartillo,* assimilated to the name of the dance) ; **spadille,** the ace of spades, 1728 (Span. *espadilla*) ; **quadrille,** a dance, 1738 (Span. *cuadrilla*) ; **bolero** 1787.

Cooking : **marinade** 1704 ; **caramel** 1725.

Miscellaneous : **cordillera** 1704 ; **flotilla** 1711 ; **carmine** 1712 ; **mantilla** 1717 ;   **auto-da-fé** 1723 (Span. *auto-de-fé*) ;   **jade** 1727 (Fr. *le jade*, earlier *l'éjade*, from Span. (*piedra de*) *ijada* ' stone for the colic ', from supposed medicinal properties) ;   **cigar** 1735 (Span. *cigarro*) ; **xebec** 1756 (Span. *xabeque*, probably of Eastern origin).

American :   Animals, plants, etc. :   **charqui,** dried meat, 1706 (Span. from Peruvian ;   from the Span. verb *charquear* comes the anglicized verb **jerk** 1707) ;   **agouti** 1731 (Span. *aguti*, from the S. American native name) ;   **cinchona** 1742 ; **gallinazo,** American vulture, 1760 ;   **alpaca** 1792 (first of the animal's wool ;   Span. from Arab. *al* ' the ' + Peruv. *paco*, the native name).   (ii) Miscellaneous :   **maté** 1717 (Span. from Quichua *mati*, a vessel made of calabash ;   later used for *yerba maté*, a herb infused in a *maté* and used for drinking) ; **sangaree,** a West Indian drink, 1736 (Span. *sangría*) ; **hacienda** 1760 ; **mesa** 1775 ; **ratoon,** new shoot from root of sugar-cane, 1777 (Span. *retoño*).

Most of the nineteenth century loans from Spanish are from the American side of the Atlantic, relating to farming in particular ; the majority of these come to England by way of the United States. Two or three words from Spain itself, it will be observed, date from the time of the Peninsular War.

Agriculture : **silo** 1835 (the verb *ensile* in 1883).

Spanish products : **cigarette** 1842 (through French) ; **esparto** (grass) 1868 ; **camisole,** a kind of jacket, 1816 ; **grenadine,** material, 1865 (Fr., from Place-Name *Granada*).

Military and political : **presidio** 1808 ' fort, garrison town ' (still used with reference to southern United States) ; **guerilla** 1809 ; **camarilla** 1839 ; **pronunciamento** 1843 ; **intransigent** 1879 (Span. *los intransigentes*, party of Extreme Left in the Cortes, and in 1873-4 the extreme Republicans).

Games and dancing : **cachucha** 1840 ; **monte,** a card-game 1850 ; **pelota,** a Basque game, but not a Basque name, 1895.

Literature and art : **picaresque** 1810 (Span. *picaresco*, from *picaron* ' a rogue ') ; **plateresque,** a style of decoration like silver work, 1842 (Span. *-esco*) ; **tilde** 1864.

American : (i) Farming terms : **lasso** 1808 (Span. *lazo*) ; **mustang** 1808 (E. Span. *mestengo*) ; **gaucho** 1824 (probably of Indian origin) ; **rodeo** 1834 ; **stampede** 1834 (Mexican Span. *estampida*, a specialized use of the Span. word meaning ' crash, uproar ') ; **lariat** 1835 (Span. *la reata*, the first word being the definite article) ; **vaquero** 1837 ; **bolas** pl. 1843 ; **quirt** 1851 ; **cinch** ' girth ' 1872 (Span. *cincha*) ; **bronco** 1883.

(ii) Plants and animals : **yerba,** for *yerba maté*, 1818 ; **guaco** 1822 ; **pichiciago,** an animal of Chile, like an armadillo, 1825 (S. Amer. Span. *pichiciego*, of native origin) ; **guacharo** 1830 ; **nutria,** the fur of the coypu, 1836 (the word originally meant ' otter ') ; **matico** 1838 ; **grama** (grass) 1851 ; **pómpano,** a fish of the West Indies and southern states, 1863 (Span. *pámpano*) ; **coquito** 1866.

Mining : **placer** 1848 ; **bonanza** 1878 (used in mining slang ; in Span. the word means ' prosperity ').

Building :   **pueblo,** an Indian village, 1818 (Span. *pueblo*
' people ') ; **patio** 1828 ; **adobe** 1834.

Miscellaneous :   **serape,** a shawl, 1847 ; **vamoose** 1848
(American slang, from Span. *vamos* ' let us go ') ; **canyon** 1850
(Span. *cañon*) ; **dago** 1888 (from Span. personal name *Diego*) ;
cafeteria (twentieth century ; in English the accent is usually
shifted from the penultimate to the antepenultimate) ;
tango 1913.

CHAPTER IX

LOANS FROM OTHER EUROPEAN LANGUAGES

A. CELTIC

Some account has been given in an earlier chapter of the Celtic loan-words which reached English during the Old English period, chiefly from British and Irish. The next words from Celtic came indirectly, through French, which derives a small section of its vocabulary from Gaulish words adopted in the Gallo-Roman period, when Vulgar Latin was displacing the Celtic language in Gaul. Of those which passed into English, the following are the most certainly of Celtic origin ; there are others which are more doubtful : **gravel, lawn** (of grass), **league, lees, marl, ouch, quay, skein, truant, vassal** (and the related **valet** and **varlet**) ; all these are found before 1450. A little later we have **toque** 1505, **javelin** 1513, **druid** 1563 (ultimately from the Old Celtic stem *druid-* ; cf. O.E. *drȳ*, from the O.Irish nominative form *drui*) ; perhaps **tan** 1604.

The next direct loans from Celtic to English are borrowings within the British Isles, from Irish, Scottish Gaelic, and Welsh ; very few are earlier than the late fourteenth century, in spite of the English invasions of Ireland in the reign of Henry II. Those from Scotland are the most numerous. Some in each of the groups have been completely naturalized, and are applied to things of English origin, but for the most part these things refer to products, persons, etc., of the country from which they come.

The first Middle English loan from Ireland appears to be **kern** (Ir. *ceithern*), which dates from about 1422 ; **lough** (Ir. *loch*) is found in the latter part of the same century (the Irish Gaelic form of this is the same as the Scottish ; see *loch*, below). Four words from the sixteenth century are **tanist** 1538 (O.Ir. *tanaiste*) ; **shamrock** 1571 (Campion's *History of Ireland* ; Ir. *seamróg* [1]) ;

---

[1] Note that Irish *s* before *e* or *i* is pronounced like *sh*.

rath 1596 (Spenser, *View of the Present State of Ireland* ; Ir. *rath*) ; **brogue** ' shoe ' 1586 (Ir. *bróg* ; J. Hooker in Holinshed : *awaie with his English attires, and on with his brogs, his shirt, and other Irish rags*). The seventeenth century gives us five : **leprechaun** 1604 (Middleton, who spells it *lubrican* : M.Ir. *luchrupán*) ; **ogham** 1627 ; **Tory** 1646 (Ir. **tóraidhe* ' pursuer ', from the verb *tóir* ' to pursue ' ; applied in the seventeenth century to certain Irish outlaws and bandits ; it is first used in English politics in 1679 ; it appears as the name of a political party in 1689) ; **galore** 1675 (Ir. *go leór* ' enough ') ; **rapparee,** an Irish pikeman, 1690 (Ir. *rapaire,* a short pike). From the eighteenth century there are only four : **pollan** 1713 (perhaps from Ir. *poll,* an inland lake) ; **banshee** 1771 (Ir. *bean sidhe* ' fairy woman ') ; **shillelagh** 1772 (from the name of a village in Co. Wicklow) ; **spalpeen** 1780 (Ir. *spailpín*) ; **planxty,** a harp tune, 1790. There are not many more in the nineteenth century : **fiorin** 1809 (Ir. *fiorthán* ' coarse grass ') ; **blarney** 1819 (originally the name of a village near Cork) ; **colleen** 1828 (Ir. *cailín*) ; **keen** ' lament ' 1830 (Ir. *caoine*) ; **carrageen** 1834 (a Place-Name) ; **crannog,** a lake-dwelling in Ireland or Scotland, 1851.

English has borrowed more words from Scotland than from Ireland. The loans begin in the late fourteenth century, the earliest appearing, as might be expected, in the English-Scottish writers of the period, Barbour, Wyntoun, Dunbar, and later Gavin Douglas. The word **loch** is in Barbour's *Bruce* 1375 ; here also is **mull,** a headland (Gael. *maol*). The next loan is from a historical document ; this is **beltane,** the festival of the first of May, in the Acts of James I dated 1424. In Wyntoun's *Orygynale Cronykil of Scotland, c.* 1425, we find **clan**   (Gael. *clann*) ; **clachan,** a small village ; **inch** (Gael. *innis* ; *I wes made priowre . . . Of the ynche wyth-in Lochlewyne*). At the beginning of the sixteenth century, Dunbar has **coronach** 1500 (Gael. *corronach*) ; **bog** 1505 (Gael. *bogach,* from *bog* ' soft ') ; and **ingle,** a fire, 1508 (probably from Gael. *aingeal* ' fire '). **Plaid** appears in the *Accounts of the Lord High Treasurer for Scotland* for 1512 : *Item, the vj day of Maij, in Air, for ane plaid to be the King ane coit* (Gael. *plaide*). Douglas's *Æneis* has **caber** (Gael. *cabar* ' pole ' : *His schaft that was als rude and squair / As it had beyn a cabyr or a spar,* 1513), and **slogan** (in

the form *slogorne* ;   Gael. *slaugh-ghairm* ' host ' + ' cry ').
Later words in this century are :   **sonsy** ' fortunate, propitious '
1533 (Gael. *sonas* ' good luck ' ;   Bellenden's Livy :   *discending
fra pe maist sonsy parte of hevin* 1533) ;   **cairn** 1535 (Gael.
carn ;   Stewart's *Chronicle of Scotland*) ;   the **cairn-**(terrier) first appears
in 1910 ;   **capercailzie, -ye** 1536 (Gael. *capull coille* ' cock of the
wood ') ;   **garron** 1540 (Gael. *gearran* ;   State Papers of
Henry VIII) ;   **strath** 1540 (Gael. *srath*) ;   **kyle** 1549 (Gael. *caol*) ;
duniwassal 1565 (Gael. *duine uasal*) ;   **ptarmigan** 1599 (Gael.
tàrmachan).

The few seventeenth century loans are all from the second
half of the century :   **strathspey** 1653 (from a Place-Name) ;
caird, a travelling tinker, 1663 (Gael. *ceard*) ;   **quaich** 1673 (Gael.
cuach ' a cup ', but this is itself a loan-word from Lat. *caucus*) ;
gillie 1681 (Gael. *gille*) ;   **dulse,** an edible seaweed, 1684 (Gael.
duileasg).   From the eighteenth century :   **whisky** 1715 (Gael.
uisge beatha, literally ' water of life ') ;   **pibroch** 1719 (in
Hardyknute, in Maidment's *Scottish Ballads* ;   Gael. *piobaireachd,*
the art of playing the bagpipe) ;   **filibeg** 1746 (Gael. *feileadh-
beag* ' little fold ') ;   **claymore** 1772 (Gael. *claidheamh mòr* ' big
sword ') ;   **cairngorm** 1794 (from the name of a mountain, Gael.
Carngorm, = blue cairn) ;   **corrie** 1795 (Gael. *coire*).   Nineteenth
century :   **sporran** 1818 (Gael. *sporan* ' purse ') ;   **glengarry** 1858
(from a Place-Name in Inverness) ;   **gralloch** n. and vb. 1882
(Gael. *grealach*).

Neither Scotland nor Ireland has given many words to English,
and words from Wales are even fewer. The earliest is **crag** (Welsh
craig), which is in the *Cursor Mundi,* about 1300.   **Pendragon**
is used by Malory in 1470 ; it means in Welsh ' chief military
leader ', and it is a compound of the Celtic *pen* ' head ' and
dragon, borrowed from Latin as the name of a standard.
Coracle appears in Salesbury's Welsh dictionary, 1547, in the
spelling *corougle,* as the English equivalent of Welsh *kwrwgyl.*
Penguin, though its etymology is doubtful, may have been introduced by Welsh sailors, and be formed from Welsh *pen* ' head '
and *gwyn* ' white ' ; it is to be found in Parkhurst's travels, in
Hakluyt's *Voyages,* 1578.   **Cromlech** is used in 1603, in Owen's
Pembrokeshire.   **Gwyniad** dates from 1611. The next loan is
more than a century and a half later :   **pennill** (pl. *pennillion*)

1784. **Eisteddfodd** (the original meaning in Welsh was 'session, meeting ') is used in an English work in 1822.

There are four words which are probably borrowed from Cornish, though there is some doubt about each of them : **gull** 1430 (in a cookery book ; perhaps from Corn. *guilan*) ; **brill** 1481 (Corn. *brilli* 'mackerel ') ; **wrasse** 1672 (Corn. *wrach*) ; **dolmen** (possibly from Cornish *tolmên* ' hole of stone ' ; first used in a French work by Latour d'Auvergne in 1796 ; in English first in Jephson's *Brittany* 1859). Another archaeological term, **menhir** 1840, is perhaps our only loan from Breton.

(B) PORTUGUESE

The introduction of Portuguese words into English has been almost exclusively the result of friendly or hostile commercial relations.   As in the case of Spanish, there are practically no words introduced from Portugal before the sixteenth century. What appears to be a solitary exception is **marmalade,** which is found as early as 1480, but comes through French, and not direct as most of our Portuguese words do.   (The Port. form is *marmelada*, from *marmelo* ' quince ' ; it was originally a quince jam, and not made of oranges.)

During the fifteenth century, Portuguese explorers had already made their way down the coast of Africa, round the Cape, and by sea to India, and when they were followed by the English trading-fleets of Elizabeth's reign they had established colonies or trading stations on the Guinea coast, on the East African coast, in India, and as far east as China.   It is in these regions that English sailors and merchants, and in later times officials and soldiers, have borrowed the greater number of the Portuguese words which we now have, though a few come from Portugal itself, and a few also from America, especially from the Portuguese settlements in Brazil and Guiana.   Very few are from the West Indies.   In fact, the sixteenth and seventeenth century line of demarcation between the Spanish area of trade and colonization in the west, and that of Portugal in the east, is very clearly reflected in the words which their English rivals adopted from each of them.

The sixteenth century gave us two or perhaps three words

directly from Portugal [1] ; **reis** 1555 and **milreis** 1589, neither of
them naturalized in English, and perhaps **padre** 1584, which
may, however, be Spanish ; this word has become fairly familiar
in England of recent years. From the west came **flamingo** (Port.
flamengo, perhaps borrowed in Portugal), found first in 1565,
in Hakluyt's *Voyages* (Sparke) : *The fowle of the fresh riuers . . .
where of the Flemengo is one, hauing all redde feathers* ; **coco**(nut)
1579, in Hakluyt's *Voyages* (T. Stevens) : *Wine of the Palme tree
or of a fruite called Cocos* ; **molasses,** still in common use in
America, 1582 (Port. *melaço*, adopted in the plural) ;   and
sargasso, the ' gulf-weed ', which still gives its name to the
Sargasso Sea, 1598 (Port. *sargaço*). The first Portuguese words
to be borrowed by the English in Africa were **madeira,** the
wine of *Madeira*, 1585, and **yam** (Port. *inhame*, probably from
a native word, though this is uncertain), which is found first
in 1588. In the same year also the first words from the Portuguese
in the East are recorded : **buffalo** (Port. *búfalo*, of the Indian
buffalo ; it is not used of the American bison until the end of
the eighteenth century) 1588, from a book on China ; **palanquin**
1588 (ultimately of Hindi or East Indian origin) ;   **typhoo**
(Port. *tufão*, probably from Urdu *tūfān* ; the present English
form has perhaps been influenced by Latin *typhonus*, from Greek
tuphōn) 1588, in Hickock's translation of Frederick's *Voyages* :
*I went a boord of the Shippe of Bengala, at which time it was the yeere
of Touffon* ;   **mandarin** 1589 (Parke's translation of Mendoza's
History of China ; Port. *mandarin*, through Hind. or Malay from
Sanscrit *mantrin* ' counsellor ') ;   **bayadère,** a Hindu dancing-
girl, 1598 (Port. *bailadeira* ' dancer ', but through French) ;
areca (Port., from Tamil) 1599, in Hakluyt's *Voyages* : *Great
quantie of Archa . . . which fruit they eat . . . with the leaf of an
Herbe which they call Bettell.*

The seventeenth century brought us another Portuguese
wine, this time from Portugal : **port,** from the Place-Name which
is now *Oporto*, really *O Porto* ' the port ' ; this is not till 1691,
when there is a reference to '*English ships that went to Bourdeaux
and took in wine, and after sailed to port O Porto, and then came
home, pretending it to be port* '. Tales of travellers in Brazil and

---

[1] These should be contrasted with the fairly numerous loans from Spain at
this period.

Guiana record four more words :   **peccary** 1613 (Harcourt,
Voyage to Guiana ;   probably originally from a native name) ;
macaw 1668 (Port. *macao*) ;   **grouper** 1697 (Dampier's *Voyages* :
Port. *garupa*) ;   **macaque** 1698 (through French from Port.
macaco, a Brazilian monkey ;   the word was borrowed again
in the Portuguese form as the name of a South African monkey,
1774).   The African name *Guinea* appears first (in the form **ginny**)
as the name of the guinea-fowl in 1620, and a little later as the
name of a coin (made from Guinea gold), in Evelyn's *Diary*,
1664.   Another West African word is **assagai** (borrowed by the
Portuguese from Arabic, and ultimately Berber), which first
appears in *Purchas his Pilgrimes*, 1625 : '*They of Myna or the
Golden Coast, their armes are Pikes, or Assagaies, Bowes and
Arrowes* ' ;   the spelling *assegai* is not found until the nineteenth
century.   The word **dodo** is from the Portuguese *doudo*, meaning
' stupid ', applied by Portuguese sailors to this bird, which is
a native of Mauritius.   It is found in English first in 1628, in
a letter written by a traveller to the island (E. Altham) :   ' *Of
m' perce you shall receue a iarr of ginger . . . and a bird called a
DoDo, if it live* '.

The year 1600 is of considerable importance in the history of
Portuguese words in English, for it was on December 31st in
this year that Queen Elizabeth granted a charter to ' The
Company of Merchants of London Trading to the East Indies '.
The regular and organized trade of the East India Company
brought about closer relations with the Portuguese traders in
the East, and the names of articles of commerce, and of things
connected with European life in India and farther east were
borrowed more freely than before.   The first word recorded in
this century is from the *First Letter Book of the East India
Company*, and is dated 1602 :   **pintado,** a coloured cotton cloth
(Port. *pintado*) :   ' 60 *ffardells . . . of blewes and chekered stuffes,
some fine Pinthadoes.*'   Other words followed quickly :   **caste,**
but in its earlier spelling **cast** (Port. *casta* ' race, descent ') 1613 ;
emu 1613 (of the cassowary, from Port. *ema*, originally of the
crane ;   it is not used of the Australian emu till 1842) ;   **com-
prador,** a native servant or house-steward in India and the Far
East, still in use in China, 1615 ;   **tank** (Port. *tanque*, from Lat.
stagnum ' pond ') 1616, in Terry's *Voyages to the East Indies* :

'*they have many Ponds, which they call Tanques* . . . *fill'd with water when that abundance of Rain fals*' ; **pagoda** 1634 (*Travels of Sir T. Herbert* ; Port. *pagode*) ; **lorcha,** a Chinese boat, 1653 ; **palmyra,** and **goglet,** a water-vessel of porous earthenware, 1698, both from a book on travel in India (Port. *palmyra, gorgoleta*).

Eighteenth century loans are fewer. From Portugal we have **moidore** from the beginning of the century (1711 ; Port. *moeda d'ouro*), and the title or form of address **senhor** from the end (1795 ; Murphy, *Travels in Portugal*). From Brazil : **pareira,** a drug obtained from a kind of Brazilian vine, 1715 (Port. *parreira*). From Africa : **palaver** 1735 (Port. *palavra* ; the first reference is to a talk or conference with natives of the Gold Coast ; later it passed into sailors' slang). From India : **joss** ' idol ' (Port. *deos* ' god') and **verandah** (Port. *varanda*), 1711, from Lockyer, *Account of the Trade with India* ; **cangue** 1727 (Port. *cango*), in Hamilton, *New Account of the East Indies* ; **ayah** (Port. *aia*) 1780.

The nineteenth century adds very little to our stock of Portuguese words : **margosa,** an East Indian tree, 1813 (Port. *amargoso*), continues the Eastern loans ; the last one is of quite a different character, and comes to us through French ; this is **massage,** first found in English in 1876, and ultimately from Portuguese *amassar* ' to knead '.

(C) SLAVONIC

English has at no time adopted many words from Slavonic and only two or three are used at the present time without direct reference to Russia, or Poland, etc. Those which are now most familiar are *sable, polka, mammoth, astrakhan,* and even these are hardly in constant, popular use. There is, however, a certain number of Slavonic, chiefly Russian, words which may be considered as more or less anglicized in form if not in application, almost all of them borrowed since 1550.

One Slavonic word has already been mentioned in the chapter on Scandinavian loan-words : the Norse loan *tapor-æx* (see p. 73), which came originally from the Russian *topor*. But this did not survive the Old English period. A Middle English borrowing is **sable,** from Old French, from Mediaeval Latin *sabelum,* which represents Russian *sobol,* the name of the animal ; this appears in English in the fourteenth century.

It was not until the middle of the sixteenth century that England came into direct relations with Russia. When Chancellour, in 1553, sailed round to the White Sea in a search for the North-East Passage, he opened up a new avenue for English trade. The Muscovy Company, established in the reign of Elizabeth, gained command of the shipping of the eastern Baltic, and English travellers as well as merchants made their fellow-countrymen acquainted with Slavonic words and customs. Before this time the Dutch had had control of the Baltic trade, and it is worth noting that at least two words have come into English from Slavonic by way of Dutch ; these are **pram, praam,** a type of boat used in the Baltic and the Netherlands, 1548 ; and the bird-name **siskin** 1562 (Dutch *sijsken,* from Slav. *czyźik*).

The first batch of direct loans from Russia falls between 1550 and 1590. They are as follows : **kvass** 1553 (recorded by Chancellour himself in his *Book of the Empire of Russia,* in Hakluyt) ; **rouble** 1554 (Hasse, in Hakluyt) ; **czar** and **verst** 1555 (both in Eden's *Decades*) ; **moujik** 1568 ; **voivode** 1570 (in Hakluyt) ; **beluga** and **sterlet** 1591 (in Giles Fletcher's *Of the Russe Commonwealth*).

After this there is a gap of nearly a century, which may be partly explained by the fact that during the first half of the seventeenth century the Eastern trade, hitherto carried on across the continent of Europe, and through Russia, became more and more a sea-borne trade, following the Cape route. The next few words of Russian origin came to England through other languages ; **calash,** earlier **calèche,** is from a French form ; it appears first in the *London Gazette,* 1666 : *The Pope taking the air in a rich calèche* ; **steppe** 1671 is apparently also through French ; **hospodar,** the title of the governors of Moldavia and Wallachia, from a Slavonic word meaning ' lord ', comes through Roumanian and French. It is after the visit of Peter the Great to England in 1697 that direct loans from Russian again begin to appear, and this visit may have been the stimulus to further acquaintance with Russian matters on the part of Englishmen.

Copeck is found in 1698 (Crull's *Muscovy*) ; **mammoth** 1706 ; **knout** 1716 (Parry's *State of Russia*) ; **ukase** 1729 (Consett, *Present State of Russia*, in the form *oukauze*) ; **astrakhan** 1766 (from a Place-Name ; first with reference to a coat-lining) ; **suslik** 1774.

A dozen more words make their appearance in the nineteenth century, all but two from the first half ; about half of them are words which are pretty generally known, the rest being less familiar : **saigon** 1801 ; **vodka** 1802 ; **droshky** 1808 ; **mazurka** (Polish) 1818 ; **samovar** 1830 ; **Uniat** 1833 ; **tundra** 1841 ; **troika** 1842 ; (manna)-**croup** 1843 (Russ. *krupa*) ; **polka** 1844 ; **tarantass,** a vehicle, 1850 ; **polynia,** an open stretch of water in an icefield, 1853 ; **zemstvo** 1865.

Then there is another interval, until the twentieth century has begun, when a small group of political words find their way to England; the chief of these are : **duma** 1905; **pogrom** 1905 ; **soviet** 1917; **ogpu** 1927; **bolshevik.** Another recent loan is **intelligentsia** 1920. Finally we may mention the word **robot,** which is Czech, from the stem of the verb *robotiti* ' to work ' (cognate with Russ. *rabótat*) ; this became familiar from the translation of Karel Capek's play, *Rossum's Universal Robots*, produced in England in 1923, and the word is now used for a machine performing the actions of a human being, or for a human being acting automatically.

(D) HUNGARIAN

The language of Hungary has given very few words to English. Two, however, are fairly old borrowings, dating from the sixteenth century. **Hussar** is found in 1532 ; it came perhaps through German, and represents Hungarian *huszar* (perhaps ultimately from Ital. *corsaro* = corsair), the name given to a body of horsemen organized in Hungary in the fifteenth century. **Coach,** earlier **coche,** from French, appears first in 1556 ; it is from Hung. *kocsi*, an adjectival form from the Place-Name *Kocs*, near Buda. The national name **Magyar** is recorded from the end of the eighteenth century, and during the early part of the present century it was popularized as the name of a particular shape in a woman's dress or blouse. **Shako** was apparently

borrowed during the Napoleonic wars ; it represents a French
form of Hungarian *csákó*, abbreviated from Hung. *csákós süveg*
' peaked cap ' ; English has it first in 1815. Finally there are
a very few recent loans, of which the most familiar are **czardas,
goulash, paprika.**

(E) MISCELLANEOUS

Other European languages have very little representation in
English. From Basque we have borrowed (through Spanish and
French) **bizarre** 1648, and **chaconne** (Basque *chucun* ' pretty ')
1685. Croatian appears in the (chiefly historical) **pandour,**
applied to one of a body of Croatian infantrymen of the
eighteenth century ; it dates from 1747 in this country ; the
word is probably ultimately from Med. Lat. *banderius,* from a
Germanic word. From Corsica comes the dialect form **maquis**
(Ital. *macchi* ' thicket '). Lapp is represented by one early loan,
morse 1475 (French, from Lapp *morsha* ' walrus '), and one from
the eighteenth century, **lemming** 1713 (Norw. from Lapp.
luomek).

To conclude we may give a small handful of words from Modern,
as distinct from Classical, Greek : **romaika,** a national dance,
1625 (Gk. *Rhōmaïkē*) ; **palikar,** the follower of a military chief,
1812 (Mod. Gk. *palikári*) ; **klepht,** a Greek brigand, 1820 (Mod.
Gk. *klephtēs*) ; **phanariot** (Mod. Gk. *phanariotēs*).

CHAPTER X

LOAN-WORDS FROM THE EAST

(A) ARABIC

It is from Arabic that English has borrowed the greatest number of Eastern loan-words, though it is true that a considerable proportion of them have not come to us direct. Of those which appear in the Middle English period, most have reached us through French (which often learnt them from Spanish), some perhaps directly from Spanish. The increasing trade with the Levant brought England into more immediate contact with the Arabic-speaking peoples of North Africa during the later fourteenth century, and in the sixteenth century trade and exploration farther east gave us a new source of Arabic loans : the Arabic element in the dialects of India. In the present section the Arabic words which we borrowed through Hindustani, etc., are not dealt with, nor are those which came to us through Turkish, which also has a fair number of words of Arabic origin ; some notes on these will be found in the sections on Indian and Turkish.

Apparently the earliest Arabic loan-word in English is the O.E. **mancus,** the name of a coin of gold, equal to the Latin *solidus* ; this represents the Arabic *man-kuš* = ' stamped (with a die) ', and may have reached English from France or from Spain ; at this time the Moors had the upper hand in Spain and southern France, and evidence that England was influenced by Moorish finance is afforded by the existence of a gold coin, minted in England in the time of Offa, which besides the title *Offa rex* bears also an Arabic inscription. *Mancus* is found in English documents, chiefly charters, from the year 799 onwards ; it does not, however, survive the Conquest. It appears in such contexts as : *ælcum messepreoste binnan Cent mancus goldes* (Charter 41 in *Oldest English Texts*, 835) ' to every priest in Kent, a mancus of gold ' ; *loca, nu þu hafast þine mancossas,*

213

þa þe þu sohtest (*Gregory's Dialogues* 65) 'look, now you have your mancuses, which you were seeking', where the Latin original has *Ecce habes solidos quos quaesisti* ; *bebohte his hors to twelf mancussum* (*Dialogues* 63) ' sold his horse for twelve mancuses ', for the Latin *equum suum duodecim aureis vendidit*. Another Old English loan is the word **ealfara,** a pack-horse, borrowed as a trading or military term from Old Spanish *alfaraz*, from Arab. *al faras* ' the horse '. This has been recorded once only : in the eleventh century *Letter of Alexander to Aristotle* : *xxx þusenda ealfarena & oxna þa ðe hwæte bæron* ' thirty thousand pack-horses and oxen which carried the wheat '. The same word, in the form *auferan*, is found in Old French, and it is possible that French was the immediate source of the English word.

The Arabic loan-words of Middle English begin at the end of the twelfth century, with the word **saffron** in the *Trinity College Homilies*, c. 1200 : *Hire wimpel wit oðer maked ʒeleu mid saffran* ' her wimple white, or made yellow with saffron ' ; this is O.Fr. *safran*, from Arab. *za'farān*. **Admiral** is found in the early manuscript of Laʒamon's *Brut*, in the sense of ' emir ' (from O.Fr., from Arab. *amir al*, abbreviated from a phrase such as *amir-al-bahr* ' emir or commander of the sea ') : *þat on admiral* : *of Babiloine he wes ældere* ' the one emir was prince of Babylon ' ; it is used first of an (English) admiral of the fleet in Wyntoun's *Cronykil*, 1423, and for the commander-in-chief of the Navy by Capgrave in 1460.

Many of the earlier Arabic loan-words have to do with science, especially mathematics, which had reached an advanced stage among the Moors. The first word in this class is the now archaic **algorism,** the name of the Arabic system of numeration, also used for ' arithmetic ' ; this is to be found in the *Ancrene Riwle* (see p. 84), and comes to us through O.Fr. *algorisme*, from Arab. *al-Khowarazmi*, the name of a mathematician. The next word is more commonplace : **mattress,** from O.Fr., probably from Ital. *materasso*, ahd ultimately from Arab. *almatrah* ' place where something is thrown ' ; also, ' a mat, bed ' : *Goth, he seide, and maketh a bed / Of quoiltene and of materasz*, Southern Legend Collection, c. 1290.

Fourteenth century loans are more numerous : **barbican,** in the *Cursor Mundi*, c. 1300 (through Fr.). In the romance of

King Alisaunder (early fourteenth century) : **acton,** a doublet of quilted cotton worn under the armour, O.Fr. *auqueton,* from Span. from Arab. *al-qutun* ' the cotton ' (see **cotton** 1381) ; **cubeb,** a spicy berry used for flavouring, also French from Span., Arab. *kabābah* ; **dragoman** (O.Fr. *dragoman, dragman,* Arab. *targumān* ' interpreter ') : *Alisaundre . . . is y-come to Arabye, / So me saide a drogman.* Other fourteenth century loans : **hazard** (in *Havelok the Dane*) ; **camphor,** earlier *camfre, camfire* (O.Fr. from Arab. *kafūr*), *Wardrobe Accounts,* Edw. II, *c.* 1313 ; **alkanet** (Arab. *al-ḥenna* ; cf. **henna,** borrowed without the Arab. definite article, 1600) 1326 ; **lute** (O.Fr. from Arab.) 1361–2 : *In uno viro ludenti in uno loyt* ' for one man playing on the lute ', Durham Account Rolls ; **alchemy** 1362, in Langland's *Piers Plowman* (O.Fr. from Med. Lat., from Arab. *al kimia,* but this is from Greek *kēmia*) ; **alembic** (O.Fr. from Arab. *al anbīq* ' the cup ', again ultimately from Greek) 1374, in Chaucer's *Troylus and Criseyde* : *This Troylus in teres gan distille, / As licour out of alambic fulle faste* iv, 520 ; **cotton** (Fr. from Span. from Arab. *qutun*) 1381–2, *Compotus of Earl of Derby* ; **almagest,** used primarily for an astronomical treatise of Ptolemy, (the Arab. word has the definite article *al* + a loan from Gk. *megíste*), *c.* 1386, Chaucer's *Miller's Tale* : *His almageste and bokes gret and smale* ; **alkali** (Arab. *al qalīy*), **tartar,** and **elixir** (Arab. *al-iksir*), all in Chaucer's *Canon's Yeoman's Tale,* note especially *The Philosophre stoon, / Elixir clept, we sechen fast echoon* ; **zenith** (Fr. from Span. from Arab. *samt (ar-rās)* ' path overhead ') 1387, Trevisa's translation of Higden's *Polychronicon* ; **azimuth** (Fr. from Arab. *as-sumūt,* ' the ' + the plural of *samt* ' path, way ', as in *zenith*), **nadir** (Ar. *naḍīr* ' opposite to '), **almanac,** all in Chaucer's *Treatise on the Astrolabe, c.* 1391 ; the last word is of doubtful origin ; it may be from a Spanish-Arabic *al* + *manākh* ' calendar ', recorded in an early sixteenth century Spanish-Arabic vocabulary, but not elsewhere in Arabic ; **ream** (Fr., from Arab. *rizmah* ' bale ') 1392–3 ; **caliph** (Fr., from Arab. *khalīfah*) 1393, in Gower's *Confessio Amantis,* again in 1400 in Mandeville's *Travels* ; **amber** (Fr., from Arab. *'anbar,* originally ' ambergris '), **syrup** (Fr. *sirop,* from Arab. *sharāb* ' wine, or other drink ' ; cf. *shrub* and *sherbet*) 1398, in Trevisa's translation of the *De proprietatibus rerum* of Bartholomaeus Anglicus ; **cipher** (Fr.,

P

from Span. from Arab. *çifr* ; cf. *zero* 1604) 1399, *Richard the Redeless* : *than satte summe, as siphre doth in awgrym, / That noteth a place, and no thing availeth.*

It will have been noted that all of these fourteenth century words are scientific or denote objects of trade. The same is true of most of the words of the fifteenth century, but now we begin to find words relating to the Mohammedan religion. *Mandeville's Travels, c.* 1400, has **alcoran** (*the holy book Alcaron*), **mosque** (Fr., from Arab. *masgid*), as well as **bedouin** (Fr., from Arab. *badāwin*, pl.), and **lemon** (Fr., from Span., from Arab. *laimūn*). An early fifteenth century medical work, Lanfranc's *Chirurgia*, has **nucha,** the spinal cord, later the nape of the neck (Med. Lat. from Arab. ; *Alle þe cordis þat comen of þe brayn and nucha*), **realgar** (Med. Lat., from Arab. *rehj al-ghar*, literally ' powder of the cave ' ; *þou schalt in no maner leie þerto realgar, ne noon violent pingis*) ; **sumac** (Fr. from Span., from Arab. *summac*). About 1430 we find **maravedi,** a coin, which represents the Spanish form of Arab. *Murabitīn*, the name of a Moorish dynasty in Spain, 1086–1147, after which the coin was named. **Caraway** is in the *Promptorium Parvulorum* of about 1440 (O.Span. *alcaravea*, from Arab. *al karawiyā*). Science is represented again by **alidade,** in an addition (dating from about 1450) in one manuscript of Chaucer's *Astrolabe.* **Genet,** a civet-cat (Fr., from Arab. *jarnait*), appears in 1481 in Caxton's *Reynard the Fox* ; **tambour** (Fr., from Arab. *tambur*) in Caxton's *Fables of Æsop,* 1484. The remaining words from this century are all trade-terms : **quintal,** a weight of a hundred pounds (Span., from Arab. *qinṭar*) 1470, *Black Book of the Exchequer* ; **antimony** 1477, in a book on alchemy ; **garble,** originally ' to sift, remove, refuse from ' (through Italian, from Arab. *gharbala* ' to sift ', perhaps itself a loan-word from Lat. *cribellāre*), 1483, in an Act of the reign of Richard III : *they will not suffre any garbelyng of theym to be made but selle good and bad at so excessyf price togedyr ungarbeled* ; **tass** (O.Fr. *tasse*, from Arab. *ṭass*, ' basin ') 1483, in Caxton's *Dialogues* ; **tare,** weight of conveyance or receptacle of goods for sale, etc. (Fr., from Span., from Arab. *tarhah*, from *ṭaraha* ' to throw away ') 1486, in the *Naval Accounts*, Henry VII : *ij barrelles Gonnepowdre conteyning in weight besides the tare Diij lbs.*

In the sixteenth century there is a reflection of the increase in

direct relations between England and North Africa, and the
Levant, in the words now introduced—words denoting Eastern
persons and rank, and animals and other products of Egypt,
North Africa, etc., besides those which became articles of
commerce. Some words still reach England by way of French
or Spanish, some through Italian, but many appear to have been
learnt by English travellers direct from Arabic speakers. **Rebec,**
a musical instrument (cf. *lute*, 1361) 1509, is a French form of
Arab. *rebāb.* Scientific terms are less common now, perhaps the
only one from this period being **algebra** (Ital., from Arab. *al-jebr,*
literally ' the putting together of broken parts '), used by Copland
in 1541. There are a few naval and military terms, none of them
directly from Arabic ; **arsenal** (from Arab. *dār accinā'ah* ' work-
shop ') appears to have been borrowed in Romance as *darsena*
whence it passed into Italian, was borrowed by French, and then
by English ; it is recorded first in 1506, in the sense of ' dock '
(for ships) ; **calibre** 1567 is French from Arab. *qālib* ' mould ' ;
monsoon, borrowed by Portuguese from Arabic, was then
borrowed by Dutch from Portuguese, and by English from Dutch;
it is found in 1584. Eastern titles, etc. : **mameluke** 1511 (Arab.
mamlūk ' slave ' ; used by Guylforde : *there was a grete Ambasset
of the Soldans towardes Venyce, that hadde in his companye many
Mamolukes*) ; **assassin** 1531 (Ital. *assassino,* from Arab.
hashshāshīn, pl., literally ' eaters of hashish '), already in its
modern sense ; **sultan** 1555 (Arab. *sultān* ; the feminine *sultana*
appears in 1585, and as the name of a kind of raisin in 1841) ;
sheikh 1577, in Eden's *History of Travayle* (Arab. *shaikh,* ' old
man ') ; **muezzin** 1585 (Arab. *mu'aðð̣in,* participle of *aðana* ' to
proclaim ') ; **mufti,** a Mohammedan priest, 1586 (Arab. *muftī* ;
in the modern sense of ' civilian dress ' it is used first in 1816) ;
cadi, a judge, 1590, in Webbe's *Travels* (Arab. *qādī*). One term
connected with the Mohammedan religion is **hegira** (Arab.
hijrah) 1590. Trade terms : **carat** (from Ital., from Arab. *qīrat,*
perhaps ultimately Greek) 1535, in Eden's *Decades of the Newe
World* ; **magazine** (Fr., from Arab. *makāzin* ' storehouses ') 1583 ;
tariff (from Ital., from Arab.) 1591, in the sense of ' list of customs
duties, etc. ; **jar** (Fr. *jarre,* from Span., from Arab. *jarrah*)
1592. Animals, plants, etc. : **saker,** a kind of falcon (Fr., from
Span. *sacro,* from Arab. *çaqr*) 1521 ; **artichoke** (from Ital.

articiocco, from Span., from Arab. *al-kharshūf*) 1531 ;   **civet** (Fr., from Arab. *zabād*) 1532 ;   **tamarind** (probably through Span., from Arab. *tamr-hindī*) 1533 ;   **tarragon** 1538 (from Span., from Arab. *ṭarkhōn*) ;   **alcohol** 1543 (Med. Lat., from Arab. *al-koḥ'l* 'the collyrium '), **senna** (Arab. *sanā*), both in a medical work, 1543 ;   **carob** 1548 (Arab. *kharrūbah*) ;   **apricot,** earlier **apricock** 1551 (Fr. *abricot* and Span. *albarcoque*, from Arabic, but ultimately from Latin) ;   **ribes,** 1562 ;   **kali** 1578 (note the earlier *alkali*, with the Arab. definite article) ;   **albacore,** a fish of the Atlantic, 1579, in Stevens's *Letters from Goa*,[1] in Hakluyt's *Voyages* (Port., from Arab. *al-bukr* ' young camel ') ;   **roc,** a fabulous Eastern bird, 1579, in Twyne's *Phisick against Fortune* (Arab. *rokh*) ; **anil,** the indigo shrub, hence a dye obtained from it, 1581 ; **sash,** earlier **shash** (Arab. *shāsh* ' muslin ') 1590, Ralph Fitch,[1] in Hakluyt's *Voyages* : *Great Store of cloth is made there fo cotton, and Shashes for the Moores* ;   **giraffe** (Fr., from Span., from Arab. *zarāfah*) 1594 ;   **zibet** (Ital., from Arab. *zabād*, cf. *civet*, above) 1594 ;   **calabash** 1596 ;   **hashish** 1598, in Phillips's *Discourse of the East and West Indies*, translated from the Dutch of Linschoten ;   **kermes,** an insect from which a dye is obtained (Arab. *qirmiz*), 1598, used first in English in a transferred sense, of the oak on which the insect lives.

During the seventeenth century more words appear which refer specifically to Eastern life and customs, and which have not acquired a wider application or become as fully naturalized as many of the earlier loan-words. Words connected with the sea : **sirocco** 1617 (Ital., from Arab. *sharq* ' east ') ;   **tartan,** a type of ship used in the Mediterranean, 1621 (Fr., from Arab. *tarīdāh*) ; **felucca** 1628 (Ital., from Arab. *falaka* ' to be round ') ;   **khamsin,** a wind which blows for periods of fifty days, 1685 (Arab., = fifty).

People : **fakir** 1609 (Arab. *faqīr* ' poor man ') ;   **imam** 1613, in *Purchas his Pilgrimage* (from Arab. *imām* ' precede ') ;   **ameer** 1614, the variant **emir** in 1625 (cf. the earlier *admiral*), from Arab. *amīr* : *Mahomet's . . . kinsmen in greene Shashes, who are called Emers* Purchas ;   **hákim** ' governor ' (Arab. *ḥākim*) 1615 ; **sayyid, said** ' lord ' 1615 ;   **marabout,** a hermit, 1623 (Fr., from

---

[1] See Sir W. Foster, *England's Quest of Eastern Trade.*

Arab. *murābit*) ; **sufi** 1653 (Arab. *çufi*) ; **hakím** ' doctor ' 1638
(Arab. *hakīm*) ; **ulema** 1688.

Trade : **sequin** 1617 (Fr., from Ital. *zecchino*—and chiefly
used of an Italian coin— from Arab. *sikkh*, a die for coining) ;
mohair, earlier *moekaire*, 1619 (Arab. *muχayyar*) ; **tabby** 1638
(Fr., from Arab. *'attābiy*, the name of a quarter of Baghdad,
from a personal name). Buildings, food, clothes, etc. : **couscous,
kouskous** (Fr., from Arab. *kaskasa* ' to pound ') 1600, in Pory's
translation of Leo's *Africa* ; **arrack** 1602 ; **mastaba** ' a bench,
seat ' (Arab. *mactabah*, probably from Persian), 1603, in Knolles's
History of the Turks ; in the archaeological sense of a kind of
tomb, in 1882 ; **sherbet** 1603 (Arab. *sharbaʰ*, perhaps through
Turkish ; borrowed also in French, whence English took *sorbet*
in the nineteenth century) ; **alcove** 1623 (Fr., from Span., from
Arab. *al qobbah* ' the vault ') ; **hammam,** a Turkish bath, and
sofa (Arab. *ṣoffah*) 1625, in *Purchas his Pilgrimes : A Sofa
spread with very sumptuous Carpets of Gold . . . upon which the
Grand Signior sitteth* ; in the modern sense in 1717 ; **madrasah**
1630 (Arab. *madrasaʰ*) ; **harem** 1634 (Arab. *haram*) ; **masjid**
1646 (Arab. *masgid* ; cf. *mosque*, borrowed earlier through
French) ; **jerid,** a javelin, 1662 ; **minaret** 1682 (Arab. *manārat*) ;
cabob 1690 (Arab. *kabāb*) ; **mattamore,** a subterranean dwelling
or store, 1695 (Fr., from Arab. *matmūraʰ*) ; **burnous** (Arab.
burnus) 1695, in a work on Morocco by Pierre Motteux.

Animals, plants, etc. : **henna** (Arab. *henna*) ; **gazelle** (Fr.,
from Arab. *ghazāl*), 1600, in Pory's translation of Leo's *Africa* ;
talc (Fr., from Arab. *talq*, perhaps from Persian) 1601 ; **colcothar**
1605 (Arab. *qolqotār*) ; **curcuma** 1617 (Arab. *kurkum* ' saffron ') ;
azarole, the fruit of the Neapolitan medlar, 1658 (Fr., from Ital.,
from Arab.) ; **jerboa** 1662 ; **albatross** 1681 (with assimilation to
Lat. *albus* ' white ', from Port. *alcatras*, from Arabic, and perhaps
originally from Phoenician, through Greek) ; **natron** 1684 (Fr.,
from Span., from Arab. *natrūn*, from Greek *nitron*).

Miscellaneous : **zero** 1604 (Fr., from Ital., from Arab. *çifr*,
cf. the earlier *cipher*) ; **salaam** 1613 (Arab. *salām*) ; **saraband**
1616 (Fr., from Span., from Arabic) ; **hadji,** one who has been
on a pilgrimage to Mecca, 1602 (Arab. *hajj* ; the Arabic name of
this pilgrimage, *hājī*, is found in English as *hadji* in 1704).

The eighteenth century brought in fewer words from Arabic ;

most of them are concerned with plants and animals, clothes, and people ; a few refer to Mohammedan religion and mythology. They are given here in order of introduction, without classification : **Allah** 1702, in Rowe's *Tamerlane* ; **tarboosh** 1702 (Arab. *tarbūsh*) ; **kiblah,** the point to which Mohammedans turn in prayer, 1704 (Arab. *qiblah*) ; **haik** 1713 (Arab. *ḥayk*) ; **abutilon** 1731 (Mod. Lat., from Arab.) ; **houri** 1737 (Fr., probably through Pers. *ḥūrī*, from Arab. *ḥawira* 'to be black-eyed like a gazelle') ; **fellah** 1743 ; **shrub,** a beverage, 1747 (Arab. *shurb* 'drink', cf. *sharāb* 'wine') ; **jinnee, genie** 1748 (Arab. *jinnī* ; the English form with *j-* first in 1841) ; **ghazi** 1753 ; **hookah** 1763 (Arab. *ḥuqqah* 'casket, cup') ; **candy** 1769 (Fr., from Arab., from Pers. *qand* 'sugar') ; **nunnation,** first with reference to a phonetic change in Arabic nouns, later used more generally, 1776 (Arab. *nūn* '*n*') ; **carafe** (through French) 1786 ; **ghoul** 1786 (Arab. *ghūl*) ; **dirhem** 1788 (Arab. *dirham*, from Lat. *drachma*) ; **fennec** (Arab. *fenek*), **simoom** (Arab. *semūm*) 1790, in Bruce's *Travels in Abyssinia* ; **durra, dhurra** 1798 ; **kohl** (cf. *alcohol* 1543) ; **coffle,** a train of slaves, etc., 1799 (Arab. *qāfilah*).

Practically all the nineteenth century loans from Arabic were, and remain (with the exception of *loofah*), words with special reference to Eastern things, plants, animals, etc., or other products ; again, they are fewer than in the previous century ; **doum** 1801 ; **afreet, afrit** 1802 ; **bismillah** 1813 ; **marabou** 1823 (Fr., apparently a special use of Arab. *murābit* 'hermit', cf. *marabout* 1623) ; **ariel,** a variety of gazelle, 1832 ; **aḷizarin** 1835 ; **shadoof** 1836 (Arab. *shādūf*) ; **wadi** 1839 ; **yashmak** 1844 ; **alfalfa** 1845 ; **razzia** 1845 (Fr., from Algerian, from Arab. *ghazwah* 'war') ; **zariba** 1849 ; **jehad** 1869 (Arab. *jihad*) ; **sudd** 1879 ; **dahabiah,** a boat used on the Nile, 1877 (the word in Arabic means 'golden', and was applied first to a gilded state barge) ; **moucharaby** 1884 ; **loofah** 1887 (Arab. *lūfaʰ*) ; **safari** 1892 (Swahili, from Arabic).

(B) INDIAN DIALECTS

English has borrowed a few words, some directly and some indirectly, from Sanscrit, and these are among the very latest and the very earliest from the East. Already in the Old English period, and previously on the Continent (as has been pointed out in Chapter II), a few Sanscrit words had passed into Germanic or English through Greek and Latin : **panther, pepper,** and the O.E. **meregrota** ' pearl ' ;   **ginger** came into Late O.E. or early M.E. through French ; so also **cendal, sendal,** a silk stuff, which appears in the late twelfth century : *wið ciclatouns and cendals and deorewurðe claðes* (see p. 111) ;   **sandal** ' sandal-wood ' (Scrt. *çandana*) probably comes through Med. Lat. *sandalum* ;   it is found first in 1400. In the eighteenth century, **avatar** seems to have been borrowed directly from literary Sanscrit (it appears in a work by Sir W. Jones in 1784) ; so also **suttee** 1786 (in the *Parliamentary Papers, E. India* ;   Scrt. *satī*) ;   **tantra,** one of the Hindu religious writings, 1799. Almost all those borrowed from Sanscrit during the nineteenth century are terms connected with Indian philosophy : **yoga** 1820 ;   **maya** 1823 ;   **karma** 1828 ; **nirvana** 1836 ;   **swastika** 1871 (Scrt. *svastika*, from *svasta* ' well-being, luck ') ;   **stupa,** a Buddhist monument, 1876.

But by far the greatest number of Indian loan-words in English are from Hindustani, which is developed from Old Sanscrit (and thus an Indo-Germanic dialect), but has a considerable admixture of Arabic and Persian words in its vocabulary. These appear first in the middle of the sixteenth century, but are rare until the very end of the century, after English traders had actually begun to come into direct contact with India by sea. The first trading voyage to the East by way of the Cape made by an English ship was that of James Lancaster,[1] in the *Edward Bonaventure*, who sailed from Plymouth to the East Indies in 1591–2. There are four words recorded first before 1600 : **lac,** a kind of resin, 1533 (Eden's *Treatise on the Newe Indies*) ; **raj** 1555 (Eden's *Decades*) ;   **maund,** a weight, 1584 Barret, in Hakluyt's *Voyages* ;   Hind. *mān*) ;   **banian** 1599 (Hakluyt's *Voyages*, in the sense of a Hindoo trader ;   it is probably Gujerati, and has passed through Arabic and Portuguese).

In the seventeenth century, with the East India Company spreading its influence gradually across India, and travellers recording their impressions of Eastern travel, Indian words are found in considerable numbers. Few, however, have become

---

[1] See the account of this voyage in Sir W. Foster's *England's Quest of Eastern Trade*, London, 1933.

really ' popular ' terms, though *chintz, tussore, dungarees, kedgeree, punch,* are pretty well naturalized, and *cot* and *bungalow* are common. Here is a classified list of the loans of this century :—
People and titles : **nabob** 1612 (Hind. *nāwwāb*), in Covete's *Voyages : an Earle is called a Nawbob* ; **guru** (Hind. *gurū*), and **mullah,** an expounder of the Koran, or a religious leader, 1613, in *Purchas his Pilgrimage : the Mulla's or Priests of the Mogores* ; **moonshee,** a native interpreter, (Hind. *munshī*) 1622 ; **vakeel** (Hind. *vakīl,* from Arab.) 1622 ; **moolvie,** a teacher (Hind., from Arab. *maulavi*), and **ryot** (Hind. *raiyat,* a farmer, from Arab.), 1625, in Purchas ; **sahib** 1627 (Hind. from Arab. *çāhib* ' friend ') ; **khansamah,** a house-steward, 1645 (Hind., from Pers. *kansaman*) ; **sice, syce** 1653 (Hind. *sāyis,* from Arab.) ; **mahout** 1662 (Hind. *mahaut*) ; **pundit** 1672 (Hind. *pandit*) ; **maharajah, ranee,** 1698, in Fryer's *Account of East India and Persia.*

Textiles, clothes, etc. : **chintz,** really a plural, from Hindi *chĭnt* (from Scrt. *chitra* ' variegated '), 1614, in Peyton's *Voyages* in *Purchas his Pilgrimage :   530 Callicoes white and coloured ... Pintadoes, Chints, and Chadors* ; cf. Pepys, *Diary,* 1663 : *Bought my wife a chint, that is a painted Indian callico, for to line her new study* ; **chuddar,** a square of cloth, 1614 (Hindi, *chadar* ; see quotation above, under *chintz*) ; **tussore** 1619 ; **dhoti,** a loin-cloth, 1622 ; **puggaree** 1665 (Hind. *pagri* ' turban ') ; **dungaree** 1696 (Hind. *dungrī*), in Purchas ; first recorded of trousers of this material in Kipling, 1891.

Animals, plants, etc. : **datura** 1662 (Hind. *dhatūrā*) ; **bummalo** 1673 (Mahrathi *bombīla*) ; cf. Fryer, *E. India and Persia : notable for a fish called Bumbelow, the Sustenance of the Poorer sort* ; **talipot,** a kind of palm, 1681 (Hind. *talpat*) ; **mongoose** 1698 (Mahrathi *mangūs*) ; **sambur,** a deer, 1698 (Hind. *sāmbar*).

Food and drink : **kedgeree** (Hindi *khichṛī*) 1625 ; **punch** 1632 (apparently from Hind. *panch* ' five ', as made of five ingredients) ; **ghee** 1665 (Hind. *ghi*), Sir T. Herbert's *Travels*) ; **pawnee** 1683 (Hind. *pāni* ' water ').

Houses, household objects, vehicles, etc. : **mussuck,** a water-skin, 1610 (Finch, in *Purchas his Pilgrimage* ;   Hind. *masak*) ; **punka(h)** 1625 ; **doolie,** a litter, 1625 (Hawkins, in Purchas ; Hind. *doli*) ; **cot** 1634 (Hind. *khāṭ* ' bedstead ' ; later in nautical use, 1769, and for a child, 1818) ; **bungalow** 1676 (Hind. *banglā*, originally an adj., = ' of Bengal ') ; **tomtom** 1693 ; **hackery**, bullock-cart, 1698 (Hind. *chhakra*).

Coins and measures : **crore,** ten million rupees, 1609 (Hawkins, in Purchas ; Hind. *karor*) ; **rupee** 1612 (Withington, *Travels* ; Hind. *rūpīya*) ; **lac, lakh,** ' a hundred thousand ', especially of rupees, 1613 (Peyton, in *Purchas his Pilgrimage* ; Hind. *lākh*) ; **pice** 1615 ; **seer,** a weight, 1618 (Hind. *sēr*) ; **cowrie** 1662 (Hind. *kaurī*).

Official : **durbar** 1609 (Hawkins, in Purchas ; Hind. *darbar*) ; **choky,** a custom or toll house, 1608 (Saris, in Purchas ; Hindi *chaukī* ; by the nineteenth century it had become a slang term for ' prison ') ; **cutcherry,** an office, 1610 (Hawkins, in Purchas ; Hind. *kachahrī*) ; **chop,** official seal or stamp, 1614 (Milward, in Purchas : *The King sent us his chop* ; Hindi *chhāp* ' impression ' ; now chiefly used in China, = ' brand, trade-mark ').

Miscellaneous : **ghât,** a mountain-pass, 1603 (R. Johnson, *Kingdom and Commonwealth*) ; **shikar,** hunting-expedition, 1613 (Finch, in Purchas ; **shikari** ' hunter ' not till 1827) ; **maidan** 1625 (*Purchas his Pilgrimes* : *The Medon, which is a pleasant greene, in the middest whereof is a May-pole to hang a light on* ; Hind. *maidān*) ; **juggernaut,** a figure of Vishnu, 1638 (Bruton, in Hakluyt ; Hind. *jagannath* ' lord of the universe ' ; figuratively in 1854) ; **pucka** 1698 (Hind. *pakka* ' ripe, of full weight ').

Here already have been examples of development of meaning in Anglo-Indian use which are foreign to the original Hindustani, etc. ; the same thing happens also in later loans, e.g. *wallah, chit, jungle, pug,* in the eighteenth and nineteenth centuries. The distribution of new words in this century is remarkable : out of thirty-five words now recorded for the first time, only four occur before 1750 ; there seems to be a slackening of interest in Eastern travel, and the East India Company was apparently carrying on much the same kind of trade as in the previous century. But in the middle of the century India and the Company were disturbed by the French bid for power, and after Clive's successful campaigns before, and after the beginning of, the Seven Years' War (1756), a renewed interest in, and growing knowledge of, India is reflected in a new period of borrowing.

Now we have again a number of words denoting persons and rank, some of them military, rather fewer concerned with textiles and clothes, a fair number of plants and animals, etc. The total number of words first recorded in the seventeenth century is fifty-one, sixteen more than in the eighteenth.

Persons, etc. : **nawab** 1758 (Hind. *nāwwāb,* cf. the earlier *nabob*) ; **ressaldar** 1758 (Hind. *risāladār*) ; **jemadar** 1763 (Hind. from Arab.) ; **Nizam** 1768 (Hind., from Arab. *niḍām* ' order, arrangement ') ; **wallah** 1776 (from the Hind. agent-suffix *-wālā*) ; **baboo** 1782 (*India Gazette*) ; **soucar,** a Hindu banker, 1785 (Hind. *sāukār* ' honest ').

Textiles, etc. : **gunny** 1711 (Lockyer, *Account of the Trade with India* : *When Sugar is pack'd in double Goneys* ; Hind. *gōni* ' sack ') ; **bandana** 1752 (Long, *Bengal* : *Plain taffaties, ordinary bandannoes* ; Hind. *bāndhnū* ' a method of dyeing ') ; **jaconet** 1769 (from a Place-Name, Jagannathi, in Bengal) ; **sari** 1785.

Animals and birds : **argala,** a kind of stork, 1754 (Hind. *hargila*) ; **myna** 1769 (Hind. *mainā*) ; **monal,** a kind of pheasant, 1769 ; **muckna,** an elephant, 1780 (Hind. *makhnā*) ; **cheetah** 1781 (Hind. *chītā* from Scrt. *chitta* ' spotted ').

Plants, etc. : **sunn,** fibre, 1774 (Hind. *san*) ; **tatty,** a kind of matting, 1792 (Hind. *ṭaṭṭi* ' wicker-frame ') ; **jute** 1746 (Bengali *jhoṭo*).

Objects of ordinary use : **anna** 1727 (Hamilton, *New Account of the East Indies* ; Hind. *āna*) ; **howdah** 1774 (Hind. *haudah,* from Arab.) ; **chatty,** a water-pot, 1781 (Hind. *chāti*) ; **chit** 1785 (Hind. *chiṭṭhi*) ; **bangle** 1787 (Hind. *bangrī*) ; **bidree** 1794 (Hind. *bidri*).

Districts : **mofussil** 1781 (Hind. from Arab.) ; **taluk** 1799 (Hind. from Arab.).

Natural features : **nullah,** watercourse, 1776 (Hind. *nālā*) ; **jungle** 1776 (Hindi *jangal* ' open desert ').

Buildings : **dâk** 1727 (Hamilton, *New Account of the East Indies*) ; **gurry,** a fort, 1786 (Hind. *gaṛhī*).

Miscellaneous : **baksheesh** 1755 ; **shampoo** 1762 (Hind. *chāmpo,* imperative of *chāmpnā* ' to press, kneed, shampoo ') ; **nautch,** a dance, 1796 (Hind. *nāch*).

Of these only *bandana, jute, bangle,* and *shampoo* have come into widespread use.

The number of loans increases in the nineteenth century, partly helped by the appearance of India in fiction as well as in further travels and memoirs. Terms for fabrics, etc., are fairly frequent, as are also names of plants and animals, and of things used in Indian life. Again only a few are at all widely used : *cashmere, chutney, dinghy, gymkhana, loot, nainsook, polo, puttee, pyjamas.*

People : **sowar,** cavalry trooper, 1802 (Hind. *sāwar* ' rider ') ; **dacoit** 1810 (Williamson, *East Indian Vade Mecum* ; Hind. *dākāit*) ; **thug** 1810 (Hind. *thag* ' deceiver, robber ') ; **moonsif** 1812 (Hind. from Arab. *munçif* ' just ') ; **chuprassi** 1828 (Heber, *Indian Journals* ; Hind. *chaprāsī*) ; **dhobi** 1860 (W. H. Russell, *Diary in India*) ; **chela** 1883 (Sinnett, *Esoteric Buddhism* ; Hind. *chēlā* ' slave, pupil ').

Textiles, garments, etc. : **puttee** 1800 (Hind. *paṭṭi* ' bandage ') ; **nainsook** 1804 (Hind. *nainsukh, nain* ' eye ' + *sukh* ' pleasure ') ; **cashmere** 1822 (Place-Name *Kashmīr*) ; **topi** 1826 ; **tat,** canvas, 1840 ; **numdah,** a kind of cloth ; **dhurrie,** a cotton fabric, 1880 (Hind. *dari*) ; **pyjamas** 1886 (Hind. *pājāma,* from *pā'e* ' leg ' + *jāma* ' garment ').

Animals, fish, etc. : **gazel,** a kind of ox, 1800 ; **gaur** 1806 ; **gavial,** crocodile, 1825 (Hind. *ghariyāl*) ; **dhole,** the Indian wild dog, 1827 ; **panda,** the cat-bear, 1835 (Himalayan) ; **mugger** 1844 (Hindī *magar*) ; **mahseer,** a fish, 1854 ; **markhor,** a kind of goat, 1867 (Pushtu) ; **krait** 1874 (Hind. *karait*).

Plants : **sissoo,** E. Indian tree, 1810 (Hind. *sīsō*) ; **toon** 1810 (Hind. *tun*) ; **munjeet** 1813 (Hind. *majīth*) ; **mudar** 1819 (Hind. *madār*) ; **deodar** 1842 (Hind. *de'odar,* from Scrt. *deva dara* ' divine tree ') ; **sola,** the pith of an E. Indian plant, 1845 (Bengali) ; **purree,** a yellow pigment, 1852 (Hind. *pōōri*).

Household objects, etc.: **lota(h),** a brass vessel, 1819 ; **charpoy** 1845 (Hind. *chārpāi* ' bedstead ', = ' four feet ') ; **tonga** 1880 (Hind. *tānga*).

Food : **chupatty** 1810 (Williamson, *East Indian Vade Mecum* ; Hindi *chapātī*) ; **chutney** 1813 (Forbes, *Oriental Memoirs,* 1813).

Military : **tana,** military post, 1803 (Hind. *thāna*) ; **kukri,** a sword, 1811 ; **gingall, jingal,** a fire-arm, 1818 (Hind. *janjal*) ; **tulwar,** kind of sabre, 1834 ; **dumdum** 1897 (Place-Name).

Miscellaneous : **pachisi,** a game, 1800 ; **zillah,** a district, 1800 ;

dinghy 1810 (Williamson ; Hind. *dengī*) ; **loot** 1839 (*Blackwood's Mag.* ; Hind. *lūt*) ; **pie,** a coin $= \frac{1}{3}$ of pice, 1859 ; **gymkhana** 1861 (Hind. *gendkhana* ' racket-court ') ; **pug** ' footprint ' 1865 (Hind. *pag* ' foot ') ; **tamasha** ' show ' 1872 (Hind. from Arab.) ; **polo** 1872 (*Daily News* ; Hindī, = ' ball ').

Some further loans which have reached English through Hindustani, but are in origin Persian, will be found in a separate section under *Persian*.

Another Indian dialect which is represented in English by a very few words only, is the language of the Gipsies, Romany, surviving in the British Isles only among the Welsh gipsies and on the borders of Wales. The word **pal** is probably from the Romany *prāl* ' brother, mate ' ; it is found in English in 1681, among the depositions in the Hereford Diocesan Registers : *Wheare have you been all this day, pall?*   **Rum** ' queer, odd ', is usually supposed to be a development of the Romany word *Rom* = gipsy ; it is found in 1774. A word which has become familiar through the writings of Borrow is **gorgio** = non-gipsy (1851) ; though it has never become naturalized in English.

Finally, there is a small group of words from Singhalese, of Southern Ceylon :   **wanderoo,** a monkey, 1681 ;   **poon** 1699 (Dampier's *Voyages* ; Singhal. *pūna*) ; **tourmalin** 1759 (through Fr., from Singhal. *tormalli* ' cornelian ') ;   **bo-**(tree) 1861 ; **beri-beri,** a tropical disease, 1879.

(C) Persian

England has also borrowed a number of words from the Persian branch of the Indo-Germanic family of languages. The earliest Persian loans are indirect, coming into Old English by way of Greek and Latin, the usual medium of transmission of Eastern culture as well as of words in early mediaeval times. Old English has **pard** ' leopard ', **tigris** ' tiger ', **paradis** (see p. 37), all of which are ultimately from Old Persian or Iranian. *Paradise* represents Greek *paradeisos* ' a park, enclosure ', which is from Persian *pairi-daēza* ' to enclose '. After the beginning of the Middle English period, Eastern words for a time come into English through French :   **scarlet** *c.* 1250 (from O.French, probably through Italian, from Pers. *saqalāt*, a kind of rich cloth, often

of a red colour) ; **tiger,** fourteenth century, a re-borrowing from
O.French *tigre* (O.E. retains the classical form *tigris*, and has
also the Latin plural *tigres*, until about 1000, when an English
plural *tigras* appears) ;   the O.Persian word from which *tiger*
is derived is apparently *tigra*, meaning 'something sharp, an
arrow ' ; Persian has also given us the chess terms **rook, check,
checkmate,** and **chess** itself, the last being from the O.French
plural *esche(c)s*, from *eschec* ' CHECK ', which comes through
Arabic from Persian *shāh* ' king ' ;   **checkmate** represents Pers.
shāh māta ' the king is dead ' ; while **rcok,** the earlier term for
a ' castle ' is from O.Fr. *roc*, from Persian *rukh*. Other fourteenth
century loans are :   **azure** *c.* 1325 (O.Fr. from Pers. *lajward*
' lapis lazuli ') ; **salamander** (from O.Fr., from Lat. from Gk. ;
cf. Pers. *samander*) 1340, in the *Aȝenbite of Inwyt* : *þe salamandre
þet leueþ ine þe uere* ' that lives in the fire ' ;   **taffeta** 1373
(Exchequer Rolls of Scotland ;   O.Fr. from Ital., from Pers.
tāftah) ; **borax,** earlier **boras** (O.Fr. from Pers. *būrah*), **arsenic**
(O.Fr., from Lat., from Gk., from Hebrew, from Pers. *zarnīka
' yellow ornament ') ; both these in Chaucer ;   **musk** (ultimately
from Pers. *musk, misk*) 1398, in Trevisa's translation of the
De proprietatibus rerum of Bartholomaeus Anglicus.   There are
four fifteenth century borrowings from Persian, still through
French and Latin :   **mummy** (Fr. *momie*, from Med. Lat. from
Arab. *mūmīya*, from Pers.) *c.* 1400, in Lanfranc's *Chirurgia* ;
balas, a kind of ruby (Fr., from Med. Lat., from the Pers. Place-
Name *Badakhshān*, near Samarkand) 1414 (York Wills) ;
nenuphar, water-lily, 1425 (Pers. *nīnūfar*) ; **bezoar** 1477 (through
Fr. and Arab. from Pers. *pād-zahr* ' antidote, counter-poison ').
A few more Persian loans through French are found in the
sixteenth and seventeenth centuries :   perhaps **spinach** 1530
(through Fr., Span., Arab., probably from Pers.) ; **jasmin** 1548
(Fr., from Arab. *yás(a)mīn*, from Pers. *yāsmīn*) ; **julep,** a sweet
drink, 1624 (Fr., from Arab. *julāb*, from Pers. *gulāb* ' rose-
water ') ; **lilac** (Fr. *lilac*, a form given by Cotgrave, now *lilas*,
from Span. from Arab. from Pers. *līlak*) 1625, in Bacon's essay
On Gardens ; **babouche,** a slipper, 1695 (Fr., Arab., from Persian).
One quite recent loan through French is **Khedive** (Fr. from
Turkish, from Pers. *khadiv* ' prince '), the title granted in 1867
(May 14) to the ruler of Egypt (Ismail Pasha), as viceroy of the

Sultan, by the Turkish government ; cf. *The Times*, May 24,
1867 : *His Highness is to be called ' Khedive ', which is regarded
as the Arabic equivalent of ' King '.*

During the early modern period a few words from Persian
are adopted in English through literary or scientific Latin :
satrap 1380 (Wyclif ;   Lat., from Gk. *satrapēs*, from Pers.
xšaθra-pāvan- ' protector of the country ') ;   **asafoetida** 1398
(Trevisa's Bartholomaeus ; from Lat., the second element being
Lat. *foetida* ' stinking ' and the first Pers. *azā* ' mastic ') ;
tiara (originally of a Persian head-dress), first in an anglicized
form **tiar,** 1513, in Douglas's *Æneis* ; *tiara* in 1555, in Watreman's
Fardle of Fashions ;   **magus,** a magician, 1555 (Chaucer has the
personal name Simon Magus) ;   **naphtha** 1572 ;   **cinnabar** 1599
in Hakluyt's *Voyages* (Pers. *zanjifrah*) ;   **gypsum** (Pers. *jabsīn*
' lime ') 1646, Sir Thomas Browne.

During the Middle Ages the trade with Persia and the Far
East had been an overland trade, which accounts for the very
roundabout route by which in this period Persian words had
reached English. But with the discovery of the seaward way to
the East, in the fifteenth century, and the expansion of English
sea-borne commerce, Englishmen came into contact with Persian-
speaking peoples, and borrowed words directly from them.
During the fifteenth century also, the control of the trade-route
to Persia passed from the hands of the Tatars into those of the
Turks, and English traders learnt a few Persian words through
Turkish.   Again, there was a considerable Persian element in
Hindustani, and English travellers and merchants began in the
late sixteenth century to bring such words home together with
other Indian loans.

Persian words borrowed through Turkish : **spahi,** a horseman
(Pers. *sipāhī*), 1562, really a literary loan, since it appears in
Shute's translation of Cambini's *Turkish Wars* ;   **giaour,** an
unbeliever, applied by Mohammedans especially to Christians
(Pers. *gaur*), 1564, Jenkins in Hakluyt's *Voyages* ;   **jackal** (Turk.
chakāl, from Pers. *shagāl*), 1603, Biddulph in *Purchas his
Pilgrimage* ;   **serai,** an inn (Pers. *serāi*) 1609, Finch in *Purchas
his Pilgrimage.*

Persian words borrowed in India :   **tabasheer,** a siliceous
substance found in the joints of bamboo, and used medicinally

(Pers. *tabāshīr*) 1598, Phillips's translation of Linschoten's *Travels* ; **sirdar** (Hind. *sardār* ' commander ') 1615, Sandys : *Travels* ; **cummerbund** (Hind. *kamar-band* ' loin-band ') 1616 ; **lashkar,** originally a camp of native soldiers, 1616, Sir T. Roe in Purchas ; **mohur,** gold coin of India, 1621 (Pers. *muhr*) ; **lascar,** an East Indian sailor, originally the same word as *lashkar,* 1625, Purchas : *I caused all my Laskayres to remaine aboord the Vnicorne* ; **zemindar,** a collector of revenue, 1683 ; **havildar,** a sepoy non-commissioned officer (Pers. *hawāl-dār,* the first element of which is from Arabic), **subahdar,** native officer, both in 1698, in Fryer's *Account of the East Indies.* There are two Persian loans from this source in the early eighteenth century, and then there is the same gap as we found in the Hindustani loans (see p. 223) until approximately the time of the Seven Years' War : **kincob,** a rich stuff embroidered with gold or silver (Pers. *kimkhāb*) 1712, in an advertisement in the *Spectator* : *One Isabella colour Kincob Gown, flowered with Green and Gold* ; **sepoy** (cf. *spahi,* above) 1717 ; **seersucker,** a fine linen fabric (Pers. *shīr-o-shakkar* = ' milk and sugar '), 1757, in Guyon's *New History of the East Indies* ; **zenana** 1761 (Pers. *zanāna*) ; **khidmatgar,** a male servant, 1765 ; **purdah,** a curtain, hence, a system of seclusion of women (Pers. *pardah*), 1800. The last two are comparatively recent : **khaki** (Hind. *khākī* ' dusty ', from Persian), first used for the uniforms of the Guide Corps (under Lumsden and Hodson) in 1848 ; recorded first in English in 1857 (of the fabric ; of the colour, in 1863) ; **nilgai** 1882 (Pers. *nīlgāw,* = ' blue cow ').

Words probably borrowed direct from Persian : Most of these are found first in books of travel ; they represent Persian titles, and names of various classes of people, coins, clothes, food, and terms of government, with, later, a few terms from Persian mythology : **shah** 1564, Jenkinson's *Travels,* in Hakluyt : *Shaw Thamas* ; **toman** ' ten thousand (men, dinars, etc.) ' (Pers. *tūmān*), 1566, Edwards in Hakluyt ; **dervish** (Pers. *darvīsh* ' poor ') 1585, T. Washington's translation of Nicholay's *Voyages* ; **divan** 1586 (M.Pers. *devān,* now *dīwān*), originally a council of state, then successively a hall, a raised part of the floor, a long cushioned lounge extending along a wall, and so on ; (cf. the Fr. *douane,* with a different sense, through Ital.

dovana) ; **caravan,** earlier **carouan** (Pers. *kārwān*), a party of travellers, with their baggage-beasts, etc., 1599 (Hakluyt) ; the form *caravan* is perhaps through French ; **bazaar** (Pers. *bāzār* ' market ') ; the earliest form in English, *bazarro*, is perhaps through Italian : *A faire place or towne, and in it a faire Bazarro for marchants*, Hakluyt, 1599 ; *basar*, probably direct from Persian, appears in 1616 (Purchas) ; **caravanserai** 1599 (Hakluyt ; Pers. *kārwān-serāi*).

Seventeenth century : **pad(i)shah,** a title applied originally to the Shah, 1612 ; **pilau** 1612 (Pers. *pilāw* ; the alternative form *pilaff* is a Turkish development) ; **mirza** 1613 (Purchas ; Pers. *mīrzād* = prince + born) ; **ban,** a ' learned ' loan (it was a title applied to the viceroy of certain military districts of Hungary, and had been introduced from Persia) ; **firman,** an edict, licence, permit, 1616 (Sir T. Roe in Purchas ; Pers., from Scrt. *pramāṇa* ' command ') ; **dinar,** an Oriental coin, 1634 (Sir T. Herbert's *Travels*, of coins in the territories of the Mogul ; Pers., from Late Greek, from Lat. *dēnārius*) ; **shawl** (Pers. *shāl*), 1662, in Davies's translation of Olearius's *Voyage* : *The richer sort have . . . another rich Skarf which they call Schal, made of a very fine stuff, brought by the Indians into Persia* ; **papooshe** 1682 (Pers. *pāpōsh* ; cf. *babouche*, above, through French) ; **peshwa** (Pers., = ' chief '), 1698, in Fryer's *Account of the East Indies*.

Eighteenth century : These are very few, and all from the second half of the century : **carboy** 1753 (Pers. *qarābah* ' large flagon '), in Hanway's *Travels* : *I delivered a present . . . of oranges and lemons . . . and 6 Karboys of Ispahan wine* ; used for chemicals, 1883 ; **peri** (Pers. *perī*) 1777, in Richardson's *Persian Dictionary* (English section) ; again in 1786, in Beckford's *Vathek* ; **bulbul** (Pers., from Arab.) 1784, in Sir William Jones's *Memoirs* ; **simurg,** a bird of Persian legend, 1786, in Beckford's *Vathek* ; **attar** 1798 (originally Arabic), in Pennant's *Hindostan*.

Nineteenth century Persian loans are even fewer : **cuscus,** the root of a grass, 1810 (Williamson's *East India Vade Mecum* ; Pers. *khas-khas*) ; **narghile** 1839 (Miss Pardoe's *Beauties of the Bosphorous* ; Pers. *nārgīleh*, from *nargīl* ' coco-nut ') ; **koh-i-noor** (Pers. *kōh-i-nūr* ' mountain of light '), the name of a diamond which became one of the British crown jewels on the annexation of the Punjâb in 1849, hence any very fine diamond ; used already by Thackeray in the general sense in 1849 ; **pashm,** soft downy fur, 1880.

(D) Turkic Dialects

The Asiatic languages known under the general name of Turkic are represented in English by words from the dialects of Tatar and Osmanli (Ottoman, or Turkish proper). Our first connexion with the Turks was overland across the continent of Europe, and the earliest Turkish loans are usually through French, sometimes also by way of a Slavonic dialect, the Slavs being the nearest neighbours of the Turks in the west. The earliest Turkish word in English seems to be the Turkish *khān* ' lord, prince ' (in O.Fr. as *can, chan, cham*), found already in *Mandeville's Travels*, *c.* 1400 : *the grete Caan of Cathay*, and thus applied to the ruler of an empire farther east than Turkey itself.[1] The word is found later in English in the forms *chan* and *cham*, and also in the Turkish form **khan.** Of the subsequent borrowings from Turkish through European languages, only *horde, tulip, bergamot* (pear), and *vampire* have become fully naturalized ; the remainder are still used almost exclusively with their original eastern application : **janissary,** one of a former body of Turkish infantry, especially a member of the Sultan's body-guard, 1529 (perhaps through Italian) ; **horde** (Turkī *ordā* ' camp ', later applied to a nomadic tribe ; the Golden Horde was the name applied to one such tribe which forced its way into Eastern Russia in the thirteenth century ; the initial *h-* appears first in Polish, whence the word passed into French, and so to English) ; first in 1555 (Eden's *Decades*), and in a general sense, of a large crowd or company, in *Purchas his Pilgrimes*, in reference to the natives of Greenland. **Tulip** is from O.Fr. *tulipe, tulipan*, perhaps through Ital. *tulipano*, from a Turkish colloquial form *tulband* ' turban ' (the flower being supposed to resemble this), probably ultimately Persian ; the tulip is first mentioned by a European in *c.* 1554, when it is referred to by the Emperor's ambassador to the East, Busbeq ; in English it appears in 1578, in Lyte's translation of Dodoneus. Seventeenth century loans through European languages are : **koumiss** (Tatar *kumiz*, coming into French

---

[1] The first European missions to the Mongol court date from the thirteenth century.

Q

through Russian) 1607, in Topsell's *Four-footed Beasts* ;
bergamot 1616 (through Ital. *bergamotta* from Turk. *beg-armudi*
' prince's pear ') ; **caique,** a skiff (through French from Turk.
kaik), 1625, in Purchas :   *when the Great Turke goeth vpon the
water, whose Caikes are most rich and beautifull to behold* ; **dey**
1659 (Turk. *daī* ' maternal uncle ') ; **shabrach,** a saddle-cloth,
1667 (probably through German) ; **odalisque** 1681 (Turk.
ōdaliq). Eighteenth century : **vampire** 1734 (from French, from
Magyar *vampir*, from Slavonic, and apparently ultimately from
Turk. *uber* ' witch ') ; **salep** (Turk. *sālep*), 1736, in Bailey's
Household Dictionary ; **caracal** 1760 (Fr., from Turk. *qarah-
qulah*). The word **begum,** which we borrowed from Hindustani,
is in origin Turkish (*bigīm*) ; it appears in English in 1634, in
Sir T. Herbert's *Travels* ; a fairly recent loan-word is **kourbash,**
a whip, 1814, from Turkish through Arabic.

During the sixteenth century, English merchants, particularly
the Levant Company, were trading with Constantinople by way
of the Mediterranean, while others made their way to Turkey by
the overland route.   At this period the first direct loans from
Turkish into English were made.   Among the sixteenth century
loan-words *turban, coffee,* and *caviare* are the best known ; most
of the words borrowed in this and the following century are names
of Turkish products, or classes of people.   During the eighteenth
century there is an almost complete lack of Turkish loans, but
a number of new words appear in the nineteenth century.

Sixteenth century : **sanjak,** an administrative district in the
Turkish Empire (Turk. *sanjāq* = ' banner '), 1537, in the *State
Papers, Henry VIII* ; **turban,** earlier also **tolipane, tulbant,**
in its original sense (cf. *tulip,* above ; Turk. *tulbant*), 1561, in
Jenkinson's *Voyages* ; the form *torbant* is used by Hickock in
his translation of Frederick's *Voyages,* 1588 ; **vizier** (Turk. *vezīr,*
but Arabic in origin), 1562, in Shute's translation of Cambini's
Turkish Wars ; **dolman** 1585 (Turk. *dōlāmān*), in Washington's
translation of Nicholay's *Voyages* : *they are clothed with a long
gowne, which they do call Dolyman, girded with a large girdle of
silke* ; **caftan,** a long tunic, **caviar(e)** (Turk. *khāvyār*), both in
1591 (the latter in the form *cavery*) in Fletcher's *Russe Commonwealth* ; **coffee** (Turk. *káhveh*), first in the form *chaoua,* in
Phillips's Linschoten, 1598, and then as *coffa* in Capt. John

Smith's *Travels and Adventures*, 1603–30 : *Their* [the Turks'] *best drinke is Coffa of a graine they call Coava* ; **bey** (= prince) 1599, in Hakluyt : *The By who is the gouernour of the Ilande*.

Seventeenth century : **aga,** chief officer in the Ottoman Empire (Turk. *aghā*), 1600, in Pory's translation of Leo's *History of Africa* ; **effendi** 1614 (Turk., but originally Greek), 1614, in Selden's *Titles of Honour* ; **kiosk,** a pavilion (Turk. *kiūshk,* perhaps through French), 1625, in Purchas ; **kaimakan,** a lieutenant, deputy, 1645 ; **pasha** 1646 ; **seraskier,** the Turkish minister of war, 1684, in the *London Gazette*.

Eighteenth century : **vali,** civil governor of a Turkish province, 1753, in Hanway's *Travels*.

Nineteenth century : **fez,** 1802 (Turk. *fes,* supposed to be from the Place-Name *Fez,* in Morocco) ; **chibouk, chibouque** (the latter from French), a long pipe, 1813, in Byron's *Corsair* ; **kavass,** an armed constable, 1819 (Turk. *qawwās* ' bow-maker ') ; **yataghan,** a sword, 1819 (Turk. *yātāghan*) ; **elchee,** an ambassador (Turk. *īlchī*), 1828, in *Blackwood's Magazine* : *so well described by an English Elchee* ; **latakia** (Turk., Place-Name), 1833, in Disraeli's correspondence ; **bosh** (Turk., = empty, worthless) 1834, in *Ayesha,* a novel by Morier, through the popularity of which the word is said to have gained currency in this country ; **tarpan,** a wild horse (Tatar) 1841 ; **kismet** (Turk., from Arab. *qismat*) 1849 ; **bashi-bazouk,** a mercenary soldier, 1855 ; **mudir,** governor of a village, a Turkish use of an Arabian word, 1864 (*Athenaeum*) ; **macramé** (Turk. *maqrama* ' towel') 1869, in a work on lace-making ; **vilayet,** a province of the Turkish Empire (ultimately Arabic) 1869 (*The Times*) ; **zaptieh,** a Turkish policeman, 1869 (Tozer's *Highlands of Turkey*) ; **irade,** a written decree (originally Arabic), 1883.

(E) DRAVIDIAN

The non-Indo-Germanic dialects of Southern India, grouped under the name *Dravidian,* are represented in English by a small number of loan-words from Tamil (spoken in south-east India and north Ceylon), from a variety of this known as Malayalam (spoken in south-west India), and from Telugu (spoken along part of the east coast of India, north of Madras). The history and chronology of these words in English is the same as that of loans from Hindustani, etc. They appear first in the sixteenth century, and are most common in the latter part of this century, in the seventeenth, and in the late eighteenth century. A few of them have passed into current English use.

Sixteenth century : **calico,** earlier also **calicut** (from the Place-Name Calicut, on the Malabar coast), 1540 (Lancashire Wills) : *a surplyse and an elne kalyko cloth* ; **betel** 1553 (Eden, *Treatise on the Newe Indies* ; through Portuguese, from Malayalam *veṭṭila*); **coir,** fibre, earlier also **cairo,** which is through Portuguese (Malayalam *kāyar* ' cord '), 1582 : *The Moores which trade to Sofala in great ships, that haue no decks nor nailes, but are sowed with Cayro,* Lichefield's translation of Castañeda's *Conquest of the East Indies* ; the spelling *coire* is found in 1697 ; **mango** 1582, in the same translation (Port. *manga,* from Tamil *mān-kāy*) ; **copra** (Port., from Malayalam *koppara* ' coco-nut ') 1584, Barret in Hakluyt's *Voyages* ; **curry,** earlier **carriel** (Port. *caril,* Tamil *kari,* probably two periods of borrowing), *carriel* in 1598 (Phillips's Linschoten), *currey* in 1747 (*Art of Cookery*) ; **coolie** 1598 (also in Phillips ; Tamil *kūli*).

Seventeenth century : **pariah,** a low caste of South India (Tamil *paṛaiyar,* pl. of *paṛaiya,* ' hereditary drummer '), 1613 : *The Pareas are of worse esteeme . . . reputed worse than the Diuell* (Purchas) ; **atoll** 1625 (probably Malayalam *aḍal* ' uniting ') ; **cheroot** 1669 (Tamil *shuruṭṭu,* through French) ; **catamaran** 1697 ; **teak** (Port. *teca,* from Malayalam *tēkka*), and **tindal,** native petty officer (Malayalam *taṇḍelu* ' head-man '), both in Fryer's *Account of the East Indies,* 1698.

Eighteenth century : **corundum** 1728 (Tamil *kurundum* ' ruby ') ; **bandy,** a cart, 1761 (Telugu) ; **anaconda** 1768 (Tamil) ; **bandicoot,** a kind of rat, 1780 (Telugu *pandi-kokku*) ; **mulligatawny** 1784 (Tamil *milagu-tannīr* ' pepper-water ').

Nineteenth century : **yercum,** a shrub, 1826 (Tamil) ; **patchouli,** a plant, also the perfume obtained from it 1845 (Tamil).

(F) SEMITIC DIALECTS

The Arabic dialect of Southern Semitic has already been dealt with in Section A of this chapter. The present section covers

Northern Semitic, including the dialects of Phoenician (long extinct as a spoken language), Hebrew, and Aramaic. There are very few traces of Phoenician in English ; the word **sack,** borrowed in Old English from Latin, which took it from Greek, is possibly of this origin, and so perhaps are the names of some of the Greek letters, which are more or less familiar in English. Many of the Old and Middle English loan-words which may be traced back to Semitic are from the Hebrew of the Bible, and reach English through Greek and the Latin of the Vulgate. In Middle English a certain number of Semitic trade terms come through French. Words borrowed directly from Hebrew or Aramaic are not very common ; they are chiefly Biblical words, adopted during the sixteenth century, and later loans connected with the observances of the Jewish religion. Some Old English loans from Latin and Greek which are Semitic in origin will be found in Chapter II. Others borrowed at this period, which survived in present-day English (though some may be later re-borrowings) are **amen, cassia, hemp, hosanna, manna, rabbi, Sabbath, Satan, tunic, seraphim, cherubim.** The word **seraph,** as a singular noun, is not found until 1667 (in Milton's *Paradise Lost*) ; **cherub** is used first by Wyclif, *c.* 1382 : *a palme bitwix cherub & cherub* ; the Hebrew form is *k'rūb.*

Middle English loans through French are **endive, jasper, emerald, coral, cinnamon, sapphire,** all of the thirteenth or fourteenth century ; **nitre** and **myrtle,** in Lanfranc's *Chirurgia, c.* 1400 ; **jubilee** (Heb. *yōbēl*) in Wyclif, 1382 ; **Pasch(al)** (Heb. *pesakh* ' passover ') 1427, in the records of St. Mary at Hill, in the sense of an Easter candle or candlestick.

Some Hebrew loans of the Middle English period are literary or scientific borrowings through Latin. A number of them are Biblical words, from the Latin of the Vulgate, found for the first time in Wyclif's translation of the Bible (1382). The word which is now *Messiah* has appeared in several different forms : **Messyas,** the Greek and Latin form of Aramaic *m'shīhā* ' anointed ' is the usual Middle English form ; the fourteenth century has also the French **Messye** ; the final -*ah*, approximating more closely to the Aramaic, is not found until 1560, in the Geneva Bible ; subsequently this is the usual form. **Galbanum,** a gum resin, is a Middle English loan from Latin, and ultimately from Heb.

chelbenāh. **Mammon,** occurring first in Langland, is late Lat., from Gk., from Aramaic *māmōn.* The following are recorded first in Wyclif :   **Abaddon** (as a proper name) ;   **babel** (Heb. *bābel*) :   *Therfor was callid the name of it Babel, for there was confounded the lippe of all the erthe* ;   in the general sense of ' confused sounds ', it is found first in Skelton ;   **behemoth** (Heb. *b'hēmōth*) ; **corban ;   ephod** (Heb. *āphad* = ' to put on ') ;   **leviathan** (Heb. *livyāthān*) :   *Whether maist thou drawen out leuyethan with an hoc* ?   **nard ;   shibboleth** (Heb. *shibbōleth* ;   in a transferred sense, in 1658) ;   **teraphim.** Later loans from Mediaeval or ecclesiastical Latin are :   **cabbala** 1521 (Med. Lat. from Heb. *qabbālāh* ' tradition ', hence the oral tradition from the time of Moses to the Rabbis) ;   in the sense of ' secret intrigue ', it is used by Clarendon (*Hist. of the Rebellion*) in 1646 ;   another form, **cabal,** probably through French, appears in 1616. **Lotus** is first recorded as used by Sir Thomas Elyot in 1540. **Gehenna** is found in 1594 (Heb. *gē'hinnōm*).

Other Semitic borrowings, the forms of which seem to be derived directly from Hebrew, belong to the sixteenth and early seventeenth centuries (mostly from translations of the Bible), and to the nineteenth century ; one or two of the latter are from the German-Jewish dialect, Yiddish. **Selah** 1530 (Heb. *selāh*) ; **hallelujah** 1535 (Coverdale) ;   **shekel** 1560 (Geneva Bible ; Heb. *sheqel*) ;   **torah** 1577 (Heb. *tōrāh*) ;   **sanhedrin** 1588 (Heb. *sanhedrīn*, which is from Greek *sunédrion* ' council ') ;   **Elohim** 1605 (Heb. *elohim*) ;   **mishna,** a collection of precepts, 1610 (Fitzherbert's *Policy and Religion*) ;   **gopher-**(wood) and **shittah** (Heb. *shiṭṭāʰ*, a kind of tree), both in the Authorized Version of the Bible, 1611 ;   **midrash,** a commentary, **tallith,** a robe (later, a scarf), both in *Purchas his Pilgrimage,* 1613. Nineteenth century : **jaal-**(goat), a wild goat, 1838 ;   **kosher** 1851 (Mayhew, *London Labour* ; Heb. *kāshēr* ' fit, proper ') ;   **oof** 1885 (*Sporting Times* ; Yiddish *ooftisch,* actually a German form, from Germ. *auf dem tische* ' on the table ', i.e. cash) ;   **schnorrer,** a Jewish beggar, 1892 (Zangwill, *Children of the Ghetto* ; another Yiddish word).

(G) Tibeto-Chinese

The Central and Eastern Asiatic languages of Tibet, Burma, and China are sometimes grouped together under one head, though the character of their relationship is doubtful. Two Tibetan words are fairly familiar in English, one from the seventeenth and one from the eighteenth century. (The first two European explorers known to have reached Lhasa were Johann Grueber and Albert D'Orville, who travelled from Peking to Nepal by way of Lhasa in 1661 ; an earlier traveller, Friar Oderic, is reputed to have penetrated to Tibet not long after the time of Marco Polo (thirteenth century), but this remains doubtful.) The word **lama** (Tibetan *blama*) is used in an English translation of Martini's *Conquest of China* in 1654 ; **Dalai-lama** in 1698. **yak** (from Tibetan *gyak*) is recorded first in 1799, by Samuel Turner, who was sent by Warren Hastings to visit the Tashi-Lama, 1783–4.

Chinese words are more numerous, though only a few have been thoroughly naturalized, the best known being *tea, ketchup, japan,* and the names of several varieties of tea, such as *pekoe, souchong*. A number of Chinese words have reached English through Japanese ; these will be given in the next section.

The earliest known Chinese word in English is **silk** (through Latin and Greek, from an early name of the Chinese ; see p. 273). Middle English has **galingale,** an aromatic root (eleventh century in the form *gallengar*, next *c*. 1305 as *galingale*) ; this is Old French, from Arab. *khalanjān*, through Persian from Chinese *Ko-liang-kiang* ' mild ginger from Ko '. The early modern English loan-words from Chinese are mostly known first through translations of foreign works. For instance, Parke's translation of Mendoza's *History of China* (1588) first records **li,** a measure of length, and **litchi** (Ch. *li-chi*) : *They haue a kinde of plummes that they doo call Lechias.* Martini's *Conquest of China,* in an English translation of 1654, has **ginseng** : *The root cal'd Gimsem, so much esteemed amongst the Chineses.* Phillips's translation of Linschoten records in 1598 the word **chaa,** the Portuguese form of Chinese (Mandarin) *ch'a* ' tea ' : *the aforesaid warme water is made with the powder of a certain hearbe called Chaa.*

But from the seventeenth century onwards Chinese words are also introduced by English travellers and traders ; R. Cocks's *Diary*, 1620, speaks of ' a China sampan ', but as used by ' Hollanders ' ; **japan,** a kind of varnish, from the Chinese name

of the country of Japan, *Jih-pun* = sunrise, appears in 1688 ;
bohea (Ch. *Wu-i,* the name of some hills in the north of Fuhkien)
in Cunningham's *Voyage to Chusan,* 1701. Meanwhile, the English
had learned to drink tea ; they took the word **tee** or **tay** from the
Dutch, through whose East Indian trade the herb was brought
to this country about 1650–5 ; Dutch *thee* is from the Amoy
dialect of Chinese : *t'e* (cf. the Mandarin dialect form *ch'a,*
above) ; already in 1658 tea is advertised in the *Mercurius
Politicus* : *That excellent . . . drink called by the Chineans tcha,
by other Nations Tay alias Tee.*

Lockyer's *Account of the Trade with India,* 1711, has the
Chinese words **pongee,** a kind of silk (apparently from North
Chinese *pun-chī* = own loom) ; **sycee,** uncoined silver (Ch. *si szě*
= fine silk) ; **ketchup** (Ch. *kôechiap* ' the brine of pickled fish ') :
the best Ketchup from Tonquin. The remaining eighteenth century
loans, all but one, are connected with trade : **pekoe** (Amoy
pek-ho), 1712, Addison, in the *Spectator* : *Coffee, Chocolate,
Green, Imperial, Peco, and Bohea-Tea seem to be trifles* ; **congou**
(Ch. *kung-fu*) 1725, *London Gazette* : *Next week will be sold, a
large Parcel of Bohee, with som Congou and Green Tea* ; **hong,**
a series of rooms used as a warehouse or factory (Cantonese
hang ' row, rank '), 1726, Shelvocke's *Voyage round the World* ;
kaolin, a kind of clay used for porcelain (Ch. *kaoling*), 1727, in
Chambers' *Cyclopaedia* ; kaolin was first made known in Europe
by d'Entrecolles in 1712 ; **hyson** (Ch. *hsi-ch'un*) 1740 ; **souchong**
(through French from Ch. *siao-chung*) in the *Annual Register*
1760 : *The East-India ships . . . have brought* 62,900 [lb.] *of
Souchong* ; **chin-chin,** in Anglo-Chinese use (Ch. *ts'ing-ts'ing*),
1795, in Syme's *Embassy to Ava* : *We soon fixed them in their
seats, both parties . . . repeating Chin-Chin, Chin-Chin, the Chinese
term of salutation.*

The nineteenth century loans from China are a varied collection,
but none indicate a close connexion with the country ; they still
include trading terms, together with words relating to Chinese
customs, government, and art : **kotow, kowtow** (Ch. *k'o-t'ou*),
1804, in Barrow's *Travels in China* ; **whanghee,** a cane (Ch.
huang), 1815, Milburn's *Oriental Commerce* ; **loquat,** a fruit
(Ch. *luh kwat*), 1814 ; **yamun, yamen,** mandarin's office, or state
department (Ch. *ya* ' official residence ' + *mun* ' gate '), 1827,

Lloyd's *Tinkowski's Travels* ; **wampee,** a fruit (Ch. *hwang-pi*), 1830, in Lindley's *Natural System of Botany* ; **oolong** (Ch. *wulung*), 1852, McCulloch's *Dictionary of Commerce* ; **kylin,** a fabulous animal represented on Chinese porcelain (Ch. *ch'i-lin*), 1857, in Marryat's *Pottery and Porcelain* ; and finally one word adopted in the present century : **tong,** a Chinese secret society, 1918 (from Ch. *t'ang,* a hall, meeting-place).

(H) JAPAN

Words from Japanese (including Chinese loan-words in Japanese) are very few indeed until the nineteenth century, and as will be seen hardly any have been really anglicized. Trade with and travel in Japan seems to have lagged behind in comparison with the corresponding discoveries in Cathay and other parts of the Far East, though a few references in the sixteenth, seventeenth, and eighteenth century translations of works of travel, and in such works written by Englishmen, show that even then a small number of Japanese words were being introduced into the language. The earliest seems to be **bonze,** adopted from the Portuguese (from Jap. *bonzô,* from Ch. *fan-seng* ' religious person ') in 1588, in Parke's translation of Mendoza's *History of China : They haue amongst them* [i.e. in Japan] *many priests of their Idols whom they do call Bonsos of the which there be great couents.* Four more words are found for the first time in the seventeenth century : **shogun,** the hereditary commander-in-chief of the Japanese army (Jap. *shōgun,* from Ch. *chiang chün*), 1615, in Cocks's *Diary* ; **kimono** 1637 ; **saké,** a liquor made from fermented rice, 1687, in Lovell's translation of Thevenot's *Travels* ; **soy** (Jap. *soy,* colloquial pronunciation of *shō-yu,* from Ch. *shi-yu*) 1696, in Ovington's *Voyage to Suratt* : *Souy the choicest of all Sawces* ; one in the eighteenth century : **mikado** 1727, in Scheuchzer's translation of Kaempfer's *Japan.*

Later loans are more numerous, but almost all still have an exclusively Japanese reference : **obi,** a sash, 1802 ; **sen** 1802 (Pinkerton's *Modern Geography*) ; **ginkgo,** a tree, 1808 ; **daimio,** a feudal noble, 1839, in the *Penny Cyclopaedia* (Jap. from Ch.) ; **hara-kiri** 1856 (*Harper's Magazine*) ; **tycoon** 1863 (Jap. *taikun*

' great lord ', from Ch.) ;   **samisen,** a kind of guitar, 1864 (Jap.
from Ch. *san-hsien*) ;   **jinricksha** 1874 (Jap. *jin-riki-sha*) ;
samurai 1874 ;   **yen** 1875 (Jevon's *Money* ;   Jap. from Ch. *yüan*
' round ', also ' dollar ') ;   **gobang,** a game played on a chequer-
board, 1886 (Guillemard, *Cruise of the ' Marchesa '* ;   Jap. *goban,*
from Ch. *k'i-pan* ' chess-board ') :   *Some of the games are purely
Japanese . . . as* go-ban.   Note : *This game is the one lately introduced into England under the misspelt name of Go Bang* ;
kakemono, a wall-picture, 1890 (*Daily News*) ;   **geisha**
1891 (Sir Edwin Arnold in the *Contemporary Review*) ;   **ju-
jutsu** 1904.

CHAPTER XI

MALAY-POLYNESIAN AND AUSTRALIAN

(A) MALAY-POLYNESIAN

The hundreds of dialects of the islands of the Pacific Ocean may be divided into four large groups, Indonesian, Polynesian, Melanesian, and Micronesian. Of these the first two are represented in English by a not inconsiderable number of words. Indonesian includes the dialects of the Malay Peninsula, of Java, of Sumatra, of the Philippines, of Madagascar, etc., etc. The first of these make their appearance in English in the second half of the sixteenth century, some of them perhaps through Portuguese, at the same time, approximately, as the first words from India (there are no very early loans from this group, however, as there are in the case of the Indian dialects, e.g. in Old English). Some of the loan-words from Malay, etc., have become very, or comparatively, familiar, such as *sago, bamboo, gong, gingham, cockatoo, launch, bantam, kapok, caddy* (for tea), *gutta percha, raffia.* Even in this list it is obvious that words from these languages denote especially animals, birds, plants (and their products). The first Malay word to appear in English is **sago** (Mal. *sāgū*) 1555, in Eden's *Decades of the Newe Worlde* (in a reference to Molucca). Other sixteenth century loans are : **kris,** a Malay sword (Mal. *k(i)rīs*), 1577, Drake, in Hakluyt's *Voyages* ; **proa** (Mal. *p(a)rāū,* a boat), 1582, in Lichefield's translation of Castañeda's *Conquest of the East Indies* ; **picul,** a weight (Mal. *pikul,* a man's load), **tael,** a weight (Port. from Mal. *tahil*), **durian,** a kind of fruit (Mal., = thorn), all in Parke's translation of Mendoza's *History of China,* 1588 ; **nipa,** a kind of toddy obtained from a palm (Mal. *nīpah,* 1598, in Hickock's translation of Frederick's *Voyages* ; **bamboo** (Mal. *bambu,* through Dutch *bamboes*), and **mangosteen** (Mal. *mangustan*) 1598, in Phillips's translation of Linschoten.

Seventeenth century words are still all from Malay ; some are

direct borrowings, others through French, Portuguese, or Dutch :
gong, earlier **gongo** (through Port. or Span. *gongo,* from Mal.
gong) 1600 ; the instrument seems to have been adopted into
English use in the early nineteenth century, cf. Scott in *The
Antiquary* : *I have had equally doubt concerning my dinner call;
gongs, now in present use, seemed a new-fangled and heathenish
invention* ; **tombac,** an alloy (Fr., from Mal. *tambâga* ' copper ')
1602, Lancaster's *Voyage to India,* in Purchas ;   **cassowary**
(Mal. *kasuārī*) 1611, in reference to a cassowary brought to
England and kept in St. James's Park ; *St. James his Ginney-
hens, the Cassawarway moreover* (Note, *an East Indian bird at
St. James*) ; **junk,** a ship (Fr. *jonque,* or Port. *junco,* from Mal.
djong) 1613, Purchas ; **gingham** (Fr. *guingamp,* Mal. *ginggang*
= ' striped ') 1615, in a letter quoted in Cocks's *Diary* :
*Capt. Cock is of opinion that the ginghams, both white and browne
. . . will prove a good commodity in the Kinge of Shashna his cuntry ;*
paddy (Mal. *pādī*) 1623, State Papers, Colonial ; **sumpitan** (Mal.
sumpītan), **cockatoo** (Mal. *kakatúa,* through Du. *kaketoe*), both
in Sir T. Herbert's *Travels,* 1634 (*Cacatoes, birds like Parrats,
fierce and indomitable*) ; **tincal,** crude borax (Mal. *tingkal*) 1635 ;
rattan, a kind of climbing palm, also a cane made of its stem
(Mal. *rōtan*), 1660, in Pepys's *Diary* : *Mr. Hawley did give me
a little black rattoon, painted and gilt* ; **amuck, amok** (Mal. *āmuk*
' rushing in frenzy to murder ') 1663 ; **catechu,** an astringent
obtained from *Acacia catechu* and other East Indian trees (Mal.
kachu) 1683 ; **lory** (Mal. *lūrī*) 1692 ; **babiroussa** (Mal. *bábi
* hog ' ; *rusa* ' deer ') 1696 ; **launch** (Mal. through Span.
lancha) 1697 ; **dammar,** a resin (Mal. *damar*), 1698 ; **orang-
outang** (Mal. *ōrang ūtan* = man of the woods) 1699.

The chief point about eighteenth century loans from Indonesian
(all but two of which are from the second half of the century) is
that we now find a few words from Malagasy, the dialect of
Madagascar ; the island had been discovered by the Portuguese
in the sixteenth century, but the words from Malagasy which
come into English are apparently through French.   **Tanrec,**
a mammal allied to the hedgehog (Mlg. *tandraka*), 1729, in Drury's
Madagascar ; **bantam** 1749, apparently from a Place-Name in
Java ; **kapok** (Mal. *kāpok*) 1750 ; **gecko,** a lizard, 1774 (Mal.
gekoq) ; **mangabey** 1774, in Goldsmith's *Natural History* (the

name of an African monkey, so called by Buffon, from the name
of a district in Madagascar, though the animal is not found in
the island) ; **pangolin,** the scaly ant-eater (Mal. *peng-gōling* =
roller) 1774 ; **aye-aye** (Mlg., perhaps named from its cry) 1781,
in Pennant's *Quadrupeds* ; **trepang** (Mal. *trīpang*) ; **upas** (Mal.
ūpas) 1783 ; **tanghin,** poison obtained from a shrub (Mlg.
tangena), 1788, in a translation from the French of Sonnerat's
Voyage) ; **caddy** 1792 (Mal. *kati,* a weight) ; **muntjak,** a deer
(Mal. *minchek*), 1798.

During the nineteenth century there is a constant, if not large,
drift of Indonesian words into English, now including words
from dialects other than Malay and Malagasy ; the majority of
them are still names of animals and plants. (The first four words
in this list are used first as English words by Sir Stamford Raffles,
Lieutenant-Governor of Java, 1811–15.) **Rasse,** the civet-cat,
1817 (Jav. *rasé*) ; **napu,** the musk-deer (Malay), **dugong** (Mal.
dūyong), 1820 ; **siamang,** a kind of ape, 1822 (Malay, *siyāmang* ;
Raffles in *Trans. Linnaean Soc.* : *I have recently procured a
living siamang, which is very tame and tractable*) ; **teledu** 1824
(Jav.) ; **rusa,** deer, 1827 (Mal.) ; **gambier** 1830 (Mal. *gambīr,*
name of plant) ; **sarong** 1834 (Mal. *sārung*) ; **manucode,** bird
of paradise, 1835 (from Buffon's French, from the Modern Latin
manucodiata, from Mal. *manuk dēwāta* ' bird of the gods ') ;
indri, the babacoote (in Mlg. the word means ' behold ' ;
Sonnerat heard it from a native, and mistook it for the name of
the animal), 1839, in the *Penny Cyclopaedia* ; **delundung,** the
weasel-cat, 1840 (Malay) ; **gutta-percha** (Mal. *getah percha*
' gum of the percha ', name of tree, assimilated to Latin *gutta*
' drop ') 1845, in the *Athenaeum* : *the Secretary described the
Substance called gutta-percha* ; **parang** 1852 (Mal.) ; **ylang-ylang,**
a tree, 1876 (Philippine Is. *īlang-ilang*) ; **babacoote,** a kind of
lemur, 1880, in Sibree's *Great African Islands* (Malagasy) ;
raffia, raphia, a kind of palm, also the fibre of this (Mlg.) 1882,
in Smith's *Dictionary of Economic Plants* ; **linsang,** a kind of
civet-cat (Jav.), 1885 ; **ramie,** a plant, 1888 (Mal. *rāmī*).

The Polynesian Islands include the most easterly and southerly
groups of the central Pacific. Closely related dialects are found
in the Tonga Islands, Samoa, Hawaii, the Marquesas, Easter
Island, New Zealand, and others. Only a small number of words

have reached English from this source, nearly all being names of animals or plants, and only two or three have become at all common : *taboo, tattoo,* and perhaps *ukulele.* The first appear in English in the late eighteenth century, as the result of Captain Cook's explorations and discoveries between 1768 and 1779. Cook's first voyage in the Pacific was made in the *Endeavour,* 1768–1771, primarily for the purpose of observing the transit of Venus. At this time he visited both Australia and New Zealand. During the years 1772–3 he sailed to the Antarctic, and then, returning north, visited New Caledonia and the New Hebrides. His last voyage, 1776–9, during which he explored the northern Pacific and discovered the Sandwich Islands, ended in his death.

During these ten years, Cook used in his Journals the following Polynesian words : **pa, pah,** a Maori fort (Maori *pà*), **taboo** (Tongan *tabu*), **tattoo** (Polynesian *tatau*), **kava,** an intoxicating beverage ; **taro,** a plant (Sandwich Is.) ; another word of this period is **kaka,** a New Zealand parrot, recorded by J. R. Forster in 1774.   The remaining Polynesian words, chiefly of Maori origin, were all but one borrowed in the nineteenth century : **kauri,** a pine (Maori), 1823, in R. A. Cruise's *Ten Months in New Zealand* ; **tapa,** cloth made from bark (Polynesian), 1823 ; **tara,** a kind of fern (Maori), 1834, in Ross's *Van Diemen's Land* ; **kiwi** (Maori) 1835, W. Yate's *Account of New Zealand* ; **rata,** a tree (Maori), 1835, also in Yate's book ; **kanaka** (Hawaiian) 1840, in Dana's *Before the Mast* ; **poi,** a dish made of tara-root (Hawaii), 1840 ; **moa** (Maori) 1842 [1] ; **kakapo,** ground parrot of New Zealand (Maori), 1843 ; **kea,** a green parrot (Maori), 1862 ; **tuatara,** a lizard (Maori), 1890 ; **ukulele** (Hawaii) 1920.

(B) Australian

The continent of Australia had been discovered in the seventeenth century, and Dampier had touched there in 1688. But it was not until after the voyages of Captain Cook had brought it again to the attention of England that any European settlements were made there, and that any native words became known in English.   The first colony, to which convicts were

---

[1] British colonization in New Zealand began in the early years of Queen Victoria's reign.

transported, was established at Port Jackson in 1788, and in the second decade of the nineteenth century the immigration of agricultural settlers began.

Apparently the first Australian word to be recorded is **kangaroo**, noted by Cook in 1770 : *The animals which I have before mentioned, called by the Natives Kangaroo or Kanguru.* Four more words are recorded in the eighteenth century : **dingo** 1789 (Tench's *Botany Bay*) ; **corroboree**, a native dance, 1793, in J. Hunter's *Port Jackson* ; **waratah**, a shrub, 1793, in J. E. Smith's *Botany of New Holland* ; **wombat**, 1798, Flinders, *Voyage in Terra Australis.* Of eleven words borrowed in the nineteenth century, eight are names of birds, animals, or trees : **koolah, koala**, the Australian bear, 1808 ; **boomerang**, 1827, in Capt. King's book on the Survey of the Australian coasts : *Boomerang is the Port Jackson term for this weapon, and may be retained for want of a more descriptive name* ; **paramatta**, a fabric (from a Place-Name), 1834, in J. D. Lang's *State of New South Wales* ; **myall**, a native (Austr. *mial* ' wild ') 1835, in Mitchell's *Expedition to Eastern Australia* ; **joey**, a young kangaroo (Austr. *joé*), 1839, in W. H. Leigh, *Voyage to South Australia* ; **myall**, a kind of acacia (Austr. *maiāl*), 1845 ; **budgerigar** (Austr., = good cockatoo) 1847 ; **mallee**, a kind of eucalyptus, 1848, in Westgarth, *Australia Felix* ; **warrigal**, the dingo (Austr. *warringin*), 1852 ; **jarrah**, mahogany gum-tree, 1866 ; **karri**, one of the blue gums, 1870, Knight's *West Australia.*

Chapter XII

THE LANGUAGES OF AFRICA

Apart from European languages now spoken in Africa, the various dialects of this continent form many and highly diversified groups. In many parts of the north Semitic dialects (chiefly Arabic) are common ; Hamitic dialects (Coptic—from earlier Egyptian—Berber, Libyan, Cushitic) are spoken in parts of the north and east. In the south there are the languages of the Hottentots, Pygmies, and Bushmen. In the huge territory occupied by African negroes there exist two great related languages, Bantu and Sudanese, each of which has several hundred varieties. Bantu is spoken to the south of the Equator (to give only an approximate boundary), Sudanese to the north. In many areas these dialects have been much affected by the influence of foreign languages, e.g. Arabic.

The earliest connexion of English with Africa is at a very early period, when a few words entered it, or its continental parent-language, from Egyptian by way of Greek and Latin. Old English (see p. 55) has the forms *senep* ' mustard ', *elpend* ' elephant ', *carte* ' paper ', all of which are of Egyptian origin. *Elpend* was superseded in Middle English by *elephant*, the French form of the Latin word which Old English had borrowed ; *chart*, another French form, again ultimately Egyptian, has replaced *carte* ; O.E. *senep* is obsolete, but another O.E. word, *næp* ' a root, turnip ', which apparently also comes (through Latin) from Greek *sināpis* (from Egyptian) survives as the second element of **turnip, parsnip. Ebon, ebony,** representing Lat. *hebenum* (Gk. *hebenon*, from Egyptian, and related to *elephant*) appear in Late Middle English, the latter first in Wyclif, who also has another Egyptian word, **ibis,** which he borrowed from the Latin of the Vulgate. **Turnip,** earlier **turnepe** (the origin of the first syllable is obscure), appears first in 1533, in Elyot's *Castell of Helthe* : *Turnepes beinge welle boyled in water, and after with fatte fleshe, norysheth moche.* Unlike so many Eastern languages,

Egyptian has no contribution to make to English in the sixteenth and seventeenth centuries. It is true that Purchas has the word **oasis** in 1613, but this is a ' learned ' word in origin, having been borrowed by Latin from Greek, and by the latter from Egyptian (cf. Coptic *ouah* ' to dwell ').

Recent loans from Egyptian have been archaeological terms, of which the best known are **canopic** (with a Latin ending), from the early Egyptian Place-Name *Canopus*, 1878, and **ushabti**, not until 1912.

It has already been pointed out (see Chapter IX) that the Portuguese had established trading-stations on the Guinea coast in the sixteenth century, and hither came Englishmen in the reign of Elizabeth to dispute the Portuguese monopoly of the West African trade. Until recent times, all the Sudanese words borrowed by English have been of West African origin, most of them apparently taken directly from the native dialects, though a few are through Portuguese or French. It was in this area of Africa, in spite of opposition, that English trade was established earliest and most strongly, the slave trade, apart from other ventures, proving a constant attraction to the Guinea coast for more than two hundred years. It is owing to the slave trade that a few African words have reached English by way of America and American-English (see below).

The earliest West African word in English appears to be **yam,** through Portuguese *inhame*, though its African origin is sometimes disputed ; it is found first in 1588, in Hickock's translation of Frederick's *Voyage to the East Indies*, where it is spelt *inany* ; the spelling *ycam* is used in 1657 ; **banana** (through Span., from the native name in Guinea) in 1597. In the seventeenth century we find three more words : **pongo,** a kind of ape, 1625, Battel in *Purchas his Pilgrimes : This Pongo is . . . more like a Giant in stature, than a man : for he is very tall, and hath a mans face, hollow-eyes, with long haire vpon his browes* ; **drill,** a kind of baboon, 1644 ; **harmattan** (through Fr. from W.Afr. *haramata*) 1671, in a section (' *Of the Harmetans in Ginny* ') of R. Bohun's *Wind* ; **greegree, gregory, grigory,** an African amulet, 1698.

The eighteenth century loans are also from the Sudanese dialects of West Africa : **potto,** a lemur, 1705 ; **okra** 1707, through

R

the West Indies; it appears first in Sloane's *Jamaica*; **chimpanzee** 1738 : *A most surprizing creature is brought over in the Speaker, just arrived from Carolina, that was taken in a wood at Guinea. She is the Female of the creature which the Angolans call Chimpanzee, or the Mockman* ; **opah,** a fish, 1750 ; **obeah, obi,** an amulet ; sorcery, 1764 ; **cola, kola,** the seed, used for chewing, etc., of a West African tree, 1755, in Nicholas Owen's *Journal* ; *with some old bags of grass or cloath to hould the good man's tabaco or cola* ; **shea** (Mandingo *si, se*) 1797, in Park's *Travels in Africa*.

The first nineteenth century loan takes us back to a West African borrowing which far antedates any other in a European language. In the fifth and sixth century Hanno the Carthaginian visited the coast of Africa, and in the Greek account of his voyage the word *gorillas* (pl.) is alleged to be an African word. This was adopted as the specific name of the ape (*Troglodytes gorilla*) by Savage in 1847 (Journal of the Boston Natural History Society) ; it is found as an English word first in 1853 : *Description of Cranium of an adult male gorilla* (R. Owen in *Trans. Zool. Soc.*). The name **guereza,** an Abyssinian monkey, is from an Eastern type of Sudanese (1859, in Wood's *Natural History*). **Gumbo** (Angolan *ki-ngombo*) appears first in America (1859). **Voodoo,** first found in 1880, is probably from Dahomey *vodu*.

The influence of Bantu on the English vocabulary is almost negligible until the nineteenth century. Three words (one of them doubtful) are found before 1800 : **zebra** 1600 (from a Congo dialect, probably through Port.), in Pory's translation of Leo's *Africa* : *The zebra or zabra of this countrey* [Congo] *being about the bignes of a mule, is a beast of incomparable swiftnes* : possibly **baobab** 1640 (in a botanical work) ; **kudu, koodoo,** 1777, in G. Forster's *Voyage round the World*.

The next Bantu word is not found until 1847, and then in the West Indies, whither it was carried from Africa in 1827 ; this is **dengue,** the name of a type of fever, from a Swahili word meaning ' sudden cramp ', but through Spanish. **Inyala,** an antelope, is found in 1848 (*Proc. Zool. Soc.*), **tsetse** (Bechuana) in 1849 (E. E. Napier's *Excursions in South Africa*). Then we have a few words from the Zulu dialect, two of which have special reference to the

Zulu War : **induna,** an officer under the king of a tribe, 1875, in Oates, *Matabele Land* ; **donga,** a ravine, 1879, in the *Daily News* ; **impi** 1879, in the *Daily Telegraph*, 16th May : *A Zulu impi . . . managed to cut off the chief's cattle* ; **indaba,** a conference, 1894, in the *Pall-Mall Gazette*, 26th Dec. : *A message was therefore conveyed . . . to the King, inviting Umtassa to come in to an indaba at Umtali.* One word from the Congo dialect dates from the beginning of the present century : **okapi,** first recorded in 1900.

Finally, we have a few words from the Hottentot language, all of which appear first in books of travel, four of the eighteenth, one of the nineteenth century : **kaross,** rug or mantle of skin, 1731, in Medley's translation of Kolben's *Cape of Good Hope* ; **gnu** 1777, G. Forster's *Voyage round the World* (*gnoo*) ; **quagga** 1785, Forster's translation of Sparrman's *Voyage to the Cape* : *One of the animals called quaggas by the Hottentots and colonists* ; **karoo** 1789 ; **kaama,** the hartebeest, 1824, in Burchell's *Travels*.

Chapter XIII

FROM THE NEW WORLD

The journeys and discoveries of Columbus in 1492 and of Cabot in 1497 opened the way for a new source of supply for the English vocabulary as well as for English markets. Something has already been said (see Chapter X) of the Spanish explorations across the Atlantic and of their settlements on the American coasts, as well as of the English traders and explorers who followed the Spanish trade routes, and, in spite of vigorous opposition, themselves engaged in trade with the native inhabitants of the Americas. A few American words which reached us through Spanish have been given in Chapter X, but a more complete list must be given here.

The Indian dialects of America number many hundreds, and their inter-relations are still a matter of much speculation. They will be divided here, somewhat arbitrarily, into two groups : (A) South and Central America, Mexico, and the West Indies, and (B) North America. There is, however, a historical justification for this division, since words borrowed from the (A) group, especially in the earlier periods, most commonly enter English through Spanish or Portuguese ; while those from the (B) group come directly from North American Indian ; the latter are all subsequent to the re-establishment of the colony of Virginia in 1607 (Raleigh's colony was founded here in 1587), while the former have already begun to enter English in the middle of the sixteenth century.

(A) South America, etc.

The chief dialects of South America to be represented in English are the Quichua dialect, from Peru, which reached considerable importance under the empire of the Incas, and spread over a considerable area in the North-West and South America ; the Guarani dialect of parts of Paraguay and the Argentine which likewise extended far beyond its original territory, and in the sixteenth century was spoken, sometimes together with a local dialect, over much of Brazil ; Mexican dialects ; and the Carib dialects (originally from the mainland of South America) of the southern West Indies.

The first American Indian word to appear in English is **guaiacum,** a Latinized form of Spanish *guayaco*, from Haitian ; this is found in an English translation (1533) of a medical work. Then we have a batch of eleven words, all but one from the West Indies, recorded in Richard Eden's *Decades of the Newe Worlde*, a translation of a work by Peter Martyr. The first we shall mention is Mexican : **cacao** (for the later *cocoa*, see 1707), the Span. form from Mex. *caca-uatl* = caca-tree : *In the steade* [of money] *the halfe shelles of almonds, whiche kynde of Barbarous money they* [the Mexicans] *caule cacao or cacauguate* ; the others are : **caclque,** a native chief (Span. from Haitian) ; **canoe** (in Eden *canoa*, from Span. from Hait.) ; **cassava** (Hait., perhaps through French) ; **hammock** (Span. *hamaca*, from Carib.) : *their hangynge beddes whiche they caule Hamacas* (cf. Raleigh's *Discovery of Guiana* : *They lay each of them in a cotten Hamaca, which we call brasill beds*) ; **hurricane,** the present form, but many variants occur in the seventeenth and eighteenth centuries ; Spanish seems to have had both *huracan* and *furacan* ; the word is originally Carib ; Eden uses *Furacan* where Peter Martyr has this form, but when translating Oviedo in the same work he gives two forms : *Great tempestes which they caule Furacanas or Haurachanas . . . ouerthrowe many howses and great trees* ; **iguana** (Carib. *iwana*, through Span.) : *Foure footed beastes . . . named Iuanas, muche lyke vnto Crocodiles, of eyght foote length, of moste pleasaunte taste* ; **maguey,** the American aloe (Span., from Hait.) ; **manatee** (Span., from Carib. *manattoui*) : *A yonge fyshe of the kynde of those huge monsters of the sea whiche thinhabitours caule Manati* ; **savannah,** earlier *zavana* (Span., probably from Carib.) ; **yucca** (Span., from Carib.).

A word now obsolete is **sapota,** an evergreen tree (Span. *zapota* from Mex. *zapotl*) *c.* 1560 (Tomson, in Hakluyt), but its diminutive, *sapodilla*, will be found later under 1697. The next word is an important one : **potato** (from Span. *patata*, from Hait. *batata* ; the Haitian form is also found in English, first in 1577) ; this appears first, with reference to the sweet potato, in Hawkins's *Voyage to Florida*, 1565 : *These potatoes be the most delicate rootes that may be eaten, and doe far exceede our passeneps or carets.* The usual modern potato, *Solanum tuberosum*, which is a native of western South America, was introduced into Spain from Quito soon after 1580, and it gradually became familiar in other parts of Europe ; the first reference to it in English is in Gerard's *Herbal*, 1597 ; Gerard, however, refers it to Virginia, where it is not indigenous.   Sparke's *Sir John Hawkins' Second Voyage* (in Hakluyt) gives us the Cuban word **maize** (Span. *maiz*, from Cuban) : *Mayis maketh good sauory bread.* The first Brazilian words are found in 1568, in Hacket's translation of Thevet's *New-found World* : **manioc,** earlier **manihot** (the latter perhaps a French spelling ; Braz. *mandioca*) : *The Americanes make meale of those rootes that are caled Manihot* ; **toucan** (Port. *tucano*, from Braz. *tucana*).   In Hawkes's *Travels* (Hakluyt) we find the tree-name **mammee** 1572 (Span. *mamey*, from Hait.).

Frampton's *Joyfull Newes from the Newe Founde Worlde* (1577) has several new words :   **cayman** (Span., from Carib.) ;   **copal,** a kind of resin (Mex. *copalli* ' incense ') : *They doe bryng from the Newe Spaine twoo kindes of Rosine . . . the one is called Copall* ; **petun,** a kind of tobacco, now obsolete, except as surviving in the plant-name **petunia** (Braz. *petỹ*, through French *petun*) ; **tacamahac,** a resin (Span. from Aztec *tecomahiyac*) ; and finally **tobacco** (Span. *tabaco*, from Hait., where it was perhaps used originally of a tube or pipe) : *This hearbe which commonly is called Tabaco, is an Hearbe of muche antiquitie, and knowne amongest the Indians* ; cf., eleven years later, William Harrison in his *Chronologie* : *In these daies the taking-in of the smoke of the Indian herbe called Tabaco, by an instrument formed like a litle ladell, whereby it passeth from the mouth into the hed & stomach, is gretlie taken-vp & vsed in England.*

Two more words conclude the sixteenth century list :   **teocalli,** a Mexican temple (Mex. *teocalli*), 1578 ;   **papaw, pawpaw** (Carib., perhaps through Span. *papayo*), 1598, in Phillips's translation of Linschoten : *There is also a fruite that came out of the Spanish Indies, brought . . . to Malacca, and from thence to India, it is called Papaios, and is very like a Mellon, as bigge as a man's fist.*

Peruvian (Quichuan) words appear first in the seventeenth

century ; these, like other South American words, are nearly
all names of animals, birds, plants, and their products. Many of
them appear in translations of Spanish or Portuguese works,
but others are recorded in the accounts of the voyages of English
sailors (often as given by Hakluyt or Purchas). **Llama** 1600
(Span. from Peruvian) : *An Indian boy driuing 8 Llamas or
sheepe of Peru which are as big as asses* (Hakluyt) ; **quipu,** one
of the knotted cords used by the Peruvians to convey messages,
1604 (Quichuan) ; **viscacha,** a rodent (Span. from Quichuan
uiscacha), 1604, in E. Grimstone's translation of D'Acosta's
History of the Indies ; the following six words are from the same
work : **guanaco** (Span. from Peruv. *huanaco*), **guano** (Span.
from Peruv. *huano*), **condor** (Span. from Peruv. *cuntur*), **chocolate**
(Span. from Mex. *chocolatl*), **jaguar** (Braz. *yaguara, jaguara*) :
*They ascribe power to another starre, which they called
Chuquinchincay (which is as much as iaguar), over tigres, beares,
and lyons* ; **tomato** (Span. *tomata* from Mex. *tomatl*) : *There
was also Indian pepper, beetes, Tomates, which is a great sappy
and savourie graine.* **Piragua** (Span. from Carib. *piragua*
' dugout ') 1609, in *Virginia Richly Valued* : *A piragua or ferrie
bote* ; **buccan,** a wooden frame for roasting meat (Braz.), 1611,
in E. Aston's translation of Lery's *History of America* ; this word
is now obsolete in English, but the agent-noun **buccaneer** (a
French formation from *buccan*) is still current ; it meant first
a hunter, later a pirate : *Not able . . . to root out a few Buckaneers
or Hunting French-men*, Hickeringill, *Jamaica,* 1661. **Puna,**
a table-land (Peruv.), **ananas** (Peruv. *nanas*), **tanager** (Braz.
tanqara), **tamandua,** ant-eater (Braz.), 1613–14, in *Purchas his
Pilgrimage.* **Coca** (Span. *coca* from Peruv. *cuca*) 1616, in Bullokar :
*an hearbe of India, the leaues whereof being bruised and mixt with
the powder of Cockles or Oysters in their shelles burnt the Indians
use in little balles to carry in their mouthes to preserue them from
famine and great dryth* ; from this comes **cocaine,** first recorded
in 1874. **Vicuna** (Span. *vicuña* from Peruv.), 1622, in R. Hawkins,
Voyage into the South Sea ; **paca** (Tupi) 1657 ; **hoatzin,** a bird,
1661 ; **chilli** (Mex.) 1662, in H. Stubbe's *The Indian Nectar,
A Treatise on Chocolata* ; **roucou,** a tree whence a dye is obtained
(Fr. from Braz. *urucu*), 1666, in J. Davies's translation of
Rochefort's *Caribby Isles* ; **urubu,** a vulture, 1672, in

Willoughby's *Ornithology* ; **jalap,** a drug, 1675 (Fr. from Span. *jalape,* from the Mex. Place-Name *Xalapan*) ; **coati** (Tupi) 1676 ; **ipecacuanha** (Port., from Braz. *ipe-kaa-guéne*) 1682, J. Pechey : *Some Observations made upon the Brasilian Root, called Ipepocoanha* ; **anatto,** a Central American dye, 1682, Sir William Petty : *Arnotto dyeth of itself an orange colour* ; **curassow,** from the name of the island of Curaçao (see this again in 1813) 1685, in L. Wafer's *Voyage* : *The Corrosou is a large black land-bird, heavy and big as a turkey-hen* ; **saki** 1687 (Braz. *çahi*) ; **calipash,** the upper shell of the turtle (Span. *carapacho,* probably from Carib. ; cf. **carapace** 1836, from Mod. French) 1689 ; **chigoe** (Carib.) 1691, the form **jigger** in 1781 ; **sapodilla,** an evergreen tree (Span. diminutive of *zapota,* q.v. under 1560), 1697, in Dampier's *Voyages* : *Where there grow great Groves of Sapadillies which is a Sort of Fruit much like a pear* ; **avocado** 1697 ; **barbecue** 1697 ; **sapajou,** a monkey (Fr., perhaps from Cayenne), 1698.

South American and West Indian words of the earlier eighteenth century are for the most part recorded first in books of travel and descriptions of the countries of the West, but towards the end of the century we find a number of them in scientific works on natural history, etc., or in works of more general instruction, such as Chambers' *Cyclopaedia* ; Goldsmith's *Natural History* is responsible for a fairly large group.

Cashew (Fr. *acajou,* from Port. from Braz. *acajoba*) 1703, in Dampier's *Voyages* (III) : *The Cashew is a Fruit as big as a Pippin, pretty long, and bigger near the Stemb than at the other end* ; the French form *acajou* is also used in English, first in Bradley's *Family Dictionary,* 1725 ; **pampa,** usually in plural, **pampas** (Span. from Peruv. *bamba* ' steppe ') 1704 ; **maqui,** a shrub of Chile, 1704 ; **charqui,** dried flesh (Span. from Peruv.), 1706 ; there is also a Spanish verb *charquear,* which is anglicized as **jerk,** first found in 1707 ; **tapioca,** meal prepared from the root of the cassava (Port. from Braz. *tipioca*), 1707, in Sloane's *Voyage to Jamaica* : *The juice evaporated over the fire gives the Tipioca meal* ; cf. Capt. John Smith in his *Map of Virginia,* 1612 : *The Chiefe roote they haue for foode is called Tockawhoughe . . . Raw it is no better than poison, and being roasted except it be tender . . . it will prickle and torment the throat extreamly* ; **cocoa** (cf. the earlier *cacao,* q.v. under 1555 ; eighteenth century also *cacoa, cocao*) 1707, in Funnell's *Voyages* : *The Nut* [of Theobroma cacao] *or kernel . . . ripens in a great Husk, wherein are sometimes 30, nay* 40 *cocoas. These cocoas are made use of to make chocolate* ; for the powder, cf. Burns's *Letters*, 1788 : *I executed your commission in Glasgow, and I hope the cocoa came safe* ; **copaiba,** a balsam (Span. from Braz. *cupauba*), 1712, in E. Cooke's *Voyage to the South Sea* ; **maté** (Span. from Braz. *mati* ' vessel made of calabash ', used for infusing the leaves of the plant known as *yerba maté*) 1717 ; applied to the shrub itself, 1758 ; **nopal** (Span. *nopal* from Mex. *nopalli*) 1730 ; **agouti** (Fr., from Span. *aguti*, perhaps from Carib.) 1731 ; **colibri** (Carib.) ; **guan,** a gallinaceous bird, 1743, in G. Edwards, *Natural History* ; **poncho** (Span. from Araucanian) 1748 ; **perai,** a fish (Tupi *piraya*), **jacaranda,** a tree (Braz.), **jacana,** an aquatic bird (Port. *jaçaná* from Braz. *jasaná*), in Chambers' *Cyclopaedia, Supplement*, 1753 ; **cayenne,** earlier **cayan** (Braz. *kyýnha*, assimilated to the Place-Name) 1756, in P. Browne's *Jamaica* ; **paramo, corozo,** 1760 ; **woorali,** a poison, 1769, in E. Bancroft's *Essay on the Natural History of Guiana*.

The next seven words are from Goldsmith's *Natural History* : **jabiru,** a wading-bird (Braz. *jabirú*) ; **cougar** (Fr. *couguar* (Buffon) ultimately from Braz. *guaçu ara* : *There is an animal of America, which is usually called the Red tiger, but Mr. Buffon calls it the Cougar*), **tapir** (Braz. *tapira*), **ocelot** (French (Buffon) from Mex. *tlalocelotl = tlalli* ' field ' + *ocelotl* ' jaguar ' ; *The catamountain which is the Ocelot of Mr. Buffon*), **coaita,** the red-faced spider-monkey (Braz.), **cabiai** (Braz., later **cavy,** 1796), **capybara** (Braz.).

Caoutchouc 1775 (Fr., from Carib. *cahuchu*) ; **tafia,** liquor obtained from molasses (probably Carib.), 1777, in the Historical Collections of Illinois ; **puma** (Peruv.), **curare** (Carib. *wurari, wurali*, see *woorali* above), both in Robertson's *History of America*, 1777 ; **tamarin** (Fr., perhaps from Carib.), **margay** (Fr., from Braz. *mbaracaia*), Smellie's translation of Buffon, 1780–1 ; **tinamou** (Fr. from Galibi *tinamu*), 1783, in Latham's *Synopsis of Birds* ; **axolotl,** a reptile (Aztec), 1786, in Rees's *Encyclopaedia* (*A singular fish found in the lake of Mexico*) ; **angostura** (from a place of this name in Venezuela, now Ciudad Bolivar) 1791, A. Brande, *Experiments & Observations on the*

Angustura Bark ;   **coypu** 1793, in Pennant's *History of Quadrupeds* ;   **pitpan,** a boat (Central America), 1798.

Twentieth century loan-words are rather fewer, but their character remains much the same : **rhatany** (Mod. Lat. *Rhatania*, from Port. from Quichuan *rataña*) 1808, in Reece's *Dictionary of Domestic Medicine* ;   **curaçao, curaçoa** (the name of an island in the Caribbean Sea), a liqueur, 1813, Moore, *Postbag* : *And it pleased me to think at a house that you know / Were such good mutton cutlets and strong curaçoa* ;   **agama,** a lizard (Carib.), 1817, in *Blackwood's Magazine* ;   **jacamar,** a bird (Braz. *jacama-ciri*), 1825, Waterton's *Wanderings in South America* ;   **quinine** (Fr., from Span. from Peruv. *kina* ' bark ') 1826 (first introduced into medical practice in 1820) ;   **mescal** (Span., from Mex. *mexcalli*), 1828, in Sir H. G. Ward's *Mexico* ;   **coumarin** (French *coumarine*, from Guiana *cumaru* ' tonka bean '), 1830, in Lindley's *Natural System of Botany* ;   **araucaria** (from *Arauco*, the name of a province in the south of Chile) 1833, in the *Penny Cyclopaedia* ;   **guarana,** a shrub (Braz.) 1838 ;   **sisal** (grass) 1843 (Place-Name in Yucatan) ;   **divi-divi,** a tree (Carib.), 1843, in the *Pharmaceutical Journal* ;   **coyote** 1850 (Span. from Mex. *coyotl*) ;   **mesquite** (Span. from Mex.) 1851, in Mayne Reid's *Scalp Hunters* ;   **pinole,** meal made from parched corn-flour (Span. *pinole*, from Aztec *pinolli*) 1853 ;   **cacoon,** a bean (perhaps Carib.), 1854, in Simmonds, *Commercial Products of the Vegetable Kingdom* ;   **tamal** (Mex.) 1856, in Olmsted's *Texas*) ;   **henequen** (Span. *jeniquen*) 1880 ;   **istle** (Mex. *ixtli*) 1883, in Cassell's *Family Magazine* ;   **pudu** (Chile) 1886.

(B) NORTH AMERICAN

It has been remarked earlier in this chapter that the first introduction of loan-words from North American Indian dialects followed the refounding of the colony of Virginia in 1607. The first borrowings are indeed from the dialects of this area, though later settlements (by 1640 it is estimated that there were 25,000 English settlers in New England) brought the English language into contact with the dialects of tribes farther north. It will be observed that words from Canadian Indian fail to appear until the last quarter of the eighteenth century, after the conquest of Canada in 1759.

Seventeenth century : **racoon** (Powhatan dialect of Virginia)
1608, in Capt. Smith's *True Relation* (in the form *Rahaugcums*) ;
opossum (Virginian) 1610, in the *True Declaration of the Colony
of Virginia* : *There are Arocouns, and Apossouns, in shape like
to pigges, shrowded in hollow roots of trees.* In Capt. Smith's
Map of Virginia, 1612, we find : **persimmon** (Powhatan) : *the
fruit like medlers* ; *they call Putchamins, they cast vppon hurdles
on a mat, and preserue them as Pruines* ; **puccoon** (Powhatan) ;
moccasin (Powhatan *mockasin*) ;   **terrapin,** earlier **terape**
(Algonquin *terape*), 1613, in A. Whitaker's *Good Newes from
Virginia* ; in *Purchas his Pilgrimage*, 1613 : **sagamore** (Penobscot
sagamo = *sachem* in other dialects ; *He obserued a feast made by
Anadabijou, the great Sagamo, in his Cabin*), **moose** (Narragansett
moos ; *Captaine Thomas Hanham sayled to the Riuer of Sagadahoe
1606. He relateth of their beasts . . . redde Deare, and a beast bigger,
called the Mus*). **Sachem,** the head of a tribe (Narragansett)
1622, *Relation of the Plantation in Plymouth, New England* ;
musquash, earlier **mussascus** (Abnaki *muskwessu* ;   the early
form perhaps from Powhatan), 1624, in Capt. Smith's *Virginia* :
A Mussascus is a beast of the forme and nature of our water Rats ;
pow-wow (Algonquin) 1624, of an Indian medicine-man, in 1812
of a conference ; **wigwam** (Ojibwa *wigwaun*) 1628, in Levett's
Voyage to New England : *We built us our wigwam or house, in
one hour's space* ; **hominy** (the exact form or dialect of the original
is doubtful) 1629, in John Smith's *Continuation of the History
of Virginia* : *Their servants commonly feed upon Homini,
which is bruized Indian corne pounded, and boiled thicke, and
milke for the sauce* ; **wampum,** earlier **wampumpeag** (Algonquin
*wampampiak) 1631. The next four are from W. Wood's *New
Englands Prospects* 1634 : **squaw** (Algonquin *squa, squaws* ;
tomahawk (Algonquin *tämähāk*) : *They beate them downe with
their right hand Tamahaukes, and left hand Iavelins* ; **skunk**
(Indian *segankw*, etc.) : *The beasts of offence be Squunckes,
Ferrets, Foxes* ; **papoose** (Algonquin) : *This little Pappouse
travells about with his bare footed mother to paddle in the Icie
Clammbankes.* **Tautog** (Narragansett *taut-auog*) 1643, in Roger
Williams's *Key to the Language of America* ; **manitou** (Algonquin
manito) 1671 ; **hickory** 1676 (Virginian *pohickery*) ; **woodchuck**
1689 (Cree *wuchak*, assimilated to *wood*).

Eighteenth century :   **sora,** the Carolina rail (? Virginia), 1705, in R. Beverly's *Virginia* ;   **catalpa** (Carolina Indian ; the tree was discovered by Catesby in 1726), 1726, in Catesby's *Natural History of Florida* ;   **totem** 1760 (Ojibwa) ;   **way-way, wav(e)y,** the wild goose, (Cree *wehweh*) 1768 ;   **pecan** (Algonquin) 1773, in P. Kennedy's Journal in Hutchins's *Description of Virginia* ;   **caribou** (Canadian French from Indian) 1774, in Goldsmith's   *Natural   History* ;   **succotash**   (Narragansett *msiquatash*) 1778, in Carver's *Travels in North America* ; **menhaden** 1792 (Narragansett *munnawhatteaûg*) ;   **quahaug,** a clam, 1794 (Algonquin *poquauhock*).   The next three from Morse's *American Geography,* 1796 :   **maskinonge,** a kind of pike (Ojibwa) ;   **pekan,** animal like a weasel (Canadian Fr., from Algonquin) ;   **kinkajou,** an animal allied to the racoon (cf. Algonquin *kwingwaage* ' wolverine ' ;   Buffon transferred the name).   **Kinnikinic,** a mixture used in place of tobacco, 1799 (Algonquin = mixture).

Nineteenth century :   **pemmican** (Cree *pimecan*) 1801, Sir A. Mackenzie, *Voyage up the St. Lawrence* ;   **wapiti** (Cree *wapitik*) 1817 ;   **toboggan** (French *tabaganne* (1691) from Canadian Indian) 1829 ;   G. Head's *Forest Scenes of North America* (*tobogin*) ;   **mugwump** (slang) 1832 (Natick *mugquomp* ' great chief ') ;   **tamarack,** the American larch (Canadian Indian), 1841, in Fenimore Cooper's *Deerslayer* ;   **chipmunk** (probably Indian) 1842 ;   **catawba** (grape) 1857 (from a river-name) ; **tepee** (Sioux *tī-pī* ' tent, house ') 1872, in W. F. Butler's *Great Lone Land* ;   **choctaw,** step in skating, (from the name of an Indian tribe) 1892 ;   **apache** (French, from the name of an Indian tribe) 1902.

(C) Eskimo

This is a very small section, which cannot, however, be included under *American Indian,* since the Eskimo dialects appear to belong to an entirely different family.   The first word is of doubtful origin, but it may be from Eskimo :   **tarrock,** the Arctic tern, 1674.   The other three are genuine Eskimo, all of the eighteenth or nineteenth century :   **kayak** 1757 ;   **umiak, oomiak** 1769 ;   **igloo** 1856 (*The hut or igloë . . . was a single rude elliptical apartment,* Kane).

Chapter XIV

LATER LOAN-WORDS FROM LATIN AND GREEK

(A) Latin

The wealth of Latin and Greek words gradually absorbed into English since the beginning of the Middle English period is of more importance from a cultural than from a historical point of view. They do not illustrate, as do most of the words which we have dealt with hitherto, the constant increase in English relations with other countries and languages, and the formation of new contacts, although they do indicate the continuous importance of Latin culture and literature in England especially under the influence of the Classical Renaissance. They are discussed here, therefore, only in outline, merely to illustrate the types of words borrowed in the Middle and Modern English periods and their usual methods of adoption and treatment.

The Latin loan-words which were included in an earlier chapter, at least those of the first two periods, were adopted directly into the spoken language from Latin-speaking people. But for two hundred years or more before the Norman Conquest the influence of the Latin of Classical literature and the Latin of religion and learning had been felt in English writing, and to some extent at least in English speech. During Middle English this process goes on,[1] The Latin forms borrowed in earlier Middle English are, as in Late Old English, usually of a technical character, very often terms of religion (e.g. *credo*, Lambeth Homs. ; *paske* ' Easter ', Trin. Homs. ; *benedicite, confiteor, dirige* (later *dirge*), *ipocrisis*, Ancr. Riwle), and this holds good of some at least of the later Middle English borrowings from Latin, many, though not all, of which still survive. We find, for instance, further ecclesiastical terms, such as *requiem, gloria, limbo, magnificat, pater(noster)*, *eremite, lector, lateran, collect, quinquagesima, diocese, bull*,

---

[1] See especially O. Dellit, *Ueber lateinische Elemente im Mittelenglischen* Marburg, 1906.

mediator, redemptor, salvator, sanctum, besides names of the books of the Bible and other words taken from the Vulgate : *Genesis, Exodus* (both ultimately Greek), *psalm, apocalipse, alleluia, magi, sabbat.*

Another source of Latin words in M.E. was the study and practice of the law, whence came such terms as *client, arbitrator, conviction, debenture, defalcation, emolument, equivalent, exorbitant, extravagant, executor, gratis, hereditament, imprimis, implement, legitimate, memorandum, mittimus, pauper, persecutor, proviso,* and many others, besides more exclusively legal words and phrases such as *alias, dedimus, habeas corpus, subpœna, prima facie.* All these appear before 1500, and many before 1400.

Terms of the schools and of writing are also common : *abecedary* (Lat. *abecedarius*), *abacus, allegory, et cetera, cause, contradictory, desk, ergo, explicit, finis, formal, incipit, index, item, library, memento, major, minor, neuter, scribe, simile, videlicet.* Scientific terms form a large group. (A) Medicine : *diaphragm, digit, orbit, hepatic, dislocate, fomentation, ligament, recipe, saliva.* (B) Alchemy, including several which are now obsolete, or have changed their meaning : *dissolve, ether, gypsus, mercury, sal effronium, acuate, aggravate* (adj.), *calcine, commixt, concatenate* (adj.), *contumulate, concrete, distillation, elixir, essence, fermentation, fixation, immaterial, liquable, obscuration.* (C) Astronomy (many of them found first in Chaucer) : *ascension, comet, conspect, dial, eccentric, equal, equator, equinoxium, equinoxial, hesperus, intercept, retrograde.* (D) Botany : *cardamom, gladiol, juniper, lupin, pine.* (E) Zoology : *asp, cicade, locust, lacert.* (F) Mineralogy : *adamant, chalcedony, chrysoberyl, jacinct, onyx, lapidary.*

But there are in addition to words of this kind some hundreds of words adopted from Latin in Middle English, which cannot be grouped under any special technical category. Many of them are abstract terms, and they may be noun, adjective, or verb : —
Nouns : *adoption, aliment, collision, collocution, colony, commissary, concussion, conductor, conflict, depression, exclamation, expedition, impediment, implication* ; Adjectives : *aggregate, alienate, communicative, compact, complete, confederate, determinate, effeminate, imaginary, immortal, incorporate, infirm.* Verbs : *accede, adjure, admit, combine, commend, commit, conclude, confide,*

discuss, dissent, distend, exclude, expend, immix, import, infect, interest, etc., etc.

It happened fairly often that the form which a French word had taken in its development from Latin remained close enough to the Latin to make it sometimes difficult to know whether a Late Middle English loan-word is from French or direct from Latin ; as, for instance, in the following words : *exemption, execution, dissimulation, distant, dispense, discipline, contrite, contract* (n.), *compress* (vb.), *exhale, expectant, impression.* Often, also, a word which was adopted from Old French is, either in Middle English or later, reborrowed from Latin, or at least refashioned on the model of Latin, either in pronunciation or spelling or both, e.g. *adventure* (earlier *aventure*), *adorn* (earlier *aorn*), *confirm* (earlier *conferm*), *debt* (earlier *dette*), or this may happen in French itself, and the French word be reborrowed (e.g. *captive,* earlier *caitiff* ; though the English word in this and other cases *may* be directly from Latin). The matter is further complicated by the fact that in the adoption of words from Latin the common Latin suffixes are replaced in English by the suffixes common in French loan-words of similar derivation. For instance, O.Fr. *-ie* represents the Latin suffix *-ia,* and it is found in many English words from Old French, such as *envy, villainy* ; hence Lat. *custodia, familia, colonia,* were anglicized as *custodie, familie, colonie* (now *-y*). The same ending (now *-y*) was used in English for Latin nouns and adjectives in *-ius, -ium* : *mercury, contradictory, dimissory itinerary, corollary.* Similarly the Latin noun stems in *-tion, -sion,* appear in M.E. as *-tioun (-cioun), -sioun* (the French form of the ending), though during the fifteenth century they are gradually replaced by *-tion,* etc , with approximation to the Latin spelling. Thus we have M.E. *inflacioun (inflation), elevacioun, cognycyoun, attencioun, diffusioun.* So also in the French suffixes *-our, -te* (later *-or, -ty*) for the Latin *-ōr(em), -tas (-tātem)* : *pastour, mediatour, rectour, captivite, actualyte, infelicitee,* etc., etc.

Sometimes, however, an Old French form has deviated so far from its parent Latin that there can be no doubt as to which is the immediate source of the corresponding English word. Often, in fact, English has two forms (doublets), one from French the other directly from the Latin form which also produced the French, though the Latin type may have been borrowed considerably after Middle English. Some examples of this (with the dates of the earliest recorded use of the Latin loan) are : *count—compute* 1631 ; *ray—radius* 1597 ; *purvey—provide* (L.M.E.) ; *spice—species* 1551 ; *sure—secure* 1533 ; *treason—tradition* (L.M.E.) ; *strait—strict* 1578 ; *respite—respect* (L.M.E.) ; *poor—pauper* 1516 ; *garner—granary* 1570.

Many Latin suffixes, including those already referred to, are generalized in English, and may be used with Latin stems other than those with which they were used in classical Latin, or even with English stems. We may mention the very common noun-suffixes *-ment* (e.g. *argument, pigment, segment, sediment* ; and with non-Latin stem, *acknowledgment, oddment*), *-tion* (e.g. *oration, conversation, definition, elocution* ; cf. *starvation,* with an English stem) ; the adjectival suffixes *-ose* and *-ous* (the latter primarily a French suffix, but used with Latin stems), from Lat. *-ōs-* (*famous, callous, copious, religious, victorious, nervous, jocose, morose, verbose,* all of which had *-ōsus* in Latin ; *arduous, spurious, various, industrious, dubious,* remodelled in English from Latin adjectives in *-us*) ; *-al* (*fatal, floral, moral, plural, capital*) ; *-ary* (*ordinary, necessary, temporary, literary*) ; *-ate* (*delicate, fortunate, laureate* ; these were once much more common than they are now, large numbers having been formed from Latin participles in *-ātus,* e.g. *obstinate, desperate,* but many are now obsolete, or have been replaced by forms in *-ated,* the English past participles of verbs also formed from the Latin participles ; cf. now obsolete adjectives such as *alienate, conflate, contaminate, expiate*) ; *-ant, -ent* (e.g. *arrogant, different, crescent, important, provident, fluent*) ; *-able, -ible* (*durable, admirable, miserable* ; *credible, horrible*). In Latin, verbal adjectives from verbs of the first conjugation were formed with *-ābilis,* from verbs of other conjugations with *-ibilis.* This relation is sometimes lost in English, and new formations with *-able* are sometimes made from English verbs adopted from Latin verbs of the second, third, or fourth conjugation, e.g. *dependable, movable.* This suffix is the most used now of all the Latin adjectival suffixes, and a number of adjectives have been made with it from English or French nouns as well as verbs, e.g. *laughable, workable, comfortable, fashionable, sizable, peaceable, likable, eatable,* and even *un-get-at-able.*

In verbs from Latin the commonest ending is -*ate*, the English forms being derived largely from the passive participle (in -*ātus*) of Latin verbs of the first conjugation, e.g. *alienate, associate, exaggerate, accumulate, frustrate, hibernate, liberate, radiate, ventilate*, etc. Many of these, as has been indicated above, were adopted first as adjectives. English verbs formed from the perfect participle of other conjugations have no specific ending, e.g. *act, collapse, correct, conflict, confuse, exempt, incense*. Many other verbs are formed from Latin present stems, e.g. *conjure, dispute, deter, defer, interfere, disturb*, etc., and sometimes we have two verbs, one from the Latin present, the other from the participle, e.g. *conduce—conduct, convince—convict, repel—repulse*, etc. Another participial form which sometimes appears in English is that of the future passive participle or gerundive in -*and*-, -*end*-, in such words as *dividend, legend, reverend, agenda, memorandum*, etc.

So far we have dealt chiefly with English words which can be grouped under special suffixes, but there are, of course, very many Latin words which have been adopted in English with no special formative or derivative suffix. They often have exactly the same form in English as in Latin, so far as the spelling goes—their pronunciation in English following the spelling, each letter being given the value it usually has in modern English (e.g. *creator, ibex*), or in the case of early loan-words the Latin sounds having shared the development of the native English ones, as in the case of other foreign words.

Latin nouns, adjectives, and pronouns have usually been adopted in the nominative case (e.g. *circus, augur, consul, genus*), but inflected forms are occasionally found (generally depending on common early use in some particular phrase), such as the ablatives *folio* (from the phrase *in folio*), *limbo, proviso, via, specie, rebus* (pl.) ; the dative plural *omnibus* ; the accusative *requiem* ; the genitive plural *quorum*. To these we may add various Latin verbal forms which have become crystallized in the same way through some frequent construction (e.g. in legal formulae), and are now often used as nouns, e.g. *deficit, exit, caveat, ignoramus, interest, recipe, veto, tenet, fiat*. Latin prepositions and adverbs are adopted direct less commonly than nouns, adjectives, and verbs, but some do occur in English, though these

s

again commonly appear as nouns : *alias, alibi, extra, interim, item, verbatim.*

It must be noted that in the literature of certain periods, or among certain groups of writers, loan-words from Latin are used especially freely. This may or may not lead to copious adoption of Latin words in ordinary use. The period of the Renaissance certainly added very many Latin words to our ordinary vocabulary, as well as introducing many which failed to receive general approval. The frequent Latinisms sometimes found in poetic diction, as, for instance, in that of Milton, and in that of the eighteenth-century poets, have had far less effect on English as a whole.

We shall conclude this sketch of Latin borrowings since Old English by giving a brief dated list of forms appearing since 1500 and still surviving (showing the first recorded appearance in English), omitting derivative verbs, nouns, and adjectives (e.g. those with the suffixes mentioned above, and those compounded with common prefixes, such as *de-, dis-, ex-, in-, inter-, infra-, per-, pre-, pro-,* etc., many of which are Latin, though some are French), and also verbs which are formed directly from Latin verbal stems without suffix. The list will therefore consist chiefly of nouns and simple adjectives, some of the nouns being adopted from other parts of speech in Latin.

It will be seen from this list that the infiltration of Latin words has been continuous since 1500, the largest numbers having been introduced during the second half of the sixteenth century and the first half of the seventeenth, and the smallest number during the last half of the eighteenth century.

1500–1549

Cadaver 1500 ; arbiter 1502 ; integer 1509 ; genius 1513 ; torpedo 1520 (of a fish ; as a term in gunnery 1775) ; pollen 1523 ; junior 1526 ; cornea, fungus 1527 ; vertigo 1528 ; acumen 1531 ; folio 1533 ; alias, mandamus, quondam 1535 ; area, exit, peninsula 1538 ; quietus, regalia 1540 ; abdomen, animal (adj.), pus 1541 ; appendix, miser 1542 ; circus 1546 ; aborigines 1547 ; interim 1548 ; augur, axis 1549.

1550–1599

Vacuum 1550 ; genus, medium, specie, species 1551 ; terminus

1555 ; caesura 1556 ; caveat, multiplex 1557 ; corona, hiatus 1563 ; innuendo 1564 ; cerebellum 1565 ; decorum 1568 ; aliquot, nasturtium, vertex 1570 ; indecorum 1575 ; ignoramus, vagary 1577 ; interregnum, mamma, nostrum 1579 ; codex, compendium, exordium, viva-voce 1581 ; nonplus, octavo, omen 1582 ; posse 1583 ; quarto 1589 ; militia 1590 ; cornucopia 1592 ; multiplicand 1594 ; radius, sinus 1597 ; albumen, arcana, delirium, simulacrum, stratum, virus 1599.

1600–1649

Toga 1600 ; premium 1601 ; nostrum, odium 1602 ; rebus 1605 ; torpor 1607 ; equilibrium 1608 ; specimen 1610 ; spectrum, series, tiro 1611 ; census 1613 ; cerebrum, plus, vertebra 1615 ; amanuensis, tenet 1619 ; literati, squalor 1621 ; affidavit, par 1622 ; arena 1627 ; apparatus 1628 ; agendum, -a, vade-mecum, veto 1629 ; fiat 1631 ; farrago 1632 ; curriculum 1633 ; forceps 1634 ; query 1635 ; gratis 1636 ; formula 1638 ; imprimatur, onus 1640 ; crux, impetus, locum (tenens) 1641 ; focus 1644 ; alumnus 1645 ; data, -um 1646 ; plebs 1647 ; insignia 1649.

1650–1699

Copula, stamen 1650 ; album, larva, viscera 1651 ; complex, desideratum, vortex 1652 ; pallor 1656 ; frustum, honorarium 1658 ; pendulum 1660 ; nebula, rabies 1661 ; tedium 1662 ; lacuna, minimum 1663 ; afflatus 1665 ; tuber 1668 ; dictum 1670 ; corolla 1671 ; residuum, serum 1672 ; fulcrum 1674 ; pabulum, vinculum 1678 ; calculus, mica, stimulus 1684 ; scintilla 1692 ; lens, lumbago, status 1693 ; antenna 1698 ; momentum 1699.

1700–1749

Nucleus 1704 ; cirrus 1708 ; caret 1710 ; inertia 1713 ; locus 1715 ; propaganda 1718 ; alibi 1727 (adv., as n. in 1774) ; auditorium 1727 ; ultimatum 1731 ; maximum 1740.

1750–1799

Minutia, -ae 1751 ; insomnia 1758 ; bonus (n.) 1773 ; extra, herbarium 1776 ; prospectus 1777 ; via (prep.) 1779 ; deficit (n.) 1782 ; tandem 1785 ; addendum 1794 ; detritus 1795 ; habitat, humus 1796.

1800–1849

Excursus 1803 ; dementia 1806 ; cognomen, opus 1809 ; candelabrum, pupa 1815 ; duplex 1817 ; stet 1821 ; ego, incunabula 1824 ; omnibus 1829 ; animus 1831 ; sanatorium 1840.

1850–1899

Aquarium, consensus 1854 ; moratorium 1875 ; referendum 1882 ; bacillus 1883.

(B) GREEK

A few Greek words discussed in Chapter II came directly into Germanic before English became an independent dialect. But many Greek words reached English before the Conquest *through Latin,* and Latin is the immediate source of the majority of the later Greek loan-words in English. In Middle English, most of the Greek borrowings came through Latin by way of French. Those that have reached English directly, and those that have come through Latin, in Middle and Modern English, have done so through literature or scientific writings, and thus are nearly all words of ' learned ' origin, though a fair proportion of them have become popularized (cf. *acrobat, alphabet, asylum, atom, bulb, camera, celery, character, chemist, chorus, comma, cycle,* and many others).

Here, again, as in the case of the modern Latin loans considered in the previous section, the interest lies mainly in the evidence of the continued influence of Greek art, and the continued tradition of Greek science, in England as previously in Rome.

The Greek technical words now in scientific use fill many pages in most dictionaries, though most of them are not in every-day use. A very large number of these are compound words, either taken from an already existing Greek compound, or, more commonly, made up of individual Greek elements (which may or may not have been used in Greek to form compounds). A comparatively small number of these words, all of which are originally ' learned ', have become ' popular ', e.g. telephone, -graph ; gramophone ; thermometer, barometer.

The present work is not intended to deal with purely technical words, and all that will be done here is to give a few examples of the type of Greek element used in these technical compounds, with a few forms derived from each, simply to indicate their characteristics. The Greek words made use of in this way are usually nouns, adjectives, or prepositions.

From Greek nouns : *anemo-* (Gk. *anemos* ' wind ') : anemo-graph, -meter, -scope. *Antho-* (Gk. *anthos* ' flower ') : anthology -chlorin, -genetic, -phagous. *Anthropo-* (Gk. *anthropos* ' man ') : anthropology, -geography, -morphic, -phagy ; anthropoid. *Bio-* (Gk. *bios* ' way of life ') : biochemistry, -genesis, -graph, -graphy, -logy, -nomics, -scope. *Broncho-* (Gk. *brogkos* ' wind-pipe ') : bronchocele, -plegia, -pulmonary, -pneumonia ; bronchitis. *Cephalo-* (Gk. *kephalē* ' head ') : cephalocaudal, -facial, -mancy, -pod, -ptera, -thorax. *Chloro-* (Gk. *khlōros* ' light green ') : chloroform, -phyll, -phane ; chlorate, chlorine, chlorosis. *Chrono-* (Gk. *khronos* ' time ') : chronogram, -isotherm, logy, meter, -phor, -thermal. *Geo-* (Gk. *geō-* ' earth ') : geodesy, -gnosy, -graphy, -logy, -mancy, -metry, -phone, -physics, -tropic. *Helio-* (Gk. *hēlios* ' sun ') : heliocentric, -chromy, -graph, -meter, -stat, -therapy, -trope, -typy. *Hydro-* (Gk. *hudr-* ' water ') : hydrocarbon, -cephalic, -chloric, -gen, -logy, -meter, -pathy, -phobia, -plane, -static. *Litho-* (Gk. *lithos* ' stone ') : lithocarp, -chromatic, -chrome, -genous, -graphy, -mancy, -phyte, -tomy. *Logo-* (Gk. *logos* ' word ') : logocyclic, -daedaly, -graph, -machia, -mancy, -nomy, -type. *Neuro-* (Gk. *neuron* ' nerve ') : neurology, -pathic, -sis. *Physio-* (Gk. *phusis* ' nature ' ; the *y* in this and other words of Gk. origin is a Latin spelling of Gk. *u*) : physiognomy, -graphy, -logy.

From Greek adjectives : *acro-* (Gk. *akros* ' topmost, extreme ') : acrocephalic, -lith, -megaly, -polis. *Aero-* (Gk. *aeros* ' of air ') : aerodrome, -dynamics, -naut, -phore, -phyte, -plane, -stat. *Archaeo-* (Gk. *arkhaios* ' ancient ') : archaeology, -nomous, -pteryx. *Auto-* (Gk. *autos* ' same, self ') : autobiography, -chthon, -cracy, -graph, -matic, -nomy, -mobile (a hybrid, the second element Latin), -toxin, -type. *Caco-* (Gk. *kakos* ' bad, evil ') : cacodyl, -epy, -ethes, -graphy, -phony. *Eu-* (Gk. *eu* ' well ') : eucalyptus, -demonics, -hemerism, -logy, -phemism, -phrasy, -phuism, -rhythmics. *Hemi-* (Gk. *hēmi-* ' half ') : hemicycle, -pterous, -sphere, -stich. *Hetero-* (Gk. *heteros* ' different ') : heterodox, -dyne, -geneous, -morphic, -nomy. *Holo-* (Gk. *holos* ' whole,

entire ') : holocarp, -caust, -graph, -phote, -spheric. *Homo-*
(Gk. *homos* ' same ') : homoblastic, -dont, -geneous, -graph,
-logy, -nym, -phone. *Idio-* (Gk. *idios* ' private, personal ') :
idiomatic, -morphic, -pathic, -syncrasy. *Iso-* (Gk. *isos* ' equal ') :
isobar, -clinic, -gonic, -pod, -therm. *Macro-* (Gk. *makros* ' long ') :
macrobiosis, -cosm, -cephalic, -cranial, -petalous, -pod. *Mega-*
(Gk. *megas* ' large ') : megacephalous, -lith, -pod, -therium.
Megalo- (Gk. *megalē* ' large ') : megalomania, -saurus. *Micro-*
(Gk. *mīkros* ' small ') : microbiology, -cephalic, -cosm, -meter,
-phone, -scope, -spore, -tome. *Mono-* (Gk. *monos* ' alone, single ') :
monochord, -chrome, -cyclic, -drama, -gamy, -gram, -graph, -lith,
-logue, -mania, -morphic, -poly, -syllable, -phthong, -theism,
-tone, -type. *Neo-* (Gk. *neos* ' new ') : neolithic, -logism, -phyte ;
neo-Classic, neo-Gothic, neo-Platonism. *Pan-* (Gk. *pán* ' all ') :
panacea, -cratium, -dect, -demic, -orma, -oply, -opticon,
-technicon. *Poly-* (Gk. *polus* ' much, many ') : polyanthus,
-archy, -chrome, -gamy, -glot, -gon, -morphic, -onymy, -phone.

From Greek prepositions, etc. : *Amphi-* (Gk. *amphi* ' on both
sides ') : amphibrach, -centric, -pod, -theatre. *Anti-* (Gk. *anti*
' against ') : antitoxin, -dote, -logy, -pathy, -pyretic. *Apo-*
(Gk. *apo* ' away, apart ') : apocope, -deictic, -dosis, -logy, -plexy,
-stasy, -them. *Cata-* (Gk. *kata* ' down from, against, over ', etc.) :
catabolism, -clasm, -clysm, -lepsis, -logue, -plasm, -ract, -rrhine,
-strophe. *Dys-* (Gk. *dus-*, with negative or pejorative force) :
dysentery, -genic, -logistic, -pepsia, -phonia, -pnoea. *Endo-*
(Gk. *endon* ' within ') : endogamy, -crine, -derm, -gen, -morph,
-plasm, -sperm. *Epi-* (Gk. *epi* ' on, over ') : epicentre, -cycle,
-demic, -dermis, -glottis, -gram, -lepsy, -logue, -scopacy, -strophe,
-style, -taph, -thelium. *Hyper-* (Gk. *huper* ' beyond ') : hyperbole,
-borean, -metrical, -trophic. *Meta-* (Gk. *meta* ' between ', often
expressing change) : metabolic, -carpus, -centre, -mere, -morphic,
-phor, -phrase, -physics, -thesis. *Para-* (Gk. *para* ' from,
against ') : parallel, -phrase, -lipsis, -digm, -dox, -graph, -logism,
-plegia. *Peri-* (Gk. *peri* ' around ') : perianth, -cardium, -cope,
-cranium, -patetic, -phrase, -scope, -spomenon, -style. *Syn-*,
syl-, *sym-* (Gk. *sun* ' with ') : synchronize, -cope, -ecdoche,
-onym, -opsis, -tax, -thesis ; syllabus, -lable, -logism ; symmetry,
-pathy, -physis, -ptom, -posium.

Even in these examples, which are but a fraction of the total number of Greek words used to form English compounds, we see several of the commoner forms used as second elements in compounds. We need only mention such forms as *-phile, -phobe (-phobia), -archy, -mania, -logy, -mancy, -gram, -graph, -scope, -phone, -morphic, -pathy, -meter (-metry)*. The commonest Greek verb suffix in English—still used as a living suffix—is *-ize*, which occurs in words directly from Greek, from Greek through Latin or (spelt *-ise*) through French, as well as in words not of Greek origin (e.g. *macadamize*). With this belong the noun-suffixes *-ism* and *-ist*, both of which are common as living suffixes.

We shall end with brief lists (A) of Greek words adopted in Middle English and up to 1500 through French (and Latin), (B) of Greek words adopted since 1500 through Latin and directly from Greek. Those under (B) will be given in chronological order.

(A) *Middle English and up to* 1500

(1) Borrowed through French :—

Academy, atom, bible, centre, character, climate, currant, diet, diphthong, dropsy, dynasty, ecstasy, emblem, emery, fancy, fantasy, frenzy, galaxy, harmony, horizon, idiot, ink, liquorice, logic, lyre, magic, magnet, melon, muse, mystery, nymph, paten, pause, phantasm, pheasant, plane, pomp, quince, resin, rhetoric, rheum, rheumatic, rhubarb, rue, scandal, schism, spasm, sphere, stratagem, surgeon, theatre, thyme, tiffany, tragedy, treacle, turpentine, type, tyrant.

(2) Through Latin only :—

Abyss, agony, allegory, amethyst, artery, asphalt, asylum, centaur, chaos, chimera, comedy, crypt, cycle, dactyl, demon, echo, ethic, halcyon, hero, history, hyaena, iris, mania, mechanic (adj.), meteor, papyrus, phial, piracy, pirate, pole, plague, prune, quinsy, siren, sphinx, syringe, theme, thesis, thorax.

(B) *After* 1500

(A word followed by (L) was borrowed through Latin ; (F) indicates borrowing through French ; otherwise the words were adopted directly from Greek.)

1500–1549

Irony (L) 1502 ; alphabet (L), trophy (F) 1513 ; elegy (F) 1514 ; drama (L) 1515 ; tome (L) 1519 ; dilemma (L) 1523 ;

gorgon (L) 1529 ; phrase 1530 ; idea (L) 1531 ; trope (L) 1533 ; enigma (L) 1539 ; scene (F) 1540 ; rhapsody 1542 ; crisis 1543 ; tragic (F) 1545 ; cynic (L) 1547 ; labyrinth (L) 1548 ; machine (F) 1549.

1550–1599

Scheme (L) 1550 ; anemone (L), clematis (L), cube (F) 1551 ; distich (L), hyacinth (L), phalanx (L) 1553 ; caustic (L), isthmus (L), nectar (L), troglodyte (L) 1555 ; rhythm (L) 1557 ; chorus (L) 1561 ; chemist (F), despot (F) 1562 ; halo (F) 1563 ; ambrosia (L) 1567 ; bulb (L), topic 1568 ; nausea (L) 1569 ; chord (L), cylinder (L), prism (L) 1570 ; basis (L) 1571 ; sceptic (L) 1575 ; meander (L) 1576 ; larynx, skeleton (L) 1578 ; pathos 1579 ; amnesty (L) 1580 ; climax (L), diatribe (F), praxis 1581 ; comma (L) 1586 ; acrostic (L), colon (L), nomad (L), philtre (F) 1587 ; critic (L), ode (F) 1588 ; epic (L), trochee (L) 1589 ; disaster (F), python (L) 1590 ; phaeton (L) 1593 ; chasm (L), cynosure (L), patriot (F), stigma (L) 1596 ; theory (L) 1597 ; energy (L) 1599.

1600–1649

Idyll (L) 1601 ; archive (L), enthusiasm (L), strophe 1603 ; acoustic (F) 1605 ; orchestra (L) 1606 ; barytone (F) 1609 ; absinthe (F) 1612 ; crater (L) 1613 ; museum (L) 1615 ; system (L) 1619 ; hyphen (L) 1620 ; colophon (L) 1621 ; clinic (L), tactics (L) 1626 ; lymph (L) 1630 ; dogma (L) 1638 ; typhus (L) 1643 ; coma, electric (Mod. L.) 1646 ; aeon (L) 1647 ; tonic 1649.

1650–1699

Cosmos 1650 ; elastic (Mod. L.) 1653 ; siphon (L) 1659 ; celery (F), disk (L) 1664 ; nous 1678 ; pharynx (L) 1693 ; botany (L) 1696.

1700–1749

Phlox 1706 ; camera (L) 1708 ; bathos 1727 ; triptych 1731 ; philander 1731.

1750–1799

Anther (L) 1791 ; thrips 1795.

1800–1849

Rhea 1801 ; phase 1812 ; pylon 1823 ; acrobat (F) 1825 ; corm, myth, rhizome 1830.

1850–1899

Agnostic 1870 ; therm 1888.

PRE-CONQUEST LOAN-WORDS FROM LATIN

(A) Words from the Continental period, up to about 400, showing early borrowing by corresponding forms in other Germanic dialects, or by their phonological form (i.e. absence of early Romance changes, or presence of sound-changes which took place before or very shortly after the settlement of the English in this country). *Note* : When no translation of the Latin words is given, they may be taken as having approximately the same meaning as the Old English words derived from them.

A (1) MILITARY, LEGAL, OFFICIAL

camp ' field, open space ; battle ' ; also **campian** ' to fight ', **cempa** ' warrior ' (cf. Mod. Eng. *camp*, which is from French). Lat. *campus*.

cāsere ' emperor '. Lat. *Caesar*.

ċearrige, -uge, a vehicle. Lat. *carrūca*, of Gaulish origin.

ċēas(t) ' strife '. Lat. *causa* ' cause, reason ; business ; judicial process '.

diht ' saying, direction ', **dihtan** ' to set in order ; direct ; dictate ' [DIGHT]. Lat. *dictum* n., *dictāre* vb.

insiġle ' seal '. Lat. *insigillum*.

pīn ' punishment, pain ', **pīnian** ' to punish, torture '. Vulg. Lat. *pēna*, Lat. *poena* ' penalty, punishment ', from Gk. *poinē*.

sċrīfan ' to allot, decree '. The ecclesiastical sense, SHRIVE, is a later development. Lat. *scrībere* ' to write ; to set down in writing ; to subscribe to ; to draft (a law) '.

sċrift ' something decreed as a penalty ' ; later, ' penance, SHRIFT ; confessor.' Lat. *scriptum* ' something written ; composition ; enactment '.

sēam ' burden ', **sēamere** ' beast of burden '. Vulg. Lat. *sauma*, *saumārius*, from Lat. *sagma* ' pack-saddle ', from Gk. *sagma*.

sinoð ' council, synod '. Lat. *synodus*, from Gk. *synodos*.

strǣt (i) ' road ; paved road, STREET ', (ii) ' bed '. Lat. (i) *strāta*, (ii) *strātum*.

trifot ' tribute '. Lat. *tribūtum*.

A (2) Trade, Measures, etc.

ċēap 'goods, price, market' [CHEAP] ; vbs. **ċēapian, ċīepan** ' to buy '. Lat. *caupō* 'innkeeper, wineseller ; small trades-man '. (The trade in wine was one of the earliest to be established in the Germanic-speaking areas (already in the time of Tacitus) and the vine was cultivated in Germany from the time of Probus—the last quarter of the third century. See Wackernagel, *Zeitschr. f. deutsches Alter-tum*, vi, 262.)

mangere ' merchant, trader ; -MONGER ' ; **mangian** ' to trade '. The suffixes *-ere, -ian* are English. Lat. *mangō* ' a dealer in slaves and other wares.'

mīl ' MILE '. Lat. *mīlle* (*passuum*) ' a thousand paces ' (about 1,618 yards).

mydd ' bushel '. Lat. *modius*, the Roman corn-measure.

(be)mūtian ' to change, exchange '. Lat. *mūtāre*.

pund ' POUND (weight or money) ; pint '. Lat. *pondō*, measure of weight.

(a)pundrian ' to weigh '. Lat. *ponder-āre*.

tolne, toll ' TOLL '. Vulg. Lat. *tol-*, Lat. *telōnium*, from Gk. *telōnion*.

A (3) Coins

cāsering ' imperial coin, drachma '. See *cāsere* under (1).

dinor ' a coin '. Lat. *dēnārius*.

mynet ' a coin ; coinage, money ' [MINT]. Lat. *monēta* ' mint, coin, money '.

trimes(se) ' drachm ; a (foreign) coin '. Lat. *tremissis*.

A (4) Metals, etc.

calc, ċealc ' CHALK, plaster '. Lat. *calc-em, calx*.

coper ' COPPER '. L. Lat. *cuprum*, earlier *aes cyprium*, from Gk. *kuprion*, named from the island of Cyprus.

ġimm ' precious stone, jewel '. (Also a form *gemme*, borrowed in the third period.) Lat. *gemma* ' bud or eye of a plant ; jewel, gem '. (Cf. Mod. Eng. *gem*, which is through French.)

meregrēot, -grota ' pearl '. Lat. *margarīta* (from Gk. *margaritēs*), but altered by popular etymology through the influence of O.E. *mere* ' sea, lake ', and *grēot, grota* ' grit, gravel '.

piċ ' PITCH '. Lat. *picem, pix*.

A (5) Dress, Textiles, etc.

belt ' BELT '. Lat. *balteus*, possibly of Etruscan origin.

bisæċċ ' pocket '. Vulg. Lat. *bisaccium* (cf. *sacc*, below).

ċemes ' shirt '. (Cf. *chemise*, which is from Fr.) L. Lat. *camisia*, from Celtic.

fullere ' FULLER of cloth '. Lat. *fullō*.

matte, meatta ' MAT '. Lat. *matta*, perhaps from Phoenician.

ōrel ' veil, mantle '. Lat. *ōrārium*.

pæll, pell ' rich robe ; purple robe ; PALL ', **pællen** adj. ' purple, costly '. Lat. *pallium* from *palla* from **par(u)la*, from Gk. *phar-os* ' mantle '.

pihten, part of a loom. Lat. *pecten* ' comb '.

pileċe ' robe of skin ', [PILCH]. Vulg. Lat. *pellicea*.

plūm-(feðer) ' down '. (Cf. *plume*, from Fr.) Lat. *plūma*.

purpur, purple ' PURPLE garment '. Lat. *purpura* ' the purple-fish ; the dye obtained from it ; purple cloth ', from Gk. *porphurā*.

pyl(w)e ' PILLOW '. Lat. *pulvīnus*.

saban ' sheet '. Lat. *sabanum*, from Gk. *sabanon*.

sacc ' SACK, bag '. Lat. *saccus* from Gk. *sakkos*, from Phoenician.

sæċċ ' sack, bag '. Vulg. Lat. **saccium*, from Lat. *saccus* (see above).

sīde ' silk '. Vulg. Lat. **sēda* from Lat. *sēta* ' hair, bristle '.

sioluc, *sil(u)c ' SILK '. Later loan than next word ; apparently also from Lat. *sēricum*.

sīric ' silk '. Lat. *sēricum*, from *Sēres*, Latinized form of name of E. Asiatic people, the Chinese.

socc ' shoe, SOCK '. Lat. *soccus*, from Gk. **sokkhos, sukkhos*.

strǣġl ' mattress, bed '. Lat. *strāgula* ' rug, horsecloth '.

swiftlere ' slipper ' ; probably for **suftlere*, changed by popular etymology through the influence of *swift*. Lat. *sub-talāris*.

sūtere ' shoemaker '. Lat. *sūtor*.

timple, an instrument used in weaving. Lat. *templa* (pl.) ' small timbers '.

A (6) HOUSEHOLD AND OTHER USEFUL OBJECTS

candel ' CANDLE '. Lat. *candēla*.

fifele ' buckle '. Lat. *fībula*.

fæċele ' torch '. Lat. *facula*.

mīse ' table '. (The form **mēse** is probably a later borrowing.) Vulg. Lat. *mēsa*, Lat. *mēnsa*.

pīpe ' PIPE ' (musical instrument or tube) ; vb. **pīpian** ' to play on a pipe '. Vulg. Lat. **pīpa*, from Lat. *pīpāre* ' to play on a pipe '.

sċamol ' bench, stool ', [SHAMBLES]. Lat. *scamellum*.
seġne ' fishing-net '. Lat. *sagēna*, from Gk. *sagēnē*.
spynġe ' sponge '. (Mod. Eng. *sponge* from Fr.) Lat. *spongea*, from Gk. *sphoggia*.
tæfl, a game played on a board. Lat. *tabula*.

A (7) FOOD, DRINK, COOKING

butere ' BUTTER '. Lat. *būtyrium*, from Gk. *boutūron*.
ċeren ' new wine '. Lat. *carēnum*, from Gk. *karoinon*.
ċēse, ċiese ' CHEESE '. Lat. *cāseus*.
must ' new wine, MUST '. Lat. *mustum*.
sælmeriġe ' brine '. Lat. *salmuria*, from Gk. *halmuris*.
seim, *seġem ' lard, fat '. Vulg. Lat. **sagīmen*.
wīn ' WINE '. Lat. *vīnum*.

A (8) VESSELS, ETC.

binn ' manger, BIN '. Lat. *benna*, a Celtic loan-word.
box (see under plants, below).
buteric ' leather bottle '. Vulg. Lat. *buta*.
bytt ' bottle, flagon '. Vulg. Lat. *buttis* (from a diminutive of this comes *bottle*, through French).
ċelċ, cælic ' cup '. Lat. *calīc-em*. (Cf. *chalice*, through Fr.)
ċetel, ċietel ' kettle '. Lat. *catellus*. (Mod. Eng. *kettle* is from O.N. *ketill*, also a loan-word from Lat.)
cupp(e) ' CUP '. Vulg. Lat. *cuppa*.
cuculer ' spoon '. Lat. *cochlear*, ultimately from Gk.
cyll ' leather bottle '. Lat. *culleus*.
disċ ' plate, dish '. Lat. *discus*, from Gk. *diskos*.
earc(e) ' chest, ARK '. Lat. *arca*.
gabote, *gafote ' small dish '. Lat. *gabata*.
ġellet ' basin '. Vulg. Lat. *gallētum*.
lebil, læfel ' cup, bowl '. Lat. *labellum*.
orc ' cup, flagon '. Lat. *orca*, possibly Phoenician.
panne ' PAN '. Vulg. Lat. *panna*, from Lat. *patina* ' dish '.
sċrīn ' chest ', later ' SHRINE '. Lat. *scrīnium*.
sester, seoxter ' jar ; a measure '. Lat. *sextārius*.
spyrte ' basket '. Vulg. Lat. **sporta*, from Gk. *spurida*.

A (9) TOWNS, HOUSES, BUILDING

ċeaster ' city '. (Also *cæster*, reborrowed at a later period.) Lat. *castra* (pl.) ' camp '. This is the usual term for a city in O.E., and is commonly used to translate Lat. *civitas*, which had acquired the sense of ' city ' by A.D. 200. It also occurs in English Place-Names, being often added by the English to Romano-British names, now ending in -*chester*, -*caster*, -*cester*. (See Crawford in *Introd. to Survey of English Place-Names* (1922), pp. 146 ff.)

ċeosol ' hut '. Lat. *casula, casella*.

clūs(e) ' enclosure '. Vulg. Lat. *clūsa*, Lat. *clausa*.

clūstor ' lock, barrier, enclosure '. Vulg. Lat. *clūstrum*, Lat. *claustrum*.

cruft(e) ' vault, crypt '. Lat. *crupta, crypta*, from Gk. *kruptē*.

cyċene ' KITCHEN '. Lat. *coquīna*.

cylen ' KILN '. Lat. *culīna*.

līne ' LINE, cord '. Lat. *līnea*.

pearroc ' enclosure '. Vulg. Lat. *parricus*. (Whence Mod. Eng. *park*, through French.)

pīl ' pointed stick '. Lat. *pīlum*.

pīle ' stake, PILE ; a mortar ' ; vb. **pīlian** ' to pound in a mortar '. Lat. *pīla*.

pinn ' PIN, peg ; pen '. Lat. *penna*. (Mod. Eng. *pen* is through Fr.)

pīsle ' warm room '. Vulg. Lat. *pēsālis*, Lat. *pēnsilis*, used architecturally of arched or colonnaded structure, specifically of vapour-baths.

port (i) ' town, harbour, PORT '. Lat. *portus* ' harbour, haven '.

port (ii) ' gate, door '. Lat. *porta*.

portic ' porch, vestibule '. Lat. *porticus*. (Mod. Eng. *porch* is through Fr.)

post ' POST '. Lat. *postis*.

pundur ' plumb-line '. Lat. *pondere*, ablative of *pondus* ' weight '.

regol ' wooden ruler '. Later used in abstract sense for monastic rule, etc. Lat. *regula*.

sċindel ' roof-shingle '. Lat. *scindula*.

tiġle ' TILE, brick '. Lat. *tēgula*.

weall ' WALL, rampart '. Lat. *vallum*.

wīċ ' dwelling, village ; camp '. Lat. *vīcus*.

ynċe ' INCH '. (Cf. later *yndse*, under C.) Lat. *uncia*.

A (10) PLANTS AND AGRICULTURE

(*a*) **billere**, a kind of cress. Lat. *berula*, of Celtic origin.

box ' BOX-tree ; box (made of box-wood) '. Lat. *buxus* ' box-tree ', *buxum*, its wood, or something made of this, from Gk. *puxos*.

byxen ' made of box-wood '. With Gmc. adjectival suffix.

ċiċeling ' chickpea '. With Gmc. *-ing* suffix. Lat. *cicer*, probably from an East European source.

ċipe ' onion '. Lat. *cēpe*. Probably from a Gk. **kēpe*.

ċesten-(bēam) ' chestnut-tree '. Lat. *castanea*, from Gk. *kastanon*.

ċiris-(bēam) ' cherry-tree '. Vulg. Lat. *ceresia*, Lat. *cerasum* (the fruit), from Gk. *kerasion*. (The Mod. forms of this and of the preceding word come through French.)

codd-(æppel) ' quince '. Lat. *cu-*, *cydonia*, from Gk. *kudōniā*.

corn-(trēo) ' cornel '. Lat. *cornus*.

cymen ' cummin '. Lat. *cuminum*, from Gk. *kumīnon*.

cyrfet ' gourd '. Lat. *cucurbita*. (The reduplicating syllable *cu-* is lost in Germanic.)

fīc ' fig '. Lat. *fīcus*, from some Mediterranean dialect. (Mod. Eng. *fig* is through Fr.)

finu(g)l ' FENNEL '. Lat. *fēnuculum*.

mealwe ' MALLOW '. Lat. *malva*.

mīl ' millet '. Lat. *milium*. (*Millet* is from a Fr. diminutive of Lat. *mil-ium*.)

minte ' MINT '. Lat. *menta*, *minthe*, probably from a S. European language.

nǣp ' turNIP '. Lat. *nāpus*, probably from Egyptian, perhaps through Gk.

pise, peose ' PEA '. Lat. *pisum*, from Gk. *pisos*, from an E. European dialect.

pīn-(bēam) ' PINE '. Lat. *pīnus*.

piper ' PEPPER '. Lat. *piper*, from Gk. *peperi*.

pirie ' pear-tree '. (Cf. *peru*, under B.) Lat. *pirea*.

plūme ' PLUM '. Lat. *prūnum*, from Gk. *proûmnon*.

plȳme ' plum-tree '. Vulg. Lat. **prunea*, from Lat. *prūnum*.

popiġ, papiġ ' POPPY '. Lat. *papāver*.

porr ' leek '. Lat. *porrum*.

rǣdiċ ' radish '. Lat. *rādic-em* ' root, radish '.

rūde ' rue '. Vulg. Lat. *rūda*, Lat. *rūta*.

sinop ' mustard '. Lat. *sinapis*, from Gk. *sināpi*.

syrfe ' service-tree '. Vulg. Lat. *sorvea*, from Lat. *sorb-us*.

ynne ' onion '. Lat. *uniōn-em*.

(*b*) **ċipp** ' ploughshare '. Lat. *cippus*.

culter ' COULTER '. Lat. *culter*.

impian ' to graft '. Vulg. Lat. *imp(utare)*.

mylen ' mill '. Lat. *molīna*.

plante ' PLANT ', vb. **plantian** ' to plant '. Lat. *planta*.

pytt ' PIT, cistern '. Lat. *puteus*.

sicol ' SICKLE '. Lat. *sēcula*.

A (11) Animals, Birds, Fish

assa, assen (fem.) ' ass '. Lat. *asinus, -a*, probably through Celtic.

culfer ' dove '. Vulg. Lat. **columbra*, Lat. *columbula*.

cypera ' salmon at the time of spawning ', [KIPPER]. Probably Lat. *copor* ' copper ', named from its colour.

draca ' dragon ', [DRAKE]. Lat. *dracō*, from Gk. *drakōn*.

elpend, ylpend ' elephant '. Lat. *elephant-*, from Gk. *elephant-*.

eosol, esol ' ass '. Lat. *asellus* ' little ass '.

mūl ' mule '. Lat. *mūlus*.

olfend ' camel '. The source of this word is doubtful. Gothic has *ulbandus*, O.H.G. *olbenda*, and it seems certain that it has some connexion with the Gk. or Lat. *elephant-*. It is possibly a loan-word which came into Gmc. through Gothic from Asia Minor.

ostre ' oyster '. Lat. *ostrea*, from Gk. *ostreon*.

pēa, pāwa ' peacock '. Lat. *pavō*, of Eastern origin.

strūta, strȳte ' ostrich '. Lat. *strūthio*, from Gk. *strouthios*.

turtle, -a ' TURTLE-dove '. Lat. *turtur*.

A (12) Disease and Medicine

(a)cōfrian ' to recover '. Lat. *(re)cuperāre*.

fefor, -er ' FEVER '. Lat. *febris*.

flītme ' lancet '. Vulg. Lat. *flētoma*, Lat. *phlebotomus*, from Gk. *phlebotomos*.

A (13) Miscellaneous

crisp ' curly '. Lat. *crispus*.

miltistre ' harlot '. Lat. *meret(rīx)*, with Eng. suffix *-estre*.

nēomian ' to produce harmony '. Vulg. Lat. *neuma*, from Gk. *pneuma* ' breath '.

pīs ' heavy '. Vulg. Lat. *pēsus*, Lat. *pēnsus*.

s(e)altian ' to dance ', **sealt**(icge) ' dancer '. Lat. *salt-āre*.

sicor ' safe '. Lat. *sēcūrus*.

sȳfre ' sober '. Lat. *sōbrius*.

turnian ' to TURN '. Vulg. Lat. *tornāre* ' to turn ', Lat. *tornāre* ' to turn in a lathe '. The date of borrowing of this word is very uncertain ; it may be considerably later.

(B) Words probably borrowed in Britain, 450–650. These are still loans from the spoken language.

B (1) Legal and Official

insegel ' seal '. Cf. earlier *insigle*.

mæġester ' master '. Lat. *magister.*
pra-, profost ' officer, steward, PROVOST '. Vulg. Lat. *prepositus,* Lat. *praepositus.*
seġlian ' to seal '. Lat. *sigillāre.*
seġn ' mark, sign, banner '. Lat. *signum.*
senoð ' council '. Cf. earlier *sinoð.*

B (2) TRADE

cystan ' to spend '. Vulg. Lat. *costāre,* Lat. *constāre.*

B (3) METALS, ETC.

pærl ' pearl '. Vulg. Lat. **perla.*

B (4) DRESS, TEXTILES, ETC.

ċelis, a kind of shoe (?). Occurs as a gloss to *pediles* in Cod. Carolsruh. Aug. IC. (Schlutter, *Anglia,* xxxvii, 45). Lat. *calceus.*
(ġe)corded ' of plain stuff '. Vulg. Lat. *cordatus,* from Lat. *chorda.*
coren-(bēag) ' crown '. Lat. *corōna.*
cugle ' COWL '. Vulg. Lat. *cuculla,* Lat. *cucullus.*
cyrtel ' garment, coat, KIRTLE ', from *cyrtan* ' to shorten ' (see under 14 below).
derodine ' scarlet dye ', Vulg. Lat. *dirodinum,* from Gk. *diarhodon.*
mentel ' cloak '. Lat. *mantellum.*
stropp ' strap '. Lat. *stroppus.*
tæpped, -et, teped ' wall or floor covering '; **tæppel-**(bred) ' footstool '. Lat. *tapētum.*

B (5) HOUSEHOLD AND OTHER USEFUL OBJECTS

cæfester ' halter '. Lat. *capistrum.*
cæfl ' halter, muzzle '.
pīlstre ' pestle '. Lat. *pīla* + *pistillum.*
tasul, teosol ' a die ;　a small square of stone '. Lat. *tessella.*
trefet ' TRIVET, tripod '. Lat. *tripod-em.*

B (6) HUNTING AND FISHING

ancor ' ANCHOR '. Lat. *anchora,* from Gk. *agkūra.*
cocer ' quiver '. Vulg. Lat. *cucurum.*
punt ' PUNT, flat boat '. Lat. *ponto.*

B (7) FOOD AND COOKING

eced ' vinegar '. Lat. *acētum.*
foca ' cake baked on the hearth '. Lat. *focus* ' hearth '.
oele ' oil '. Vulg. Lat. *oli,* Lat. *oleum.*

B (8) Vessels

byden ' bushel ; barrel '. Vulg. Lat. *butina*.
cæpse ' coffer '. Lat. *capsa*.
ċest ' CHEST '. Vulg. Lat. *cesta*, Lat. *cista*.
copp ' cup '. Vulg. Lat. *cuppa*.
cȳf ' vat, cask '. Vulg. Lat. *cūpia*, Lat. *cūpa*.
cȳfl, cūfel ' tub '. Vulg. Lat. *cūpellus*.
mortere ' MORTAR '. Lat. *mortārium*.
pæġel ' PAIL '. Vulg. Lat. *pagella*.
pott ' POT '. Vulg. Lat. *pottus* (?).
tunne ' cask, TUN '. Vulg. Lat. *tunne*.
turl ' ladle, trowel '. Lat. *trulla*.
tynċen ' small barrel '. Probably diminutive of *tunne*.

B (9) Towns, Houses, Building

ċeafor-(tūn) ' hall, court '. Vulg. Lat. *capreus* ' timber, spar, rafter '.
cæster ' town '. (Cf. earlier *ċeaster*.)
cylene ' town '. (In Place-Names.) Lat. *colōnia*, through British.
mūr ' wall '. Lat. *mūrus*.
pǣl, pāl ' post, stake '. Lat. *pālus*.
solor ' upper room '. Lat. *sōlārium*.
torr ' tower '. Lat. *turris*.

B (10) Plants and Agriculture

(*a*) **æbs** ' fir-tree '. Lat. *abiēs*.
ċerfelle ' CHERVIL '. Lat. *cerefolium.·*
coccel ' corn-COCKLE '. Vulg. Lat. *cocculus*.
coelender, celendre ' coriander '. Lat. *coriandrum*, from Gk. *koriannon*.
consolde ' comfrey '. Vulg. Lat. *consolida*.
cost ' COSTmary '. Lat. *costus*, from Gk. *kostos*.
croh, crog ' saffron '. Lat. *crocus*.
elehtre, elotr ' lupin '. Lat. *electrum* ' amber ; the metal electrum ', from Gk. *ēlektron*. (The plant owes its name to its colour.)
eofole (?) ' dwarf elder '. Lat. *ebulus*.
eolone ' elecampane '. Lat. *inula*.
glædene ' gladiola '. Lat. *gladiola*.
humele, hymele ' hop-plant '. Vulg. Lat. *humulus*. (Possibly from Slavonic.)
leahtroc ' lettuce '. Lat. *lactūca*.

T

laser ' tare '. Lat. *laser*.

lent ' lentil '. Lat. *lent-em*.

lufestice ' lovage'. Vulg. Lat. *luvestica*, Lat. *ligusticum*.

mōr-, mūr-(berie) ' mulberry '. Lat. *mōrum*.

næfte, nefte ' catmint '. Lat. *nepeta*.

ōser ' osier '. Vulg. Lat. *ōsāria, ausāria*. (Mod. *osier* is through Fr.)

pere ' PEAR '. Lat. *pirum*.

petersilie ' parsley '. Lat. *petroselinum*. (Mod. *parsley* is through
  Fr. *persel*, though probably influenced by the O.E. ending.)

pipeneale ' pimpernel'. Vulg. Lat. *piperīnella*.

pollegie ' pennyroyal '. Lat. *pūlegium*.

pyretre ' pyrethrum '. Lat. *pyrethrum*, from Gk. *purethron*.

sæppe ' spruce-fir '. Lat. *sappīnus*.

senap ' mustard '. (Cf. earlier *sinop*.)

solsece ' heliotrope '. Lat. *sōlsequia*.

(b) **pil** ' hair of plant ', vb. *pilian* ' to PEEL, skin '. Lat. *pilus,
  pil-āre*.

fann ' winnowing-FAN '. Lat. *vannus*.

forca ' FORK '. Lat. *furca*.

fossere ' spade '. Lat. *fossōrium*.

mattuc ' MATTOCK '. Vulg. Lat. *mat-io*.

pāl ' spade '. Lat. *pāla*.

B (11) ANIMALS, BIRDS, FISHES

catt(e) ' CAT '. (?) Vulg. Lat. *cattus, -a*. Origin doubtful.

cocc (i) ' cock '. Vulg. Lat *coccus*.

cocc (ii) ' cockle '. Vulg. Lat. *cocculus*. Lat. *concha* from Gk.
  kogkhē.

lempedu ' lamprey ', [LIMPET]. Vulg. Lat. *lamprēta*.

muscelle, muscle ' MUSSEL '. Lat. *mūsculus*.

pīne-(wincle) ' winkle '. Lat. *pīna*, from Gk. *pîna*.

rēnġe ' spider '. Lat. *arānea*.

trūht ' TROUT '. Lat. *trūcta*.

B (12) MEDICINE

(for)stoppian ' to STOP up '. Vulg. Lat. *stuppāre*, Lat. **stuppa**
  ' tow ', from Gk. *stuppē*.

lafian ' to bathe, wash, LAVE '. Lat. *lavāre*.

trifulian ' to grind to powder '. Lat. *tribulāre*.

B (13) RELIGION AND LEARNING

dīlegian ' to cancel, expunge '. Lat. *dēlēre*.

gloesan ' to interpret, gloss '. Lat. *glōssa* ' a foreign word needing
  explanation ', from Gk. *glôssa*.

græf ' a style '. Lat. *graphium*, from *graphion*.

læden ' Latin ; language '. Vulg. Lat. *Ladīnus*, Lat. *Latīnus*.

munuc ' MONK '. Lat. *monachus*, from Gk. *monakhos*.

myneċen ' nun '. Vulg. Lat. *monic-* (as preceding word) with Gmc. feminine suffix.

mynster ' monastery, MINSTER '. Lat. *monasterium*, from Gk. *monasterion*.

nunne ' NUN '. L.Lat. *nonna* ' old lady, nun '.

pinsian, pīsian ' to reflect, consider '. Lat. *pensāre*.

relic ' RELIC '. Lat. *reliquia*.

seġnian ' to make the sign of the Cross ', from *seġn* ' mark ', see *seġn* under (1) above.

traht ' text, passage, commentary ' ; **trahtað** ' commentary ' ; vb. **trahtian** ' to expound '. Lat. *tractus, -ātus, -āre*.

B (14) MISCELLANEOUS

cūsc ' chaste, modest '. Lat. *cōnscius*. Perhaps through Old Saxon, in which the word occurs as *kūskō*.

cyrtan ' to shorten '. Lat. *curt-us*.

cyrten ' beautiful '. Vulg. Lat. *cōrtīnus*, from Lat. *cohorta* ' cohort, company '. (For meaning, cf. *courteous*, and Germ. *höflich* and *hübsch*.)

īsel ' island ' (in Place-Names). Lat. *insula*.

munt ' mountain '. Lat. *mont-em*.

pyngan ' to prick '. Lat. *pungere*.

sætern-(dæġ) ' SATURDAY '. Lat. *Saturnī* (*dies*). The only day of the week whose name is not of Gmc. origin.

(C) After 650. Late loan-words, including those of learned origin introduced through the written language (marked L).

C (1) MILITARY, LEGAL, OFFICIAL

arce-, ærce- (L) ' arch- ' (in titles). Lat. *archi-* from Gk. *arkhi-*.

carc(ern) ' prison '. Lat. *carcer*. (The O.E. ending is *ærn, ern* ' house '.)

centur (L) ' centurion '. Lat. *centuriō*.

consul (L) ' consul '. Lat. *consul*.

cōorte (L) ' cohort '. Lat. *cōhorta*.

(ā)cordian ' to reconcile '. Vulg. Lat. *ac-cordāre*.

(ā)cūsan ' to accuse '. Lat. *ac-cūsāre*.

legie (L) ' legion '. Lat. *legiō*.

mīlite (L) ' soldiers '. Lat. *mīlitēs* (pl.).

-spendan ' to SPEND '. Lat. *expendere*.

C (2) MEASURES

cubit (L). Lat. *cubitum* ' elbow ; measure of length '.
sescle ' sixth part '. Lat. *sextula*.
tālente (L) ' talent '. Lat. *talenta*.
yndse ' ounce '. Lat. *uncia*.

C (3) METALS, ETC.

amber (L) ' ambergris '. Vulg. Lat. *ambra*.
āðamans (L) ' diamond '. Lat. *adamant-em*, from Gk. *adamas, -mant-*.
cristalla (L) ' crystal '. Lat. *crystallum*, from Gk. *krustallos*.
gagāt (L) ' jet '. Lat. *gagatēs*, from Gk.
ġeaspis .(L) ' jasper '. Lat. *jaspis*, from Gk.
marman-, marmel-(*stān*) ' marble '. Lat. *marmor*.
platung ' metal plate '. Vulg. Lat. *platta*.
pumic (L) ' pumice '. Vulg. Lat. *pōmice*, Lat. *pumic-em*.
spalder, spelter ' asphalt '. Lat. *aspaltus*, from Gk. *aspalathos*.

C (4) DRESS, TEXTILES, ETC.

albe (L) ' alb '. Lat. *alba*.
calc (L) ' shoe, sandal '. Lat. *calceus*.
cāp ' COPE '. Vulg. Lat. *cāpa*, Lat. *cappa*.
cāsul (L) ' cassock '. Lat. *casula*.
cilic (L) ' hair-cloth '. Lat. *cilicium*.
corōna (L) ' crown '. (Cf. earlier *coren*.) Lat. *corōna*.
dalmatice (L) ' dalmatic '. Lat. *dalmatica*.
planete (L) ' chasuble '. Lat. *planeta*.
purs ' PURSE '. Lat. *bursa*, from Gk. *bursa*.
stōl ' long outer garment '. Lat. *stola*, from Gk. *stolē*.
tunece ' coat, tunic '. Lat. *tunica*, of Semitic origin.

C (5) HOUSEHOLD AND OTHER USEFUL OBJECTS

cāma ' bridle '. Lat. *cāmus*.
casse ' hunting-net '. Lat. *cassis*.
cwatern (L) ' four on dice '. Lat. *quaternus*.
ferele ' rod '. Lat. *ferula*.
formelle (L) ' bench '. Lat. *formella*.
pīc ' PIKE '. Vulg. Lat. *pīcus*.
press (L) ' wine-PRESS '. Vulg. Lat. *pressa*.
sponge (L) ' sponge '. (Cf. earlier *spynġe*.) Lat. *spongea*.
tabele, tablu (L) ' table, tablet '. (Cf. earlier *tæfl*.)
torcul (L) ' wine-press '. Lat. *torcular*.
tracter ' funnel '. Lat. *tractārius*.

C (6) Music, Poetry, etc.

antefn (L) ' anthem '. L.Lat. *antefana,* from Gk. *antiphōnē.*
cantere (L) ' singer '. Lat. *cantor.*
cantic (L) ' song, hymn '. Lat. *canticum.*
chōr(a) (L) ' dance ; chorus '. Lat. *chorus.*
cimbal(a) (L) ' cymbal '. Lat. *cymbalum,* from Gk. *kumbalon.*
citere ' cither '. Lat. *cithara,* from Gk. *kithara.*
fers ' verse '. Lat. *versus.*
fiðele ' FIDDLE '. Vulg. Lat. *vītula.*
mēter (L) ' metre '. Lat. *metrum,* from Gk. *metron.*
organ (L) ' song '; **organistre·** ' organist '; vb. **orgnian** ' to
   sing to an accompaniment '. Lat. *organum* ' instrument ;
   musical instrument ', from Gk. *organon.*
orgel ' organ '. Lat. *organum.*
reps, respons (L) ' liturgical response '. Lat. *responsōrium.*
salm, psalm (L) ' psalm, song '. Lat. *psalm,* from Gk.
sallettan ' to play on the harp, sing psalms '. Lat. *psullere.*
sōn (L) ' musical sound '. Lat. *sonus.*
timpane (L) ' tabret, timbrel '. Lat. *tympanum,* from Gk.
   tumpanon.
ymen (L) ' hymn '. Lat. *hymnus,* from Gk. *humnos.*
ymnere (L) ' hymn-book '. Lat. *hymnārium.*

C (7) Food and Cooking

cōc, cōcere ' cook '. Vulg. Lat. *cocus,* Lat. *coquus.*
mōrað ' mulberry wine '. Lat. *mōrātum.*
sicera (L), an intoxicating drink. Lat. *sicera,* from Gk. *sikera.*

C (8) Vessels

āmel ' vessel for holy water '. Lat. *āmula.*
ampulle (L) ' vial, flask '. Lat. *ampulla.*
cālic (L) ' cup '. (Cf. earlier *ćelć.*)
cāul, cāwel ' basket '. Vulg. Lat. *cavellum.*
scutel ' dish ', [SCUTTLE]. Lat. *scutula.*

C (9) Towns, Houses, Building

castel (L) ' village, small town '. Lat. *castellum.*
clauster (L) ' cloister '. (Cf. earlier *clūstor.*) Lat. *claustrum.*
columne (L) ' pillar '. Lat. *columna.*
fenester ' window '. Lat. *fenestra.*
pālent, -ant ' palace '. Vulg. Lat. *palantium,* Lat. *palātium.*
pālentse, -endse ' palace '. Vulg. Lat. *palantia.*
plætse, plæce ' open place in a town ; street '. Lat. *platea.*

tempel (L) 'temple'. Lat. *templum*.
ðēater (L) 'theatre'. Lat. *theātrum*, from Gk. *theatron*.

C (10) PLANTS

alewe 'aloe'. Lat. *aloe*.
amigdal (L) 'almond'. Lat. *amygdala*, from Gk. *amugdalē*.
aprōtane (L), **prutane** 'southernwood'. Lat. *abrotonum*, from Gk. *abrotonon*.
armelu 'wild rue, moly'. Lat. *harmāla*.
balsam (L) 'balsam, balm'. Lat. *balsamum*, from Gk. *balsamon*.
berbēne 'verbena'. Lat. *verbēna*.
bēte 'BEETroot'. Lat. *bēta*.
bētonice (L) 'wood-betony'. L.Lat. *betonica*.
calcatrippe, a kind of thorn ; 'CALTROP'. L.Lat. *calcatrippa*.
cāric (L) 'dried fig'. L.Lat. *carica*.
cāul, cāl, cāwel 'COLE'. Lat. *caulis*.
cēder (L) 'cedar'. Lat. *cedrus*, from Gk. *kedros*.
celeðonie (L) 'celandine'. Lat. *celīdonium*, from Gk. *khelīdonion*.
centaurie (L) 'centaury'. Lat. *centaurēum*, from Gk. *kentaureion*.
coliandre (L) 'coriander'. (Cf. earlier *coelendre*.)
cucumer (L) 'cucumber'. Lat. *cucumer-*.
cucurbite (L) 'gourd'. (Cf. earlier *cyrfet*.)
cuneglæsse 'hound's-tongue'. Lat. *cynoglossā*, from Gk. *kunoglōssē*.
cunel(!)e (L) 'thyme'. Lat. *cunīla*.
cypresse (L) 'cypress'. Lat. *cyparissus*, from Gk. *kuparissos*.
drācentse, -conze 'dragon-wort'. L.Lat. *dracontea*.
fēferfūge 'FEVERFEW'. Lat. *febrifugia*.
lactūc(e) (L) 'lettuce'. (Cf. earlier *leahtroc*.)
laur, lāwer 'laurel'. Lat. *laurus*.
lilie 'LILY'. Lat. *līlium*, from Gk. *leirion*.
magdala-(trēo) 'almond-tree'. See *amigdal*, above.
mārubie, -fie 'horehound'. Lat. *marrubium*, from Gk.
menta 'mint'. (Cf. earlier *mint*.)
nard (L) 'spikeNARD'. Lat. *nardus*, probably from an Eastern language.
organe 'marjoram'. Lat. *origanum*, from Gk. *origanon*.
palm(a), pælm 'PALM'. Lat. *palma*.
pānic (L) 'a kind of millet'. Lat. *pānīcum*.
peonie (L) 'peony'. Lat. *paeōnia*, from Gk. *paiōnia*.
persic (L) 'peach'. Lat. *persicum* = Persian.
perwince (L) 'periwinkle'. Lat. *pervinca*.
polente (L) 'parched corn'. Lat. *polenta*.

prūtene. See *aprōtane*, above.
rōse ' rose '. Lat. *rosa* from Gk. *rhodon.*
rōsmarin (L) ' rosemary '. Lat. *rōs marīnus.*
sāfine (L) ' savine '. Lat. *sabina.*
salfie (L) ' sage '. Lat. *salvia.*
saturege (L), **sæ ðerige** (not before 800) ' savory '. Lat. *saturēia.*
sīgle ' rye '. Lat. *secale.*
spīca (L) ' spikenard '. Lat. *spīca.*
stōr (L) ' frankincense '. Lat. *storax*, from Gk. *sturax.*
sycomer (L) ' sycamore '. Lat. *sycomorus*, from Gk. *sūkomorus.*
ðimiama (L) ' incense '. Lat. *thȳmiāma*, from Gk. *thumiama.*
ȳsope (L) ' hyssop '. Lat. *hyssōpum*, from Gk. *hyssōpos.*

C (11) ANIMALS, BIRDS, FISHES

aspide (L) ' asp, viper '. Lat. *aspidis*, from Gk. *aspid-.*
basilisca (L) ' basilisk '. Lat. *basiliscus*, from Gk. *basiliskos.*
camel(l) (L) ' camel '. Lat. *camēlus* (Vulg. Lat. *camellus*), from Gk. *kamēlos.*
cancer (L) ' crab ; cancer '. Lat. *cancer.*
delfīn (L) ' dolphin '. Lat. *delphīnus*, from Gk. *delphînos.*
felefor ' bittern '. Lat. *porphyrio*, from Gk. *porphuriōn.*
fěnix (L) ' phoenix '. Lat. *phoenix*, from Gk. *phoinix.*
lamprēde (L) ' lamprey '. (Cf. earlier *lempedu*.)
lēo (L) ' lion '. Lat. *leōn-*, from Gk. *leōn-.*
lōpust (L) ' locust '. Lat. *lōcūsta* (influenced by O.E. *loppestre* ' lobster '.
palðer, pandher (L) ' panther '. Lat. from Gk. *panthēra.*
pard (L) ' leopard '. Lat. *pardus*, from Gk. *pardos*, probably from Persian.
pellican (L) ' pelican '. Lat. *pelicūnus*, from Gk. *pelekan*, an Eastern word.
spilæg (L), a poisonous fly. Lat. *spilagius.*
tiger (L) ' tiger '. Lat. *tīgris*, from Gk. *tigris*, ultimately Persian.
turtur. (Cf. earlier *turtle*.)
ultor ' vulture '. Lat. *vultor.*

C (12) MEDICAL

ciper-(sealf) ' henna salve '. Lat. *cyprus.*
flanc (L) ' side '. Vulg. Lat. **flanca*, a loan from Gmc.
mamme ' breast '. Lat. *mamma.*
plaster (L) ' a plaster '. Lat. *emplastrum*, from Gk. *emplastron.*
rabbian (L) ' to be mad, rage '. Vulg. Lat. *rabiāre*, Lat. *rabere.*

scrōfel (L) 'scrofula'. Lat. *scrofula*.

sideware 'zedoary'. Lat. *zedoārium*.

temprian 'to mix, mingle'. Lat. *temperāre*.

tīriaca 'a medicine'. L.Lat. *tiriaca*, Lat. *thēriacum*, from Gk. *thēriakon*.

ūf (L) 'uvula'. Lat. *ūvula*.

C (13) RELIGION

abbod 'abbot' Vulg. Lat. *abbādem*, Lat. *abbāt-em*, from Gk.

abbudesse 'abbess'. Vulg. Lat. *abbādissa*, Lat. *abbātissa*, from Gk.

acolitus (L) 'acolyte'. Lat. *acoluthus*, from Gk. *akolouthos*.

alter, altāre (L) 'altar'. Lat. *altar, altāre*.

apostata (L) 'apostate'. Lat. *apostata*, from Gk. *apostatēs*.

(a)postol 'apostle'. Lat. *apostolus*, from Gk. *apostolos*.

ælmesse 'ALMS'. Vulg. Lat. *almosina*, from Gk. *eleēmosuna*.

bæzere, bæōzere 'baptist'. Lat. *baptista*, from Gk. *baptistēs*.

clēric, -oc (L) 'clerk, clergyman'. Lat. *clēricus*, from Gk. *klērikos*.

crēda (L) 'CREED'. Lat. *crēdō* 'I believe'.

crisma (L) 'chrism'. Lat. *chrīsma*, from Gk. *khrīsma*.

crismal (L) 'chrisom'. Lat. *chrīsmāle*.

crūċ (L) 'cross'. Lat. *cruc-em*.

culpe 'guilt, fault'; vb. **culpian** 'to be guilty; to cringe'. Lat. *culpa*.

cumǣdre 'godmother'. L.Lat. *commāter*.

cumpæder 'godfather'. Lat. *compater*.

dēcān 'one in charge of ten monks; a dean'. Lat. *decānus*.

dēmōn (L) 'demon'. Lat. *daemōn*, from Gk. *daimōn*.

diacon (L) 'deacon'. Lat. *diāconus*, from Gk. *diakōn*.

discīpul (L) 'DISCIPLE'. Lat. *discipulus*.

domne 'lord'. Lat. *domine* (vocative).

eretic (L) 'heretic'. Lat. *haeriticus*, from Gk. *haieretikos*.

fals (L) 'falseness'. Also as adj. of weight or coinage. Lat. *falsus*.

grād (L) 'step; rank'. Lat. *gradus*.

idol (L) 'idol'. Lat. *īdolum*, from Gk. *eidolon*.

letanīa (L.) 'litany'. Lat., from Gk. *litanīa*.

mæslere 'sacristan'. Vulg. Lat. *mansiōnārius*.

mæsse, messe 'MASS'. Romance *messa*, Lat. *missa*.

martir (L) 'martyr'. Lat., from Gk. *martur*.

noctern (L) 'nocturn'. Lat. *nocturnus*.

nōn (L) ' ninth hour ', [NOON]. Lat. *nōna (hōra)*.
nonn(e) ' monk '. Lat. *nonnus*.
offrian ' to OFFER, sacrifice '. Lat. *offerre*.
oflǣte, -āte ' oblation ; sacrificial wafer '. Lat. *oblāta*.
orc ' evil spirit '. Lat. *orcus*.
pāpa ' POPE '. Lat. *pāpa*.
paradīs (L) ' PARADISE '. Lat. *paradīsus*, from Gk. *paradeisos*.
passiōn (L) ' story of the Passion '. Lat. *passiōnem*.
postol. See *apostol*, above.
prēdician (L) ' preach '. Lat. *praedīcāre*.
prīm (L) ' prime '. Lat. *prīma (hōra)*.
prīor (L) ' prior '. Lat. *prior*.
sabbat (L) ' sabbath '. Lat. *sabbatum*, from Heb. *sabbāt*.
sācerd ' priest '. Lat. *sacerdos*.
sanct ' saint '. Lat. *sanctus*.

C (14) BOOKS AND LEARNING

accent (L) ' accent '. Lat. *accentus*.
ātrum ' black pigment '. Lat. *ātramentum*.
bærbær ' barbarous.'. Lat. *barbarus*.
biblioðēce (L) ' library '. Lat. *bibliothēca*, from Gk. *bibliothēkē*.
brēfian (L) ' to state briefly '. Vulg. Lat. *breviāre*.
cānon (L) ' canon, rule '. Lat. *canon*, from Gk. *kanōn*.
cāpitol(a) (L) ' chapter '. Lat. *capitolum*.
carte ' paper, deed '. Lat. *c(h)arta*, from Gk. *khartēs*.
circul (L) ' circle '. Lat. *circulus*.
cranic ' chronicle '. Lat. *chronica*, from Gk. *khronikon*.
dēclīnian (L) ' to decline ' (gram.). Lat. *dēclīnāre*.
(e)pistol ' letter '. Lat. *epistula*, from Gk. *epistola*.
grammatic-(cræft) (L) ' grammar '. Lat. *(ars) grammatica*,
    from Gk. *grammatikē*.
graðul ' gradual ; Mass-book '. Lat. *graduāle*.
lātīn (L) ' Latin '. Lat. *Latīnus*.
māgister (L). (Cf. earlier *mæġester*.)
mēchan(isċ) (L) ' mechanical '. Lat. *mēchanicus*, from Gk.
    mēkhanikos.
nōt (L) ' note, mark '. Lat. *nota*.
nōtere (L) ' notary '. Lat. *notārius*.
paper (L) ' paper '. Lat. *papȳrus*, from Gk. *papūros*.
part (L) ' part '. Lat. *part-em*.
philosoph (L) ' philosopher '. Lat. *philosophus*, from Gk.
    philosophos.

pigment (L). Lat. *pigmentum*.
pistol. See *epistol*, above.
prōfian ' to regard, consider '. Lat. *probāre*.
punct (L) ' point '. Lat. *punctum*.
scōl ' SCHOOL '. Lat. *schola*, from Gk. *skholē*.
sott ' fool '. Vulg. Lat. *sottus* ' fool ', perhaps from Gmc.
studdian ' to see to, take care of '. Lat. *studēre*.
tītol (L) ' title, superscription '. Lat. *tītulus*.
trămet (L) ' page '. Lat. *trāmit-is*.
tropere (L) ' service-book '. Lat. *tropārium*.

C (15) CALENDAR AND ASTRONOMY

bīses (L) ' leap-year '. Lat. *bissextus*.
cālend (L) ' month '. Lat. *calendae* ' calends '. The use of
the word in the sense of ' month ' is found in Roman poets,
e.g. Ovid, Martial.
comēta (L) ' comet '. Lat. *comēta*, from Gk. *komēta*.
epact (L) ' epact '. Lat. *epactae*, from Gk. *epaktai*.
termen (L) ' fixed date '. Lat. *terminus*.

C (16) MISCELLANEOUS

centaur (L) ' centaur '. Lat. *centaurus*, from Gk. *kentauros*.
crōc(ed) (L) ' yellow '. Lat. *croc-us*.
flōr(isċ) (L) ' floral '. Lat. *flōridus*.
gīgant ' giant '. Lat. from Gk. *gigant-*, *gigas*.
tonian ' to thunder '. Lat. *tonāre*.

NOTE ON THE PHONOLOGY OF LATIN LOAN-WORDS IN OLD ENGLISH

In loan-words from Latin, it must be remembered, the stress was often shifted in Old English to conform to the English habit of stressing the stem syllable ; thus Lat. *tribútum* becomes *trífot*, *secúrus* becomes *sícor*, *offérre* becomes *óffrian*, and so on. In some cases, of course, the Latin already had the stress on the stem (e.g. *fefer*, Lat. *febris* ; *pāpa*, Lat. *pāpa* ; *mealwe*, Lat. *malva*, etc.).

Latin words, like other loan-words, were adopted with each sound represented by the nearest corresponding sound in English or Germanic when they were borrowed in the spoken language. Most of these correspondences are quite straightforward.

Lat. *a* was adopted as *a*, and in words borrowed sufficiently early (in the first, or even in the second period) they underwent the normal development of Gmc. *a* in English :—

(i) it appears as *a* or *o* before a nasal : *candel*, *condel* ; *ancor*, *oncor* ;

(ii) it became *æ*, which normally remained : *tæfel*, *pægel*, *fæcele* ; but :—

(iii) it was retracted to *a* before a back vowel : *draca*, *gabote* ;

(iv) it was fractured to *ea* before *h* or *r* + consonant : *leahtroc*, *earca*, *ċearruge* ;

(v) it was either fractured to *ea* or retracted to *a* (according to dialect) before *l* + consonant : *sealm*, *salm* ; *mealwe*, *malwe* ;

(vi) it was diphthongized to *ea* in some dialects after *ċ*, *sċ* : *ċeaster*, *ċeafor-tūn*, *sċeamol* ;

(vii) it was raised to *e* when followed by *i* : *ċelċ*, *ċeren* (from Vulg. Lat. **carīn-*).

In words borrowed after the period when *a* became *æ*, but before the period of *i*-mutation, *a* became *æ* before *i* : *cæfester*, *cælic* (a reborrowing).

Later loans did not undergo these changes, but kept *a* : *fals*, *carte*, *plaster*, *castel*, *cancer*.

Latin *i* remained in the earlier loan-words : *pipor, pise, disċ, insiġle, bisċop, sinoð*.

In later loan-words this vowel was borrowed as *e*, partly perhaps because it had been lowered slightly in Vulg. Lat. and Romance, partly because in Old English the Gmc. *e* had become tense : *seġlian, seġn, ċest, peru, senoð*.

The latest loans from Latin again had *i*, being mostly from Classical Latin, in learned loans : *citere, ciper, discipul*.

Latin *u* remained in the earliest loans : *fullere, purpur, turl, must* ; before *i* this was fronted to *y* : *pylwe, bytt, cyrfet*.

In later words (again partly on account of a Vulg. Lat. change) *u* appears as *o* : *box, copp, torr*. But in late loans from Classical Latin *u* is found again : *punct, scutel, pumic*.

Latin *e* remains in Old English apart from certain combinative changes : *fefor, sester* ; but

(i) before a following *i*, *e* becomes *i* : *ciris, pilce, pirie* (from **cerisia, *pelice, *peria*) ;

(ii) before a nasal + another cons., *e* appears as *i*, either because they were borrowed early enough to share in this Gmc. sound-change, or through sound-substitution (O.E. not possessing the group *e* + nasal + cons.) : *minte, timple, ġimm, binn*. But late loans have *e* : *templ, centur*.

(iii) Vulg. Lat. *e* shortened from Lat. *ē* in words where it preceded the chief accent (e.g. *secūrus*, from Lat. *sēcūrus, denārius* from Lat. *dēnārius*) becomes O.E. *i*, since it was a tense vowel, and thus approximated more to O.E. or Gmc. *i* than to *e* : *sicor, dinor*.

(iv) In some later loans, Vulg. Lat. *e* appears to have been borrowed as *æ* : *pærl, næpte*.

Lat. *o* commonly appears as *o* : *porr, post, socc, apostol, offrian, rose, ostre, mortere* ; *solor, morað* (the last two from Lat. *ō* shortened in Vulg. Lat.) ; but

(i) Before nasal + cons. *o* becomes *u* : *pund, nunne, punt, munt*, except in the latest loan-words, such as *domne*.

(ii) When followed by *i, j*, in the next syllable, *o* becomes *u*, later *y* by *i*-mutation : *mylen* (from **molina*), *mynet* (from **munit-*, Lat. *monēta*), *cycene* (**cocina*, Lat. *coquīna*), *spynge* (**spongia*).

Latin *ā* appears in Old English as *ǣ*, if borrowed before the period in which West Gmc. *ā* became O.E. *strǣt, nǣp* (non-West Saxon *strēt, nēp*). Lat. *cāseus* became first **kǣsj-*, then **ċǣsj-*, then, through the West Saxon diphthongization after *ċ*, **ċēasi*, and finally by *i*-mutation *ċīese*. In non-West Saxon, by the ordinary change of *ǣ* to *ē* it becomes *ćēse*. In later loan-words Latin *ā* remains : *pāpa, pāl.*

Latin *ī* remains in Old English whatever the date of borrowing : *prīm, pīn, pīpe, scrīn, wīn, fīc.*

Latin *ū* remains in Old English : *mūr, rūde, clūstor, plūme, bemūtian.* But when followed by *i* it becomes *ȳ* : *plȳme* (from *plūmj-*).

Latin *ē* is represented in O.E. by *ī* ; the Vulgar Latin *ē* must have been a tense *ē*, approximating more nearly to the English *ī* than to the (rare) O.E. *ē* : *sīde, clīroc, tīgle.* In late learned words *ē* remains : *crēdo, bibliothēce, clēroc* (reborrowing). The same applies to Vulg. Lat. *ē* from Lat. *oe* or *ēn(s)* : *pīn* (Lat. *poena*), *mīse (mȳse* ; Lat. *mēnsa), pīslic* ; cf. the late *fēnix* (Lat. *phoenix*).

Latin *ō* remains in Old English : *nōn, mōr-(bēam).* When followed by *i* or *j, ō* is fronted to *ǣ*, later *ē* : *glēsan.*

There are some special rules of quantity which have to be observed with regard to the ' learned ' loan-words from Latin in Old English. If the position of the chief stress remains the same in English as in Latin, a short vowel remains short, in a closed syllable (e.g. *sanct, circul*) ; but if the stressed vowel was in an open syllable in Latin, it was pronounced in the school-Latin of the early Middle Ages with a long vowel if it stood in the penultimate syllable, with a short vowel if it stood in the ante-penultimate, whatever the quantity may have been in classical Latin, and this process was followed in Old English : Lat. *crēdō, coquus, sonus, nōna, schola* : O.E. *crēda, cōc, sōn, ṇōn, schōl* ; but Lat. *fībula, būtyrum, līlie, clēricus, calicem, cithara* : O.E. *fifele, butere, lilie, cleric, calic, citere.*

If the position of the accent was shifted in Old English to the first syllable, a short vowel in this syllable became long if the syllable was open ; Lat. *magister, sacerdos, columna* : O.E. *māgister, sācerdos, cōlumne.*

There are not very many words in Old English in which the vowels are derived from Lat. diphthongs. Lat. *ae* (borrowed in the period before Gmc. *ai* became O.E. *ā*) became *ā* : Lat. *caesar,* O.E. *cāsere.* Lat. *au*, together with Gmc. *au*, became O.E. *ēa* : Lat. *caucus,* O.E. *ćēac* ; Lat. *caupō,* O.E. *ćēap* ; but later ' learned ' words retain the *au*, or develop this to *āwe* : Lat. *caulis,* O.E. *caul, cāwel* ; Lat. *laurus,* O.E. *lāwer.*

In regard to the Latin consonants the chief points to be observed have to do with certain developments in Gallo-Roman and Romance. Latin intervocalic *p* became *b*, and *t* became *d*, and later still, in Romance, these became respectively *ƀ* and *đ*.

In the earliest loan-words (and in late loans from classical Latin) the *p* and *t* are retained : *copor, næp, pipor* ; *mynet, strǣt butere* ; but later words show the voiced form of the consonants, (for *b*, which did not exist in O.E. between vowels, O.E. used *ƀ*, written *f*, as in the still later loans from Romance, which are indistinguishable in this respect from loans of the Gallo-Roman date) : *cæfl* Lat. *capulus, cæfester* (Lat. *capistrum*) ; *abbod* (Lat. *abbātem*), *eced* (Lat. *acētum*), *sīde* (Lat. *sēta*), *byden* (Lat. *butina*), or still later, from Romance : *fiðele* (L.Lat. *vitula*), *moраð* (Lat. *mōrātum*).

Lat. intervocalic *b* became *ƀ* in Vulg. Lat., and this remains in O.E., written *f* : *fifele* (Lat. *fībula*), *tæfl* (Lat. *tabula*), *trifot* (Lat. *tribūtum*), *fefor* (Lat. *febris*).

Finally we must note a distinction between the consonants used at different periods of Old English to represent Lat. *c* (*k*). Early loans with this consonant have the same development as Gmc *k* in O.E., i.e. *c* (*k*) becomes *ċ* before front vowels (*i, e, æ*) but remains otherwise : *ċest, ċeaster, ċetel, ynċe, pileċe*, etc. But later loans keep the *c* (*cæppe, castel*), with the exception of words borrowed from Romance after about 600, at which time Lat. *k* had become *ts* before *i, e* in Romance, and is represented by this group in O.E. : *yntse* (Lat. *uncia* ; cf. earlier *ynce*), *drācentse* (L.Lat. *aracontea*), *plætse* (Lat. *platea*).

SCANDINAVIAN VOWELS IN OLD AND MIDDLE ENGLISH

Several of the Old Norse vowels existed already in Old English (though not necessarily in cognate words), and these shared the normal development of the O.E. vowels in Middle English. Other O.N. vowels and diphthongs, however, were not found in O.E. ; these usually became assimilated to the nearest corresponding native form.

In the following list the nearest corresponding etymological form in O.E. is given after the O.N. vowel, and then the form in which the latter appears in Old or Middle English.

SHORT VOWELS

O.N. *a* (O.E. *æ*, etc.) remains as *a* : *awe, anger, carl, kasten, hap.*

O.N. *e* (O.E. *e*, etc.) remains as *e* : *geten, nevnen, brennen* ; so also *e* for *i*-mutation of *a* : *egg, leg, ketel.*

O.N. *i* (O.E. *i*) remains as *i* : *skin, grip, hitten, ill, prift.*

O.N. *o* (O.E. *o*) remains as *o* : *pogh, scot, odd, score.*

O.N. *u* (O.E. *u*) remains as *u* : *bule, ugli, sum, skulle.*

O.N. *y*, through *i*-mutation of *u* (O.E. *y*) develops like O.E. *y*, mostly to *i*, since most of the Scand. loans appear in the north-east : *flutten, flitten* ; *brunie, brinie.*

O.N. *y*, through *u*-mutation of *i* (O.E. *i*), develops as the preceding vowel : *big, biggen, sister.*

O.N. *ǫ*, through *u*-mutation of *a* (O.E. *æ*, etc.), usually becomes *a* : *lagu* (O.N. *lǫg*), *rag* (O.N. *rǫgg*).

SHORT DIPHTHONGS

O.N. *ia, io* (O.E. *e, eo*) appear in M.E. as *e* : *sterne* (O.N. *stiarna*), *skerre* (O.N. *skiarr*), *ket* (O.N. *kiot*).

LONG VOWELS

O.N. *ā* (O.E. *ǣ*) appears as *ā* in O.E., and as *ā, ǭ* in M.E. : *lāh, lōh* ; *wāre, wōre* ; *bāþe, bōþe.*

O.N. *ē* : M.E. *ē* : *sēr.*

O.N. *ī* (O.E. *ī*) remained as *ī* : *nīðing, tīðende, þrīven.*

O.N. *ō* (O.E. *ō*) remained as *ō* : *bōnde, blōme, bōn, bōþe.*

O.N. *ū* (O.E. *ū*) remained as *ū* : *droupen, boun.*

O.N. *ǣ* becomes *ę̄* : *gēten, skēr.*

O.N. *ø* becomes *ę̄* : *slēȝmen, sēmen.*

O.N. *ȳ* develops like O.E. *ȳ* : *bī, fīle, mīre, skī, tīnen.*

Long Diphthongs

O.N. *ei* (O.E. *ā*) remains as *ei* : *swein, beisk, beiten, heil, greipen.*

Pr. O.N. *ǫu*, O.N. *au* (O.E. *ēa*) appears as *ou, au, ō* : *coupen, goulen, lous* ; *laus, gaulen* ; *lōpen, windōge.* These differences reflect partly distinctions in Scandinavian dialects, partly different periods of borrowing, but their distribution in English words is not clear.

O.N. *iu, io* (O.E. *ēo*) became *ēo* and developed like the same diphthong in native words, usually to *ē* : *skēt, mēk.*

O.N. *øy* (O.E. *ē*, W.S. *īe*) usually became *ei* : *beisten, keiren.*

NOTES ON THE PHONOLOGY OF FRENCH LOAN-WORDS IN MIDDLE ENGLISH

Accent

The chief change in French loan-words adopted in Middle English was the shifting in the position of the accent to the stem-syllable in those words where French had placed it on the final syllable and not on the stem, e.g. *hónour, pítē, énvie, vírtu*, in place of *honóur, pité, envíe, virtú*. The change was not at first universal, the French accent being retained for some time by bilingual speakers, and even in the fifteenth century poets varied between the English and the French mode of accentuation.

In the case of verbs with prefixes (such as *recórden, commánden, aváuncen*), the accent follows the system of accentuation of native verbs with this formation (such as *arísen, āwáken, forȝíven*).

Quantity

(1) Old French *a, e, o* appear as long vowels in dissyllabic words in which the first syllable is open, or if there are two medial consonants both belonging to the second syllable, and also in trisyllabic words having the accent on the penultimate : *fāme, dāme, rōbe, cōte, appēren* ; *hāste, fēste, cōste* ; *tāble, fēble, nōble* ; *brōche, āge, plāce (ts, later s)*. With the accent shifted in English : *bācun, bāsin, māson, lēver, trēsour, pōstern*.

(2) O.Fr. *i, u*, in the same position, appear as long vowels in English if the position of the accent remains the same as in French : *bíble, desīren, attīren, houre, spouse, cīdre, poudre, jousten*.

If, however, the accent is shifted from the last to the penultimate syllable, the French *i* is treated like English *i* in open syllables, that is, it remains *i* in some dialects, and becomes *ę̄* in others, especially in the north and east, giving alternative forms in M.E. : *cítē, cę̄tē* ; *prísoun, prę̄soun* ; *miróur, mę̄rour*, etc.

(3) Lengthening seems to take place before *r* + consonant, e.g. *art, force, source*, which, with other words, sometimes appear

to have a long vowel ; but this lengthening is not carried out consistently.

Note.—(i) A number of words retain a short vowel in M.E. where a long vowel might be expected : *maner, palais, profit, forest,* etc. It has been suggested that these depend on a class-dialect, perhaps an upper-class pronunciation influenced by the original French, and used by bilingual speakers.

(ii) Verbs sometimes retain a short vowel in the conditions indicated above (under 1 and 2), e.g. *passe, cacche* ; perhaps the influence of trisyllabic inflected forms in English (e.g. *passede*) kept the vowel short, since English did not pronounce long vowels in this position.

QUALITY

French *a.* (A) (i) Short in closed syllables : *barre, part, large hardi.* Occasionally long before *r* + consonant, as shown by such spellings as *aart.*

(ii) Long before a single final consonant : *debāt, bās, pās,* etc.

(iii) Long in open syllables (see above, under Quantity) : *dāme, escāpe, āble, tāste, plāce, āge, bāsin, sāvour, nātur, nātioun* (pronounced as dissyllable).

(B) (i) Before a nasal, O.Fr. *a* appears as *au* in Anglo-Norman (C.Fr. *ä*) from the early thirteenth century, and this passes into M.E. : *chaunce, daunce, graunten, laumpe.*

(ii) This *au* before *mb, ndž,* is monophthongized to *ā* : *strānge, dānger, chāmbre.*

French *e.* (i) Short in closed syllables : *lettre, serven, certain, servaunt, tempest, gentil, (en)tent.* (Occasionally long before *r* + cons.)

(ii) Long in open syllables, *ẹ̄* from Fr. *ẹ, ę̄* from Fr. *ę̄* : *apẹ̄len, bẹ̄ste, prẹ̄chen ; āpẹ̄ren, fẹ̄re, degrẹ̄.*

(iii) Long before a single final consonant : *bẹ̄k* ' beak '.

Note.—(i) The French *ẹ* was apparently very tense, as it sometimes appears as *ī* in M.E. ; thus M.E. has both *frēre* and *frīre* (Mod. Eng. *friar*), *quēr* and *quīr* (Mod. Eng. *choir*).

(ii) A.N. retains the distinction between O.Fr. *en* + cons. and *an* + cons., whereas C.Fr. levels both under *ä* ; an occasional C.Fr. form (with M.E. *am, an,* from *ā*) appears in later M.E., e.g. *amperour.*

French *i.* (A) When the accent remains : (i) Short in closed syllables : *simple, prince.*

(ii) Long in open syllables : *arrīven, dīnen, crīen ; bīble, vīce.* (But short before *ch* : *riche.*)

(B) When the accent is shifted : (i) Short in closed syllables.

(ii) Short also in open syllables, except in certain dialects, especially of the north and east, where it becomes $\bar{e}$: *pitē, rivēr, diner* ; *pētē, rēver, dēner*.

French *o*. Whether the accent is shifted or not : (i) Short in closed syllables (except occasionally before r + cons.) : *cofre, propre, cors* (but sometimes *coors*, etc.).

(ii) Long in open syllables : *rọbe, cọte, clọsen, nọble, rọsten, apprọchen, ọdour*.

(iv) Long before single final consonant : *clọs, grọs, stọr*.

(v) Long and tense before or after lip-consonants : *pọvre, mọven, prọven, fọl, bọte*.

French *u*. (A) When the French accent remains : (i) Either long or short in closed syllables : *scurge, scourge* ; *disturben, -tourben* ; *sours* ; but

(ii) Usually long before nasal + consonant (where A.-N. *u* = C.Fr. *o*) : *count, mount, fountain, pouncen, confound*, etc., but *numbre, spunge, plungen*, and a few others, are short.

(iii) Long before a single final consonant.

(iv) Long in open syllables : *route, houre, vowe, pouche, double, couple*. (But short sometimes before cons. + l : *duble, cuple, truble*.)

(B) When the accent is shifted : Short : *super, mutoun*.

French *ü*. (A) When the accent remains : (i) Short in closed syllables : *jüggen, jüstice*. This vowel remains *ü* in those areas in which O.E. *y* was retained (written *u*) ; both were retracted to *u* by the fifteenth century. In those areas in which O.E. *y* had been unrounded, Fr. *ü* was probably retracted earlier (perhaps even at the time of adoption, in which case it may be regarded as an example of sound-substitution rather than sound-change).

(ii) Long in open syllables : *ūse, rūde, sūre* ; also before single final consonant : *pūr, dūk*. The vowel remained *ū* in those areas in which O.E. *ȳ* had been retained. Elsewhere it may have been quite early diphthongized to *ēu*, later *iu*, as it was eventually everywhere (together with O.E. *ȳ*). In Late M.E. it was certainly levelled under *iu* from M.E. *ēu, ēu*.

(B) When the accent is shifted : Usually short in both closed and open syllables ; but long occasionally in open syllables ; cf. *stüdy, dücat, düchess*, with *hŭmour, cŭrate, mŭsic* (the modern forms of which show length in M.E.)

French *ai*. This diphthong was in process of being monophthongized in Norman-French at the time of the Norman invasion of England ; therefore M.E. has forms with *ai* and with *ẹ*. The diphthong remained longest (and is most frequent in loan-words in English) before *l*, *m*, or *n*, when final, and before a vowel : *grain, plain, saint, remainen, claimen* ; *rai, gai* ; *paien, assaien.* Cf. *pẹ̄s* (earlier *pais*), *ẹ̄se* (earlier *aise*), *rẹ̄sun* (earlier *raisun*), *sẹ̄sen, sẹ̄sun, plẹ̄saunt, ẹ̄gle, glẹ̄ve* (earlier *glaive*). A few words have *ai* pretty regularly in M.E. : *waite, plaice, caitiff, aide, traitre.* French *ai* includes a new *ai* (already developed at the time of the Conquest) from *a* before *li, ni*, the *i* [j] fronting the consonant and then disappearing : *tailor, failen, availen, Spaine*, etc.

French *ei*. This diphthong was levelled under *ai* in Anglo-Norman, remaining usually in M.E. before *l*, *n*, or *m*, when final, or before a vowel ; but otherwise appearing in M.E. as *ẹ̄* : *recẹ̄t, encrẹ̄sen* ; *preie (praie), obeien* ; *air, faire, peine.* In Central French, Old French *ei* became *ọi* in the twelfth century (later *oẹ*, and by the sixteenth century *oa, wa*). A few Central French words with *oi* from this source were adopted in M.E. during the fourteenth century : *esploit, poise, royal*, etc.

French *ọi*. This diphthong occurred in both A.-N. and C.Fr. It remained in M.E. : *noise, joie, choice, cloistre.*

French *ọ̈i* seems to have become *ui* in A.-N., and *ọ̄i* in C.Fr. by the twelfth century. M.E. has sometimes *oi* and sometimes *ui* ; some of the spellings with *oi* may be really *ui* forms (*o* being a common spelling for *u*), but some of them are almost certainly non-Norman forms : *puint, puison, juinen, builen* ; cf. *point, join, voice, moist, broil, toil*, etc.

French *üi*. This diphthong was pronounced in A.-N. either as a rising or as a falling diphthong. The latter, which was the commoner, was monophthongized in A.-N. and followed the same lines of development in M.E. as the vowel *ü*, i.e. remained or became *ẹu* : *fruit, destruien, annuien, pü* ' pew '. The rising diphthong appeared chiefly after back consonants, and became *wi* in M.E. : *quiver, squirrel* (O.Fr. *cuiver, escuireuil*).

French *ie*. This (rising) diphthong was monophthongized in A.-N. to *ẹ̄*, and was borrowed as *ẹ̄* in M.E. : *chēre, fērs, relēf, chēf, fēvre, nēce.* The *ie*-spelling which is found in many of these words to-day (*chief, relief, fierce*, etc.) reflects the influence of French scribes who followed the practice of dialects in which monophthongization did not take place. It is rare before the fifteenth century.

French *ue*. This (falling) diphthong was monophthongized in A.-N. to *ǣ*, and was borrowed in this form in M.E. It was levelled under the native *ǣ* which had developed from O.E. *ēo*, and with this was unrounded to *ē* in most dialects, but preserved as a rounded vowel for a considerable period (probably until Late M.E.) in the west. The spelling varies between *eo, oe,* and *e* (occasionally *u* in the west) : *poeple, people, peple* ; *preoven, preven* ; *boef, bef.*

French *au, ou, eu*. These diphthongs arose in O.Fr. through the vocalization of *l* before a consonant, e.g. *auter* (from *alter*), *sauve* (from *salve*), or (more rarely) through the vocalization of *v*, e.g. *ewer* (= *euer*) from earlier *ev-* (Lat. *aqu-*). The diphthongs remained in M.E. : *faut, assaut, sauf, faucoun, souden, peutre* ' pewter '. But before lip-consonants in the early fourteenth century, the diphthongs were monophthongized through the loss of the *u*, and the remaining vowel was lengthened : *sāf, bāme, sāmoun*. Later forms with *al, ol,* in place of the *au, ou*, either in pronunciation or in spelling, are due to Latin influence on English or to reborrowing from a Latinized form in French : *fault, falcon, solder.*

French *uei*. This triphthong usually became the diphthong *üi* in French dialects, and as this diphthong was treated in English as *üi* from other sources. (See above.)

French *ieu*. This became monophthongized in Norman-French to *iu*, and was eventually levelled in English under the *iu* from *ęu* (Fr. *ü̆* or English *ę̄u*).

French *eau*. This was reduced to *ęu* in A.-N., and in M.E. is finally levelled under *ęu* : *beauty, beuty*. Before a lip-consonant or *š, tš,* the diphthong is monophthongized to *ę̄* : *Bę̄champ*, from *Beuchamp, Bēvoir*, from *Beuvoir,* etc. (Hence Mod. Eng. [*ī*] in such words, where the spelling is *eau,* or *ea.*)

The points of chief interest in the adoption of French consonants in English are concerned with differences in the French dialects, especially those which differentiate the northern French dialects from those spoken farther south. The following are the most important distinctions between Norman-French and Central French which are reflected in the Middle English loan-words :—

(i) N.-F. *w* : C.Fr. *g* (from Gmc. *w*). M.E. *werre, waste, waite, warisoun, wicket* : *garisoun, gīle, gerdoun, gernement,* etc. The *g*-forms appear chiefly in and after the fourteenth century.

(ii) N.-F. and Picard *k* before *a* : C.Fr. *ch.* (But the *ch*-type developed also in part of Normandy, and so some of the earlier *ch*-forms may be from this area, and are not necessarily Central French.) M.E. *casten* ' chasten ', *cacchen, cariteþ, caudron, catel, carpenter, market*:   *chasten, chācen, charite, chaudron, chatel, chair, chēf*, etc.

(iii) N.-F. and Picard *g* : C.Fr. *j* [*dž*]. M.E. *garden, gaol* : *joy, jest, jail*, etc.

(iv) N.-F. and Picard *ch* [tš] : C.Fr. *ts* (later *s*). M.E. *chisel, chīme, cherry, cacchen, perche, winche* : *wince, chace, perce, celle, citē*, etc.

(v) E.N.-F. and Picard *š* : C.Fr. *s*.   M.E. *punishe, norishe, anguish, cuisshin* : *rejoice*.

Another special French development which affected loan-words in English was the disappearance of Fr. *þ* (earlier *t*) and *đ* (earlier *d*) between vowels and finally after a vowel. These consonants remained longer in Anglo-Norman than elsewhere, and appear in some earlier borrowings, e.g. *cariteþ* (later *carite*), *plenteþ* (later *plente*). See p. 108 for further examples.

Latin initial *h* disappeared in Vulg. Lat., and consequently most of the French loans in M.E. had no initial *h*, except in the spelling, where it was influenced by classical Latin. In French loan-words from Gmc., however, at least such as were borrowed after the loss of Vulg. Lat. *h*-, the initial *h* remained, and was adopted in M.E. : *haste, heraud, hardy*, etc.

The French development of *s* + consonant is reflected in Middle English. In the eleventh century O.Fr. *s* disappeared before voiced consonants, and is therefore not present even in the earliest English loans : *dīnen, māle, fantōme*. (Before *l* and *n* early A.-N. has *d*, perhaps one stage in the development of *s* before its disappearance, and this is found in one or two English words, e.g. *medle*, O.Fr. *mesler*.)

O.Fr. final *n* becomes *m* by dissimilation after a point consonant : *venim* (O.Fr. *venin*), *velim* (O.Fr. *velin*), *ransum* (O.Fr. *ransun*), *pilegrim* (O.Fr. *pilegrin*).

SELECT BIBLIOGRAPHY

(In chronological order)

BOSWORTH-TOLLER. *Anglo-Saxon Dictionary.* Oxford, 1882. Supplement, 1928.

BRATE, E. *Nordische Lehnwörter im Ormulum.* Halle, 1884.

Oxford English Dictionary. Oxford, 1884–1928.

POGATSCHER, A. *Zur Lautlehre der griechischen, lateinischen und romanischen Lehnwörter im Altenglischen.* Quellen und Forschungen, lxiv. 1888.

SKEAT, W. W. *Principles of English Etymology.* 2nd Series. *The Foreign Element.* Oxford, 1891.

STRATMANN-BRADLEY. *Middle English Dictionary.* Oxford, 1891.

SVIEDO, F. H. *French Elements in Middle English.* Oxford, 1899

BJÖRKMAN, E. *Scandinavian Loan-Words in Middle English.* 2 Vols. Halle, 1900, 1902.

BEHRENS, D. *Französische Elemente im Englischen.* In Paul's *Grundriss*, 1², Strassbourg, 1901.

MACGILLIVRAY, H. S. *The Influence of Christianity on the Vocabulary of Old English.* Halle, 1902.

VISING, J. *Franska Språket in England.* Gothenburg, 1902.

HOEVELMANN, K. *Zum Konsonantismus der altfranzösischen Lehnwörter in der mittelenglischen Dichtung des 14. und 15. Jahrhunderts.* Kiel, 1903.

YULE, H., and A. C. BURNELL. *Hobson-Jobson, A Glossary of Colloquial Anglo-Indian Words and Phrases.* New ed. by W. Crooke. London, 1903.

DEROCQUIGNY, JULES. *A Contribution to the Study of the French Element in English.* Lille, 1904.

DELLIT, O. *Über lateinische Elemente im Mittelenglischen.* Marburg, 1905.

REMUS, H. *Die kirchlichen und speziellwissenschaftlichen romanischen Lehnworte Chaucers.* Halle, 1906.

RÖSNER, F. *Die französischen Lehnwörter im Frühneuenglischen.* Marburg diss., 1907.

METTIG, R. *Das französische Element im Alt- und Mittelenglischen.* Englische Studien, xli, 1909–1910.

LUICK, K. *Zu den Lateinischen Lehnwörtern im Altenglischen.* Archiv, cxxvi, 1911.

FUNKE, O. *Die gelehrten lateinischen Lehn- und Fremdwörter in der altenglischen Literatur.* Halle, 1914.

EKWALL, E. *Scandinavians and Celts in the North-West of England.* Lund, 1918.

KEISER, A. *The Influence of Christianity on the Vocabulary of Old English Poetry.* Univ. of Illinois Studies in Language and Literature, v. 1919.

NÖJD, R. *The Vocalism of Romanic Words in Chaucer.* Uppsala, 1919.

FÖRSTER, M. *Keltisches Wortgut im Englischen.* Halle, 1921.

FUNKE, O. *Zur Wortgeschichte der französischen Elemente im Englischen.* Englische Studien, lv, 1921.

LUICK, K. *Über die Betonung der französischen Lehnwörter im Mittel-englischen.* Germ.-Rom. Monatsschrift, ix, 1921.

FÖRSTER, M. *Englisch-Keltisches.* Englische Studien, lvi, 1922.

TOLL, J. M. *Niederländisches Lehngut im Mittelenglischen.* Halle, 1926.

BENSE, J. F. *A Dictionary of the Low-Dutch Element in the English Vocabulary.* Pts. i–iii. *Aam—Plash.* The Hague, 1926–1932.

RITCHIE, L. GRAEME. *Early Instances of French Loan-Words in Scots and English.* Englische Studien, lxiii, 1928.

PRAZ, MARIO. *The Italian Element in English.* English Assoc., *Essays and Studies,* xv. Oxford, 1929.

SMOCK, J. C. *The Greek Element in English Words.* Ed. by P. W. Long. London, 1931.

BENTLEY, H. W. *A Dictionary of Spanish Terms in English, with Special Reference to the American Southwest.* New York and Oxford, 1932.

WYLD, H. C. *The Universal English Dictionary.* London, 1932.

HOLTHAUSEN, F. *Altenglisches etymologisches Wörterbuch.* Heidelberg, 1932–3.

KSOLL, A. *Die französischen Lehn- und Fremdwörter in der englischen Sprache der Restaurationszeit.* Breslau, 1933.

TAYLOR, W. *Arabic Words in English.* (S.P.E. Tract xxxviii.) Oxford, 1933.

Shorter Oxford Dictionary. Oxford, 1933.

SUBJECT INDEX

WORD INDEX

[Old and Middle English words are given in italics. They are included when strikingly different from the modern spellings.
In the alphabetical order, æ follows a, ȝ follows g, þ follows t. Middle English th and ð are counted as þ, ei as ai, vocalic y as i, consonantal i as j and u as v.
The Latin and Greek words in the last chapter are not indexed, nor are the foreign words in the long M.E. passages in Chap. III.]

arrack 219
arrive 118, 128, 143
arroyo 197
arsenal 217
arsenic 227
arsmetike ' arithmetic ' 130
arsoun ' saddle-bow ' 119, 142
artichoke 183, 188, 217
article 126
artisan 185
asafoetida 228
asaumple ' example ' 126
asaut ' assault ' 141
ascape(n) ' escape ' 120, 143
asise ' assize ' 137
ask ' ash ' 91, 99
asottien ' be foolish, mad ' 116
aspic 165
aspide ' asp ' 4, 40, 43, 285
aspien ' espy ' 120, 124, 143
asprete ' bitterness ' 125
ass 23, 57
assa ' ass ' 23, 57, 277
assagai 208
assail 123, 128, 132, 143
assald ' ass ' 36
assassin 217
assault 123
assay 137
assemble 137
assent 137
assets 156
assize 136, 137
assoil 135
assumption 123
astat ' estate ' 126
astrakhan 209
astronomy 118, 130
asur ' azure ' 141
at ' that ' 94
atelier 166
atiffen ' adorn ' 123
atir 120
atoll 234
attaché 166
attaché-case 166
attack 190
attar 230
attente ' attempt ' 126
attic 162
attire 120
attitude 191
attlen ' intend, purpose ; go ' 80
apamans ' adamant ' 24, 282
aubade 162
aubergine 164
auctorite ' authority ' 137
augrim ' arithmetic ' 126

auk 103
aunt 136
auter ' altar ' 129, 131
auto-da-fé 200
autorite ' authority ' 126
avail 137, 138
avalanche 164
avancen ' advance ' 124
avatar 221
avaunse ' advance ' 138
ave 123
aventure ' adventure ' 126, 128, 135
aventurine 166
aviroun ' round about ' 144
avocado 200, 254
avocet 191
avoid 127
avow 137
await 124
awe 81, 82, 87, 91, 94, 97, 99, 102
axolotl 255
ayah 209
aye 81, 87, 90, 94, 99
aye-aye 243
azarole 219
azimuth 215
azure 141, 156, 227

æbs ' fir-tree ' 279
æced ' vinegar ' 23
ælmesful ' bountiful ' 49
ælmesse ' alms ' 19, 22, 28, 286
æstel ' bookmark ' 60

babacoote 243
baban ' baby ' 121
babel 236
babelinde ' babbling ' 124
babiroussa 242
baboo 224
babouche 227
baccarat 166
bachelor 136, 139
bagatelle 191
bain ' obedient ' 97
bain-marie 167
bairn 94, 96, 98
bait vb. 82, 91
bait n. 95
baiten ' feed ' 91, 102
(a)baite ' entice ' 100
baksheesh 6, 224
balance 143
balas 227
balcony 190
baldachin 188
baldo Rom. 12
ballet 162

x

calash 210
calc ' chalk ' 272
calc ' sandal ' 37, 282
calcatrippe ' kind of thorn ' 47, 284
calèche 210
calend ' month ' 21, 44, 288
calenge ' challenge ' 123
calenture 198
calibre 217
calic ' cup ' 23, 31, 32, 49, 116, 283
calico 10, 234
calipash 254
caliph 215
calix ' cup ' 39
caliz ' cup ' 122, 131
call 68, 77, 79, 88, 90, 93, 95, 96, 98,
    99, 100, 102
caltrop 156, 284
calu ' bald ' 47
cama ' bridle ' 282
camaraderie 168
camarilla 201
cambric 10, 173
camel 6, 129
camell ' camel ' 35, 36, 54, 285
cameo 189
camisole 201
camorra 183, 193
camouflage 158, 169
camp n. ' fight ' 18, 271
camphor 215
campian ' to fight ' 47, 271
canaille 163
canard 168
can-can 166
cancelere ' chancellor ' 107
cancer ' cancer ' 32, 285
cancre 127
candel, condel ' candle ' 19, 30, 31, 273
candelmæsse ' Candlemass ' 49
candelstæf ' candlestick ' 37, 38
candle 19, 30, 31, 50, 144
candy 220
cangue 209
canker 127
cann ' cognizance ' 66
canna ' reed ' 43
canne 48
cannibal 198
canoe 251
canon 107, 128, 131
canon ' law ' 28, 287
cañon 8
canonie ' canon ' 107
canoniel ' canonical ' 122
canopic 247
cantabile 192
cantaloup 193

cantata 192
cantatrice 193
canteen 164
cantel-cap ' cope ' 49
cantere ' singer ' 283
cantic ' song ' 39, 283
canticle 129
canto 189
canyon 8, 202
canzone, -et 189
caoutchouc 255
cap ' cope ' 282
capelein ' chaplain ' 107
capellan ' chaplain ' 49
capercailzie 205
capital 126
capitol ' chief ' 47
capitol, cap(i)tel ' chapter ' 28, 45,
    108, 287
capitula ' chapter ' 49
capon 105, 130
caporal 168
capot 162
capriccio 189
caprice 189
captive 5
capun ' capon ' 105
capybara 255
carabineer 162
caracal 232
caracole 199
carafe 220
caramel 200
carapace 254
carat 6, 188, 217
caravan 230
caravanserai 230
caravel 188
caraway 216
carbine 162
carboy 230
carbunculus 25
carcern ' prison ' 21, 25, 31, 281
cardinal 107, 117
cargo 199
caribou 258
caric ' dried fig ' 41, 284
carillon 166
carite(þ) ' charity ' 108, 114, 120
carl ' man ' 72, 102
carmagnole 163
carmine 200
carnival 186
carob 218
carol 138
carouse 180
carp ' talk ' 95, 96, 102
carr ' rock ' 57

delay 120, 138, 143
delfin ' porpoise ' 48, 285
delice ' delight ' 125
delight 125
deliver 135, 143
delundung 243
démarche 163
demeinen ' behave ' 143
demere ' delay ' 143
demi-monde 168
demoiselle 160, 161
demon 286
demur 156
demure ' delay ' 134
dengue 248
denim 162
dénouement 164
deodar 225
deofol ' devil ' 18, 52
deol ' sorrow ' 120
depart 124, 134
depeinten ' portray ' 127
depôt 163
derf ' bold ' 90, 95, 96
derodine ' scarlet ' 278
dervish 229
des ' dais ' 140
descriven ' describe ' 126
desereten 140
desert 123, 129
desceyve ' deceive ' 138
desheriten ' disinherit ' 131
desperado 199
desiderata 7
deskumfit 126
desman 103
desperance ' despair ' 125
despite 137
despoil 124
desputen ' dispute ' 110
destrier ' steed ' 142
destroy 138, 143
détour 165
de trop 169
dette ' debt ' 122
Deuleset ' God knows ' 127
devil 18, 52
devise 128
devotion 125
devout 125
dey 232
dhobi 6, 225
dhole 225
dhoti 222
dhurra *see* durra
dhurrie 225
diablerie 165
diacon 22, 286

diadem 136
die 69, 70, 76, 77, 80, 82, 85, 86, 88,
    93, 94, 96, 97, 99, 100, 101, 102
diegan ' die ' 70
diet 125
dihtan ' order, dictate ' 33, 37, 271
dil ' hide ' 95
dilegian ' cancel ' 280
dilettante 192
diligence 164
diminuendo 192
dinanderie 166
dinar 230
dine 144
diner, -or ' penny ' 35, 272
dinghy 226
dingo 245
dinner 137, 144
dirhem 220
disc ' dish ' 17, 18, 274
disciple 114, 121, 137
discipline 114, 126
discipul 28, 35, 36, 39, 286
discrive ' describe ' 143
discure ' discover ' 143
disgrace 186
dish 17, 18, 274
dishabille 163
dishonour 133
dismember 138
dispend 138
display 156
dispute 110
disputing 129
dissever 135
distinction 126
distingué 168
distrait 165
disturb 124
ditto 191
diva 193
divan 229
divers 135
divi-divi 256
doble ' double ' 144
doce-amur ' sweetheart ' 139
dock 175
dodo 208
doge 183, 186
doit 175
dol ' sorrow ' 128
dolman 232
dolmen 206
domineer 176
domino 200
domne ' lord ' 28, 33, 286
don 197
dona 199

fantasia 192
fantesme ' phantom ' 126
fantoccini 192
farcost ' condition ' 80
farnian ' prosper ' 68
farouche 165
fashion 143
fasoun ' fashion ' 143
fauchon ' falchion ' 141
faucoun ' falcon ' 128, 142
fausien ' make false ' 120
fauteuil 164
faux pas 163
fæcilae ' torch ' 18, 273
feast 116, 123, 128, 130, 132, 138
feble ' feeble ' 143
feblesce ' feebleness ' 124
feeble 116, 124, 130, 132, 143
feebleness 138
fefer, -or ' fever ' 26, 277
feferfuge ' fever few ' 284
feȝen ' cleanse ' 90
felage, felau, -aw ' fellow ' 88, 93, 97, 98, 99
felaushepe ' fellowship ' 100
fel(d)spar 181
fellah 220
fellow 65, 77, 85, 86, 93, 94, 97, 98, 99, 101, 102
fellowship 100
felon 134, 137, 139
felony 133, 134
felucca 190, 218
femme de chambre 164
fenester ' window ' 33, 283
fenix ' phoenix ' 21, 285
fennec 220
fennel 17, 276
feolaga ' fellow ' 65
fe(o)lufer ' bittern ' 17, 285
fer ' sound, whole ' 88, 95
fer, a kind of fur, 135
fer-de-lance, 167
fere ' power ' 83
ferele ' rod ' 282
ferret 188
fers ' verse ' 29, 32, 42, 45, 283
fess 156
feste 116, 123, 128
fête 8, 165
feu de joie 164
feute ' fealty ' 140
fever 26, 50
Feverer ' February ' 112
fey ' faith ' 133
fez 233
fiacre 162
fiancé 8, 168

fiasco 193
fic ' fig ' 26, 276
ficelle 167
fichu 167
fiddle 283
fierce 137
fifele ' brooch ' 47, 273
fig 123
figer ' fig-tree ' 123
figurant 164
figure 130
figurine 193
fiken ' hurry about, fidget ' 85, 90
fil ' villain ' 95
filibeg 205
filibuster 175
filigree 191
fin ' end ' 130, 134, 138
finale 192
fin de siècle 166
fine 8, 130, 143, 157
fine ' to end ' 128
finugl ' fennel ' 17, 276
fiord 103
fiorin 204
firkin 173
firm 193
firmament 129, 138
firman 230
fisicien 121
fitch 176
fipele ' fiddle ' 283
flair 168
flaket ' flagon ' 142
flambeau 162
flamboyant 166
flamingo 207
flanc ' side ' 285
flâneur 168
flasce ' bottle ' 37
flaun ' flan ' 132
flaunch 156
flautist 193
flench, flense 179
flit 82, 86, 88
flitme ' lancet ' 277
flitten ' flit ' 88
floe 103
floege ' little ship ' 64
flom see *flum*
flor ' flower ' 128
florin 184
florisc ' floral ' 288
florys ' flourish ' 138
flotilla 200
flour 123, 130
flourish 138
flower 128, 132, 134

garb 156, 186
garble 216
garboard 177
garçon 166
garen, geren, ger 88, 91, 95, 96, 97, 98
garibaldi 194
garite ' watch-tower ' 140
garret 140
garron 205
garrot 199
garsoun ' boy ' 139
garsum see *gersum*
gate 86, 89, 91, 93, 95, 96, 97, 98, 99, 102
gauche 165
gaucho 6, 201
gauntlet 103
gaur 225
gauze 160
gavial 225
gavotte 158
gay 143
gazel 225
gazelle 219
gazette 189
gæte see *gete*
gear 97, 102
geaspis ' jasper ' 54, 282
geaunt ' giant ' 127
gecko 242
gehenna 236
geisha 240
gelatine 193
gellet ' basin ' 274
gelus ' jealous ' 125, 129, 130
gem 14, 156
gemel 156
gemsbok 178
genappe 167
gendarme 167
genealogy 137
generalissimo 190
generally 137
generation 137
genet 216
geneva 178
genge ' retinue, company ' 92
genie 220
genius 7
genre 168
gent ' noble ' 133
genteel 161
gentelerie 113
genterise ' nobility ' 125
gentile ' gentle ' 125
gentle 113, 125, 137, 161
gentleman 138
gentleness 7

gentry 138
georgette 168
ger(en) see *garen*
gere ' gear ' 97
gerner(e) ' granary ' 115, 122
gersum, gærsum ' treasure ' 73, 79, 80, 85, 93, 96
gesso 189
gest ' guest ' 100, 102
gest ' story ' 133
gestning ' entertainment ' 88, 93
get 92, 95, 96, 97, 98, 99, 102
gete, gæte ' care, heed ' 83
gete(n) ' to watch, guard ' 92, 96, 97
ghât 223
ghazi 220
ghee 222
ghoul 220
giant 127, 139
giaour 228
gibbet 122, 136
gien ' guide ' 144
gigant ' giant ' 19, 23, 39, 288
gigour ' player on the gigue ' 127
gildre ' snare ' 98
gile ' guile ' 113, 120, 125
gillie 205
gimm 15, 19, 20, 23, 272
gin 178
gin ' trap, device ' 112, 118, 120, 128, 129, 130, 134
gingall see *jingal*
ginger 118, 123, 221
gingham 241, 242
gingifer, -ver 106, 118, 123
ginkgo 239
ginseng 237
giraffe 218
girandole 191
gisarme ' battle-axe ' 119, 129, 132
giste ' lodging ' 122
giuegoue ' gewgaw ' 124
give 76
givelen ' heap up ' 132
glacé 158, 167
glacen ' slip ' 143
glacier 164
glacis 162
gladiolus 7
glaive ' sword ' 132
glædene ' gladiolus ' 47, 48, 279
glee 16
gleg ' quick ' 96
glengarry 205
glenten ' gleam, glance ' 88
glint 88
glissade 166
gloesan ' to gloss ' 16, 280

moonsif 225
moose 257
moquette 165
mor ' mulberry ' 41, 280
moraine 164
morale 165
morass 177
morap ' new wine ' 48, 283
morbidezza 191
morceau 164
mordent 193
more ' parsnip ' 47
morello 190
morgen 180
morgue 166
Morocco 10
morse 212
morsel 137
mortar 279
Moselle 10
mosque 216, 219
mosquito 198
moss-bunker 178
mot 168
motif 166
motto 189
moucharaby 220
moujik 210
moulin 166
mount 119, 129
mountain 137
mountebank 186
mousse 167
mousseline 162
moustache 161
move 135
muckna 224
mudar 225
mudir 233
muezzin 217
muff 175
mufti 217
mugger 225
muggy 103
mugwamp 258
mul ' mule ' 23, 277
mulatto 198
mule 115, 137, 142
mull 204
mullah 222
mullet 156
mulligatawny 234
multiply 113
mum vb 176
mummy 227
munjeet 225
munt ' hill ' 23, 36, 37, 38, 47, 48, 281
muntjak 243

munuc ' monk ' 28, 281
mur ' wall ' 21, 279
musclan scel ' mussel ' 17, 280
muscovado 200
music 24, 130, 137
musk 227
musket 187
musketoon 190
muslin 162, 190
musquash 257
mussel 17, 280
must n. 30, 274
mustachio 161, 186
mustang 201
mutian ' change ' 22, 272
myall 245
mydd ' bushel ' 27, 272
mylen ' mill ' 276
myna 224
mynecen ' nun ' 41, 281
mynet ' coin ' 17, 41, 272
mynetere, miyniteri ' moneyer ' 17, 33
mynster ' monastery ' 22, 28, 281
myrtle 235

nabob 222, 224
nacelle 168
nadir 215
nag vb. 103
nai ' nay ' 87
nainsook 225
naïve 163
Nankin 10
naphtha 228
napu 143
nard 37, 236, 284
narghile 230
naseberry 200
nasturtium 7
nation 136
nativitep 108, 109
nativity 123
natron 219
nature 135, 137
nape ' grace ' 84
naut ' oxen ' 97
nautch 224
nawab 224
nay 79
næp ' turnip ' 17, 246, 276
næpte ' catmint ' 48
nebula 7
necromancy 138, 144
née 168
nefte ' catmint ' 46, 280
négligé 156, 167
negro 198
nenuphar 227

perceive 137, 138, 143
perdu 160
pere ' pear ' 280
perfection 125
pergola 190
peri 230
peril 135, 137, 143
perish 135
perseven ' perceive ' 143
persiennes 166
persiflage 165
persimmon 257
persoc, -ic ' peach ' 48, 284
person 121, 136
pert 130
peruke 186
pervince ' periwinkle ' 48, 284
pes ' peace ' 112, 116, 129
peshwa 230
peso 197
petersilie ' parsley ' 46, 280
petunia 252
phanariot 212
philosoph ' philosopher ' 27, 287
physic 144
physician 121
physique 167
piaffe 165
piano 191
pianoforte 192
piastre 190
piazza 188
pibroch 205
pic ' pinnacle ' 36
pic ' pitch ' 31, 272
picador 200
picaresque 201
picaroon 199
picayune 159
piccaninny 199
piccolo 193
pice 223
pichiciago 201
pick-axe 138
pickle 174
picnic 165
picot 167
picturesque 192
picul 241
pie ' magpie ' 128, 138
pie (coin) 226
piece 143
pied à terre 169
pierrot 164
pietà, 191
pigment 288
pihten, part of loom 273
pike 36, 282

pikeis ' pick-axe ' 138
pilare 122
pilaster 188
pilau, pilaff 230
pilch 49, 273
pile 20, 275
pile ' mortar ' 26, 275
pilece see *pylece*
pilgrim 109, 113, 117, 121, 128, 136, 139
pillar 122, 129, 133
pillow 273
pilot 160
pilstre ' mortar ' 48, 278
piment ' spiced wine ' 123, 132
pimento 200
pin 275
pin ' pine-tree ' 276
pin ' torment ' 14, 271
pince-nez 167
pinewincle ' winkle ' 47, 280
pinian ' to torment ' 14, 34, 271
pinole 256
pinsian ' consider ' 16, 26, 44, 281
pintado 208
pioneer 160
pip 174
pipe 44, 50, 273
pipeneale ' pimpernel ' 280
piper ' pepper ' 276
pipere ' piper ' 35
pipette 167
pipistrelle 192
pipor ' pepper ' 13, 43, 54
piquant 161
pique 157, 161
piqué 167
piragua 253
pirie ' pear-tree ' 276
pirouette 164
pis ' heavy ' 277
pis aller 163
pisé 164
pise ' pea ' 17, 54, 276
pise ' piece ' 143
pisle ' warm room ' 48, 275
pislic ' heavy ' 36, 38
pistol 187
pistol ' epistle ' 40, 287
piston 192
pit 23, 36, 50, 276
pitch 31, 272
piteous 137
pitpan 256
pittance 125
pity 134, 138
pizzicato 193
placard 174

z

sapodilla 251, 254
sapota 251
saraband 199, 219
sardonix 134
sargasso 207
sari 224
sarmun ' sermon ' 127
sarong 6, 243
sarsaparilla 198
sash 218
sassafras 198
Satan 235
satchel 156
satrap 228
Saturday 35, 37, 42, 281
sauerkraut 180
saundoute ' doubtless ' 144
sauté 167
sauter ' psalter ' 115, 123, 131
savagene ' savage ' 140
savannah 251
savant 164
savate 168
save 137, 138, 143
saviour 141
savoir faire 168
savour 112, 125
sæc(c) ' sack ' 23, 273
sælmerige ' brine ' 274
sæppe ' spruce ' 280
sætern(es)dæg 35, 37, 42
sæperige ' savory ' 48, 285
sbirro 190
scab 103
scabbed 92
scaglia 192
scalle ' scab ' 102
scamol ' stool ' 46, 273
scandle ' scandal ' 126
scant 103
scantling 133
scape ' escape ' 128
scaramouch 191
scare 82
scarlatina 193
scarlet 135, 226
scarn n. 118, 120
scarnen ' to scorn ' 113
scathe 89, 90, 100, 102
scatheless 82
scatter 76
scaur 103
scegþ, a light ship 64
scena 193
scenario 193
scene 161
sceppe, a measure 73
sceptre 136

schauntillon ' scantling ' 133
scherzo 193
schipperke 179
schnapps 182
schnorrer 236
school 13, 27, 33, 50, 288
schooner 178
schorl 181
schottische 182
scindel ' roof-shingle ' 275
scinn ' skin ' 69
sclavyne ' cloak ' 128
scogh ' wood ' 96, 97
scol ' school ' 13, 27, 33, 288
scolle ' skull ' 100
scomfit 141
scone 175
scope 186
score 69, 73
scorge ' scourge ' 124
scorn 118, 125
scorn vb. 138, 144
scorpion 123, 137
scoru ' score ' 73
scot ' tax ' 101, 102
scourge 124
scow 178
scrag 103
scrannel 103
scrap 103
scrape 100
scribun ' they decreed ' 17
scrifan ' decree ' 19, 271
scrift ' confessor ' 21, 271
scrin ' shrine ' 13, 33, 37, 42, 274
scriptor ' writer ' 39
scrofel ' scrofula ' 286
scrowe ' scroll ' 127
scrub 103
scrutnian ' examine ' 46
scud 103
scudo 190
scuffle 103
scutel ' scuttle ' 13, 283
scuttle 13, 283
scyrtan ' shorten ' 46
seal n. 140
seal vb. 110
sealmscop ' psalmist ' 14
s(e)altian ' dance ' 277
sealticge ' dancer ' 31
seam ' wallet, burden ' 37, 38, 43, 45, 271
seamere ' pack-animal ' 271
séance 167
secco 193
sece ' cease ' 138
seck ' sack ' 89